THE SOURCES OF MODERN ART

I

Robert DELAUNAY
The Cardiff team
(1912-1913)

THE SOURCES OF
MODERN ART

Jean Cassou   Emile Langui   Nikolaus Pevsner

52 colour plates

333 black and white plates

51 line drawings

THAMES AND HUDSON

LONDON

TRANSLATED BY KATHERINE M. DELAVENAY
AND H. LEIGH FARNELL

CONTENTS

Epochs of European Art

THE EXHIBITIONS organized by the Council of Europe, every year, in one of the member countries, have each concentrated upon some particular epoch of European civilization. A number of publishers have joined together in order to produce, in several languages, a volume devoted to each of these outstanding occasions and so to preserve the achievements and impressions of them permanently. The first volume of this series was *The Age of Rococo,* corresponding to the exhibition in Munich in 1958.

In the same way the present volume takes as its starting-point the exhibition held at the Musée d'Art Moderne in Paris, from November 9th 1960 to January 23rd 1961, and called *Les Sources du XXᵉ Siècle. Les Arts en Europe de 1884 à 1914.* The task of presenting the subject as a whole — the political movements, the industrial and social revolutions of the time, and also the scientific ideas and the intellectual trends that characterized it — was given to me, in my capacity as *Commissaire Général* of the Exhibition. The chapter on the visual arts and that on architecture and the applied arts during the same period, were undertaken by Emile Langui and Nikolaus Pevsner respectively, both of whom were members of the organizing committee of the exhibition. Since we had all three already co-operated on the actual exhibition, we naturally found it easy to work together in presenting the same material in another form — a book. The years of the last quarter of the 19th century and the beginning of the 20th, with their variety of events, their wonderful mixture of ideas, feelings and themes, where assuredly some of the richest and most fruitful in the whole history of the human spirit.

JEAN CASSOU

THE CLIMATE OF THOUGHT

Between the Franco-Prussian War of 1870-1871, which laid the foundations of the German Empire, and the First World War of 1914 stretches a period of peace which may be called the period of Balance of Power in Europe. A precarious balance, a constantly imperilled peace, but at least a period during which the status quo was maintained. Among western European powers wars were a rarity. Such conflicts as the Russo-Turkish War of 1877-1878, the Chinese-Japanese War of 1889-1895; the Spanish-American War of 1898, the Russo-Japanese War of 1904-1905, the War between Italy and Turkey of 1911-1912 and the Balkan War of 1912-1913 took place outside the European theatre, as did all the other colonial wars. All were, in fact, the result of imperialist expansion radiating from the centre towards the periphery, on which were situated all the vital danger points — such, for instance, as the Balkans, where the interests of the pan-Slav Empire of the Tzars clashed with those of the twin Austro-Hungarian Empire giving rise to the famous Eastern Question. At the uttermost parts of the earth the great maritime and commercial power of the British Isles exercised its constant restless vigil, the heroic dominion established by its explorers, soldiers and sailors sometimes conflicting with the no less vast and powerful epic of the French colonial Empire. The same expansionist impetus later inspired Germany and Italy, while the United States, strong in the first formidable flush of youth, inevitably thrust outward in its turn, with a dynamism first directed at the expense of the last Spanish possessions, and later spread throughout the Pacific and extended to the whole of the South American continent by means of the jealous promulgation and application of the Monroe Doctrine. Inter-state rivalries were of an economic order: each state having a surplus population to be distributed, sources of raw materials to be secured, markets to be created for its merchandise. All this remote and eccentric activity was the direct result of the capitalist phenomenon then in full expansion. The question was whether they would be forced to come to direct grips at home, on their own soil. This was indeed a dangerous perspective, an apocalypse constantly staved off until the future. Sometimes — Fashoda, Agadir — it seemed as if the flames had reached the powder barrel. Negotiation, however, won the day. The play of various alliances — the Triple Alliance (1882), the Franco-Russian Alliance (1893), the Entente Cordiale (1904), the Triple Entente (1907) — established a balance between conflicting appetites, or rather a permanent state of tension, always on the edge of, but never quite reaching, breaking point. Meanwhile, pending the time when Europe itself became the theatre of the struggle, when risk was transformed into reality, and tension snapped for good, European history was played out over the whole surface of the globe and peace became an armed truce. Armaments were piled up, militarism was rampant, yet peace subsisted, and to this peace human consciousness became accustomed.

A second danger — that of revolution — also assailed the consciousness of man, but this, too, was relegated to the dim and distant future. The final revolution of the century — and the XIXth century had in its time seen many revolutions — had been the French Commune. French public opinion was divided between a panic-stricken horror and a feeling of malaise.

This convulsion, together with the burning of Paris and the massacres of the Parisian populace, had led to the establishment of a bourgeois republic which, after a period of struggle, finally assumed a distinctly democratic and liberal complexion. But the Commune, although defeated, had sown its seed, and the French, shaken by this bloody shock, found their horror at the experience mingled with a certain guilty conscience. They would have liked completely to efface its memory. On the cover of the history of the Commune published by Lissagaray in 1896 were inscribed the words *Pour qu'on sache* (Lest we forget), for it was indeed being forgotten, and deliberately so. History, of course, consists not only of events but also of the repercussions of such events in the minds of men, of the memory retained of these events and of the meaning that is ascribed to them. It consists, too, of the hopes and fears inspired by the possible consequences of such events. The Commune, and, with it, the political and social revolutions of the XIXth century, and the ideas of Proudhon, Marx and other theorists continued to lead a secret and disquieting life beneath the surface of the prosperous and peaceful years of the final decades of the XIXth century and the beginning of the XXth. Already a ghost was stalking Europe. Socialism, the International, Syndicalism were all taking shape. The proletariat was everywhere becoming more and more strongly organized, its power increasing by the development of action both by means of strikes and by parliamentary tactics. The Russian revolution of 1905 showed the practical possibilities of such action. But in this sphere, too, public conscience preferred to stifle its misgiving and remain complacent.

Meanwhile the efficiency of the capitalist machine was elsewhere proving a source of enormous satisfaction. The XIXth century had been torn by war and revolution, but it had also seen the birth of a great dream, the triumph of science and of constant progress. This dream was now in process of realization. Thanks to speed, man had achieved a new disposition of his two main co-ordinates: time and space. By means of the railway, the ocean liner, and the submarine, the globe was becoming ever more closely encompassed. A prodigious new toy, the motor car, had succeeded the bicycle. Another miracle — the aeroplane — was in process of invention. In 1909 Bleriot had crossed the Channel in a single hop. To these new vehicles, constantly progressing and improving on their own performances, had been added other instruments of communication; the telegraph and the telephone, so that it seemed that there was nothing left to be discovered or invented to complete or expedite man's mastery of the world. This mastery was not only immediate and concrete, but was also confirmed by picture. Man was no longer content to possess the world more completely, to penetrate more and more swiftly, if not instantaneously, into its uttermost parts, either by conveying himself there in person or by projecting his voice or thoughts, he also felt the need to see for himself these distant parts, to acquire an image of their reality. The progress of photography, finally achieved with the use of collodion in 1851, opened up this visual empire. The extraordinary Nadar, a character straight from the pages of his friend Balzac, combined this discovery with various aeronautical exploits and, in 1858, from a balloon, succeeded in securing the first aerial photograph.

In 1893-95 it was the turn of the undersea world to be explored. By 1880 photography had already entered the world of the commonplace with the advent of the earliest picture postcards, and in 1885 it was received into the temple of art itself, crossing for the first time the threshold of the Paris Salon.

Hitherto drawing, engraving, painting, sculpture and modelling had portrayed reality, while still remaining arts, that is to say interpretations (with the obvious exception of modelling, which, however, is strictly limited in scope). Photography, on the other hand, was the exact reproduction of reality, its ambition, even in those cases where it attained the dignity of art, still being to remain faithful to reality, while revealing certain latent though none the less existant spiritual virtues. By microphotography and enlargement it thus revealed the hidden aspects of things, so serving science, that is to say, the knowledge of reality.

The photograph can, however, reveal only fixed flashes of reality. A second invention — the cinema — soon came to catch its fleeting motion. From the moment of invention of the phenakistoscope by the Belgian, Joseph Plateau, whose over-bold attempts to pierce the secrets of the sun cost him his sight, the Promethean trail was blazed from the experiments of Muybridge — encouraged curiously enough by the ex-pioneers of the Californian gold rush recently transformed into millionaires — to the work of Marey, Reynaud, Edison and of Marey's pupil Demény. Industry then took over, bringing new technical improvements. In Lyon, Auguste and Louis Lumière, manufacturers of bromide plates, were passionately interested in these experiments, and maintained contact with Demény, Marey, and Reynaud. ' I cannot recall without emotion ', Auguste Lumière was later to recount, ' those far distant days when Edison's kinescope was first publicly revealed and it occurred to my brother and myself how interesting it would be to be able to show on a screen to a whole roomfull of people animated scenes faithfully reproducing moving things and persons. In the few moments ot leisure left us by the management of our business, we proceeded to tackle this problem and I myself was engaged on the construction of an apparatus, the exact principles of which I have since forgotten, when, one day, towards the end of 1894, I visited my brother who had been slightly indisposed and was confined to bed.

' He told me how, in the calm of the night, unable to sleep, he had worked out the conditions prerequisite to achieving our aim and had conceived a device capable of fulfilling these conditions. This, he explained, consisted of making a claw move up and down in front of a gate frame by means of a mechanism similar to that of the presser-foot of the sewing-machine, the claws fitting at the top of their throw into perforations made in the edge of the image-bearing film, which was thereby pulled along, and subesquently retracting at the bottom, leaving the film absolutely immobile during the upward movement of the claw.

' This was a revelation, and I immediately understood that it only remained for me to abandon the precarious solution on which I had been working. In the course of a single night, my brother had invented *the cinématographe.*' [1]

This supremely important mechanical invention led to a concentration of all the experiments on which various men of genius had been engaged, giving impetus to the system. Other inventions followed, enriching it and allowing maximum utilization of its possibilities, not, however, followed by immediate industrial and commercial exploitation. By the time of the 1900 Exhibition, it was already fully, if rudimentarily, equipped, already in possession of all its potentialities, even, for example, to the point of ' talking '. It was, however, to remain silent for many years to come: perhaps a good thing in so far as this limitation enabled it to develop its specific properties to the full, and thereby rapidly to become an art. For this invention which, like photography, its elder sister, appeared at first to be no more than a miraculous device for capturing and reproducing reality in all its movement and vitality — in this lay its superiority over photography — was immediataly to be employed in the service of the imagination and to display in this unlimited and arbitrary domain a quite fantastic power. As soon as the technical improvements, with which science had endowed it from its earliest days but which were to be industrially exploited only by subsequent degrees, had given it complete mastery over reality — sound, colour, relief, and every possible spatial dimension — it had already achieved every conceivable effect in the sphere of unreality, that is to say of pure fantasy and of art.

Thus the latest mechanical invention in the service of reality, destined subsequently to play its true scientific role to such perfection, proved simultaneously to be an art possessing potentialities so immense and properties so unique that it not only embraced but surpassed all other arts. The cinema is at once an instrument of complete exactitude and a great poetical spell-binder: a mirror of truth, a dreamer of dreams and a worker of miracles. The reproduction of some slice of life such as closing time at the Lumière factory or a train steaming into a station was, of course, a subject of surprise to the public of the day, henceforward able to see, to re-see, and to reproduce events at will, to have, in fact, at its disposal a perpetual duplication of the whole expanding and evolving universe. That this same instrument in the hands of a Georges Méliès should also have created the wildest phantasms to satisfy our magic-seeking souls, provides us with a singular piece of insight into current human consciousness. Contemporary astonishment and enthusiasm for the fresh victories of science over nature, was accompanied, in the case of the latest of these victories, by a lyrical emotion, which, in turn, reflected upon all previous triumphs. XIXth century prophesies and hymns to progress had been fully justified: it was almost impossible not to feel a certain jubilation at the fabulous powers already achieved.

A similar note of exaltation had already been heard in the ' fanfares industrielles ' dear to the heart of the St. Simonists and the engineers of the *Ecole Polytechnique* — a name implying in itself a programme of multiple research and action — a note subsequently re-echoing down the years from Victor Hugo to Jules Verne, and heard again on the eve of the 1914 War in the *Vates* of Apollinaire. It was, of course, a splendid thing to be alive in a time so rich in prodigies, a time which perceived no limit to its own potentialities. The future lay wide open and there could be no holding back. Utopias were attained on every hand. The scientific age proclaimed by Auguste Comte was in process of accomplishment. Thanks

---

[1] Georges SADOUL: *L'invention du Cinéma*, Paris, Denoel, 1946.

ESSAI
sur
LES DONNÉES IMMÉDIATES
de
LA CONSCIENCE

THÈSE POUR LE DOCTORAT
PRÉSENTÉE
À LA FACULTÉ DES LETTRES DE PARIS
PAR
Henri BERGSON
Ancien élève de l'École Normale supérieure,
Professeur de philosophie au Collège Rollin.

PARIS
ANCIENNE LIBRAIRIE GERMER-BAILLIÈRE ET Cⁱᵉ
FÉLIX ALCAN, ÉDITEUR
108, boulevard Saint-Germain, 108
1889

EINE NEUE BESTIMMUNG
DER MOLEKÜLDIMENSIONEN

INAUGURAL-DISSERTATION
ZUR
ERLANGUNG DER PHILOSOPHISCHEN DOKTORWÜRDE
DER
HOHEN PHILOSOPHISCHEN FAKULTÄT
(MATHEMATISCH NATURWISSENSCHAFTLICHE SEKTION)
DER
UNIVERSITÄT ZÜRICH
VORGELEGT
VON
ALBERT EINSTEIN
AUS ZÜRICH

Begutachtet von den Herren Prof. Dr. A. KLEINER
und
Prof. Dr. H. BURKHARDT

BERN
BUCHDRUCKEREI K. J. WYSS
1905

DIE
TRAUMDEUTUNG
VON
Dr. SIGM. FREUD.

»FLECTERE SI NEQUEO SUPEROS, ACHERONTA MOVEBO.«

LEIPZIG UND WIEN.
FRANZ DEUTICKE.
1900.

Henri BERGSON, *Les Données Immédiates de la Conscience.* Title-page (1889)

Albert EINSTEIN, *A New Determination of Molecular Dimensions.* Title-page (1905)

Sigmund FREUD, *The Interpretation of Dreams.* Title-page (1900)

to the unbridled progress of capitalism it was now possible, for the achievement of *positive* ends, to combine and compound conditions, opportunities, occasions and conjunctures, and to organize effective collaboration between industrial and financial interests and the plethora of patents then being taken out by inventors springing up on every hand, many of them obscure, self-educated men, and every one inspired by the demon of adventure. It was indeed a period which had every reason to be proud of its achievements, and proud it certainly showed itself to be. Such pride found expression in the Universal Exhibitions organized in Paris in 1889 and 1900, and in Chicago in 1893: exhibitions which constituted in their way a balance sheet of the whole period.

These very words appeared, proudly and triumphantly, in the introduction to Hachette's Guide to the 1900 Exhibition:

' The 1900 Exhibition, world-wide and universal, is the magnificent result, the extraordinary balance sheet of a century which has not only proved to be the most fertile in discovery and the most prodigious in scientific invention, but which has also revolutionized the economic order of the Universe.

' The centenary museums scattered here and there in the various sections of the Exhibition, demonstrate the forward march of progress from the mail-coach to the express train, from the messenger to wireless telegraphy and the telephone, from lithography to radiography, from the earliest burrowings for coal in the bowels of the earth to the aeroplanes now seeking to open up the highway of the sky.

' Our Exhibition is that of the great century now drawing to its close and which ushers in a new era in the history of humanity '.

Brilliant philosophical and scientific theories founded this confident enthusiasm on new representations of Cosmos. The *Origin of Species*, the basic work of Darwinism published in 1859, had already spread the idea of evolution, destined — in spite of many variations and controversies — to such far-reaching influence. Its fundamental concept, which had already gained general acceptance, had reinforced man's growing consciousness that he no longer simply ' was ', but like the universe itself, was in process of ' becoming '. In 1889 Bergson published his thesis on the *Données immédiates de la Conscience*, followed in 1907 by *L'Evolution créatrice*. Once again motion was the key, with man himself moving, feeling, living in that motion. This philosophy was intimately and vitally connected with all the intellectual and artistic tendencies of the period; and we shall return to it later in the course of this essay. In the period following the 1914 war and during our own times, in the heart of the twentieth century, three other systems — relativity, psycho-analysis and atomism — were, however, to develop and produce results. In 1904, Einstein published his *Outline of a generalized theory of relativity*. The year 1891 saw the first works of Freud, whose *Interpretation of Dreams* appeared in 1900. In the same year Planck announced his *quantum* of energy and its universal constant h: ' Energy no longer seems anything other than discontinuous, jumping mysteriously from one state to another with no infinitesimal intermediaries ' [1].   The human mind was thus henceforward obliged to conceive un-representable cosmogonies, logics of indetermination, and mysterious actions which, even in the obscure zones of the psyche, operate each in its own particular and intrinsic fashion, without reference to the laws of classical reasoning applied to natural phenomena as a whole.   The conceptions of time and space, of pure consciousness, of finite and infinite, were thus complicated by conceptions of time-space, of the unconscious, and of the transfinite.   The repercussions of all this was translated in literary terms by the concept of the absurd, and in the realm of the plastic arts by the aesthetics of the abstract and the *informel*.   Roughly and briefly speaking, it seems as if human consciousness took refuge in the abyss of molecular isolation, in a profusion of moments, of *existences*, each with its own behaviour pattern, ambivalent, poly-valent as the case might be, but in any event totally unrelated to the comprehensible traditional universe.   It must, however, be repeated that the time had not yet come when these experiments, revolutionizing the image of the universe to such a fantastic degree, were to react upon the consciousness of men: this was left for the mid-twentieth century.   It must also be observed that late XIXth century society, by a curious paradox, providing yet further evidence of its overweening folly, while delighting in all practical progress, was highly suspicious of anything resembling speculative boldness.   Its idealism could not allow science to progress too far on the path of hypothesis and discovery.   While it was encouraged to achieve prodigious triumphs in the field of industry and commerce, it was permitted to shake neither the foundations of common sense and positive reasoning, nor the equally solid bases of religious belief, or yet to disturb man's spiritual yearnings.   In 1895, Brunetière, a reactionary vulgarian famous in his day but now long since forgotten, proclaimed ' the bankruptcy of science ' thus insulting that very science whose audacity was bringing man such rich rewards.   Let us now return to the 1900 Exhibition.

The period which sang its own praises in this Exhibition was thus a period of charming irresponsibility and genial self-suffi-ciency: in short, a happy era and one now looked back upon with a certain melancholy — ' the good old days ', ' la belle époque ', etc.   Fortified by its technical and economic triumphs, confident in a future stretching peacefully before it, pros-perity was the keynote of the age.   Stable currencies, stable values, stable everything.   The danger of war and revolution was pushed aside.   Inventiveness, although confined to the practical and contributing only to everyday life and comfort, was, indeed, extremely fertile.   This period forms a homogeneous and self-contained entity.   The declaration of war in 1914 broke in upon it with the full force of a *catastrophe*.   And from the date of this apalling rupture, humanity entered a new era.   The age of uncertainty had begun.

Happy peoples, it is often said, have no history.   The same is true of happy eras.   Lack of events is indeed their distin-guishing mark.   In his posthumous *Clio*, Péguy reflected on the life he had led during an uneventful, unhistoric period, not knowing that it was to terminate in an event, a historic event, a thunderclap which laid the way wide open for an event-ful, historic, appallingly historic period.   The period of Péguy's lifetime, however, was marked by no historically significant event, no *chronological* milestone, nothing by which a man could reckon his aging or his age, no *articulation* or turning point in time such as those which compose the glorious chronology of the XIXth century, particularly the glorious XIXth century in France.   'A man who had seen 1814 and 1815; 1830; 1848; December 2nd, 1870 and 1871; or, if it is preferred to count the hills and valleys, a man who has seen the Empire; the Restoration; Louis Philippe; the Second Republic; and, after the turning point of the Coup d'Etat, the Second Empire; and, after the twin turning point of the war and the Commune, the Third Republic — such a man can boast not only of having seen many things (such is not my present meaning), but of seeing almost too much for the human condition, too much for the human dimension, too much for human span, too much for man considered as a temporal unit, too much, indeed, for the human unit considered in the absolute.   He can also boast that his life has been not only marked out but firmly and constantly entrenched.   He is like a ceiling, a splendid vaulted ceiling, divided up into symmetrical panels ornamented with symmetrical mouldings.   Such a man can certainly not complain of any lack of ribbing or arcading ' [2].

A man of this period is indeed a figure clearly situated in time, whose age may be measured according to the passage of

---

[1] Stéphane LUPASCO: *Les trois Matières*, Paris, Julliard, 1960.
[2] Charles PÉGUY: *Œuvres en prose*. Vol. II (1909-1914) Gallimard, Bibliothèque de la Pléiade, Paris, 1947, p. 299.

time — a venerable figure of a man. The same cannot be said of men who live their lives in an unmeasured, unpunctuated, stagnant period, during which no event provides a point of reference. All they have, so says Péguy a few lines further on, is ' water-diviner events ', that is to say that if they must have events in order to feel themselves alive, they must seek deep down below the surface of the visible world, in what Miguel de Unamuno, another great observer of his age, has called ' sub-history '. We, for our part, shall now try to plunge into the sub-history of this extra-historic period in order to discover such events.

These will, of course, be events of a spiritual order.

Before leaving the surface let us for a moment try to understand and share the confidence of a solidly established bourgeois society thoroughly pleased with its enterprises, its profits, its works, with all its pomp and circumstance. To this must be added the inevitable profusion of its culture, its literature and its arts.

Books were read, music heard, plays applauded. All were tailor-made by skilled confectioners; their production aided by the criticism, witticism and advice of brilliant journalists. The comedies and novels in which this society delighted never raised acute or disturbing problems. Doubtless, in order to avoid boredom, they were obliged to comprise some elements of conflict but these never exceeded certain permissible limits, just sufficient to whet the curiosity and to satisfy the need for imaginary emancipation and for rêverie. The resolution of problems, the disentanglement of crises, the unravelling of ' cas de conscience ' must never be subversive, never call in question those accepted fundamentals upon which it was agreed that the universe as a whole was firmly based. If she was a young lady of good society, the heroine of these novels might carry the spirit of revolt to the point of saying so bad a word as ' Dash ! ' Unlike Nora, however, she could never leave her doll's house. So scandalous an act could only be presented by a foreign, nordic, anarchistic genius, and even then only on the tiny stage of a progressive theatre.

Thus fashionable novels and comedies stuck to the safe problems of divorce, adultery, military service, the fluctuations of religious faith, the union of lovers of differing social status, the career of young men of good family brought to ruin, or fallen into debauchery and evil ways, of rakes and card-sharpers of less elevated, possibly Balkan, origin, of unfortunate young ladies obliged to seek employment as governesses in foreign lands, the vicissitudes of powerful bankers or bull-necked politicians, or the sentimental peregrinations of naval lieutenants.

The music which ravished this society was that of opera: a heteroclite genre providing opportunities for classical, medieval or far-eastern reminiscences, combining orchestral colour, splendid scenery and costumes, the noisy assertions of the chorus, and the voluptuous flutterings of the ballet. Such an incongruous medley was characteristic of current taste, also to be found in contemporary furniture and architecture. Both of these were composite, compact of various historical styles. Their buffets were Henri II, their bedroom suites Louis XV, while the facades of their houses embraced all styles: Renaissance, XVIIIth century, and even an occasional graceful XVth century projecting turret. In the America of the 1880's at the height of the triumph of the great millionaires — the Vanderbilts, Morgans, Goulds and Rockefellers — when a ball might cost as much as 100,000 dollars [1], this deliberately archaic style reached new heights of delirium imputable to the fact that America was without a past. Greedily it battened on the past of the old world, with a peculiar predilection for the châteaux of the Loire and the palaces of the Italian Renaissance. A number of creative artists of genius did, however, emerge to grasp the fact that it was precisely this lack of past that would make it possible for America to become the champion of the future.

Meanwhile time stood still in the mind of American as well as European society. Recourse was made to the catalogue of the past, to all the bric-à-brac of history, and eclecticism inevitably became the key to taste. Nothing new was made, but everything that had already been made was admired. Everything that existed was thereby justified and deemed worthy of reproduction. The field was thus extensive and its variety much admired. It extended not only backwards into time but also sideways into space, thus providing men with an allusion of universal being. But, beneath such superficial variety lay always the same thing; the same, pre-determined, reassuring, almost ritual plan, the costumes and

---

[1] Cf. Oliver W. LARKIN: *Art and Life in America*, Holt, Rinehart & Winston, New York, 1960.

décor alone showing variation. It was, however, precisely the changes of décor which delighted and the costumes which dazzled contemporary audiences for whom all interest, all piquancy lay in the picturesque.

The picturesque thus predominated over painting, which is substantial creation. Painting, indeed, was forgotten, and its very concept abolished. That of the picturesque, on the contrary, carried all before it. The artist, or rather the functionary entrusted by society with organizing its aesthetic relaxation, devoted his career to the search for the picturesque. Disguised as an artist, he filled his studio with exotic objects: armour, chests, Venetian chandeliers, Chinese curios, Japanese lanterns, Turkish slippers and Persian carpets. His work consisted in discovering, by travel or in books, subjects which could suitably be decked out in exotic costumes and placed against an operatic backdrop. Opera, always more opera — with its costume and accessory shops, its stereotyped lighting effects, its never-varying scenario furbished up successively in Carthaginian, Greco-Roman, Byzantine, Slav, Turkish or Provençal style.

The Universal Exhibitions came to the aid of opera by adding fuel to the fire of enthusiasm for archaic styles and picturesque accoutrements. From one pavillion to another the superficial sensuality of the public was tickled by a mixture of ever increasing piquancy. The Universal Exhibitions were not merely the balance-sheet of the admirable progress achieved by technique and by industry: they were also the balance-sheet of all the settings of all the centuries and of all the contemporary décors of all the remotest corners of the planet. The 1893 Chicago Exhibition was particularly intoxicating in this respect: presenting an array of colonnades, cupolas, minarets, obelisks and gondolas, not to mention unspeakable imitations in the style of the Paris *Ecole des Beaux-Arts*.

But while cosmopolitanism thus constituted one of the principal sources of gratification to the bourgeoisie of the period, it represented also one of its greatest audacities. Societies of this nature might have been expected to fall into a chauvinistic isolation. They were, however, sufficiently sure of their own power to be able to appreciate foreign artists, to welcome them and to do them honour. For in this nationalistic Europe reigned also an atmosphere of internationalism. Various distant countries were taken up, simultaneously or successively, becoming temporary *fashions*. Thanks to the colour-print and the stereoscope, views of the Far East, of Andalusia or of Venice became as familar as the most famous national beauty spots. Moreover, such exotic evasions, such exciting sallies into worlds different from their own, the touch of risk and freedom, introduced an element of instability: an idea of the possibility of *something different*. To this feeling of lively curiosity we owe the piquant exhibitions of the gallery run by Georges Petit. There, in a setting of purple, gold and onyx, enhanced by the bright lights of opening nights, Parisian society tasted the delights of strange wonders, mingled with occasional samples of even more audacious ' modernist ' works, with the result that it gradually became accustomed even to Impressionism. However self-satisfied this society may have appeared, it none the less delighted in such new and piquant delicacies as Japanism, Pre-Raphaelitism and Whistlerism.

The Italians, Boldini and De Nittis, and the Belgian Stevens were as popular as the members of the *Institut*, as were also the Spanish Zuloaga, the Hungarian Munkaczy, the Swede Zorn, the Englishman Lavery, the anglicized Hungarian de Laszlo, and the anglicized Dutchman Alma Tadema. Moreover many of the leading lights of contemporary German art exhibited in Paris and were much appreciated: Leibl, Von Uhde, Menzel and even Max Liebermann, a vigorous personality generally classified as a German Impressionist. The latter demonstrates the contamination unconsciously undergone by the French public at this time under the influence of social life and the cult of foreign artists. This xenophilia was primarily a form of that cosmopolitalism which constituted one of the salient characteristics of the time. Official art, academism — or, to call it by its true name, conventionalism — was in itself an international phenomenon. It was dominant in every country, wallowing in its own stagnancy, the only flicker of movement coming from the tiny ripples caused by certain minor temerities launched by fashionable society. Repeated glimpses of the painting of neighbouring countries, left an impression of something slightly different, a spark, an after-taste, a fleeting suspicion of something more surprising and diverting, so that eventually, in every country, there came about a compromise, a gradual familiarization with preceding revolutionary movements such as Naturalism and Impressionism. In Germany, the names already quoted clearly illustrate this state of affairs. But in spite of novelties appearing in Munich or Berlin, in spite of the initiatives of other artists such as the idealists Feuerbach and Hans von Marées, or the pre-expressionist Corinth, the power remained in the hands of the academists and the dominant taste was for anecdotic art, the merry peasant, trite *Gemütlichkeit*, portraits in the style of Lenbach, and landscapes à la Hans Thoma. Naturally battle scenes, corporation frescoes and other historical paraphernalia also played their part, notably in Belgium with the followers of Wappers and de Leys, in Spain with those of Fortuny, in Russia with Repine and Verechtchaguine, not to mention what was going on in France itself. In England, the Royal Academy remained one of the strongest pillars in the Victorian temple, its members going solemnly about their task of portraying members of the Royal family and the English gentry, their dogs, their horses, and their rolling acres. The English soul possesses an extraordinary faculty for poetic rêverie, capable of attaining the highest spheres of spiritual music, but also liable to run riot in an extraordinary Christmas calendar art suitable only for retarded maiden ladies, as was the case with the Pre-Raphaelites; it can also clip its own wings and confine itself within the bounds of solemnity, tradition and good manners, hence acquiring that old-fashioned and phlegmatic charm which it is difficult not to appreciate in the works of official English artists.

Not enough attention has been paid to the official art of the late XIXth century: indeed, it has never been properly studied at all. Naturally it was reviewed in contemporary newspapers, magazines, and books, but always as if it were the whole of art, as if it were, in fact, Art itself. In reality, — always supposing that we accept the hypothesis that official art has any real connection with art and, indeed, deserves name of art at all — it must always be remembered that it was the art of a certain definite society. For this reason it should be analysed with complete scientific, historic, ethnographic and sociological objectivity, in the same way as the art of the Etruscans, the Vikings, the Batsileles, the Chinese of the Sung Dynasty or the Flemish cities of the XVth century. Thus the French bourgeoisie of the late XIXth century possessed its own official,

The judges' panel for the Paris salon (1885)

government-accredited, public art. The opening of the Salon was as much a part of the official ceremonies of the Third Republic as was the *Revue de Longchamps* on the 14th of July. The career of the artist was a regular career, marked by a series of regular steps and official recognitions: a young man entering the service of art served his apprenticeship at the *Ecole des Beaux-Arts*, competed for the *Prix de Rome*, returned from the Villa Medici ready to paint or to sculpt whatever was required of him, exhibited in the Salons, accepted commissions and medals, and was finally received into the *Institut*, whence he could, in turn, supervise the proper working of the system.

Like his literary, theatrical, musical and journalistic colleagues, the artist obeyed the rules of his chosen calling, treating a certain number of themes and subjects, venturing only with caution within the confines where, as we have seen, certain outposts of high society were becoming familiar with the eccentricities of a certain piquant modernism, with luminous, open-air pictures and, even, eventually, with Impressionism itself.

By wisely remaining within the heart of the system it was possible to lead a glorious and untroubled life by painting the portraits of the great, by carving marble allegories and representing scenes of battles, livestock and other themes of *genre* painting. In another context, I have quoted the career of the artist Gérôme as typical of such careers. Let there, however, be no mistake about it, such a career was neither despicable nor ridiculous: it was that of an artist genuinely interested in his art, as in many other things, a conscientious worker following his chosen path without, indeed, ever finding it tedious. While he may have painted things which seem to us dull, it should not be imagined that for this reason they were boring to the artist. Gérôme was a man of integrity, a faithful craftsmen, having his own tastes, his own ideas, his own store of knowledge, his own ambitions, his own passions and his own dreams. He was pupil of Paul Delaroche, a competent and authoritative master, perfectly capable of directing him in his chosen path. He earned the praises of Théophile Gautier: the romanticism of his *Jeune-France* days had left him with a taste for picturesque exteriors, local colour, *espagnolade* and masquerade. With the advent of the Parnassians, this taste turned rather towards the marmorean and the chiselled, and when Gréco-Roman art, at which the young Gérôme excelled, was restored to popularity he turned out numbers of pagan and Anacreontic scenes. Being of an inquisitive turn of mind, he then took to travel, and visited Russia, where he happened upon the Crimean war, which naturally proved a fruitful source of battle scenes. In Egypt, orientalism lay ready to his hand. Travel being even better than Universal Exhibitions, Gérôme went to see for himself, a fact which must be counted to his credit. On this score, indeed, there is nothing with which he can be reproached: Gérôme was an artist who took his artistic career with the greatest of seriousness. The only problem raised is the nature and object of the artistic career as it was then understood, and the *artistic* value of the artist who 'went to see'. Of the enthusiasm of his quest there can be no doubt, it is the object of the quest which is contestable. What was it that he sought, pursued, and hunted with such zeal in the course of his exploration of the diversity of the world, of the episodes of history, and even of contemporary events? Quite simply, 'subjects' for his art. And when he painted 'Louis XIV chez Molière', or 'Napoleon III receiving the envoys of Siam' he was convinced that he had found subjects worthy of his talent. Let us leave for a moment this world-wide quest for subjects to consider another itinerant artist, another perpetual traveller: Paul Gauguin. What in the world was Gauguin looking for? Was he too in search of subjects? To Charles Morice's query as to what had brought him to Brittany, and what it was that he was seeking there, Gauguin's reply was 'sadness'. We have also seen the other kind of sadness, a sadness mingled with a primitive primordial, all-embracing, joy — that cosmogonic *immemorial* joy, which, to quote Ségalen, another Oceanian traveller, he sought in Tahiti. At once we see the yawning gulf which separates a bourgeois master-painter travelling round the world in much the same way, let it be repeated, in which a tourist visits a Universal Exhibition, thumbs through a magazine or rummages round an auction saleroom, never penetrating below the surface, interested only in the superficial, in externals, in the frills and furbelows, from the painter — in the sense which this term is understood today — who flings himself passionately into the hidden depths of such and such a country, in an attempt to reach the very heart of things, to reach the core, the hidden core, the idea behind the external aspect, and who paints — who furiously and insatiably desires to paint — all that he discovers. It must, however, also be repeated that Gérôme too, was certainly inspired by passion and that his search for subjects was animated by a spirit of adventure. To cite one more proof of his enormous energy: laying aside his paintings (was he merely a little tired, or had he, by any chance, begun to wonder, whether what he was doing could be considered painting?) he turned to sculpture, and worked, after the heteroclite fashion of the time, in polychrome or gold and ivory — another instance of the influence of the Parnassians and of the chiselled sonnets of José-Maria de Hérédia. Can we then, by examining every point, every initiative, every aspect of the life and works of an artist like Gérôme, succeed in penetrating the mind of an artist of this type, and thus hope to understand the true nature of late XIXth century official art? At the cost of a certain amount of effort, it can probably be done, leaving us, however, still somewhat at a loss to grasp its strange and singular nature. For things were meanwhile happening elsewhere which clearly belong to the world of what we generally accept as art. By this I do not mean to suggest that art must necessarily be in conflict with the needs and requirements of society: there have been cases in which it has been possible for art to develop in reasonable harmony with society. In every case, however, art always brought in certain variations, something different or something extra, by which its specific contribution could be recognized. Sometimes, however, there has been tremendous contradiction, a complete irreductibility, attributable to the genius of the artist. In such cases society is either shocked or subjugated, and when the period is over it is seen that it is precisely the genial originality of the artist which has marked the period, establishing its reputation and often giving it its very name. Franz Hals and Rembrandt painted ' corporation ' pictures which were not too well received by XVIIth century Dutch bourgeois society. In the long run, however, the Dutch school of the XVIIth century, which is generally taken to express and represent XVIIth century Dutch bourgeois society is known entirely by Franz Hals and Rembrandt. Occasionally the conflict between art and society is even more acute, as was the case at the end of the XIXth century. In such cases there are, in point of fact, two arts, which taken at their extremes, are completely incompatible. We are therefore forced to conclude that this particular era was the era of Renoir and Cézanne and not the era of Gérôme. This implies not a difference of talent, but rather a difference in the very conception of art, of the nature of art and of artistic activity.

What then was the conception of art held by bourgeois society in France, and other civilized countries, towards the end of the XIXth century? It was conceived not as *creation* but as *production*: the two conceptions being, of course, completely distinct. Bourgeois society at the end of the XIXth century devoted all its activity — and all the ends and means of this activity — exclusively to production. It was a capitalist society, the sole aim of which was to produce, and which, to this end, exploited scientific progress, invented machines, won colonies, and explored unknown territories. To this end it was constantly totting up the balance of its discoveries, making an inventory of its equipment, taking stock, counting its acquisitions, calculating its profits and its losses. The work of its scholars, engineers and technicians was immediately utilized for the increase of production, and the same was true of the work of its artists, for artists, too, were producers and their works products which, as such, were immediately entered, like any other product, on the credit side of the balance sheet of the *Society* — this term inevitably assuming the double meaning of social group and industrial company. It may be objected that if such were the case, then these products of artistic labour would have been expected to bring in more tangible profits, not only for the account of the artistic producer but also for that of the Society in general. To this it may be replied that a well-run business also has its supernumerary activities, its publicity and entertainment expenses: and that it was under this head that it entered its artistic and spiritual products. For man did not live by bread alone; his sentimentality and his idealism were catered for by battle scenes and landscapes, by statues and paintings celebrating the work, the achievements, the power and the glory of the régime to which he belonged, and of its leading figures, its favourite sons and daughters. Everything was basically considered as a product: and like all production everything was subject to a regular rhythm and was called upon to supply standardized objects in response to constant needs and to a demand formulated in invariable terms. Government institutions established the rules in accordance with which products were to be manufactured and which guaranteed consistent quality. The products were therefore completely homogeneous, in compliance with what is, of course, the basic requirement of all production. Seascapes, beach, woodland or harvest scenes, portraits, victories and defeats (according to the nationality of the artist), vespers in the village or fancy dress balls in high society, statues of Trade, Industry and Thrift, of marshals, presidents and kings — all bore the marks of similar inspiration, all were identical, without the slightest sign of any variant, any heterogeneous factor capable of introducing an element of life. Science and philosophy alike teach us that identity, homogeneity is death. A substance always identical with itself pursues a process of homogenization and is thereby absorbed to the exclusion of any possibility of change or differentiation, thus attaining a state of inertia and death. Is it possible that the ' production ' society with which we are here concerned, however inventive in other fields, was,

Design for the Palace of Electricity at the Paris Universal Exhibition (1900)

in the spiritual sphere, producing only death? This is the logical hypothesis arising from the observation that in this sphere, too, everything was production and not creation. If these works are stripped of their character as 'products' and considered only for any possible creative element, the impression is, in fact, one of a tremendous conceptual lag, of an incompatibility as fundamental as that of life and death.

One conception completely excludes the other, and Gérôme is immediately wiped out, reduced to zero, annihilated and forgotten. It is easy to understand why he and his colleagues, Meissonier, Roybet, Bouguereau, Cormon, Detaille and company, and their equivalents in other countries, with their musketeers, their swathed or naked ladies, their biblical, patriotic, moralizing, gallant or idiotic allegories were eradicated from our memories. All these good men were producers and their works were products and every schoolboy knows the difference between a tree introduced into the production cycle by being sectioned into planks countable by and remunerative to the wood merchant, and the tree as seen by the poet, which is a free creation of nature and of its vital impulse.

No society is, however, so hermetic that it fails to experience some anxiety concerning the existence of the other, creative sphere, however foreign this may seem. A break may occur in the wall of complacency transforming it into an *uneasy conscience*. No doubt it is a matter of considerable gratification to any society to possess its own accredited, official art, an honoured art which in turn brings honour to society, displayed and vaunted in exactly the same way as its agricultural and industrial products. Sooner or later, however, its lack of originality will become apparent, for pleasure, after all, depends upon originality to provide the spice of life, and perhaps even to supply the breath of life itself. Were not the fantastic new inventions on which it prided itself in the technical domain originalities? And was there not bound to be boredom

15

in the sphere of taste and arts if fashion consistently refused to introduce either surprises, or new and piquant elements? Granted that exoticism, Japanese curios, and Cambodian dances, constituted a somewhat unexpected element. They were, however, bound to cloy rapidly unless treated as something other than a mere diversion, unless there was some attempt to go beyond the external appearance of these curiosities and to investigate them more deeply. Moreover, the resuscitation of Henri II and Louis XIV, the junk-shop eclecticism, the perpetual agglomeration soon wore very thin, largely because it was already threadbare. The only new things made were reproductions of antiques and there is always something foolishly paradoxical about such fashionable revivals of new antiques.

How was it possible for a century which had produced so many startling miracles to remain so sordidly senile and degenerate in everything concerning its décor, its homes, its furniture, its everyday objects, its personal adornment, its outward extravagance and its external aspect? Was it possible that its much vaunted industrial achievements should have no influence at all on its appearance? These achievements, so original that the century felt itself completely different from all preceding centuries and even from the first half of the XIXth century, and proclaimed its own *modernity*: a century fully conscious of its singularity and its topicality. This modernity was not a continuation or conclusion, but a beginning, the first chapter of a new age for man, the dawn of a whole new era: the industrial era, the age of the machine. It was impossible for industry and the machine not to extend their influence into every sector of existence, transforming their appearance and eventually making themselves felt in the artistic sector too.

Such an idea may at first have appeared shocking, almost sacrilegious. The spheres of industry and of beauty were irreconcilable. A factory chimney and a steam engine were ugly and prosaic. Members of the *Institut* were inspired by an ideal of beauty in pursuit of which they painted seductive nudes and touching sunsets. An ideal of beauty also inspired the lady readers of Paul Bourget and Pierre Loti and the female audiences of the Opéra and the theatres du Boulevard in accordance with which they modelled their choice of furniture on that of Madame de Pompadour. This ideal of beauty had to be protected from the incursions of industrial progress and ' materialism '. At the time of the Universal Exhibition of 1855, in an article published in the *Journal des Débats* and entitled *Poésie de l'Exposition* [1], Renan had already deplored the triumph of a civilization which took pleasure only in utilitarian festivals and had forgotten the cult of true poetry so admirably celebrated by the Ancients and the Renaissance. Poetry was a spiritual luxury, a gratuitous embellishment entirely unrelated to all the progress from which a degenerate society sought only to draw profit. The ideas of Ruskin, the Pre-Raphaelites and William Morris were not so very different.

A duality of conception thus subsisted even in the minds of those who were nevertheless beginning to dream of a reconciliation between art and industry. The old principle of the distinction between the major arts and the minor, mechanical or menial arts was slow to die. Its roots lay in far distant past, in the mediaeval conception of work as unfitting for gentlemen and — to borrow Rimbaud's metaphor — of the superiority of sword over tool and plough. Over the centuries, this conception had come to be tainted with Manicheism, and an ethnic connotation was added to its historical origin. Works of art were commendable, but all industrial work was base, vile, bad and vulgar. Thus, before recognizing the honorability of industry and the possible beauty of machines an attempt was made to integrate into the realm of beauty certain non-collective, individual handicrafts and to rehabilitate the simple tool, hallowed by long tradition and constituting, as it were, a humble intermediary between the hand and the object which it fashioned. Such direct, rustic, almost natural objects corrupted neither mind nor heart but, on the contrary, induced in the craftsman respectable and salutary virtues. They also led, moreover, to a certain familiarity with the idea that beauty might not be the exclusive property of the plastic arts: a vase, a piece of cloth, could also be considered beautiful. And since beauty was endangered by a world threatened by the clamour and glitter of industrial exhibitions, the least that could be done to protect it was to offer it refuge in one's private life and in the home, whether rich or poor, which was in future to be decorated not by furniture and curios imitated from the past but by the work of a few honourable contemporary artisans, now admitted to the temple of the arts, since they, as much as any follower of Zeuxis or Praxiteles were creating ' things of beauty '. Thus the rehabilitation of handicrafts became the indirect means of broaching the reconciliation of art and industry.

---

[1] *Journal des Débats*, 27 November, 1855, article reprinted in *Essais de morale et de critique*.

All these views, if not all these arguments, found expression among the Pre-Raphaelites, above all in the ideas of that truly great man, William Morris. It is always pointed out, and rightly so, that Morris was a socialist. It is also true that it was a logical consequence of his doctrine that bourgeois society should glorify the products of its industry, regarding the works of its artists both as products and as susceptible of possessing rich spiritual value and ideal dignity. Socialism, however, brought to light a rather different concept: that of the dignity of work itself, of all work, that of engineer and workman as well as that of artist, especially of that particular brand of workman represented by the craftsman. The emphasis was now on τεχνη. The opposition between the term 'fine arts' and those of minor, mechanical, manual, menial arts tended to disappear and to be replaced in France by that of *Arts et Métiers*, in England by that of *Arts and Crafts*, while Germany evolved the concept of *Kunsthandwerk*.

Thus the idea of creation crept in and began gaining ground. For, if men of understanding were prepared to attribute to a piece of pottery or a chair that quality of beauty formerly reserved for a few privileged objects such as statues and pictures, it was because these objects had a common element: all were fabrications — the work of *homo faber*. Statues and pictures were fabricated according to certain sacrosanct rules, according to certain noble canons, for the exclusive enjoyment of certain chosen creatures in their sublimest moments, or, to put it more realistically, to decorate the apartments in which these chosen creatures rested from their labours and received their guests, to decorate the public buildings in which the regime, on which depended the livelihood of these same creatures, conducted its administration and proclaimed its principles and its achievements. The potter, the cabinet maker, the weaver did not presumably aspire to arouse such rare emotions and the work of their hands was destined for daily usage and intended, first and foremost, to be useful. But its maker, in the depths of his innocent soul, had surely harboured some secret ambition, that of making an object agreeable to both eye and hand, practical in form, and, for that very reason, pure and simple. He too, moreover, had behind him a long training and tradition, which, however, had never been codified in any doctrine, but remained local and natural and which he was at liberty to modify in accordance with his own common sense, his own good taste and, eventually, his individual genius. Surely this was true creation?

The idea of creation leads naturally to that of style. Style is the physiognomy, the outward face and countenance of an era. Composed of features visible in all the acts and intentions of that era, not only in the creations of its plastic arts but also in its common objects, its buildings, its décor, its literature and its taste. A style is not a style merely because it is different from that found in preceding periods. The world of bourgeois plastic arts of the last twenty years of the XIXth century had no style, no mark by which it might be distinguished in the panorama of the centuries, a fact which may perhaps, explain its true monstrosity. For to be faceless is indeed to be a monster. Not only art but also everyday objects, buildings, décor, everything lacked a face, and it was the realization of its lack in this particular respect which began to make the period so cruelly conscious of its anonymity. The uneasiness started not with regard to painting or to sculpture, which satisfied its artistic needs, but in relation to its vesture. Its first impulse was to change its skin completely, to transform its houses, its furniture and its personal adornments. Its accredited purveyors, its academic masters could be of no assistance, and recourse was therefore had to the professional — the craftsman, and the labourer. They alone could supply the lacking style, the specificity, the hallmark of its individual existence. In discussing any given style — Henri II, Louis XV — among the first things of which we think are the facades of its buildings, its armchairs, and its personal adornments. The Baptismal Certificate of an era is drawn up from just such elements and the 1870-1900 period was now eager to be baptized.

In England, as we have already seen, the need for style had been particularly strongly felt and the resulting contradictions had caused some confusion. On the one hand its congenital aesthetism bristled at the thought of mechanical invasion. Inherent in the teachings of Ruskin, in the poetical aspirations of the Pre-Raphaelites, and, broadly speaking, in the sensitivity and feeling of the people, as well as in their social structure, their art of forming élites, (and within these élites those strikingly original or even eccentric figures which supply their savour) in the basic aristocratism, dandyism, snobbery of the English — inherent in all this lay an ardent desire to preserve the beautiful and to set it apart from material, industrial and prosaic vulgarity. On the other hand, the British soul is also full of generosity and we have already pointed out, apropos of the valiant pioneering figure of William Morris, the vital role played by this generosity in the birth of socialism. It is a soul inspired by religion, possessed of a reforming, proselytizing spirit. Something of this spirit entered the great movement which now urged them to put beauty into all things, even into those that are indubitably technical products and play so important a role in our domestic and private lives, in our homes, and in our gardens. Putting beauty into these things, into books and posters, into illustrations and typography, led to the recognition of beauty in other things, no longer the product of the workshop but of industry itself — wicked, insolent industry — and of metallurgy with its iron bridges, its factories and its workers' cities. The work of the Arts and Crafts movement and of the successful Glasgow school, were to contribute greatly to the reconciliation of art and industry, and to the birth and propagation of many new concepts such as that of industrial aesthetics.

In France similar conceptions also had their origins in socialism and its forerunners Fourierism and Saint Simonism. Under Napoleon III, in 1863, the *Union Centrale des Beaux-Arts appliqués à l'Industrie* had been created with the object of ' cultivating arts aiming at the combination of the beautiful and the useful .' In 1882, this merged with the Society responsible for the foundation of the *Musée des Arts Décoratifs* and became the *Union Centrale des Arts Décoratifs*. The activities of this society, housed in the *Pavillon de Marsan*, within the hallowed walls of the Louvre, were to prove highly regenerative. In 1887, the former *Ecole de Dessin*, which dated from the XVIIIth century, became the *Ecole des Arts Décoratifs*. Political, industrial and society figures, as well as critics such as Roger-Marx became actively interested in these developments. Painters and sculptors lost their sacred privilege, and manual trades were received into the sanctuary. The tendency was towards an inclusive concept of art, and in Germany the idea of *Gesamtkunstwerk* so stimulating to the ever-powerful German faculty for synthesis was on its way. In 1901, another great pioneer, the tireless organiser and creator van de Velde of Antwerp, was invited by the Grand Duke of Saxe-Weimar to direct in this spirit of synthesis his *School of Arts and Crafts*, out of which, at the close of the 1914 war, and in the changed context of new aesthetic concepts of the post-war years, emerged the *Bauhaus* of Walter Gropius.

Thus the desire to create an individual style for the period originated not in the field of the plastic, or so called major arts, but in that of the minor, the mechanical, manual, artisanal arts, and with the object of increasing collaboration between art and industry and of bringing about an integration of the utilitarian and the beautiful.

The style evolved was the *fin-de-siècle*, 1900 style, or, as it has been called in various places *Art Nouveau*, *Modern style*, *Liberty*, *Sezession*, *Jugendstil*, etc. It flourished in England, in France, in Germany, in Austria, in Holland, in Italy, in Spain, in Scandinavia: it was, in fact, an international phenomenon. Concerned only with the external aspects of collective life, it was, as we have already emphasized, an effort on the part of a bourgeois society to constitute an individual style. By so doing it marked a change of direction in the spirit of that society, a feeling of dissatisfaction in regard to its own sclerotic artistic production, a change of spirit which was in itself a revolution. This revolution, however, was not extended to the plastic arts. In this sphere the revolution was accomplished differently and by means of more basic innovations, beginning at an earlier date and having no connection with *Art Nouveau*. Certain points of contact did, however, exist between *Art Nouveau* and these fundam-

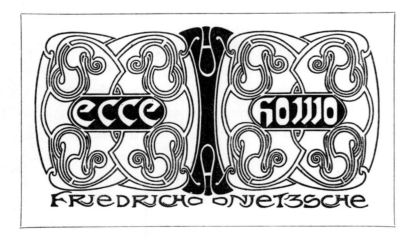

NIETZSCHE, *Ecce Homo. End-papers, designed by van de Velde* (1908)

ental revolutions and these will be considered later on. No doubt such points of contact were no more than secondary: their very existence is, however, worthy of attention. *Art Nouveau* was born of society's desire to change its décor, no longer to borrow its style from a series of historical styles, but to have an individual, characteristic, essentially *new* style of its own. This new style being a decorative style, placing its emphasis on ornament — the framework of existence — on lines and linear rendering, naturally sought its inspiration in life — in certain natural forms, particularly in that of vegetation. It was a sinuous, floral style. A similar sinuous line is to be found in Munch, in Gauguin, Toulouse-Lautrec, and in the Nabis. Moreover this style — voluntarily created by society for its social life — is an intimate style, a

18

style demonstrating the intimacy of man and his surroundings, whether these be private or public, in the home or in the street or in his places of entertainment. This concern with the intimate was also apparent in the work of the revolutionary plastic artists of the time, in the work of the creators (not the producers) who embarked on tapestry, interior decoration, poster work, street decoration, not to mention design for theatrical productions, or became, like Vuillard, painters of *interiors*.

These analogies and similarities become clearer if we recall the general state of sensitivity to which both *Art Nouveau* and the great plastic revolutions of the era owe at least something of their origin. This general sensitivity found expression, broadly speaking, in two major manifestations: in Impressionism and in Symbolism. Impressionism was essentially a naturist and sensualist movement, emphasizing the relationship between consciousness and the mobility and diffluence of the elements, their changes in time, and everything that, in our cosmic immanence, eludes fixation, contour, massive crystallization and angularity. Certainly the naturism of *Art Nouveau* had its roots in Impressionism, itself a profoundly revolutionary movement which, though rejected with much sarcasm by a bourgeoisie infatuated with an evanescent and aquatic vegetation, nevertheless exercised a continual subconscious influence.

Symbolism, though equally disparaged, was also in the air and certain of its emanations, too, came inevitably to be absorbed though mainly in its deliquescent, decadent aspect, the mannerism resulting from the use of obvious techniques and the depths of affectation and pretension to which it sunk in the boulevardizations of Jean Lorrain or the mondanities of Comte Robert de Montesquieu-Fesensac. Before reaching this stage, however, and while still in the first flush of youth, Symbolism did indeed create an atmosphere, somewhat confined no doubt, the stench of which was repellent to a society nevertheless unable to exclude it completely from its salons and its boudoirs. *Art Nouveau* was undoubtely indebted to Baudelaire and to Verlaine and, vice versa, even Mallarmé, *poète maudit* though he was, was not insensitive to the refinements of the taste for 'modern style'. The knick-knacks adorning his poet's retreat — and transfigured in his poems into the furnishings of his mental universe — came in all probability from Bing's or from the Nancy workshops.

> *Surgi de la coupe et du bond*
> *D'une verrerie éphémère*
> *Sans fleurir la veillée amère*
> *Le col ignoré s'interrompt...*

No doubt the swooning arabesque, the linear flight towards the infinite, the transparent insubstantiality of some Gallé vase had just appeared and disappeared. Mallarmé's taste for *Art Nouveau* is proved by a perusal of *La Dernière Mode*, the little magazine — so meticulous, so graceful and so futile — which he published in 1874 for the benefit of the ladies of society, or of certain prose pieces written later on, when *Art Nouveau* was at its height. Far from revolting against contemporary taste, this prince of solitude, this metaphysician, did not disdain even the most superficial, artificial and obvious of its delights, which today seem so far removed from his speculations that they only raise a smile.

Yet the distance between delights and speculations was perhaps, after all, not so great, for if *Art Nouveau* can be said to have had a philosophy at all, we shall certainly discover its origins in Symbolist philosophy. Their common denominator, their guiding principle, was woman. Both were essentially erotic. Both expressed the universal attraction of Eternal Women, of the nymph of the *Après-midi d'un Faune* and so many other shadows, images and Platonist phantom-figures which she rejoins in her flight towards the Buddhist-cum-Schopenhauerian Maya of Jules Laforgue :

> *Si mon air vous dit quelque chose*
> *Vous auriez tort de vous gêner ;*
> *Je ne la fais pas à la pose :*
> *Je suis la Femme, on me connaît.*

Woman, yes, in the full dignity of the philosophical concept, but also woman in her incidental, fashionable form: the little woman of *La Belle Epoque*, midinette of the Boulevards or star of the Moulin Rouge, her pale little face illuminated by

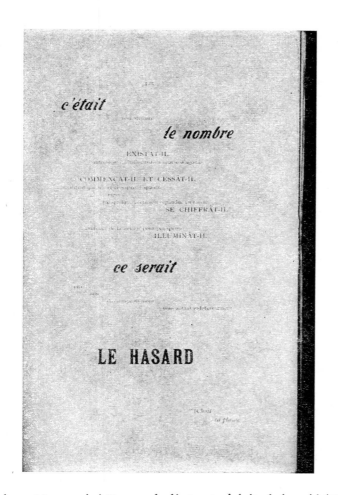

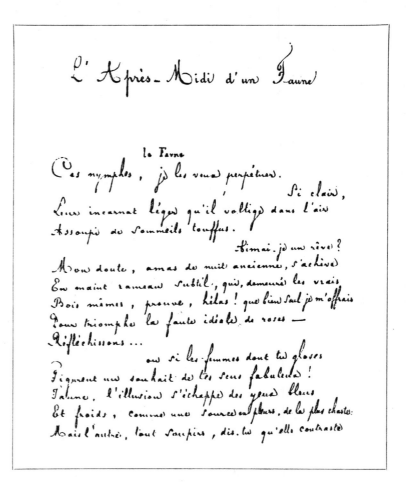

Stéphane MALLARMÉ, ' *Un coup de dés jamais n'abolira le hasard* ' (1897)
Title-page.

Stéphane MALLARMÉ, *Autograph copy of 'L'Après-Midi d'un Faune'* (1876)

gas-light, her uplifted *frous-frous* gleaming in the footlights, her black stockinged toe pointing up towards the chandelier. This woman, Laforgue's haunting ' *petite Eve* ', the subject of so many sketches by Toulouse-Lautrec, Degas, Seurat, so wildly adored, in the person of Loïe Fuller, by Mallarmé and many other great minds of the time: the symbolic and triumphant Parisienne of the 1900 Exhibition with her corseted waist and swirling skirt. In pursuit of this same chimera the greatest geniuses of the Symbolist movement drew upon all the resources of their most audacious and ironical metaphysics, from the most subtle and hermetic lyricism, to the newest forms of musical expression and the rarest of all musical novelties — free verse — with its sinuous inflexions and unexpected falls. For her too *Art Nouveau* projected its curvilinear flights, transposing into its bowls, jewels, lamps, cushions, sofas and beds, indescribably thrilling undulations and sighs of insatiable desire.

Thus *Art Nouveau* received its letters patent and its consecration. It was never a completely preposterous or isolated phenomenon but corresponded to some fundamental need, resulted from some demand of popular consciousness and closely bound up with other things inherent in the climate of the age. It undoubtely suffered from the fact that its only manifestations were in the décor of life and in its ornament, in no way an expression of all that is most vital in the heart of life itself: a fault which was, moreover, responsible for its forward stride. *Art Nouveau* ennobled those crafts catering for the décor of living, where no décor had previously existed. Any décor was certainly better than none. It could, however, be no more than a décor.

In this controversy, which often seems as tangled as the intertwinings of the so-called ' Noodle ' style itself, it can never be too much emphasized that the very fact that so much determination, ingenuity and talent was devoted to the creation of a décor, of a purely decorative style, constituted in itself a major progress. In the process, the barriers between art and craftsmanship were demolished, craftsmen becoming eminently worthy and artists themselves gaining glory by turning their hands to craftsmanship. Gauguin made pottery, Toulouse-Lautrec designed posters and bound books, Maillol and all his Nabi friends took to tapestry, as well as to designing posters and programmes for the *Théâtre de l'Œuvre*. It is in such fields as these that the analogies between *Art Nouveau* and the style of the great plastic artists of the time is most clearly seen, Cheret's posters being in exactly the same spirit as Toulouse-Lautrec's or those designed by Bonnard for the *Revue Blanche* or *France-Champagne*.

This common inspiration was perhaps even more evident in the Germanic countries. *Jugendstil* was an extremely fruitful experiment, the vital spring out of which later flowed the great Expressionist movement. Kandinsky and Klee, in their youth, both passed through the workshop of Franz von Stuck. The same violent current animated the dynamism of *Jugendstil* and that of its prolongation, Expressionism. We have already pointed out the vital importance of the idea of the synthesis of the arts, an idea born in international *Art Nouveau* but which, being in fundamental conformity with the German genius was to have special repercussions in that country, where it underwent constant new developments.

This same alacrity, this curiosity, this happy idea of uniting various crafts in the same creative flight — in fact all the virtues standing to the credit of European *Art Nouveau* may be explained by the revolutions then developing in architecture, thanks to the appearance of new materials and also in response to urgent practical and social needs. A transformation in housing was essential and this transformation was effected. *Art Nouveau* was bound to offer its services to this transformation and naturally its first throught was for its décor. The collaboration between the decorative dynamism of *Art Nouveau* and the renewal in architecture in response to new constructional requirements became, in certain circumstances, even closer. Moreover, most of the *Art Nouveau* artists being architects were, for this very reason, at least as much interested in the shell as in its contents.

The word 'architect' followed the signature of Hector Guimard, on the entrances on the Paris Metro stations, though to our eyes the engaging metal flowerered porticos resting on a similarly ornamented rectangular railing now appear to us purely ornamental. Purely decorative, yet poetic, and at the same time marvellously graceful. Yet Hector Guimard was right in claiming for this work his status as architect, for the architectural problem they presented was entirely without precedent. Architects had hitherto been required to make doors for buildings, whereas here, for the first time in the history of the world, they were required to made an entrance to a hole — a gate of hell in the middle of the Paris pavement. A functional problem, treated ornamentally no doubt, but treated none the less, and it is possible that the majestic floral scrolls designed by Guimard the 'architect' may have been due to his consciousness of the sensational novelty of the architectural problem involved, and to his perception of the need for pompous and portenteous decoration, for some solemn hall-mark for a subterranean entrance destined for a hitherto entirely unknown purpose and into which the mortal herd elected to descend in order to be transported at full speed by the most singular of vehicles.

We have here an example of the difficulty of estimating — at more than half a century's distance — the real value of *Art Nouveau* style. It has provoked much mockery as well as no-less-disdainful expressions of affection. It has been dismissed as out-of-date, irremediably out-of-date, and as belonging to a never-to-be-rehabilitated fashion, a fashion which will never find a place in history or in fame. A fashion so ridiculous that while forming part of history it will have no further place in it. The whole thing doubtless to be attributed to some unfortunate mistake. There is, of course, some basis for such condemnation, and first and foremost was the fact that *Art Nouveau* was a restricted style, having no repercussions on the totality of the artistic creation of its age, corresponding only to a few of the artistic, spiritual and moral aspirations of the time, born of a limited concern with the external aspects of communal life, its furniture, its jewellery, its entertainment, and not with its deepest aspirations or with its creative imagination. It was thus impossible for it to be anything but a decorative style, its inventors — who were in fact decorators — exercising their genius and their inventive faculties only in the field of décor and by the use of decorative forms and methods. At this point, however, major transformations came about in the house itself — the major element in social life — and architecture was swiftly and irreversibly carried along by a stupendous movement of renewal from which it emerged as the predominant medium, the pivot of all other activity in the artistic hierarchy. Henceforward emphasis was to be upon construction and on structure. Technique had in fact triumphed over decoration. At this point a dialogue was engaged between these two forces. The work of the architects and decorators of *Art Nouveau* — in spite of the predominance of decoration and arbitrary proliferation — began to show signs of functional intention, of concern with the practical comfort of the customer. Simple plans, straight lines began to win the day, as can be seen in the works of van de Velde, Horta, Mackintosh, Behrens, Hoffmann and in those of his vehement Austrian compatriot, Adolf Loos, whose campaign for a rational purge was to prove decisive.

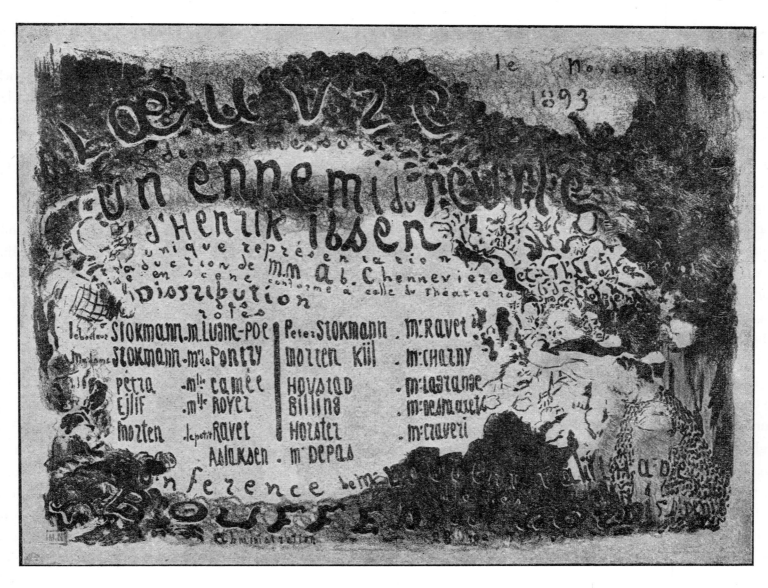

Bonnard's poster for 'An Enemy of the People' by Henrik Ibsen. Théâtre de l'Œuvre (1893)

To do full justice to *Art Nouveau* it is, however, essential to judge it objectively for what it really was, that is to say something totally irrational, whose very paradoxes and excesses lead to an absolute triumph of decoration, and to follow to their logical conclusions its deficiencies, its errors, its gratuitous and foolish wanderings. The artists who went to these extremes may have been architects — and even architects of learning or of talent — but their learning and their talent were deliberately and exclusively consecrated to success in decoration, to the victory of those elements which constituted the very essence of *Art Nouveau*. Such an architect indeed exists: one of the most original figures of the whole *fin de siècle* era, Gaudí.

We have already seen how the vital impulses of *Art Nouveau*, like those of Symbolism, arose from a profound emotionality. Both were inspired by an eroticism, or more broadly speaking, a poeticism, an exuberant poeticism related to the forces of vegetable growth, of cosmic waves. This poeticism was apparent in every activity of the encyclopaedic artist, Gaudí, in his aspirations towards a synthesis of arts and crafts visible in all his works: his furniture, his interior and exterior decoration, his design for the Güell Park, and also in his buildings — his great houses and the gigantic, fabulous cathedral of the *Sagrada Familia*. Naturally he was also faced with truly architectural problems and these he solved by geometry and by technique as well as by the preposterous and, logically enough, by providing such solutions with lyrical, even theological support. I have been told that each storey of the Casa Batlló, for instance, corresponded in his mind to a Mystery of the Rosary. The architect Francesco de Paula Quintana, his collaborator, has recorded how, for Gaudí, the hyperbolic paraboloid was, in fact, a geometrical representation of the symbol of the Holy Trinity. ' Two straight lines situated in space, both infinite and identical in kind; a third line also infinite and identical in kind, insinuating itself between the other two and uniting them: *Patre filioque procedit...* ' [1] parabolic and hyperbolic arcs, set, unlike the usual solidly established arc, across an infinite span, helicoidal columns, subtler and more abstract sisters of the salomonic rope-moulding — all these mathematical creations were also the children of a spiritual union. We may, indeed, ask ourselves whether the Batlló, Güell and Milá houses may really be considered houses? Houses perhaps, but also fantasies and visions, particularly the last — known in Barcelona as the ' stone sickness ' — an instantaneously congealed convulsion which accomplishes the remarkable feat of utilizing not a single angle. Le Corbusier, the functionalist, has rendered hommage to Gaudí, the ' constructor ' [2]. The term ' constructor ' was here deliberate for, besides recognizing in Gaudí's delirious poetry, consonant with all his own passionate poetry and romanticism, Le Corbusier also saw in him the constructor. Even the delirium of his poetry had its landmarks, its fixed vocabulary and thematic patterns, all combined within a strict constructional system. We have just cited some of Gaudí's deepest thought, so typical of the preposterous and arbitrary character of the Spanish genius. If we look more closely we shall, however, find beneath the surface an ancient, fundamental concept known to all great civilizations since the dawn of history, namely that architecture is a language and the temple both a representation and an expression of man himself. When the great civilizations spoke of the sacred character of numbers, they made no distinction between the constant, abstract, fundamentally quantitative function of these numbers and a more mysterious function, which, without in any way affecting the precision of the first, is connected with the play of universal organic forces as well as with that of rhythm on the human heart and mind. It is therefore not surprising if the equations forming the basis of a monument conceived according to architectural science, are also symbols.

At one time the mention of the name of Gaudí served only to raise a laugh, and was, indeed, quoted only by those who had seen Barcelona for themselves. The Catalans alone were proud of their compatriot, never dreaming of classifying him as the extravagant representative of a ludicrous style. The construction of the *Sagrada Familia*, like that of the great mediaeval cathedrals, was a national enterprise, the work of a whole people. In the articles in which the great poet Joan Maragall recounts how, in the course of his walks, he watched the colossus rising from the soil of the city and soaring skyward, there is no mention of the peculiarities of its style — his tone is that of poetry, the work itself being poetic: ' not architecture ', he wrote, ' but architectural poetry ' — without reference to any possible eccentricity on the part of this poetry. This eccentricity is, of course, exactly what strikes the eye of the foreigner, in Gaudí's work. He sees in it not only an old-fashioned style now judged ridiculous but also a kind of absurdity usually imputed to the excesses of the Spanish temperament. In an article published in the magazine *Formes* in 1933, I was, I think, the only person in France to speak seriously of Gaudí's work. Today, he has become a centre of interest, doubtless because it has finally been understood that, as has been pointed out above, it was possible for the mechanical discipline of the art of construction to be combined with a secret, symbolic and vitalizing aim, so that we are now prepared to see, behind Gaudí's paradoxical creations, the master hand of the humanist who rediscovered the principles of major art and applied them in his own inimitable fashion. Even this fashion is now in process of rehabilitation: the moment is now ripe for the understanding of *Art Nouveau* and for recognition that it was — particularly when carried, as in the case of Gaudí, to its ultimate point of expressiveness — an avatar of the eternal Baroque. Baroque now has its accepted place in our mind, taste and appreciation: it is seen to be one of the principal directions in which civilization, in which humanism, may develop. According to an aesthetic concept which reappears from time to time in the history of world culture, feeling, imagination, the vital impulse, and gratuitousness have greater rights than reason, which subordinates everything to certain fixed purposes, and than intellect which calculates the adaptation necessary to ensure strict equivalence to a pre-established aim, and is therefore, in the last resort, and in the broadest possible sense of the term, utilitarian. Baroque excludes the utilitarian in the same way that it excludes categorization. Genres are intermingled. Artifice is made to resemble nature and nature to resemble artifice; contradictions are harmonized; planes, lines and intersections are constrained; the subtle and the hazy are cast in bronze and set in stone; music is injected into the solid, colour into the air, and even soul into mathematics.

---

[1] Francesco de PAULA QUINTANA: *Les formes guerxes del temple de la Sagrada Familia.* La Ciutat i la Casa, n° 6, Barcelona, 1927.
[2] Preface by Joaquin GOMI and J. PRATS VALLÈS: *Gaudí,* ed. R.M., Barcelona, 1958.

The *Art Nouveau* experiment was, in fact, a revival of the Baroque spirit. At its most inspired it surmounted the opposition of what is known as good taste, and even in its more ordinary and humbler manifestations, it constituted a salutary effort on the part of a period desirous of creating its own style, and in its own always restricted domain, provided an accompaniment in a minor, sometimes discordant, key, to the immeasurably greater efforts of contemporary architecture.

The architectural experiment did not, like that of the decorative arts, remain a mere side-line, a separate phenomenon, susceptible of separate consideration. It is, on the contrary, an epic not yet fully told but which reveals at each step new perspectives, opens up new futures.

All was transformed by the advent of iron and concrete. Their requirements cut short the fanciful flights of *Art Nouveau*, imposing a framework from which all ornamentation was effaced, and excluding all superfluous statuary and all convolution, the only problem remaining being that of the concept and distribution of space itself. The new materials called for new techniques to which it was necessary to become accustomed and which, by a natural process without any preconceived ideas, evolved an aesthetic of their own. The style of the period was produced by architects, and also — since the new type of architecture demanded engineers — by engineers. In spite of Gaudí, in spite of the paradoxical, romantic, completely Spanish yet profoundly humanistic exception of Gaudí, all that was incomplete, inadequate, in the attempt of *Art Nouveau* to create its own style at once became evident: the new style — like any other style worthy of the name — could find expression only in the monumental.

The first monuments of the new style were thus sensational, and the story of the use of iron — already so long past but which had developed with such triumphal speed — opened with the Forth Bridge (1888), brilliant offspring of the famous grandfather of all English bridges, the Iron Bridge of 1779; the Garabit Viaduct (survey 1880-84, trial 1888), a chef d'œuvre of the engineer Eiffel, no less remarkable than that by which he is remembered; the Engineering Halls of 1867 and 1878, followed by that designed by Dutert for the 1889 Exhibition; and finally — highlight of this same Exhibition — the Eiffel Tower itself, surviving its original purpose to grace forever the Parisian skyline. There followed Horta's *Maison du Peuple* in Brussels (1896-98), Berlage's Amsterdam Stock Exchange in 1898, and Otto Wagner's Vienna Savings Bank (1905). The invention of cement by Vicat in 1820 and other preliminary phenomena were followed, in the history of concrete, by the sale of Monnier's patent to Germany and Austria in 1880, and by the subsequent exploits of Cottancin, Coignet and Hennebique. In 1893 Coignet constructed the Archères aqueduct, followed in 1893 by Hennebique's first concrete railway bridge. Concrete was employed by the architect Baudot in the construction of the church of St. Jean de Montmartre in 1897-1902, and, in 1902, this same material was utilized for the first time by the Perret brothers in the construction of a block of flats, the now famous 25 bis Rue Franklin, ' simultaneously transposing into the new material the structural system and drawing the plastic consequences of its use ' [1].

Parallel with all these ventures, another no less brilliant venture was taking place in the United States, against the background of a combination of circumstances then sweeping that country forward on the path towards a future infinite in possibilities. Out of this was born a prodigious creation — the skyscraper — of which it is no impiety to say that it is to our century what the cathedral was to the Middle Ages. At first it was regarded as something of a monster, but the Eiffel Tower too, had met with odium: even before its construction a fiery protest had been raised against ' the hateful column of bolted metal ', against the ' gigantic black factory chimney, barbarously overshadowing Notre Dame, the Sainte Chapelle, the Tour St. Jacques, the Dôme des Invalides, the Arc de Triomphe, humiliating all our monuments, and dwarfing all our architecture, all of which will come to fade in face of this appalling nightmare '. Among the signatories of this burst of rhetoric were a number of men of distinguished intelligence whom we are amazed to find involved in such an outbreak of stupidity. On the other hand, and in illustration of the tremendous impression made by the skyscraper on the old world, one might quote the testimony of a newly-elected academician, favorite author of the most hide-bound French bourgeoisie — Paul Bourget, whose notes on his travels in the United States, published in 1895, are remarkable for the sympathy and discernment they display.

---

[1] J.B. ACHE: *La charpente métallique et le béton armé dans l'architecture*. (Catalogue de l'Exposition des Sources du XXme siècle, Musée National d'Art Moderne, Paris, 1960).

L'ILLUSTRATION

Prix du Numéro : 75 Centimes.   SAMEDI 2 NOVEMBRE 1907   65ᵉ *Année.* — Nᵒ 3373.

LES HOMMES VOLANTS

En haut : M. Henri Farman volant, à une vitesse de 88 kilomètres à l'heure, sur le champ de manœuvres d'Issy-les-Moulineaux.
En bas : M. Esnault-Pelterie expérimentant son aviateur à Buc, près Versailles.

Voir l'article, page 296.

2
Bleriot's aircraft
(1908)

3
' *La Fusée* '
Electric locomotive, Heilmann system
(1894)

4
A Renault automobile
(1912)

5
A Ford automobile 'T'
(1908)

6
A Dion-Bouton
automobile
(1898)

7

*First series of 34 Décauville railway posters
at the Paris Universal Exhibition 1889*

8

Paris Universal Exhibition 1889

9

Paris Universal Exhibition 1900

10

Paris Universal Exhibition 1900
Detail of the ' Château d'eau' in the Champ de Mars

11

Paris Universal Exhibition 1900
Title-page of ' L'Encyclopédie du Siècle' devoted to the exhibit.

12
Chicago Universal Exhibition 1893: the Golden Gate

13
Paris Universal Exhibition 1900: the entrance

14

M. Carpezat

Decor for 'Salammbô' by Reyer

15

A. Roller

Decor for 'Rosenkavelier' by Richard Strauss (1911)

16
' *Le Point* '
A page from number 37
devoted to official art

BERTHIER   LE PORTRAIT

GAILLAC   DANS L'ATELIER

BOMPARD   UN DÉBUT DANS L'ATELIER

Pose ... poseurs ... poseuses.

LEFÈBVRE   CAUSERIE

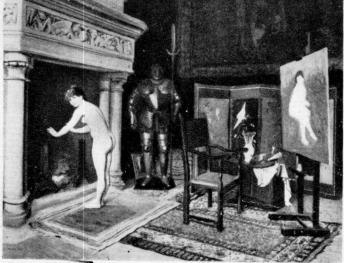

DUMAS   LE MODÈLE FRILEUX

17
Jean-Léon GÉRÔME
Sarah Bernhardt

18
Georges-Antoine ROCHEGROSSE
The Fall of Babylon

19

*A page from no. 1126 of
' Münchener Bilderbogen'
(1895)*

Die Welt in Bildern.
Sechsundvierzigster Bogen.
Deutsch-Ostafrika.

Überfall einer Karawane durch ein Rhinoceros.   Euphorbien (Wolfsmilchbäume).

Boote der Eingebornen.   Landungsplatz einer deutschen Station am Victoria-See.

Mais-Pflanzung.   Höhlenbewohner in der Gegend von Iraku.   Arabische Karawane.   Phönix-Palmen.

Münchener Bilderbogen.   Nro. 1126.   Herausgegeben und verlegt von Braun & Schneider in München.
(Alle Rechte vorbehalten.)   Kgl. Hof- und Universitäts-Buchdruckerei von Dr. C. Wolf & Sohn in München.

20

*A page from no. 1182 of ' Münchener Bilderbogen'
(1895)*

Simples relations de voyages.

On les vit dévorer l'espace sur un coursier indompté. M. Fenouillard, relégué à l'arrière par madame Fenouillard, profite de l'occasion pour affirmer à ses filles, après M. de Buffon, que le cheval est la plus noble conquête de l'homme. Ces demoiselles manifestent par leur attitude qu'elles ne sont pas convaincues de la conquête.

On vit M. Fenouillard, condamné aux galères par son épouse, faire voguer sa famille sur l'onde azurée des grands lacs et des rivières, dans un canot fait de peaux de bêtes. Ce genre de locomotion plaît infiniment à mesdemoiselles Artémise et Cunégonde, dont la figure et l'attitude expriment un état voisin de la béatitude.

Tout serait pour le mieux si, en Amérique, les rivières n'avaient pas des rapides agrémentés de roches à fleur d'eau, ce qui compromet la stabilité de l'appareil, le métacentre ayant alors, chose déplorable, une tendance à se placer au-dessous du centre de gravité. Comme M. Fenouillard ne manquerait pas de l'expliquer à ses filles s'il le savait.

On les vit plus au nord, au milieu des frimas, en panne, dans un traîneau à voile, grâce à un calme aussi subit que plat, et malgré les efforts désespérés de M. Fenouillard, qui tente par un ingénieux moyen de suppléer à l'insuffisance du vent.

On les vit fendre l'air dans un traîneau attelé de chiens ; malheureusement la famille tombe sur un attelage qui est venu au Jardin d'acclimatation, et y a puisé des principes d'insubordination jusqu'alors inconnus dans ces régions hyperboréennes.

On affirme même les avoir vus, toujours plus au nord, utiliser un moyen nouveau et fort original de locomotion. Mais quoique nous devions tout attendre de l'ingéniosité de M. Fenouillard et de sa famille, nous n'osons garantir l'authenticité du fait.

Le gouvernement change de main.

Madame Fenouillard n'est pas pleinement satisfaite. Elle le manifeste hautement en invectivant cet excellent Fenouillard. Puis, elle se déclare en insurrection contre son seigneur et maître et se charge de diriger dorénavant les mouvements stratégiques de la famille.

Madame Fenouillard saisit aussitôt les rênes du gouvernement et, calme, digne, solennelle, prend la tête, suivie de ses deux demoiselles. Tel un consul romain suivi de ses licteurs. Monsieur voudrait bien aller changer de vêtements ; mais il n'ose en demander l'autorisation au consul !

A l'aspect de la mer, madame s'enthousiasme, ces demoiselles aussi. « Que c'est beau ! dit-elle, l'immensité, c'est le commencement de l'infini ! » M. Fenouillard ose émettre timidement l'opinion que la mer est une grande nappe d'eau ; madame lui lance un regard courroucé. M. Fenouillard retire aussitôt son opinion.

« Tout le monde à l'eau, commande madame Fenouillard d'un ton qui n'admet pas de réplique. Monsieur obéit, tout en se disant à part lui, que, venant récemment de prendre un bain, il se dispenserait volontiers d'en prendre un second.

M. Fenouillard, homme prudent, trouvant que sa famille s'aventure trop loin, pousse l'audace jusqu'à en faire l'observation. Cette velléité d'indépendance lui attire un second regard courroucé de son épouse et l'injonction d'avoir à rejoindre son monde immédiatement sous peine d'être qualifié de poltron.

M. Fenouillard, qui a été caporal dans la garde nationale, ne connaît que la discipline. Au moment où il s'apprête à obéir, une vague irrespectueuse le roule avec toute sa famille, et il disparaît dans l'onde amère en articulant ces mots : « Honneur au courage malheureux ! »

21-22
 ' La Famille Fenouillard '
(1889-1893)

23
E. FRIANT
All Saints' Day
(1888)

24
Wilhelm LEIBL
Peasant interior
(1890)

25
Hans THOMA
Taunus landscape
(1891)

26

Jean-Léon GÉRÔME

Dancing Derviches

27

Paul GAUGUIN

The King's Wife

(1896)

28
Jean DAMPT
Grandmother's kiss
(1892)

29
John LAVERY
Spring

30
Giovanni BOLDINI
Portrait of Robert de Montesquiou-Fezensac
(1897)

II

Jules CHERET

Pantomimes lumineuses au Musée Grévin (poster)
(1892)

31

Henri DE TOULOUSE-LAUTREC

Misia Natanson

(1895)

32

Pierre BONNARD

France-Champagne (poster)

(1892)

33
A.H. MACKMURDO
Textile
(about 1884)

35
August ENDELL
Armchair
(1899)

34
Émile GALLÉ
Cup
(1884)

marteau-pilon à la forge de grosses-œuvres. (L'énorme pièce à forger sort éblouissante du four; les hommes manœuvrent pour l'amener sous le lion.) — Dessin de F. Bonhomme d'après nature.

36
Power-hammer
(about 1860)

37
' Hammond ' typewriter
(1887)

38
Edison phonograph with cylinder
(about 1900)

39
The first Diesel engine
(1897)

40

Two electric radiators

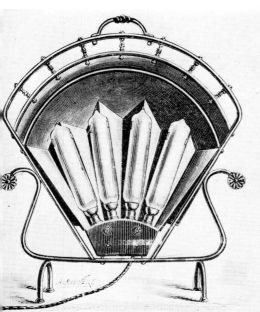

Fig. 51. — Radiateur de salon de la Compagnie de chauffage par l'électricité.

Fig. 52. — Cheminée radiateur de la Compagnie de chauffage par l'électricité.

41

Mouchot and Pifre

Solar machine
(about 1880)

42

Gustave EIFFEL

Garabit viaduct
(1880-1884)

43

John FOWLER and Benjamin BAKER

The Firth of Forth bridge near Edinburgh
(1881-1887)

44

Antoni GAUDÍ

Entrance to the Güell Park, Barcelona
(1900–1914)

45
Hector GUIMARD
Entrance to a ' Métro ' station in Paris
(1889-1904)

46
Otto WAGNER
The ' Karlsplatz ' Station in Vienna
(1899-1901)

III

Eugène Grasset

Stained-glass window: 'Spring'
(1884)

All the new and powerful poetry, the tremendous, youthful, optimistic adventure of the American millions, the whole great American legend, the whole great American myth, were understood and expressed by Paul Bourget. He also grasped the significance of the drive to the West and all the epic, romantic, lyrical themes with which we have since become familiar thanks to American films and books. He understood, too, the folklore of the Western, the convict songs, the tales of the harsh and brutal hazards of the pioneering life. Improbable as it may seem, this society novelist must be considered one of the first discoverers of the new America, and it is from his work that I should like to quote in order to convey as adequately as possible the beauty and significance of the skyscraper phenomenon.

' ... Suddenly there are buildings on every side. Buildings scaling the sky with their eighteen or twenty stories. The architect who built, or rather ' engineered ' them, has renounced the use of columns, mouldings, and all other classical embellishments. He has accepted once and for all the condition imposed by the speculator: to multiply the greatest possible number of times the value of the small plot of ground at the base, by multiplying the number of floors superimposed upon it. While this might be supposed to be a problem of interest only to the engineer, it is however not at all the case. Sheer necessity is so much a principle of beauty, and is so forcefully expressed by these buildings, that they arouse in the spectator a remarkable degree of emotion. A new kind of art is here beginning to take shape, a democratic art, made by the mass and for the mass, a scientific art in which the certitude of natural laws confers upon what appear to be the wildest audacities, the tranquillity of geometrical forms ' [1].

The skyscrapers which so astonished Paul Bourget were at most some twenty stories high. Their successors attained far more astronomical dimensions. Already, however, they sprang fully armed from the brain of the human Jupiter and their very principle, the whole of their unique, their revolutionary character is conveyed in these few lines. We have already seen how, less than ten years after proclaiming, in his *Avenir de la Science*, his boldly revolutionary thoughts of 1848, Renan confessed his terror of industrial invention and his failure to understand the ' poetry of the Exhibition '. In Bourget — on the other hand — we find a future reactionary doctrinaire who face to face with the skyscraper, immediately accepted the idea of its reconciliation of art with utilitarian needs, as well as that of the lyric quality of scientific and technical progress and of its infinite potentialities, conceiving the existence of beauty — yes, of beauty — in things no longer having anything in common with the tradition of the classical column but arousing admiration in totally new and unaccustomed ways — an authentically, vitally up-to-date, modern, and — let us admit the term — *democratic*, beauty.

Thus the skyscrapers mounted ever higher to the greater glory of the New World then in the melting pot. Their increased height was due to the steam elevator or lift invented by Elisha Graves Otis in the middle of the century, becoming electric some thirty years later, thanks to W. Siemens. A new conception of the city then arose in which the principal element became the skyscraper, now considered as a ' unit ' (a term which has met with much success) with its specific structure, its metal skeleton, its towering rectangular bulk, the play of light first upon its horizontal windows and before long upon its weightless all-glass walls, and finally its whole complex internal organization, its blood stream, its intricate machinery, all adapted to the multiple and various functions of human activity.

To the Chicago school of William Le Baron Jenney and Louis Sullivan, future master of Frank Lloyd Wright, must go the credit for giving impetus to the tremendous architectural expansion of the United States. The vital energy characteriz-ing this creative work, so perfectly attuned to the American genius, cannot be over-emphasized. No doubt the Exhibition held in this same mushrooming city of Chicago in 1893 demonstrated that the new masters were still a prey to a ludicrous nostalgia for the Old World. A healthy and original spirit, however, triumphed with the growing conviction, natural to a people of immigrants, settlers and pioneers, for whom no enterprise was too bold, that the virgin land of America must work out its own pattern, its own destiny — a destiny as unique as each of the individual destinies of which it was com-pounded. The symbol, the poet of this America, was Walt Whitman. Sullivan was his fervent admirer and it is impossible not to draw a parallel between Whitman and the other great architect then on the threshold of his career, the extraordinary Frank Lloyd Wright — obstinate, capricious, proud, indomitable, Frank Lloyd Wright — American to the very marrow

---

[1] Paul BOURGET: *Outre-mer, notes sur l'Amérique*, Paris, Lemerre, 1895.

of his bones, who, moreover, was by no means a fanatic of the skyscrapers, but on the contrary endeavoured in his ' prairie style ' to attune his constructions to nature, to American nature, a feeling for nature borne within himself and to which, like Jean-Jacques Rousseau in Europe before him, he was able to convey life. It is no accident that his name should spring to mind immediately after that of another solitary, Whitman. It is essential to note that the revolutions dictated by the Goddess Reason, the rational and rationalistic revolutions — and notably the positivist, mechanical, industrial revolution with which we are here concerned — were accompanied by a revival of feeling for nature, a reintegration of vital, primitive and cosmic forces. It would, indeed, be a very superficial error to see in the American phenomenon only concern for practical efficiency and for earning dollars, or as no more then a spirit of system reinforced by industrial methods. It was also profoundly emotional, naïvely naturist and humanitarian, philosophically daring and utopian, in a word — Romantic. This romanticism embraced the whole continent, characterising also Latin America, and it must not be neglected in any attempt to understand the twentieth century, in which the spirit and destiny of America have played so great, one may almost say so preponderant, a part.

We have already spoken of the city and the new concept of the city at which man had arrived during the last third of the XIXth century. Not only must man become engineer and architect, and engineer-cum-architect, but also town planner and architect-cum-town planner. Here, too, a certain romanticism, and a vigorous effort of imagination, was required. Proof of this can be found in the figure of one of the forerunners of town planning, Claude-Nicolas Ledoux — unquestionably a poet, and a poet of the imagination — as also in the dreams of the first French and English socialists. These were followed by the theories, designs and realizations of the first garden city planners and of their master Ebenezer Howard, by Tony Garnier's superb project for an industrial city. The contemporary world was stifling in great cities, created and developed as a result of historical and geographical hazards and upon which the industrial revolution was imposing conditions to which it was becoming more and more difficult to adapt. Certain routines, justified by false conceptions of personal and family comfort, had become established and there was little inclination to see them disappear. Noxious slums, the anarchistic and ugly growth of the suburbs, complicated existence, increased the difficulties of both work and leisure. How to maintain a balance between the urban and rural activities, how to regulate the ever-increasing circulation of people and of goods, how to locate industry in the place most fitted to its efficiency and expansion? Not only was it necessary to reform everything already in existence and everything that, in the older countries, had led to such inexorable congestion, but even in countries where space was available, it was essential to create, and to create with the most prudent and farsighted provision for future development. Such were the problems which, with all the financial, administrative and political considerations involved, faced the ingenuity of man at the end of the XIXth century, and upon the solution of these problems depended the entire future of the inhabitants of our planet.

At this point in our investigation, it may be observed that three levels of artistic creation have so far been examined . The first — production rather than true creation and subject to the injunctions of a dominant social class well satisfied with its power and its stability — was a bourgeois, official, state-approved art, generously remunerated and upheld by public favour, in which there appeared no variation, no originality, no daring unless it were for certain faint signs of contamination on its outer fringe, due to certain superficial influences and passing fancies. On the second level the somnolence of this same society was troubled by the stirrings of a confused nostalgia for creation, by the perception of a need, of a desire to possess an individual style, to mark its own place in the history of styles. This style, which affected only immediate, everyday objects and external décor, was, of course *Art Nouveau*, in which the role of the artist was no longer that of producer but of true creator. For invention now became imperative. An entirely novel situation faced these new inventors, who, gifted with creative imagination, were determined, come what might, to offer their creations on the market of contemporary society. A number of new factors — fashion, snobbery, taste, criticism — testify to the birth of a certain new artistic life in those very areas where, during the reign of official production, there had existed no such life. The new type of artist, who was well worthy of the name of artist, was above all an artisan. He had earned the name of artist while rehabilitating that of artisan. Not only must he invent forms, but he must also concern himself with materials and techniques previously scorned and relegated to the realm of industry. He practised ceramics, weaving, tapestry, stained-glass work, all crafts employing tools and even rudimentary, highly traditional and primitive machines. Finally, a conciliatory step was taken towards industry — that industry whose progress had seemed so marvellous on the strictly technical plane and so fearsome on the moral and aesthetic level. The taboo was broken: the barriers protecting the sacred reserve in which the beautiful had hitherto been conserved as carefully as if it were an intangible and invariable value, guaranteed to satisfy the idealistic needs of men interested also in other more realistic and immediately profitable values, the prices of which are quoted on the Stock Exchanges of the world. This contradiction was resolved by the intermediary of the *industrial arts*, society admitting creation and creation becoming integrated into social activities. These social activities, so profitable to man's contemporary and future way of life, were thus augmented by a new activity which was to prove equally necessary to modern man, assisting him in the creation of his décor and the organization of his luxury.

Artistic genius had also, however, a more fundamental part to play in the activities of society and in the transformations of the human way of life, thus bringing us to our third level of perspective. Such transformations constituted a gigantic whole, an immense concerted action and their elements were reciprocally connected, none susceptible of being subtracted and considered on its own as a separate self-sufficient entity, providing its own specific interest and enjoyment. All distinction between the beautiful and the useful was effaced, as was that between the enthusiasm inspired by industrial prodigies and that which only a chair-leg or a Japanese screen were considered worthy of inspiring. Modern man built his bridges, his buildings, his towns, his factories, his aerodromes and suddenly all this was art, all this was beauty. A new but nevertheless irrefutable beauty. An art, undoubtledly, even if curiously hybrid. An art to be taken as it was, utilizing arithmetic and every kind of scientific and technical knowledge, co-operating in powerful and complex enterprises, dependent upon all the realities involved in the development of Capitalism, including all its contradictions: human and social realities, the welfare of the worker, the comfort and convenience of all men. The reign of architecture had begun, and with it the reign of social art. Naturally this term must be stripped of all idea of any particular art descending from the empyrean to 'join the people'. It must be taken in its overall sense and understood that art, in the form of the modern architectural epic, was, indeed, a social art in which it is impossible to isolate artistic creation from the concept of human society in process of transforming its earthly condition: impossible to separate it from the *world*. Art participates in a universal action of this nature without it being possible to define its participation, to segregate its individual contribution. An Eiffel, a Sullivan, a Perret were not specialists invited by society to perform certain specified tasks. They were pervading universal spirits, advisers, directors and agents of earthly progress, their activities embracing the whole machinery of such progress. And the result of their activities presented certain qualities which can only be summed up by the word 'beauty.' Thus it is only at the end of a tremendous mechanism of preliminary measures, a great combined launching operation, that art appears casting its retrospective light upon what had gone before. It may well be objected that architecture has always been a multiple activity implying a certain number of activities in no way connected with art, and that architects had long since built great ensembles, founded cities, and participated in princely enterprises such as wars and festivals. All this is true, but never in history had multiplicity of architectural practice been so great, because history has never previously experienced a revolution so decisive as the industrial revolution of our time, completely transforming the material conditions of the life of man, as well as all his work and all his tools. A single art presided at this revolution, an art which is the algebra of all the arts, but also the algebra of every variety of craft and skill: the art of architecture. It is *par excellence* a social art; now more basically, more completely and more magnificently social than ever before. This conclusion is all the more striking in that it applies to a period when the concept of art itself and the art of contemporary society were without any possible relationship. Society was satisfied with an art which was not art at all, and subsequently made for itself an art expressly for its minor pleasure. By the happy expedient of promoting the artisan to the dignity of artist, this art became, indeed, a real art, though limited to the decorative sphere, an art in which the triumph of mind over the material, nature and justification of things remained, however, far too sporadic and unbalanced — an art of paradox and of caprice. This art must also be called social, but only timidly, hesitantly social, since even in a time of tremendous industrial ferment, it showed itself only in minor crafts or, when in the major register, by inflated, pompous buildings, covered with superfluities. Finally, during this same period, art revealed itself unreservedly and completely in the form of architecture: completely social, entirely worthy of the era, keeping perfect step with its development, and making of its own development the real history of the era, the history of contemporary man on the march towards new and extraordinary destinies.

Thus architecture, which, from every point of view, merits not only the name of social art, but that of art itself, entered at last into its own and it is therefore not surprising that we should find analogies and interrelationships between architecture and other contemporary arts, that is to say the plastic arts now restored to their true function. We shall see later how this restoration was brought about, and how, despite a hostile society, the revolutions by which painting and sculpture regained their true functions came to be effected. We cannot, however, leave the subject of the architectural revolution without giving some idea of its spiritual relationship to the revolutions accomplished in painting and in sculpture. The choice of the word 'spiritual' is deliberate, for it was indeed spiritually, in the spirit, in parallel spiritual aims that we must look for resemblances between the new architecture and, for example, the geometrical, discontinuous and reasoned forms of Cubism. The same spirit inspired both these transformations. It can, in fact, be observed that there was something of the engineer in the spirit and the resolution of the Cubists, in their reconstitution of separate parts, their reduction of the subject into working drawings. The Cubism of Léger in particular, with the tubular forms resulting from his close acquaintance with the French field guns of the 1914 war, and later, with his wheels, driving rods, ropes, his pieces of machinery and his pieces of pieces of machinery, certainly provides the most striking conceivable pictorial expression of our industrial age. But even before this particular development, Cubism had, from the very outset, revealed itself as the art of the industrial age by its analytical and conceptual character and its determination to construct. The very term construction, the whole idea of structure, were familiar to the Cubists, and architecture, which had become more than ever before the art of construction and of structure, emerged as the major art — the sign and symbol governing all plastic revolutions effected in contemporary France. And the master dominating all these common trends and searchings was Paul Cézanne, the great constructor whose ambition was nothing less than the reconstruction of nature itself.

Thus painting, like architecture, felt the need for a thorough clean-up, an asepsis. All extraneous suggestion of ambiant nature was to be eliminated, as were all sensitive and sentimental influences, and all ornamental adjuncts. The planning and setting up of structures required an inexorable resolution to denude, as well as linear rectitude, discipline and simplicity. Lines, figures, planes and volumes are all objects of precision, admitting no admixture, no ambiguity. The complicity of Cubism and of modern architecture was to appear more clearly when, at the close of the 1914 war, it became possible to measure their full effect. It was, however, already implicit in the profound necessity determining both the first manifestations of modern architecture and the birth of Cubism, namely the need for a world of clarity. This internal clarity was an intellectual, a spiritual clarity: a clarity recognized by the spirit itself and communicated by it to the world. Hence the predominance of the intellectual faculty over all the others.

A similar predominance was to be found in the works of Mondrian, and in those of the architect J.J.P. Oud, as well as in the Dutch *Stijl* group, created during the 1914 war. As early as 1913 one of the leaders of this group, Van Doesburg, had, indeed, proclaimed that they had 'replaced a brown world by a white'. We can never sufficiently deplore the disappearance of the Strasbourg *Aubette*: archetype of classical architecture, the work of François Blondel, its interior redecorated by Van Doesburg, Sophie Täuber and Arp, and constituting a veritable group manifesto. The members of this group, whose theories come under the heading of Neo-Plasticism, carried to its logical conclusion a determination not only to ordain in accordance with strict geometrical and architectural principles the whole of natural creation, but also to submit to the same discipline the domestic and social life of man. Doubtless this passion for authority, incorruptibility and hygiene on the part of the Neo-Plasticists is to be attributed to the obstinate Calvinist traditions of predestination and Iconoclasm. This, however, is but one particular aspect of a general phenomenon, the tendency of all contemporary arts to place themselves under the aegis of architecture, and to accept from this supreme and universal science — acknowledged master of all knowledge and all its applications — a decisive lesson of order and of purity.

This same lesson was taught at the *Bauhaus*. Its founder was the great architect Gropius, inheritor of the concept of community art previously held by van de Velde and by so many others, the dominant conception, in fact, of the whole era, ever since its first tentative appearance. Community art, an art embracing all the arts and integrating them into social activity, was both taught and practised by the *Bauhaus* group, and the keystone of all this teaching and practice was architecture, itself a community art, dedicated to the community, a collective and synthetic art, an art in the service of mankind, calling for the collaboration of all the arts, and supplying them with unity of doctrine, of resolution and of spirit. Architecture was not merely one of many genres, one of several disciplines brilliantly cultivated at the end of the XIXth and throughout the XXth century; it was also a philosophy.

Reference has already been made to Symbolism — the major spiritual phenomenon of the last twenty years of the XIXth century — apropos of the insidious and malignant influence which it exercised on *Art Nouveau*, by which Impressionism was prolonged and expanded in literary form, and provided with philosophic expression. Impressionism was in reality the art of mobility; founded exclusively on sensation, it conveyed to our senses the perpetual changes of light, the ceaseless action of the fluid elements — air, water, hours and seasons — making us completely dependent on the power of time. As soon as this dependency was achieved, things began to lose their outline, appearing henceforward ephemeral and confused, without fixed aspect, and the cosmos in which we participate by our successive optic perceptions was thus a continual *becoming*, and hence a delectable illusion. This same doctrine of mobility was also proclaimed by sculpture, despite the fact that sculpture is an art of mass and gravity. Thanks to the genius of Menardo Rosso, sculptural matter began to flow in the same way as pictorial matter while Rodin, in his determination to convey the impression of non-fixed, continous action, created flexion by the use of shadow. This dynamism, the theory of which is lucidly and admirably expressed in the interviews of the master with Paul Gsell, shared some of the aspirations of Impressionism, as did also the music of Debussy. Bergson gave these ideas their shape and system. And it is certain that in yet another form they appear in Symbolism, in the half-tints and ambiguities of its sensibility, its taste for the ephemeral and for all that is conveyed by the word ' *chute* ' or ' fall ' [1], the intuitive and musical flexibility of its free-verse, and finally in the basic vitalism, which, while delighting in following the declining curve to the vertiginous brink of absence, also acceded in other forms of expression to the ultimate heights of joy. Thus it is not surprising to find that the man best able to put Impressionism into words should have been the Symbolist poet, Jules Laforgue. Every great period of art, let it be observed, has its own poet, who always proves a more profound and illuminating aesthetician than the critics. The previous period had had Baudelaire, the following was to have Apollinaire. Impressionism, then, was miraculously well understood and analysed in the posthumous notes of Jules Laforgue — the Symbolist poet par excellence (and the inventor of free-verse). His role was, in fact, to demonstrate that the Symbolist philosophy followed logically on Impressionist philosophy. While Impressionism, however, had been purely French, Symbolism overflowed the frontiers of France to become a universal phenomenon.

One of its antecedents was thus that particular manifestation of the French genius called Impressionism: on the literary plane its origins were also French — first and foremost Baudelaire, followed by those other great poets — whose names must figure among the greatest of the great — Verlaine, Rimbaud, Mallarmé. While not yet calling themselves Symbolists, these poets were the masters of Symbolism, Laforgue himself belonging to the first generation of declared Symbolists, already convinced of the exceptional intentions of their movement, of the renaissance it was effecting and of the place it was carving out for itself in the glorious history of French lyricism. A few dates are here in order. In 1884 — the year of the sale of Manet's studio, of the foundation of the *Salon des Indépendants*, of the first *Salon des XX* in Brussels — Huysmans published *A Rebours* in which he proclaimed his admiration for Mallarmé, Redon and other '*frissons nouveaux*'. In 1887 appeared in the *Revue Indépendante* the nine fascicules composing the *Poésies Complètes de Stéphane Mallarmé*. The same year saw the death of Laforgue. In 1896, followed that of Verlaine and in 1897, in the May number of the magazine *Cosmopolis*, Mallarmé published his *Coup de dés*, the climax of a prolonged metaphysical and poetic ascetic exercise. Meanwhile in 1886, Valéry had published his *Soirée avec M. Teste* and in 1889 appeared both Maeterlinck's *Serres chaudes* and Bergson's Thesis on the *Données immédiates de la Conscience*. In 1890 Albert Aurier published in the *Mercure de France* the first article devoted to Van Gogh.

---

[1] ' ... car depuis que la blanche créature n'est plus, étrangement et singulièrement, j'ai aimé tout ce qui se résumait en ce mot: chute '. (MALLARMÉ : *Plainte d'automne*).

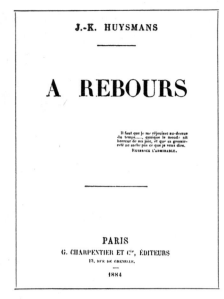

J.K. HUYSMANS, *A rebours.*
Title-page (1884)

Maurice MAETERLINCK, *Serres chaudes.*
Title-page (1889)

Paul VALÉRY, *La soirée avec Monsieur Teste.* Title-page (1906)

The reader will doubtless have observed in this enumeration a number of synchronisms between events in the intellectual life of France and that of Belgium : it was, in fact, in Belgium that French symbolism awakened its first echoes, and, indeed, not only echoes, but true harmonies.   Symbolism was to become the true expression of a Belgium then in the throes of a fervent renaissance leading to the creation, out of the depths of its national genuis, of an art and literature of its own.   While it is only fair to emphasize the active and brilliant role played in the creation of this literature by the Walloons, so geographically close to France and so deeply imbued with its history and its literature — the important magazine founded in 1886 by Albert Mockel even bore the title *Wallonie* — it must also be recognized that this creation was for the most part the work of Flemings writing in the French language and thereby subjecting this language to certain turns of phrase, certain distortions, certain subtleties which might never have been discovered had it not been for this necessity of expressing things conceived and experienced on the confines of its territory.   If Symbolism constituted so deep an enrichment for French sensitivity and for the French language, this was undoubtedly due in large part to the remarkable contribution of the new Belgian literature.   Born in France, Symbolism rapidly became naturalized in Belgium, where it found a favourable soil for redoubled and vigorous new growth.   By its very nature, Symbolism seemed to respond to the deepest and most specific properties of the Belgian genius, and particularly to Flemish complexion of the Belgian genius.   There was, moreover, a simultaneous renaissance of Flemish language and lyricism — its magnificent vigour revealed by Guido Gezelle, and above all by the great poet Karel Van de Woestijne.   The vital point to be considered here, on account of the European repercussions involved, is, however, the meeting of Flemish genius with French literature, the injection of Flemish blood into French literature, with the result that Symbolism, born, it must be repeated, in France, assumed a certain aspect, followed a certain development, acquired a certain meaning, becoming what it was and all that it was — becoming, indeed, Symbolism itself — thanks to the vital contribution of poets by the name of Maeterlinck, Verhaeren, Elskamp and Van Lerberghe.

This constitutes a first important reason for the universalization of Symbolism, a universalization which extended to Germany, mainly through Stephan George, disciple of Mallarmé, who in turn adopted the search for a hermetic poetry, cultivated in isolation, accepted only by an infinitesimal élite.   It invaded the young schools of poetry throughout the world, including Russia with Bryusov, Biely, the early Blok, and Latin America, where the greatest poet of the continent, Ruben Dario, under Parisian influence, transformed the lyricism of the whole peninsula: a remarkable détour, providing an excellent illustration of the expansive force of Symbolist poetry.

Symbolism must not, however, be studied only as a poetical phenomenon.   To do so would be to fail both to penetrate its doctrine, and to grasp the full extent of its power.   Symbolism was not merely a revolution in human sensitivity, which, following upon Impressionism, led to a new appreciation of the fleeting quality of instants and of objects, to the dawn of

54

a kind of cosmic sentiment, a bemused and musical pantheism, an exquisite communion with universal time. To advance yet a little further into the philosophical sphere, we must, to borrow its own terminology, recognize in Symbolism also a certain *idealism*. If the emphasis is placed upon the word *symbol* from which the movement took its name, we shall discover the fundamental nature of the mystic quest of Mallarmé the Platonist, as well as that of Gauguin, who appears in such deep reaction against impressionist art, an art so sensual, so materialist, that he declared it to be ' acephalous ', adding that it contained ' no place for thought '. From this flux, this deliquescence, this entanglement, Gauguin's aim was to disengage thought, which to him, as a plastic artist, signified line. Mallarmé's quest for Idea was thus closely paralleled by Gauguin's search for Style.

This idealistic aspect of symbolism appealed primarily to the nordic spirit. Hegelian philosophy had prepared the ground, as had also a lack of true plastic tradition, a congenital want of skill in seizing semblances and giving them the dignity of form, a fundamental impossibility to obtain from such exercises the same satisfaction as the Latins who bring to them the full severity of their taste and of their culture — and, on the other hand, a desperate need of unreality, or rather of a moral explanation of reality. It is thus scarcely surprising to find that in Germany the influence of Puvis de Chavannes was as great as that of Gauguin. Both these artists tended in the same direction, towards a two-dimensional, simplified, linear vision. In France, however, where the requirements of plastic quality are extremely high, Gauguin's was the vital lesson, whereas the allegorical imagery of Puvis was ignored, in spite of his official success, in spite of the approval of certain men of taste such as Mallarmé himself, who composed a sonnet in his honour. In Germany, on the other hand, the lesson of Puvis served to complete that of Hans von Marées and certain other avant-garde leaders, and there was no hesitation in placing him on the same plane as Gauguin.

Similarly — to the eternal surprise of the French — the Germanic countries also followed the teachings of the Swiss artist Hodler. His gigantic figures hacked out with a woodcutter's axe and his allegories were taken to be symbols and, as such, extolled to the German skies. There exists a Protestant tendency to accept figures only when they can be found to yield some moral meaning. It is, of course, impossible to deny the importance of Holder in the history of Swiss art, which was, indeed, created by Hodler and imposed by him on a whole section of the European continent. In the art of Hodler the Swiss soul found expression, his rough and uncouth genius proving particularly successful in rendering his native mountains, also hewn out, as it were, by axe-like strokes, like a series of gigantic diamonds glistening in a resplendent sky. This alone might have justified his role and his success. In order to understand the full significance attached to Symbolism by the German genius, eternally obsessed with the ideal, consideration must, however, be given to his work as a whole: both to those elements which seem to us plastically complete and to that which, beneath its monumental proportions conceals also a spiritual intent.

We are immediately led to recognize the link existing between Wagnerism and Symbolism. This time the term ' symbol ' is interpreted in its fullest and its richest sense, devoid of all suspicion of vulgar, facile allegory. Were not the leitmotifs, the very elements of Wagner's art, also symbols? A concept, an emotion, a passion, a character, a vital impulse, an object, each and everyone embodying the absolute irradiance of the music, are set to work upon our souls both as individuals — recognizable at each successive appearance — and also in an infinite capacity. Thus it is with youth, redemption, death, desire, the strong father, fallen king, vile woman, monster, forest, sea, night, sword and cup. In another northern dramaturgy, that of Ibsen, we find a similar proceeding, that of an art based on symbol — or rather the same concept of an art which is, in fact, actually composed of symbol. Just as Wagner's symbolism must be interpreted not by any literal and restricted allegorical interpretation, but by all the limitless, discursive, ineffable, mystic suggestions of the music, so with Ibsen, symbolism is presented to our minds through all the myriad paths of human destinies and of the emotive word, poised on the brink of silence. Here, too, every object evoked, down to the last minor accessory, participates in the general transfiguration: the tower, the sleigh, the duck, the bed of the dying mother, the light of the last cigar.

Whether Symbolism is considered as what it really was: a revolution in French poetry, or whether its empire is taken to include the contemporary aspirations and creations of the rest of Europe, the definition is the same: a representation of the world by resonance and mystery. But it is an exploration, rather than an explanation. This leads us to emphasize the importance, second only to that of the great French metaphysical poets, Rimbaud, Laforgue, Mallarmé, of the great figure of

Maeterlinck. Maeterlinck's role was capital. In France after a certain amount of friendly or foolish mockery of his symbolist mannerism, Maeterlinck has been somewhat neglected. He has, in fact, often been regarded merely as the author of the text — one is almost tempted to say the ' libretto ' — of *Pelléas et Mélisande* set to the music of Debussy, and this text has remained in public memory because it is so closely identified with the sonorities of Debussy's music. This very identification, this remarkably happy identification, was, however, the result of a miraculous meeting of two equally perfect talents, two equally creative geniuses. We must also take into consideration Maeterlinck's commanding influence outside France, on extremely divergent types of intellect not all pertaining to the world of literature, and, in particular, on the Expressionist painters. Maeterlinck is one of the rare names quoted in the writings of Kandinsky, one of the ' voyants ' from whom he claims descent in his quest for the ' spiritual '. Lounacharsky, Commissar of Education in a later revolutionary Russia favorable to artistic revolution, devoted an article to Maeterlinck in the magazine *Obrazo-vanie* in 1902. The representative character and significance of his influence will no doubt be more fully appreciated if we examine the analogies existing between his art and that of the great German poet Rainer Maria Rilke. Maeterlinck and Rilke shared a love of the humble and the lowly, both were gifted with the same faculty of attention: that subtle, scrupulous, almost painful force of sympathy applied to the minutest detail of daily life, to human scenes, human interchanges, the infinitesimal actions of nature, flower and beast. In all this they discerned and revealed a new language. All this composed a living entity from which neither poet would exclude death itself. For death also has its revelations, which are the same as those of life.

The highly representative and universally influential figure of Maeterlinck helps us to appreciate the full force of Symbolism and to realize that this movement, spiritual as well as literary, marking the last twenty years of the XIXth century, was one of the greatest movements in the history of human civilization. The strange lyricism of Maeterlinck, the tragic puppets of his theatre, his absolute pity transcending rational judgment, his curiosity concerning the faintest stirrings of the vegetable world, of stone or insect, of child, saint or mystic, his respect for the humblest destiny and his search for wisdom, the whole new science which he introduced, the science of silence — or, as it should be called and as, indeed, he himself has called it the science of the soul — gives, as no other work of the period can give, a complete picture of contemporary culture, and of the atmosphere with which this culture was imbued. It also makes it easy to understand how it was that music came to occupy a place of such importance.

For this period music represented both a method of knowledge and a moral act: a truth later established by Romain Rolland. Music constitutes the final and the highest representation of the world: the Germans, from Schopenhauer onwards, could not fail to subscribe to this contention, and Symbolism, from the time of Verlaine and Mallarmé and the poets of the *Revue Wagnérienne*, as well as Bergsonian speculation, were bound also to lead to the same conclusion. The era was above all one of music. In addition to the renaissance of national schools — Russian, Czech, Scandinavian and Spanish — the applications of ' Verism ' to Italian opera, Wagner's immediate successors in Germany and Austria — the last and brilliant outcrop of musical romanticism — we must pause to consider, in France itself, the miraculous intimate outpourings of Fauré and of Chausson, and render homage to the profound lesson of the sacred works of César Franck. Above all, however, we must consider the tremendous revolution — in perfect harmony with the most secret and fundamental purposes of Symbolism — effected by the music of Debussy. Human expression — we may almost say human thought — found, in this heaven-sent moment, a particularly satisfactory expression in music, and the genius of Claude Debussy endowed this already admirable language with yet another, newer idiom. A new language breaking down the ritual framework with its repetitions, recurrences, oratorical developments and foregone conclusions and which, transcending all these ruins, reached straight to the heart of truth. To truth through science, an exquisite newly invented science, just as the savage genius of Mussorgsky had reached straight to the heart of truth, not through science but through ignorance, a fantastic and creative ignorance. Thus to the young Debussy, *Boris* and *The Nursery* constituted vital revelations resembling, as he wrote in the *Revue Blanche*, ' the art of some curious savage discovering music in every step traced by his emotion ' [1]. This same discovery of music, of pure musical truth, due not to the savage innocence of a Mussorgsky but to the most subtle and crystalline of methods, was responsible for the creation of the new syntax of Debussy, his rare harmonies, smothered by

---

[1] Claude DEBUSSY: *Monsieur Croche antidilettante*. Dorbon aîné and Nouvelle Revue Française, 1921, Paris.

dissonance, quarter tones and diminished sevenths, his evasive, unresolved lines, his unforeseeable and hence overwhelmingly expressive prosody — an infinitesimal syntax, expressing the instantaneous, dividing the orchestral mass in the same way as the brush of the Impressionists divided light, exploring all the aerial and sub-marine aspects of nature, ephemeral, capricious and powerful as the obsessive presence of the sea, exploring, too, all that is mysterious, passionate, deep and instinctively dancing in the human soul. The miracle was that such a precious, delicate, highly quintessential art, constituting so tremendous a technical revolution, should have produced no upheaval leaving in its wake no chaos, no problems of adaptation, but the instantaneous achievement of a total, obvious and luminous *perfection*. Moreover, in spite of its delicacy, Debussy's art was capable also of greatness and of drama, of plumbing the secrets of the universe as deeply as is possible for the genius of man.

Pelléas et Mélisande dates from 1902. A second date of capital importance is that of Arnold Schönberg's *Pierrot Lunaire* in 1912. Another revolution, another invention of a language. In 1903, Schönberg had also composed a *Pelléas*, first performed in 1905 in Vienna under the direction of Gustav Mahler, his old master. The overwhelming polyphonic force revealed was bound to appeal to Mahler's grandiose and truculent nature. The paroxysmal tendency combined with a passionate need for enquiry, for objective discipline and absolute lucidity, was to lead Schönberg's unique genius, by means of atonality, to a system based on the equality and independence of the twelve sounds, to dodecaphonism and to serial music. This music has subsequently been compared to Existentialism. Analogies with the basic concepts of Expressionism, and the experiments of Klee and Kandinsky are also to be found. As a young man, Schönberg had, indeed, participated, as a painter, in the *Blaue Reiter* group.

Schönberg and his Viennese School forced music to conform to a new code of constraints, a minute and almost Chinese code, which, despite its mathematical discipline, despite the skilled pulverisation by which it reduced the sound sequences of the former modal universe, by introducing us into a world, completely strange, completely beyond the bounds of pleasure and displeasure, attains to the wildest and most sombre depths of human pathos. Though our minds may be simultaneously fascinated and bewildered, and our nerves shattered, our hearts, at all events, are indubitably conquered.

Lastly, on the eve of the 1914 war, came the dazzling splendours of Russian music, the folklorism of the Five, the savage genius of Mussorgsky, the first wave of the Diaghilev Ballet to reach Western Europe, and a third red-letter date: 1913, the year of *Le Sacre du Printemps*. Igor Stravinsky was still in the grip of the Russian popular genius, with its luxuriant colours, its fresh and irresistible impetuosity. The will to utilize such popular inspiration to effect a complete revolution of musical language was, however, already fully evident. After *Petrouchka*, *Le Sacre du Printemps* revealed a fierce explosion of that pan-rhythmism which constitutes the basic principle of Stravinsky's genius. Original orchestration, unaccustomed timbres, sustain the ardours of the constantly new and astonishing tumult of his *perpetuum mobile*. Yet another violent revolution — jazz — had, at the late date at which we have now arrived, gained acceptance as a fashion. A fertile fashion destined to exercise a profound influence on the sensitivity of succeeding years. Meanwhile new interest and enthusiasm had been developed by the bold and humorous sallies of a 'naif' musician, a former friend and companion of Debussy — the unique, completely, preposterously original figure of the pure and marvellous composer Erik Satie. His occasional brief works, calm with the quiet truth which, so said Nietzsche, is borne upon the feet of doves, introduced irony into the art of music: an extremely precious innovation. Last, but not least, came the entry of the Six.

The evolution of music in the years leading up to 1914 constitutes a remarkably rich phenomenon, marked at every turn by a series of impelling breaks, of fruitful innovations. Its whole force, however, sprang from the first faint murmurs of anxiety which, in the torpid morass of state opera and academic musical instruction, stirred music into reawakening and thanks to the pervading atmosphere of Symbolism, led to its predominance.

Let us now return to another stagnant area, that of the plastic arts, — and recall for a moment the specious, unreal, obsolete, and putrid products which passed for painting and for sculpture in the eyes of late XIXth century bourgeois society. A faint suspicion that there might have been some mistake led this society to create *Art Nouveau* for its delectation. The novelty of this revolution — for revolution it was — remained limited to external décor. Painting and sculpture were not involved. The work of the Impressionists and of Rodin had met with mockery, refusal and disdain. Literature had

Jean COCTEAU,
*Stravinsky composing
the ' Sacre du Printemps '* (1913)

followed a similar course. For this society had also its official literature, no less artificial than its art, and was unable to accept Symbolism, save for certain minor and purely decorative aspects. Something of the Symbolist poison had, however, infiltrated with the floral langours of *Art Nouveau*, as well as with the capricious meanderings of the clouds and fishes of contemporary music, the same clouds and fishes as were incrusted on its lacquer vases, or embroidered on its screens. Still only décor was involved.

Society, therefore, remained in total ignorance of the fact that in the plastic arts and mainly — indeed, exclusively — in painting, creations of the greatest possible importance had occurred. In this domain disagreement was both total and profound. Not only were its roots deep-set but a very particular combination of circumstances had created in this field a major problem. On the one hand painting had awakened to an understanding of its true nature — that of pure painting. On the other hand, bourgeois society, since it was bourgeois and therefore based on positive canons, clung jealously to the dogma — vital to its survival — that painting was a representation of the actual world. Between these two points of view, no compromise was possible.

The misunderstanding began with Courbet, that is with what was, in effect, still realism. Realism was the title given by Courbet himself to his art and to his school of painting, before the writers, headed by Zola, adopted that of Naturalism. This brand of realism shocked society not by its determination to express reality — which was in accordance with the trend expected of painting by bourgeois society. There seems to have been no problem concerning the painting in itself. The questionable element was interpretation of reality as projected in Courbet's realism; a reality portrayed by him as trivial and ugly, without embellishment, without any attempt to make it acceptable or pleasing, insisting rather on its rustic, popular and topical — modern — aspects, on everyday objects, on nature which is part of reality and which he believed to be truly natural, that is to say savage, free, powerful and true. Every time realism reappears in the course of history, the effect has been that of a revolution. Truth has always been embarrassing, for society always deludes itself with an image of the world which it believes to be true but which, in fact, is no longer anything but a convention. This is what happened in the case of Courbet. His realism was bound to shock. The principle of realism was, however, not rejected. Courbet was reproached for his political opinions. Realism, while always somewhat disquieting in itself, is often accompanied, as if to make its intentions doubly clear, by political opinions tending towards a demand for popular progress, and those of Courbet led to his condemnation for dismantling the *Colonne Vendôme* during the Commune and eventually to his death

58

in exile. On the purely aesthetic plane, however, he did not inspire absolute horror: he was not accused of the crime of pure painting, that is to say of painting anything other than a representation of reality; rather he was reproached with selecting from reality only such elements as produced uncouth and ugly pictures. In the reign of Napoleon III indeed, M. de Nieuwerkerke, Director General of Museums and Intendant of Fine Arts, went so far as to make certain gracious advances towards him, and the Minister Marius Richard offered him the *Légion d'Honneur*. This he refused. He did, however, accept from the King of Bavaria the Cross of the Knight of the Order of Merit of St. Michael (First Class) which carried with it the title of Baron. In Belgium and in Germany he was triumphantly received. Fame, though always a bitterly disputed fame, was his.

The fundamental conflict broke out with Manet. In his case too the government of Napoleon III had attempted a concil-iation by creating, in 1863, the *Salon des Refusés* in which was exhibited the *Déjeuner sur l'herbe*. An indignant public, however, confirmed the verdict of the jury. Yet Manet gave the public no supplementary grounds for identification as a dangerous and subversive individual. He came of excellent family and belonged to high Parisian society, and the scandal he provoked was therefore purely on the aesthetic plane. Yet Manet was a realist painter, whose realism bore no trace of aggressiveness, not being deliberately restricted to the sordid aspects of reality. He was indeed so deeply interested in reality that no one aspect drew him more than any other. There was no knowing where his choice might fall for, in his eyes, anything might justify the act of painting and demonstrate its power. Courbet had topped the old dictionary with the red Phrygian bonnet. Manet, for his part, added no bonnet, red or any other colour, but took the dictionary as it was, neglecting neither its noble phrases nor its common words, but making a random choice of words, or rather subjects, convinced that the choice was of no importance, that only painting and its intrinsic problems were of any consequence. Painting-for-painting's sake had seen the light of day and was launched on a career which was eventually to lead it to Serusier's ' Talisman ' painted in the Bois d'Amour under Gauguin's direction in 1888, and to Maurice Denis' dictum that ' before becoming a battle horse, a naked woman or any other kind of scene, a picture is essentially a flat surface covered by colours assembled in a certain order '.

The Impressionists, too, practised painting-for-painting's sake. They, too, were realists, naturalists attaching importance to reality and to nature, though not so much nature as seen ' through a temperament ' as in accordance with a *plastic* theory of nature. Their theory was based on a special understanding of light inspired by contemporary science. The works of Chevreul and other physicists in no way scandalized a public to whom, they, like all other scientific works, brought a more accurate view of exterior reality. The public, however, refused to admit that their effect was to transform the accepted plastic representation of this external world. The painters, for their part, on the contrary, were to utilize these scientific discoveries for plastic ends. On their authority they based a truly plastic revolution, the inauguration of a new way of painting, a revolution exclusively concerned with painting and which, therefore, only served to confirm painting in its isolation. This new way of painting, this new technique — in short, Impressionism — corresponded to a new con-ception of the universe, a philosophical conception based on scientific principles, leading not to an imitation, a reproduction, a representation of the universe, and certainly not to a representation such as that to which the public was not only accustomed but determined not to relinquish. This requirement was, however, no longer observed: its day, in fact, had gone forever. From now on painting was to pursue its own path. Aesthetic revolutions introduced new conceptions of the universe, corresponded to such and such a scientific or philosophic system, attuned themselves to such and such contemporary trends, aspirations, ideas, feelings and states of consciousness, but, in spite of this, they remained, however, fundamentally strictly aesthetic revolutions characterised by changes in the language of form.

So it was with the Impressionist revolution: the artists responsible were expressing a relationship between man and nature, and nothing but this relationship, since they claimed sensation only as the basis of their art, being, in fact, essentially sensualists. This relationship was, however, expressed in their works, which, of course, were paintings and in which the public, uncomprehending and derisive, recognized nothing natural, or rather nothing of that nature which its official painters had accustomed it to see quite differently represented.

Succeeding revolutions were based on other systems and on other principles. After the primacy of the eye, proclaimed by Impressionism, came that of pure colour, proclaimed by the Fauves, followed by that of instinct in the form of

Expressionism, of geometrical principle in Cubism, and of the unconscious and poetic imagination in Surrealism. Each revolution in turn was concerned purely with painting and its intrinsic manifestation.

The imperative and complete emancipation of painting, followed by a precipitous and dazzling series of revolutions, each producing a movement and creating its own school, which could only have been accomplished by true strokes of genius and men of great creative genius, inevitably isolated, rejected and hounded by society, did, indeed, arise. Naturally, the historian must study these plastic, aesthetic, revolutions, together with their principles, theories, systems, the mechanisms by which the various systems are connected, completed, or opposed, and their particular dialectics. He must, however, also consider the individual creative men of genius who determined such and such a dialectic, analysing both their personalities and their histories. Such personalities were exceptional because they possessed genius and their destinies were unique, full of adventures, vicissitudes and drama, largely because they were played out in conditions of isolation and of contradiction. The historian must thus operate on two planes: one horizontal, on which unfolds the dialectical succession of the history of forms, the other vertical, on which the historian must examine in turn each of these men of genius, their individual personalities and the circumstances determining their individual histories. These are the personalities who, by their meteoric apparition and dazzling presence, by their very existence even, were influential in inspiring those transformations in painting, those plastic and aesthetic revolutions of which we have already spoken. At the origin of each revolution, in the particular background from which such revolutions sprang, stood a single strong and startling personality, an individual whose motives must be studied — not only those external motives attributable to race, family or to social circumstances, but also the most intimate, secret motives, including those which psycho-analytical methods have now taught us to uncover. The work of Toulouse-Lautrec has its place in the history of forms and must therefore be examined by the historian of forms: but it is also the concern of the psychologist whose domain is the infinite domain of subjectivity. The life of this provincial aristocrat, transformed by a cruel physical deformity into a pariah who found his true home only on the fringes and in the gutters of society, amid the pleasures of Parisian night-life, the *caf' conc'* and the brothels, evolving there his own brand of wisdom — a terrible, truculent wisdom: such a singular destiny must also be considered in any attempt to explain everything in his art that is of a general order, that is to say, relevant to the history of forms.

This process is all the more necessary in that such creative individuals continued to pursue their own way, their own development, after participating in the movements which they had produced or helped to produce. Other paths were beckoning, other quests and other consequences, resulting partially, no doubt, from the movement and revolution engendered by the individual, but also and above all from the contribution of his particular subjective nature to this revolution: that is to say the deep impulsions of this same subjective nature. Bonnard, by reason of his subjective nature, of his personal temperament, of his genius, participated effectively, decisively even, in the Nabi movement, but subsequently went beyond this movement and remained himself. The Nabi movement was over, but Bonnard remained Bonnard, more Bonnard in fact, than ever before, concerned with his own relationship, his candid and novel relationship with the teeming expansion and dazzling manifestations of cosmic elements. Similarly, we can no more leave Matisse or Dufy after their participation in the Fauvist revolution, for which they were largely responsible, than we can leave Picasso or Braque after Cubism, or Kandinsky and Klee after the *Blaue Reiter*. The work, the career of each of these painters of genius is a chapter in itself, a history within a history, the glorious history of painting itself.

Seurat was the last Impressionist and also the first great creative personality among those determining the plastic revolutions of our time. The last Impressionist, certainly, but so constituted that intellect and intellectual will were the predominant faculties of his particular genius so that he was therefore not content to be a mere Impressionist. It was he who, retrospectively, formulated Impressionist theory, and, in consequence, introduced into that purely sensual, intuitive and apparently spontaneous art — not only for the present but also for the future — certain lucid aims and accepted rules. Impressionism thus became a reasoned art, and impressionist pictures began to be composed, becoming marvels of hieratism and of style — no longer Impressionist, but Neo-Impressionist, Divisionist, Chromo-Luminarist or Pointillist, all of them quite different from Impressionism. Painting had passed on to a further stage. While recognizing this fact, however, we must, simultaneously and on the vertical plane, direct our attention to the subjectivism of Georges Seurat, a genius struck down before his time, not, however, without first accomplishing, in full conformity with the traditional methods of French classicism, the splendid feat of combining the spirit of finesse with the spirit of geometry, and that with an assurance so silent and discreet that it awakens in the soul an emotion similar to that roused by the echoes of some perfect piece of music.

A similar recall to reason after the sensual delights of Impressionism is clearly heard in the message of Paul Gauguin, though directed, in his case, towards linear composition, symbol, synthesis and style. This, in turn, led to the Nabis, who combined this lesson with the constructivist teaching of Cézanne, from whom the Cubists also drew their inspiration. All these phenomena of descent, all these genealogies are a magnificent subject for historians, historians of painting, historians of what the great Focillon has called 'the history of forms' — morphologists. But once again, in addition to historians of painting, we need psychologists of painting to apply themselves to what another great master, Elie Faure, has called 'the spirit of forms'; for all the circumstances, conditions, moods and accidents of destinies such as those of Gauguin and Cézanne merit particularly close attention. To them, we shall constantly return, as also to those other moods and accidents constituted by the formidable figure of Van Gogh. An entirely different direction was imparted to painting by this artist, that of the mystic power of pure colour, a direction followed by the Fauves. The example of Van Gogh could not fail to incite young painters inspired by a true vocation to lend an ear to his hidden lesson, that of depth of soul : out of which arose yet another change of direction leading this time to Expressionism. This was just the thing for the Germanic genius, appealing to all its deepest properties, and resulting in the outbreak of a movement of very great importance : the *Neue Künstvereinigung*, the *Brücke* and the *Blaue Reiter*. In all this the influence of the Dutch Calvinist Van Gogh was to prove decisive. We have already noted the influence of Gauguin, Puvis de Chavannes and Hodler, as well as, most important, that of Edvard Munch, the major figure of the Norwegian school. For Scandinavia had now taken its place in the spiritual concert of Europe. Into literature was introduced the sometimes elusive, sometimes wonderfully innocent, but always strange and irresistible magic of Ibsen, Björnson and of so many others. To literature, too, belongs the Swedish Strindberg, not only the remarkable writer with whom we are all familiar, but also the painter in the stormy torment of whose pictures — forerunners of the abstract — are found all the characteristics of his written work.

Strindberg's *inferno* was lived in Paris, where his work was published in the *Mercure*, and where he made the acquaintance of Gauguin, with whose refractory spirit the soul of Strindberg, like that of Van Gogh, came into explosive contact.

In Paris Lugné-Poë and Suzanne Desprès opened the *Théâtre de l'Œuvre*, where Ibsen's plays were performed and which became, in fact, an Ibsen theatre. This deliberate step was of the greatest possible importance in the international life of the period. The whole of the Nabi movement grew up around this theatre. Vuillard figures with Lugné among its founders and all the Nabis, as well as Toulouse-Lautrec and Munch himself during his Parisian séjour, contributed to the design of its programmes. Munch executed a lithographed portrait of Mallarmé. In a word, Paris had at this point become a focal point for the radiation of the Scandinavian genius. The influence of Munch, one of the principal interpreters of this genius, was, however, exercised only in Germany, becoming decisive after the exhibition of his works held in the Berlin *Künstlerverein* in 1892, which, however, stirred such a tempest that it was forced to close after just one week. There was

LE CHEVAL.

Mes durs rêves formels sauront te chevaucher,
Mon destin au char d'or sera ton beau cocher
Qui pour rênes tiendra tendus à frénésie,
Mes vers, les parangons de toute poésie.

Raoul Dufy, *Illustration for Guillaume Apollinaire's 'Bestiaire'* (1911)

however a profound analogy between the genius of Munch and a certain saturnine and grating criticism of current social activity practised by the Paris circles of l'*Œuvre* and the *Revue Blanche*, by the Nabis, Vallotton, Toulouse-Lautrec, and Degas. While the latter's picture '*Le Viol*', painted around 1874, must no doubt be related to immediately preceding Naturalist 'slices of life' it is, I find, extremely close in inspiration to Neo-naturalism, certain aspects of which were cultivated by the artists of Nabi period, and certainly to the expressionist Naturalism created by Munch, with his heavy interiors in which black figures droop and languish, torn by sexual torment, devoured by some weird and sinister melancholy, always crouched on the brink of some hysterical cry. Meanwhile the art of Munch had profound repercussions on the art of Central Europe. His impact was that of a great artist: his art of creating the extraordinary figures of which we have just spoken, was

Edvard
MUNCH,
*Portrait
of Mallarmé*
(1896)

remarkable, not only for his settings, in so many ways reminiscent of Ibsen's drama, so heavily charged with all that is left unspoken, all that can, indeed, never be conveyed except by pregnant silences, but also for his portraits. Moreover, he achieved an art of composition and of space, a highly original segmentation of perspective visible in his view of somnambulistic crowds advancing down Karl-Johan Street. The highly accomplished plastic skill and knowledge underlying these hallucinatory scenes gives them a force of conviction which explains the full effect of the influence undoubtedly imputable to Munch, to whom must be ascribed the remarkable merit of having introduced into painting the element of anguish, already introduced into metaphysics by another great Scandinavian, Sören Kierkegaard.

This anguish weighed above all upon German Expressionism, particularly in the early days, and particularly in the work of the *Brücke* group: Kirchner, Schmidt-Rottluff and Nolde. Their painting was cruel, imbued with a sense of

inescapable doom. If man was predestined, then painting was predestined too. It could no longer escape evil, that is to say — in the language of painting — ugliness. This feeling of ineluctable ugliness, was absolute, and the German artists felt it in their very act of creation. Ugliness became in itself an aesthetic value. Ugliness existed not only in the creative subjectivity of the artist: it was inherent in the world and it was of the world — the world itself was ugly. Particularly ugly were the manifestations of contemporary German bourgeois society. For this reason the ugliness of a certain number of German Expressionists, of Otto Dix, of Beckmann, of the *Novembergruppe*, of the caricaturists of *Simplicissimus*, of Grosz, was a satirical ugliness. In this domain the Germanic genius revealed a truly terrifying virulence.

With the artists of the *Blaue Reiter*, true plastic values were reaffirmed and out of confusion and despair appeared a new chance of salvation. Marc, Macke, and the young artists and poets of the *Sturm*, were consumed with that thirst for the future, that joy, which, on the eve of the 1914 world

Ernst Ludwig KIRCHNER, *Manifesto of ' Die Brücke'* (1906)

catastrophe, was breaking out all over Europe. To paint, to participate in the great adventure of painting was a salutary act, an act of faith and fervour. The same emotion, in spite of the repudiation of the public, inspired first the Fauves and then the Cubists. It burst forth in the jubilant prophesies of Apollinaire, in the Orphism of that robust and gay inventor Robert Delaunay, always in such close contact with his comrades of the *Blaue Reiter*. At this point arose two other great figures, Kandinsky and Klee, whose work has remained influential down to the present day, and both of whom demand a halt for individual consideration. Kandinsky carried the adventure of autonomous and free painting to its final, abrupt and decisive conclusion — that of pure abstraction, the logical consequence of the intuitive passion of Expressionism. It was, of course, inevitable that in the process, he should find a legitimate outlet for his personal preoccupations, which were those of a mystic, a man of the spirit enamoured of the spirit and pursuing it always by spiritual means. As a painter he was to identify these means with plastic methods, and to attain spiritual expression by the use of line, point and colour. Klee, too, in the sphere of his own culture, which was that of a contemplative, a philosopher, a musician, trained in the most intricate speculations of Germanic thought, culminated also in the spiritual. Hence his prodigiously original and precious work, composed of tiny pictures, each a poem in itself, a meticulously elaborated microcosm of form and matter. For the moment, that is to say at the outbreak of the 1914 war, Klee was still at the stage of those felicitous discoveries made in Tunisia, in company with Macke and Molliet.

The history of modern painting is thus seen to be a vast spiritual drama, in which the actors are not only aesthetic movements but also artists of genius, each of whom played out his own adventure within the limits of the great adventure common to them all. A drama constantly revived, constantly reanimated. Expressionism was by no means limited to Germany: the great Belgian renaissance must not be forgotten, nor the advent of James Ensor who, after an admirable period of inti-

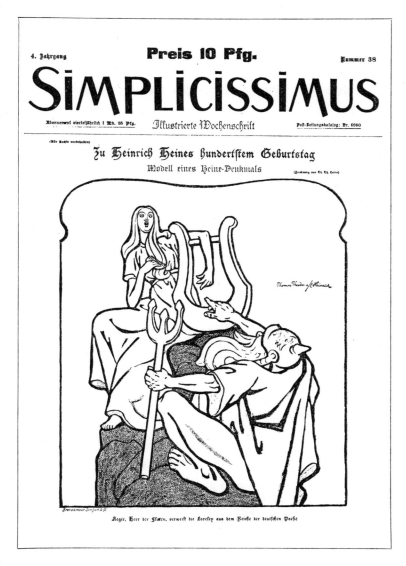

A cover of the weekly 'Simplicissimus'

Cover of no. 14 of the review 'Der Sturm' (1910)

macy similar and slightly anterior to that of Vuillard, discovered 'la peinture claire' almost contemporaneously with Van Gogh. His *Entry of Christ into Brussels* dates from 1888, the year that Van Gogh and Gauguin lived and worked in Arles. The personal fantasy of Ensor, with its elements of burlesque, sarcasm, fear and imagination must also be considered. Ensor is a man of fetishes, pass-words, witchery, of contact with occult forces and vivid likes and dislikes. His pictures lead us straight into the man himself, and a certain degree of adjustment is essential. Munch, however, had already demanded a similar adaptation, not merely to the specific properties of his plastic universe, but to the specific moral properties by which this universe was motivated. The same, no doubt, is true of Redon — another magician, whose diary bears the significant title: 'To oneself'.

With Rouault we come to French Expressionism. No doubt the personal genius of this artist obeyed laws and patterns different from those followed by the creators of Scandinavian, German or Flemish Expressionism. Rouault must be situated in a purely French tradition, that of the Romanesque and Gothic image makers, of François Villon and of French Catholicism, leading, however, in his case, to a pathos which cannot be qualified as anything other than Expressionist. Moreover, the whole trend of the *École de Paris* illustrated by Modigliani, Soutine and Chagall also appears to be Expressionist. To take the case of Chagall only, the Expressionist characteristics of his genius must no doubt be traced to the inspiration of his mixed Slav and Jewish ancestry, the urgent, nostalgic and expressive power of which is always present in his work. Quite apart from this congenital factor, it is however essential, for Chagall, as for the other individuals of genius of whom we must attempt to sketch a brief moral portrait, to direct attention to those completely individual characteristics — his tremendous emotional voltage, his leaning towards the epic, the myth, the fabulous and the legendary, his lyrical and religious vocation, his innocence of heart, his need to love — so many separate elements serving to compose a unique individuality and explain how, in the prevailing atmosphere of contemporary French painting there should arise a work incontestably Expressionist in character.

For, in France, in the meantime, had occurred an event of considerable importance, in complete conformity with the specific national genius: namely, Cubism. This had been preceeded by the great outburst of colour known as Fauvism. All the arbitrary gusto of these skilled and brilliant distractions was to be disciplined by Matisse to produce a truly masterly artistic output ranking among the most glorious of the century. Then came Cubism: Cubism, product of a civilisation fundamentally and exclusively French in character, to which, however, so many foreign artists of genius — Picasso, Gris, Marcoussis, Reth, etc. — were to make their contribution. The determination of painting to be pure painting attained here one of its greatest heights. Reason was the basis of everything. Intellect triumphed over instinct, over the caprice of poetry, the prestige of mystery, the frenzy of colour and everything involved in our relationship with the world of objects, and with their situation in space and light. Their place depended only on indications conveyed by our overall conceptual knowledge: a dissecting and analysing knowledge, so that the pictures resulting from these operations were themselves objects, that is to say, no longer designed to bear a particular name, to evoke a particular use, a particular memory or emotion, but to satisfy our need for aesthetic pleasure by strictly aesthetic means. Here, too, arose outstanding artistic personalities endowed with their own individual genius, their own characteristics, their work extending beyond the boundaries of Cubism save when, as in the case of de la Fresnaye or of Raymond Duchamp-Villon, it was interrupted by the war: Braque, Léger, Delaunay, Villon and the most miraculous inventor of them all, the truest and most outstanding genius of our age, Picasso.

Italian Futurism, with Severini, Balla, Carrà and Boccioni, the painter and sculptor who was killed in the war, was inspired by a different ambition, one which was to lead to a new turning point in the history of art: the desire to express the lyric emotion awakened in man by his participation in the boundless power, the originality, the exhilaration of the industrial age. This was not far removed from the revolt which, accelerated by the monstrous carnage of the war, was finally to lead to the total negation of Dada. Nor was it far distant from the kinetic and '*simultanéiste*' experiments combined in Orphism. One of the basic characteristics of new plastic phenomena, which at this point succeeded one another at an ever-increasing, ever more precipitous pace, was their sudden, complete, and absolute originality. One is surprised to find that all sorts of present day developments had their beginnings before the 1914 war, and that these beginnings often took the form of ephemeral and capricious phenomena arising independently, often without the

64

existence of any precise relationship between their various authors. Abstraction, for instance, was invented not only in Germany, but also in Paris and in Moscow with the advent of Rayonnism, Suprematism and Constructivism. Mention must also be made of the deliberate inventions of a most original artist, an erratic genius capable of the most dazzling flights of creative temperament: Francis Picabia. Another highly original genius, Mondrian, whose work — the very reverse of capricious — was the outcome of patient and systematic meditation, conceived the first elements of his doctrine of neo-plasticism. Survage's projected film *Coloured rhythms*, Marcel Duchamp's *Nude descending a staircase*, and Kupka's *Amorpha* were all milestones on the road leading to an unknown future. Refusing all figuration, painting had become entirely self-absorbed.

It is impossible to overemphasize the importance of a sociological study of this new departure at its very starting point, the last quarter of the XIXth century. We have already noted the situation of Courbet and Manet in relation to the social régime of their time. Courbet, as we have observed, was spurned on personal rather than on artistic grounds, and more on account of certain specific aspects of his art than for its principle, which was that of realism. When his *Burial at Ornans* and *Studio of the Artist* were rejected by the jury of the 1855 Universal Exhibition, he decided to exhibit his works on this official occasion in a hut constructed at his own expense. The same thing happened at the 1867 Exhibition, when Manet was forced to adopt the same solution. The immense hilarity aroused by the first Impressionist Exhibition in 1874, the articles of Albert Wolff and other shining lights of the wit of the Boulevard, the discussions provoked by the Caillebotte legacy in 1894, are common knowledge. Only a portion of this legacy was accepted and that with the greatest reluctance. Renoir's *Moulin de la Galette* managed somehow to remain in France. However, innumerable works of art by Cézanne and others departed to enrich American and German collections and even in these countries they were not received without protest. Kaiser Wilhelm II, discovering one day that a number of French Impressionist pictures had been introduced into the Berlin Museum by Hugo von Tschudi, burst into a rage and demanded the resignation of the over-bold Curator on the spot. In the United States the first blows at the philistinism of the commercial bourgeoisie were delivered, remarkably enough, by a photographer, Alfred Stieglitz, who, in the last few years of the century, became the apostle of photography as an art. What hope could there be of instilling the first faint glimmerings of art into the solid, unwavering, consciousness of a new traditionless society, but a society clinging all the more tenaciously to those traditions it had brought from Europe? Precisely that of inducing it to spare a glance for that reality in which it lived enclosed as in a fortress, but which, in reality, was life, nature, humanity, complexity — all, of course, potential subjects for art itself. National schools of art are often launched by realism, that is to say by a realistic art, a realistic formula of art. Artists of the lowliest degree, the type of artist whose first instinct is to look around himself and to find his models in familiar landscapes and scenes, are often to be found at the origin of national schools. It was thus natural that the new school of America, the land of a mechanical civilization, should have come into being through the intermediary of a mechanical technique such as photography. Photography was to reveal America's specific reality. By its means art was to brave the rejection and ignorance of American society. In 1892-1893, Stieglitz took his famous photograph of Fifth Avenue and his *Terminus*, depicting horses in front of Astor House in the melting snow. His collection of photographs, his magazine *Camera Work*, the exhibitions held in the gallery which he founded in 1905 at 291 Fifth Avenue revealed the beauty of New York, of true and humble American life. Sadakichi Hartmann perceived this in his *Plea for the Picturesqueness of New York*, which appeared in 1900, as did Charles Caffin in his vehement *Is Photography an Art?* A whole new movement of ideas opened up to young *avant-garde* painters, to the group stigmatized under the name of the Ashcan school who had exhibited their work in the William Macbeth Gallery in New York the same year (1908) in which Stieglitz exhibited in his Gallery a number of drawings and lithographs by Matisse. The American school was launched on its glorious career. Concurrently certain others such as Walter Pach and Gertrude Stein were exploring the forbidden areas of European art. In 1913, the celebrated Armory Show revealed to America the principal movements of European art from Neo-Impressionism to Expressionism.

All this constituted a vigorous awakening of consciousness, a series of forward steps achieved in spite of resistance, sarcasm and scandal. Small wonder then if in Europe itself the noise of scandal continued. At the inauguration of the Universal Exhibition of 1900, the artist Gérôme, Member of the *Institut* — whom we have already taken as typical of the contemporary official artist — when conducting the President of the Republic on his official tour of the Palace of Painting, restrained him on the threshold of the room in which the Impressionist pictures were displayed, barring the doorway with the broad expanse of his morning coat and crying ' Go no further, Monsieur le Président, France is here dishonoured! ' In 1916, to prevent similar dishonour, the *Institut* dispatched a delegation to the Minister begging him to refuse to accept Rodin's will, bequeathing his work to the nation. A long debate took place in Parliament, which might have been supposed, since France was in the middle of a war, to have had preoccupations of a different order. All the authority of Clemenceau, far-sighted friend of Rodin and of the Impressionists, was required to persuade France to accept so glorious a treasure. Fauvism, Cubism, Expressionism — not one of the movements behind the creation of modern art was to receive any better welcome on the part of either public or officialdom.

At this point we must once more insist on the uniqueness of the men of genius responsible for the creation of modern art and emphasize again the importance of their several destinies. Their art is explained by their personalities and by their lives. These stand out against an empty background, and if we seek to throw them into relief it is because in such a setting their very existence is a form of natural relief. An outstanding personality, engaged in activities contradictory to normal activity, is isolated to the point of appearing as a solitary figure. The life of such a figure will follow its own fatal course, will react in its own way to conditions, to circumstances, whether these be positive or negative, obligations or obstacles. For this reason the lives of such personalities require separate examination, as an individual destiny, or, to put it another way, as an individual adventure making its own contribution to the great story of painting for painting's sake.

Events are the landmarks on the path of adventure. Events are the very stuff of which adventure is shaped, composed and constituted. Events are happenings which can be recounted. A happy period has no events, and this explains the stagnant, reiterative, consistent, homogeneous, extra-temporal and extra-historical character of the last years of the XIXth century. There were, however, events in the lives of the great creative painters during this period just as there were events in the history of painting. Like their immediate predecessors the *Poètes maudits* — the great generation of creative poets, Baudelaire, Rimbaud, Verlaine, Mallarmé, Tristan Corbière and Lautréaumont — these painters, were also outcasts of society.

An outstanding event in the history of poetry, remarkable enough in the history of the world, and in the history of the mind, to be considered an event in itself, was the meeting of Verlaine and Rimbaud. From the encounters of two such persons, exceptional even among so many exceptional figures, was bound to emerge the most extraordinary of events. No less dramatic, no less explosive, was the meeting of Gauguin and Van Gogh, though the elements entering into its composition were different, the sexual element, for example, being absent from this relationship, unless, as seems plausible, we seek to discover in the two antagonists in the drama of Arles a psychic relationship of Damned Bridegroom to Foolish Virgin, or male and female poles. However this may be, the phenomenon was essentially the same. Two unique personalities of exceptional dimensions, inspired with an equal creative passion in one and the same sphere of creation surrounded by the mediocrity, the routine, the banality, not to say nullity of the universe could not fail to feel an irresistible mutual attraction. They were alone in the universe, alone in the world, and their drama was played out without spectators. It was therefore incomprehensible, with that incomprehensibility characteristic of what we call events. Evidence of these events we do, however, possess — the art of Verlaine, Rimbaud, Gauguin and Van Gogh, through which we may attempt to comprehend the incomprehensible and to study certain decisive turning points in the history of poetry or of painting.

Nor did the event end with the drama of Arles, pursuing its singular course with the flight of the two protagonists each to the antipodes of our society: these antipodes being, in one case, geographical, and in the other, mental. Tahiti for one, madness and suicide for the other. No less exceptional was the rarified atmosphere, the isolation, the absolute solitude in which the work of Cézanne was accomplished in spite of the fact that the career of the artist was, in this case, entirely uneventful. Thanks to a small personal fortune, it was provincial both in setting and in character, the artist finding in the Provençal countryside, at the foot of the Montagne Sainte-Victoire, both his spiritual home and the solution to his artistic problem. Nevertheless the scorn which weighed upon him, the silence enveloping the creation of so decided and so eventually decisive an art, only reinforced its inevitable eccentricity, throwing into relief its predominant characteristic of intellectual effort, forcing it to the extreme limits of its true domain, that of intelligence, and revealing with the clarity of a chemical analysis, the solitude here involved, a *cerebral* solitude comparable to that in which Descartes, in his ' poêle ' achieved the revelation of his *cogito ergo sum*.

It was thus outside any given milieu, away from all beaten paths, from all *terra cognitae*, independent of any relationship with anything or anybody, that contemporary painting sought and found itself. It is therefore hardly surprising that, some years later, Jarry, Apollinaire, the Fauves and the Cubists should discover manifestations of beauty in hitherto forbidden spheres — in the art of savage peoples as did certain of their German contemporaries, or in that of ignorant, naif, self-taught artists. As Rimbaud had already proclaimed in the course of his tumultuous existence ' I have loved stupid paintings, door mantels, theatre and circus backdrops, painted signs, popular illustrations .' Certainly a curious taste, understandable only in a world surfeited to the point of utter boredom, exhausted to the point of death. Nothing could have been more obscure or more likely to be subject to derision if by any chance they had been known, than the paintings of the unfortunate Douanier Rousseau. Their discovery was therefore also an event, and one which was to prove extremely fertile. Today the Douanier Rousseau is in his rightful place, the Louvre.

A sphere was thus constituted, a strictly spiritual sphere transcending that of public life, in which events were represented by the union of souls, vocations, talents, ideas, and theories. In this magnetic field a whole new sphere of attractions and polarizations entered into play. Groups, brotherhoods and cults were formed, which created contemporary art just as truly as in previous eras art had been moulded by social pressures, stimulated, maintained, governed and administered by the aristocratic salons, ruling classes and princes, encouraged by popular applause, exposed to the judgment of the public as well as of the élite of critics and other leaders of opinion, subject also to the dictates of current fashion.

Symbolism had already had its little magazines, its left-bank cafés and Mallarmé's Tuesday afternoons. In Germany these were emulated by the *Kreis* of Stefan George. Gauguin's Breton isolation had been relieved by the companionship of Sérusier, Émile Bernard and the rest of the Pont Aven Group, a company of recluses, a band of hermits, who were joined by the Danish painter Willumsen, and by the Dutch artists Meyer de Haan and Verkade. The latter, as a result of this community experience, entered a religious order and continued his generous enterprises by establishing a centre of sacred art in the Benedictine monastery at Beuren, on the Upper Danube, where he was eventually rejoined by Meyer de Haan. The Nabis retained the view that artistic creation was a spiritual operation comparable to prayer, best carried out in the pure and strict climate of a brotherhood. In a similar spirit Maurice Denis, the Nabi painter, founded, in company with Georges Desvallières, his own Studio of Sacred Art. The very term Nabi (Hebrew for prophet), the mystery with which this group deliberately surrounded itself, comparable to that of the Rosicrucians, though not without a trace of antic humour, the fervent respect with which was adopted the message of Gauguin incarnated in ' The Talisman ', bear witness to the conventual spirit, the conviction that the creative action of a group of new artists should be inspired not only by a common consciousness, but also by some kind of secret bond.

This feeling, in various forms, was to inspire other colonies of artists and of poets : that of Worpswede in Germany, that of Laethem-Saint-Martin in Belgium, both holy places of the new spirituality. In Worpswede, graced by the presence of Rainer Maria Rilke and of Paula Modersohn-Becker, there was evolved an art sensitive to the simplicity of nature, a humble, profoundly human work, a moving forerunner of certain Expressionist experiments. At Laethem-Saint-Martin, on the banks of the Lys, in one of the calmest and most beautiful of Flemish settings, where the posts of Deputy Mayor, Burgomaster, and Community Secretary were held successively by the candid Van den Abele, better known as Binus, the first group of hermits consisted of the Flemish poet Karel Van de Woestijne, his artist brother, Gustave, Valerius De Saedeleer, and the sculptor Georges Minne. All these men lived and worked at the imitation of nature, communing with one another in a spirit of peace and faith, seeking a style of art which was also a style of life and in which the spirit of Symbolism was combined with the grandeur and purity of the Flemish primitives. A second wave, including the powerful Permeke, deliberately steered the Belgian school into the path of Expressionism. Expressionism had meanwhile also come into being in Munich, Dresden and Berlin through the meeting of young German artists engaged in a mutual search and eager to communicate to one another their restless and subversive aims. Expressionism was created by groups formed as the result of chance meetings, of secessions — minorities separating from over-academic groups — of heretical sects impatient to prove their total originality by issuing manifestos and holding scandalous exhibitions. This same will to dissidence, but even more aggressively expressed, inspired the noisy efforts of the Italian Futurists. The feeling of isolation, of obscurity, of underground activity forced upon creative artists by the social system of the 'happy era' rapidly developed into a vital need for association for the purpose of positive revolutionary action, and the way was paved for Dada.

The most interesting groups now to be considered are those formed in Paris in the early 1900's, through which plastic revolutions in France are intimately bound up with the extraordinary phenomenon known as the *École de Paris*. Fauvism, too, originated in the meeting of certain young artists, some of whom were fellow pupils in the studio of Gustave Moreau, or fellow-citizens, like Friesz and Dufy in Le Havre, others meeting more fortuitously, as for instance Derain and Vlaminck at Chatou. The origin of Cubism was marked by one of those momentous and far-reaching events which we consider so vitally important, the meeting of Braque and Picasso, two artists of widely dissimilar genius, but who for a time worked in close contact, exchanging and comparing their discoveries, their challenges, their fantasies. Daniel-Henry Kahnweiler, an art dealer and man of profound culture and great intelligence, endowed with the gift of anticipation, who understood that such mutual sympathies were the very flesh, fire and essence of intellectual movements, endeavoured to foment such sympathies, assembling in his newly-established gallery artists from both left and right banks, fully aware of all that art stood to gain from the encounter of Braque and Picasso, Léger and Juan Gris. The influence of the poets, Apollinaire, Max Jacob, Reverdy, Cendrars, Salmon was the final decisive factor, for poets have an intuitive comprehension of the springs and mechanisms of life, its internal necessities, and its hidden explanations, and it so happened that the same kind providence which presided over the encounters among painters, presided also over those among the poets. Apollinaire, above all, was to exercise a felicitous influence, devoting all his passion to the stimulation of the men and ideas necessary to create a society of the intellect, however much despised by the only existing serious society, but inspired with so much joy and controversial dynamism that it finally attained reality. The little world invented by the strategems of this man of faith came to be considered life itself, and what was happening at Montparnasse and Montmartre became more important that anything that may have been happening elsewhere.

This explains why artists hurried thither from every corner of the earth. This is the vital factor to be considered in any study of the phenomenon of the aesthetic revolutions taking place in France at the beginning of the present century. Such revolutions are attributable not only to French creative artists, grouped together by chance encounters or in response to youthful enthusiasm, but also to young creators from other countries, driven from their homeland by political circumstance, as in the case of the Jews, or leaving them voluntarily because they failed to find sufficient stimulus for the development of their talent, attracted one and all by the fame and brilliance of Paris. A fame and a brilliance, which, however, must have been relatively dim, since these youngsters were the only ones to appreciate it, contemporary Paris being, on the artistic plane, as bourgeois and conventional a metropolis as any other, quite as conservative, cautious, mistrustful, self-satisfied and complacent as the England of Victoria or the Germany of Wilhelm II. Yet to Paris flocked Picasso, Kupka, Gonzales, Marcoussis, Brancusi, Pascin, Reth, Gris, Modigliani, Severini, Csaky, Survage, Lipchitz, Zadkine, Chagall, Kisling, Chirico, Foujita, Soutine, Pevsner and so many others. They set up their studios in outlying quarters, Montmartre, Montparnasse, Vaugirard or Puteaux, some of which, like the *Bateau Lavoir* and *La Ruche*, were destined to become legends in themselves. After the war the *bistros* where they gathered — the *Rotonde* and the *Dôme* — were expanded becoming fashionable cafés. But for the moment they were no more than the setting for an epic drama of poverty and bohemianism. To participate in this epic drama all these young artists converged on Paris, inspired by a common impulse and responding to an irresistible appeal, dreaming of some fraternal, difficult, heroic existence, at once free and concentrated on a common goal, totally impervious to anything outside or beyond this goal. Paris alone, with its unique experience of the subversive and the controversial, was the place best calculated to satisfy so strange an aspiration, a place touchingly defined by Chagall as *lumière-liberté* or compound of light and liberty. A painters' definition, for light is the concern of the painter, and the light for which Chagall experienced so deep a need was that of the Ile-de-France and the Mediterranean — the light of Corot and the Impressionists. A human definition, too, since man must also thirst and hunger after spiritual light, knowing that such light can shine only in the keen and salutary air of liberty, consonant with a tradition — a French tradition — of independence and revolt, without which all is threatened with sterility.

All these things were felt rather than expressed, their subtlety in direct contradiction to the full horror of all that society in general then understood by French tradition: breaths of fresh air, snatches of blue sky appearing furtively here and there between the chinks in the overall opacity of the atmosphere. These insidious draughts, these bright patches were, however, sufficient to attract to Paris this great flock of variegated pilgrims, each with his own jargon, his own message, his own childhood memories, a powerful and heterogeneous charge of poetry, which, enriching as well as harmoniously combining with the powerful native genius, gave rise to one of the most glorious moments in the history of French civilization, proving yet once more its humanism and its universalism.

Retrospectively, such a claim is possible, but at the time, at the actual moment of gestation, all that was visible was the obscure, clandestine, disparaged aspect of the phenomenon, which had, however, already begun to acquire the properties of what can only be termed an *avant-garde*, a new conception, which, in the general confusion, was in process of coming forward and even of gaining acceptance. These *avant-gardes* alone were responsible for the creation and progress of art. Art was a combat against a society which in the first place rejected art, because one of its dearest maxims was the non-creative character of art, and, in the second place, rejected individual works of art with scorn and indignation because they bore no resemblance to what it believed to be art, to the products of its own official art, considering such works, on the contrary, to be affronts to its dignity and to its moral code, a social danger and an outrage. Such *avant-gardes* arose not only in France, in Germany and in Belgium, but were on the increase throughout the world. In America, the acquisition and example of so many European works of art had kindled the enthusiasm of certain wide-awake, curious and undaunted spirits, and stimulated the vocation of young native artists eager to create a truly American school of painting. In Russia shortly before the October Revolution, poets and artists were impatiently shrugging off the yoke of the apalling bad taste of the Tsarist era, and intoxicated with self-searchings, with new and passionate theoretical discussions, were generating a whole series of magnificent new movements, schools and *isms*. In England, the obvious religious and sectarian nature of the Pre-Raphaelite movement — the Pre-Raphaelite Brethren — with their cult of beauty, their proselytism, and their concern for ethical and social reform, was in full accordance with the spirit of Protestantism. Not long afterwards, despite the forces of inertia still weighing so heavily on the immediately post-Victorian era (and accepted by the English with such apparent complaisance) other forces arose, equally typical, it must be admitted, of the British genius, namely the forces of eccentricity of which the *Vortex* group, founded on the eve of the 1914 war, was perhaps the most powerful expression. In Barcelona, then a hotbed of anarchism, an open harbour for every variety of cosmopolitan seduction, seethed the picturesque Bohemian world of Picasso's childhood. In Switzerland, the group responsible for the *Cahiers Vaudois* also constituted an avant-garde, somewhat unexpected in a country normally a bastion of the spirit of conservatism, and where the meeting between Igor Stravinsky and the great, solitary figure of Ramuz must be considered a very considerable event. Everywhere *avant-garde* movements were making themselves felt. Art was created exclusively through their intermediary, so that, as soon as we can no longer distinguish any such obvious *avant-gardes*, armed with programmes and manifestos, inspired by the demon of subversion, we are actually surprised and obliged to envisage the possibility of new problems. Such a situation would indeed suggest that, by such devious means as snobbery, commercial speculation, the power of the press, and the dictates of fashion, the social contradiction had diminished or even disappeared, that the social conditions of creation had changed, and some sort of compromise achieved between creation and society. The value of such compromises must then be examined with a view to determining how far they can be said to guarantee the virtues proper to creation, how far they prove acceptance by society of the full efficacy of such virtues, an acceptance, which, after all is said and done, must be deemed desirable. If such acceptance has been reached, then we can salute the advent not of a new ' happy era ' — we know how little that is worth — but of an era which somehow, and at least in this respect, enjoys internal harmony. Any such reasoning is, however, extremely complex and must be approached only with the greatest prudence.

The era with which we are here concerned happens, however, to be a past era, a period of open conflict between society and creation, or, to put it yet more clearly, an era during which creation was effected completely outside society, and under entirely *extraordinary* conditions. Under such conditions, how could the vocation of any young artist express itself?

Certainly not in the famous ' anch' io ' uttered by Correggio at the sight of a Raphael picture. Correggio presumably meant that his wish was simply to repeat the ' act of painting '. A whole battery of principles and practices was at his disposal to sustain and uphold him during such an undertaking. All the better for him, of course, if by virtue of his genius, he could introduce some astonishing new variation into the exercise of an honoured and honourable art. For the young artist of the modern era, however, art had no longer any accepted physiognomy, any accepted face or profile. Even its technique, the very stuff of which it must be made, was no longer either taught or learned. As Degas, I think it was, once said ' It is curious to think we spend our lives in the exercise of a profession of which we are entirely ignorant '. Technique had to be freshly invented every time. So that in the artistic vocation itself there was an element of the unknown, a door opening into the indefinite and unforeseeable, an interrogative *quid* had replaced the affirmative *quod*. Creation and nothing but creation was the order of the day. The vocation of Van Gogh was particularly remarkable in this respect. This unhappy man, unhappy in every sense of the word — including that understood by metaphysicians when they speak of an 'unhappy conscience', — experienced from the very outset an appetite which he was unable to fix on any object. He therefore called it in turn by a number of successive names, including that of God, the vaguest and, no doubt, the most sublime. To this appetite we can now give the other, equally resounding name of love. After a number of experiences of love of this order, that it is say of a spiritual order, its true aim was revealed under the name of painting. But what exactly was meant by painting? An element of mystery remained, escaping and eluding his grasp. An element of mystery which, in this case, was light. No doubt the light of France, the light of the Impressionists, and it was they who, for Vincent, represented what the mastery of Raphael had represented to Correggio. Mastery, however, was not the object of Vincent's quest, as it had been that of the Italian Renaissance artist. What then was he seeking, if it was neither light, ' la peinture claire ', the study of light, nor yet the knowledge and dexterity which may be acquired in the practice of such study, and which can be taught by masters to those who seek to become masters in their turn? Something *else* again, something to be found *elsewhere*. No doubt farther to the south, in some ideal country which he called Japan and which, according to his letters, he thought that he had found in Arles, thus demonstrating that an *elsewhere* was perpetually rediscovered in the *elsewhere* of each successive halt. Adventure is an everlasting quest.

It is thus, from the view point of its absolute quality that we must consider each adventure, the individual quest of every one of the great creators of modern art. The same absence of preconceived purpose, of predetermined guiding principle, the same indetermination of the aim pursued can be observed in each of the schools, or rather movements, which they promoted — Fauvism, Cubism and Expressionism. No doubt each of these movements represented a conscious and deliberate break with conventional academism, and also with the theories and techniques of the preceding movement, as for example, the break of Cubism with Impressionism. As a result their protagonists were well aware in what direction their experiments were tending: in this case, in that of intellect and geometry as opposed to that of sensation. But this was merely a confused reaction, biological rather than rational: a kind of natural mutation. And this very mutation was the all important factor, the vital necessity for originality which constituted the creative project. The upheaval of Cubism was so fertile, so various, that its vitality outran its major inventions which might have determined a system and an orthodoxy, putting out new sheets in all directions . Hand in hand with the desire to restore to painting some sort of rational order and to create a new form of classicism, thereby accomplishing a deliberate act dictated by the need for harmony between the rhythm of life and the logic of the mind, went a desire to do something — anything — simply, in fact, to *do*. Something of this desire was apparent in the passing craze for *papiers collés*, which no longer belonged to the domain hitherto regarded as that of painting, not merely by the bourgeois academicians but by all the world from the very beginning of the history of art. It was not only a question of launching painting on a new chapter of the history of painting, that of autonomous painting, reduced to its very essence, but also to create, in relation to painting and on its outer fringes, original objects revealing nothing but the desire and ability to create — objects in which we are tempted to see something more than pictorial creation, namely creation for creation's sake. The same desire is apparent in the contemporary fabrications of certain sculptors, Laurens, for example — works of pure sculpture in that they constitute a sculptural challenge obliging the spectator to transcend the stage of surprise and indignation and to ask himself the question ' and why not? ', thus recognizing in such curious fabrications the presence of an undirected impulse, caring nothing for classic materials or any other sacred canon, but a purely creative force, blowing where it would. The same force was to carry the great forerunners of Abstract art, Delaunay, Kupka and Picabia and the Expressionists, Marc and Kandinsky, to the critical point where their formula, already attuned to the violence of cosmic reality, became yet another formula in which violence fed exclusively on violence.

The whole epoch was thus condemned to genius.

This is a very grave conclusion. The use of the term *condemned* is here deliberate: the epoch was indeed condemned to the ignominy of seeing itself represented by creators whom it abhorred. They, in turn, were condemned by their own epoch, condemned to their own genius, relegated, abandoned to their own devices. Van Gogh's only issue was to be Van Gogh, Cézanne's only issue was to be Cézanne, the Cubists and Expressionists had no alternative but to devote themselves to their own distractions, the inventors could do nothing but invent. Nothing, in fact, but to invent inventions.

The phenomenon of the isolation of the creators of modern art from their social milieu extended also to literature, the transcription of thought itself. We have already seen how Symbolist poetry and the great inventors Baudelaire, Verlaine, Rimbaud, Mallarmé produced their work in an atmosphere of relative obscurity and scorn. Similar conditions were experienced by the European writers of the closing years of the century, Ibsen and Strindberg, of whom we have already spoken, Nietzsche, Tolstoy, in spite of his fame, and Dostoevski. What strike us are the great dimensions of each of these figures, their sheer, clear cut outlines, each following its own intrinsic destiny, each constituting what we may well describe as an individual ' case '.

The same is not true of another giant figure in the world of literature, who was born before all these others, but whose figure dominates the whole century and whose death in 1885 was a kind of national and universal calamity. His figure dominated the whole century, reflecting its every line. He himself was fully conscious of the remarkable measure of coincidence between his own destiny and the various chapters of the history of his century. He, indeed, was privileged to be a man of history, one of those men firmly entrenched in time so bitterly regretted by Charles Péguy. Born when ' the century was two years old ', he was to remain almost to the end its faithful companion. Too young to have lived its most epic moment, the Napoleonic saga, he made himself its bard, which was indeed another way of living it. All the rest he lived in person, playing not only the passive role of poet and of witness, but also the active one of participant and hero. Victor Hugo was a national figure in the history of France, and in him France recognized her image at every step of his career up to the final moment in which every figure reaches its fulfillment, the moment of death itself and the night of the funeral wake. It is rare, miraculous even, to find a poet identified with all the deepest aspirations of his compatriots and with the historic genius of his country. Victor Hugo, however, accomplished this miracle, in the full light of day, and to the constant accompaniment of a well-earned glory. Something deep in the heart of Victor Hugo's thought and lyricism was, however, revealed only afterwards, and the blaze of glory, the constant rounds of public applause, the posthumous legend itself, proved in the end to fall just slightly short of absolute identification. It is, in fact, only today that the full reality, the exact content of Hugo's philosophy, the full and profound meaning of his spiritual message has been discovered. So that it seems as though, however brilliant and apparently all-revealing the light illuminating an accepted, recognized, triumphant genius, there remains within that genius some depths of hidden mystery. In the case of Hugo, such mystery was in no way contradictory to the main action of his genius; but lay rather below its surface, influencing his action in the same positive direction. His contemporaries seem to have been aware of this without however actually recognizing it: probably a good thing in itself since the genius of Hugo, like the sculpture of Rodin, required some such element of mystery and secret power of shadow. The tremendous originality of his genius was, in the long run, all the more strongly emphasized. A similar originality is what we must also stress in our ' cases ' — those disputed, rejected figures which, far from the all-night lights of the Arc de Triomphe, nevertheless emerged towards the end of Hugo's century.

The case of Nietzsche, for example, is totally obscure. This sickly professor of Greek, obsessed with those physical disorders which were to end in madness, could count few friends, one of them, however, being Wagner — a colossus endowed with so strong a will to power and so well armed for power and glory that, for fear lest they should smother him, he thrust them violently and offensively aside. Nietzsche's thought, on the other hand, could circulate only through private, secret channels, working its ineluctable termite-like way, sapping the very foundations of the ancient edifice of Christianity. Its progress was imperceptible, but one fine day illusions were shattered, and with them all fictions, prejudices, masks, and accepted values. In the resulting chaos, nothing remained unquestioned. Through a criticism as sharp as that of Voltaire, as clear and lucid as that of the Greeks, shone an extraordinary lyricism restoring the true face of life and awakening bewildered man to the knowledge that he no longer knew anything of life, that all that had previously gone by that name had been mere shadow, and that God was dead. Other promises were held out to man merely to envisage which involved a joyful acceptance of catastrophe: a risk which must be run, and ind the course of which the soul itself was liable to break asunder. Such was, indeed, the fate of Nietzsche's soul. Certain deviations, certain misapprehensions — and a similar fate lay in store for nations too, and in particular the German nation. The issue of tragedy may well be tragic, and a tragic genius cannot be reproached for pointing to such issues. The dignity of mankind is, on the contrary, enhanced by the production of such a tragic genius. Thus, out of the prevailing chaos of the dying century, among so many remarkable men of genius, emerged Nietzsche, the most startling genius of them all — Nietzsche who, obedient to the laws of his own fate, to his love of fate, his *amor fati* and endowed with hitherto unknown power, forced human thought into limitless, ever-open paths of possibility, as terribly creative and destructive as the dance of Siva.

Ibsen too, was marked by a similar savage individualism, heedless of all barriers imposed by social convention and of all inflexible moral codes, proclaiming a new life and a new humanity. Protestantism and anarchism combined to compose this ' stubborn ' figure — to use the words of Rilke — and to enable him to carry us with him, as Suarès was to say, up to the very ' glaciers of intelligence '. The era was, we have said, condemned to genius, and by this it should be clearly understood that it was condemned to genius at its most advanced, at the point where, after a salutary purge, it opens up the way to totally unknown perspectives. The contemporary purge had been all the more thorough in that the epoch itself had been so stagnant, mediocre, senile and self-satisfied, producing an art which had become bourgeois not only on the economic and social levels, but also on the moral level. On all these levels the need for a forward step had become imperative. The analyses of Karl Marx had predicted a growing alienation of conscience and a regime more and more solidly based on profit, terminable only by a Revolution opening up the way to a new humanity. If, to the messages of Ibsen and of Nietzsche, we add the extraordinary adventure of Rimbaud, the attempt of Mallarmé to ' give the words of the tribe a purer meaning ', that of Cézanne to re-invent painting from the very beginning, Van Gogh's wild quest, and Gauguin's endless flight, we cannot fail to form a synthetic picture of a totally unprecedented project of the human spirit. Completely demystified, voluntarily dispensing with the crutches of society, of religion, and of language, no longer feeling the faintest solidarity with these broken mouldering props, the foolish and false appearances of which had been made mercilessly clear, it was now ready to turn unreservedly and freely towards an unknown future.

The case of Tolstoy is highly complex and contradictory. In Europe, the revelation of Tolstoy was accompanied by the revelation of the immense phenomenon generally known as the Russian novel, but then also called ' Slav enchantment ' or ' the soul of Russia '. In point of fact, what was at stake was the whole imperial apparatus, now shaken by powers emanating from the depths of the Russian nation, in complicity with Russian intellectuals. The Western public was keenly interested in the Nihilist drama, to which police repression had lent a flavour of conspiracy and of romanticism. After the Russo-Japanese War, itself a thunderclap in the calm sky of universal peace, came the 1905 revolution, a second clap of thunder and the first revolution of the twentieth century, occuring at a time it was generally believed that revolutions had ended with the Commune, the last revolution of the XIXth century. The attention of the world was thus concentrated more than ever on that immense, distant and sprawling, half-Asiatic land, now stirred by strange and rumbling currents. Against this background rises the great figure of Count Tolstoy. A young aristocrat, master of a rich domain and of innumerable serfs and domestics, enamoured of reading, love and happiness, excellent dancer, passionate gambler, brilliant officer of the Caucasian, Danubian and Sebastopol campaigns, had been endowed with the most extraordinary gift of writing ever known. Only the greatest, the most exceptional novelists of universal literature — Cervantes, Stendhal Balzac — have ever rivalled his faculty for recreating events, characters, facts and reality, for communicating life itself in all its detail. Having become a novelist of incomparable merit, having attained the height of human genius, Tolstoy was seized by a tragic sense of disquiet at the sight of universal injustice and at the power of the spirit of evil in the world. Repudiating his work as a writer, seeing in it only complicity with evil, he aspired henceforward only to serve humanity.

47
Victor Horta
'La Maison du Peuple' at Brussels
(1896–1899)

48

Hendricus Petrus BERLAGE

Interior of the Stock-Exchange at Amsterdam
(1898–1903)

49
Otto WAGNER
Interior of the Savings Bank at Vienna
(1904–1908)

52
John MARIN
Sunset
(1914)

53
Max WEBER
Chinese restaurant
(1915)

54
Burnham and Root
Monadnock Block at Chicago
(1889–1891)

55

D.H. BURNHAM and Co
Reliance Building at Chicago
(1895)

IV
Tony GARNIER
Industrial city
(1904–1917)

56
Auguste RODIN
The Gate of Hell
(begun in 1880)

58
Menardo Rosso
The Bookmaker
(1894)

57
Eugène CARRIÈRE
Maternity

59
Ferdinand HODLER
Eurythmie
(1895)

60
Pierre PUVIS DE CHAVANNES
Sacred grove of the Arts and the Muses
(1884)

63

Igor STRAVINSKY
First page of the manuscript score of 'Sacre du Printemps'
(1913)

64
Suzanne VALADON
Erik Satie
(1893)

65
Théo Van Rijsselberghe
The Reading
(1903)

66
Maurice Denis
Homage to Cézanne
(1900)

V

Georges SEURAT

La Grande-Jatte

(1884–1885)

67
Henri DE TOULOUSE-LAUTREC
Au Salon
(1894)

68
Paul GAUGUIN
Calvary
(1889)

69

Vincent Van Gogh

Flowers in a garden

(1888)

70

Vincent Van Gogh

View at Auvers

(1890)

73
James ENSOR
The Entry of Christ into Brussels
(detail)
(1888)

74

Georges ROUAULT
The Holy Face
(1912)

75

Paula MODERSOHN-BECKER

Portrait of Rainer Maria Rilke
(circa 1906)

76
August STRINDBERG
The Town
(1900–1907)

VI
Wassily KANDINSKY
With the black arch
(1912)

77
Carlo CARRÀ
The funeral of the anarchist Galli
(1911)

79
Nathalie GONTCHAROVA
Electric lamps
(about 1912)

80
Casimir MALEVITCH
Cubist rose
(1912)

81
François KUPKA
Amorpha
(1912)

VII
Paul KLEE
The carpet of memory
(1914)

He did so not by action but by setting an example of asceticism, by assuming a new personage, the personage of a saint. To this effort of self-destruction and reconstruction there contributed, undoubtedly if somewhat obscurely, certain primary and moralizing factors inherent in the Russian temperament aided by other factors of a more personal nature, resulting from the composition of his own peculiar dominating, capricious and devouring temperament, and, lastly and most impotant of all, from the strange and tempestuous nature of his conjugal life. This fantastic confusion ended in the flight of the great old man into the snow and his death in the little station of Astapovo.

This extraordinary saga had a tremendous impact on the conscience of the century. Following closely upon the curiosity aroused by the revelation of what was taking place in Russia, it furnished the example of an individual revolt, effected not in the name of the rights of the individual, not in that of any autonomous, imperious individual thought. This dramatic, tragic revolt was carried out in the name of humanity and in the cause of humanity, revealing in the deepest recesses of our mental world another flame, no less devouring than the pagan flame of Nietzsche, but diametrically opposed to it — the flame of human pity. Tolstoy's personal and proclaimed defiance of the authority of the Tsars, of governments, churches, police, social conventions and also of the preeminence of art, of thought and all accepted civilized values, was inspired by humanitarianism, by a jealous, savage religious passion, stripped down to the bare essentials of the Gospel lesson.

The message of Dostoevski tended, by and large, in the same direction, and was certainly no less complex and involved. A former Siberian convict, Dostoevski led the harsh life of the vagabond, for which his impenitent gambler's temperament must be held partially responsible. Many dramatic hazards attended the execution of his literary work. A fundamentally unhappy man, his characters are also unhappy men, victims not so much of external fate, as of their own internal fates, having tasted of the fruit of knowledge of good and evil, particularly of evil, of absolute evil, the existence of which raises an insoluble philosophic problem. The doubt he cast upon the reality of life was thus as fundamental as any of the questions raised by any of the other great rebels of the century. Pronounced, however, in the name of sin and supported by the arguments of sin, it could be solved only on the same dialectic level and by a religious reversal, an escape into childhood, innocence, evangelism. The Russian reactionary tradition was very much alive in Dostoevski, finding support in his restless, jealous pan-slavism. Dostoevski's thought must not, however, be reduced to such a simple pattern, for it was far from being so systematic. It was, indeed, a perpetual dialogue, a debate between the devil and man's liberty: the author often allowing great latitude to the former — such was the power of his inexorable genius — driving the liberty of man into the furthermost corner, and permitting the triumph of all the most horrible motives of evil. Arrived at this extreme, he seems, at times, as in *The Possessed*, to foreshadow the criminal absurdity of certain political movements which, in our own time, have convulsed the world by the logic of their perversion. But if only by the problematic aspect of his work, by the exposition of problems involving infinitely audacious and pathetic consequences, the philosophy of Dostoevski was bound to cause profound disturbance in the minds of men.

This problematical character was, indeed, typical of the whole era. The various figures of genius who stand out from, and dominate the period appear to be engaged in a tremendous controversy among themselves, just as each individual among them, for his own particular reasons, is engaged in controversy with the era. The era, on the contrary, having repressed such problems from its consciousness, had become convinced that none existed. Hence, its ' happiness '.

Catastrophe, however, lay in wait, in the form of the outbreak of the 1914 war. This date, as we have pointed out above, marked the birth of world insecurity. Currencies, regimes, frontiers, ideas — nothing was stable any longer. And this catastrophe in turn engendered others so that the situation of the world itself became catastrophic and man had perforce, to adapt himself to living in it.

As the fatal date drew near, the whole of Europe underwent a politicalization of feelings and ideas. The feelings and ideas discovered in the work of little known, and little understood authors, authors who had hitherto merely aroused curiosity or set a superficial fashion, and who, in any case, had seemed total strangers to public and official trends on which they had exercised so little influence, now became harnessed to concrete, practical immediate ends. Nietzscheism, with its ' will to power ', its exaltation of vital forces, found practical application in re-awakened nationalisms, as did Russian humanitarianism in the great forward spurt of socialism and internationalism, while Bergsonian vitalism, largely issued from the pragmatism of William James, found itself invoked for the justification of every sort and kind of action. Action now became the main concern of man's impatient spirit. Sometimes a bridge was even thrown across the gap between two contrary doctrines, as for instance that of Nietzscheism, with its accent on subconscious and biological elements, and that of fraternal socialism with its defence of the lowly and of oppressed classes. Such a gap was bridged by Georges Sorel in his *Réflexions sur la Violence* (1908) in which he propounded a thoroughly Nietzschean theory of revolutionary syndicalism and its tool, the general strike. His subsequent reconciliation of the cults of Lenin and of Mussolini thus caused no surprise.

War and revolution were therefore possible. This possibility, now felt to be growing rapidly nearer, gave new impetus to ideas. Doctrines, such as that of the *Action Française* which, up to that time, had been no more than doctrines, and therefore relatively inoffensive, were revealed as more and more active and aggressive. Similarly, in Germany, closer examination of various intellectual speculations, and in particular of those of Nietzsche, revealed the germs of a nationalism destined, at a later stage, to take the form of Nazism, and inevitably to claim descent from Nietzsche's Superman. Italian Futurism had already laid such claim, and in its proclamation of war as ' the hygiene of the world ', and other such noisy manifestos, could already be heard the warning notes of subsequent Fascist hectorings and bluster.

If we were to attempt to find the common denominator of the various exceptional adventures, the dramatic case histories of Rimbaud, Gauguin, Van Gogh, Ibsen, Nietzsche and of Tolstoy, we should certainly find the concept of revolt: revolt and anarchy. Such was the *trend* and significance of the era: a trend inevitably assuming many different forms, each highly emphatic and intense since each case history was completely original and outstanding. Their common trend is, however, equally outstanding: to go *against* the current, diametrically to oppose society, its institutions, its establishments and its possessions, its system, its morality and its order. This character becomes even clearer if we consider, as I have done above, the case of Victor Hugo, equally outstanding but encompassing the whole of the XIXth century. Victor Hugo's revolt, however, his social and political opposition took a *positive* direction. His rebellion was in harmony with the deepest aspirations of his own and other peoples, tending towards an ideal, a Utopia even: Utopia — a truly XIXth century term — being a distant but realizable ideal, an ideal in the achievement of which it was possible to believe. For the XIXth century this ideal was the universal, democratic republic. The same phenomenon was visible in America, in the symbolic figure of Walt Whitman, another giant, and another giant of the XIXth century; another rebel too, self-schooled, a pure, untamed spirit and even sexually abnormal. His heart also beat in unison with all the strength of all the States of the young starspangled Republic, temporarily torn asunder by the Civil War, but later reassembled within the wide sweep of the great Lincoln's telescope — O Captain! My Captain! — for the forward bound into the uncharted waters of a prodigious common future. A XIXth century phenomenon, as was, after all, Marx himself. Child of 1848, in harmony with all the revolutionary humanitarianism of the XIXth century, the deductions and prophesies of which were to require much harsh revision on the part of the succeeding century.

The phenomena heralding the new century were fundamentally different in character: based on revolt, devoid of any immediate echo or repercussion, they were doomed to exaggeration or to desperation.

As the 1914 cataclysm approached, the politicalization to which we have already referred gave to such revolts a more positive appearance. But how could negation become affirmation or anarchism take its place in history, attaining to the dignity of a political movement? Only by means of deviation, contradiction, compromise, trickery, excess and outrage, or, alternatively, by failure, renunciation, and disappointment. We have already seen how such appeals to life, to its mysterious, unconscious or panic forces, as also to its strength and its vitality had served to nourish growing nationalisms. The opposite tendency, that of revolt in the name of a just and fraternal humanity, took political form in the heroic but vain manifestations of anarchism proper, that is to say by the explosion of scattered bombs, and — more reasonably, more systematically, and in closer conformity with the historical conditions of the era — in the tremendous ferment of socialism and in the high hopes inspired by the International. The latter, with Liebknecht and Rosa Luxembourg in Germany, Jaurès in France, showed every sign of becoming a radiant humanism, only to collapse in brutal disillusionment. Socialism failed to resist the tidal wave of war and of the ' sacred unity ' votes of the *Reichstag* and the *Chambre des Députés*. Jaurès was assassinated on the very day on which war was declared. Some few years later, in Russia, on the contrary, socialism was to strip itself of all humanistic tendencies and to petrify into the strict realism of Leninism, thus accomplishing one of the most extraordinary revolutions in all history, and subsequently to accentuate this realism even further, adding a pedantically orthodox doctrine and degenerating into Stalinist imperialism, with its vaunted material successes, obtained at the cost of who knows what monstrous holocausts, the gross simplifications of its bureaucracy and its police, falling finally into a short term machiavellism equally unprofitable to humanity and to the individual.

In following the course of ideas in the new century and examining the part they played in the political doctrines which prepared the way for the catastrophe, capital importance must be attributed to Nietzscheism. We have already found signs of this doctrine in the revolutionary syndicalism of Sorel, in nationalism and in Futurism. It is reflected again in the glorious and adventurous figure of Gabriele d'Annunzio, in his heteroclitic and glittering lyricism, his violent hedonism, his triumphal and magnificent thirst for life. It reappears also in the immoralism of Gide, the romantic dilettantism of Barrès, in his cult of ' la terre et les morts' the French nationalistic formula roughly equivalent to the German *Blut und Erde*. Nietzsche's thought was exceedingly complex. Its immediate results seem, however, to have taken the form of practical application, of stimulation to action, and of a cynical justification of all forms of collective exaltation and of pragmatism. All of which must be linked in turn with the overall tendencies of a period which had elected energy as its guiding principle. The influence of Bergsonism — a vitalism, a revelation of the subjective notion of time, a philosophy of movement, a philosophy of creative energy — had already made itself felt. A dynamism to which the individual soul adheres with all its force, and which also attracts the adherence of nations, races and of classes. A new grip on reality had been offered, on the reality of *becoming*. On this new temporal perspective, Proust was shortly to base the whole psychology of a soul sequence which must rank among the most original and powerful ever written. The decisive nature of such a reversal of human consciousness cannot be overrated. A new ordering, a new tension, a new pattern of behaviour were required: an assimilation of the extraordinary new notion of energy. Energetics were the basis of Futurism, as of Expressionism, particularly of Expressionism carried to the point at which it leaps forward into the subconscious impulsions of the Abstract. In considering the inspiration of the artist and his creative action, capital importance was attributed to the initial gesture of creation. ' A line ', said Van de Velde, ' takes its strength from the energy of the draughtsman. ' Apollinaire expressed his preference for ' the most energetic art '. Everything had, in fact, become a question of energy. Energy became the principle of every order of knowledge and of progress. Energy was put to every use, including the most stupid and the most ferocious.

Physics became entirely directed towards the transformations of matter into energy, and a prodigious cosmogony emerged, doubtless beyond man's comprehension, yet, at the same time coinciding in some obscure way with man's fundamental aspirations.

We began this panorama with the spectacle of a happy era, a spectacle on which we dwelt with some complaisance. This complaisance, this insistence, may have appeared to correspond to a purely theoretical necessity, to the scholastic rule of discourse, requiring that all discourse be preceded by an *exposition*. This preamble was, however, also fundamentally true: and we therefore felt justified in employing it as a stylistic exercise, an element of composition — the better to convey the precursory rumblings of the thunderbolt about to strike the world, obliging it to live in a state of convulsion, of permanent convulsion — complete, inevitable, long expected and desired.

Thus, as the static beatitude of the 1800's drew to a close and on the eve of all these changes, not only ideas but also reality assumed new forms. New conflicts were engendered, the consequences and repercussions of which are easy to foresee. The white man's colonial expansion, which at first appeared in the form of an adventure illustrated by such powerful human figures as Livingstone and Stanley, revealed certain defects, certain contradictions which were one day to make of colonialism a system as condemnable as it was condemned. The iniquities of Dutch colonialism in Indonesia, sanctioned by State and Church, had already aroused the accusing voice of Multatuli. Reaction against Belgian prosperity, augmented by the ambitious enterprise of Leopold II in the Congo, had led to the rapid rise of the Belgian *Parti Ouvrier*. The continued expansion and vicissitudes of the British Empire were proving for that tiny island centre the major problem of the age — a problem of life and death. England found herself obliged to retain these possessions by every available means: by force or by compromise, by accepting a certain measure of disintegration while maintaining those bonds, however loose, binding to the island its peripheral parts, accepting the transformation of the concept of Empire into that of *Commonwealth*. The Empire, above all India, had long constituted a school of phlegmatic and brutal stoicism for the younger sons of noble families. Its distant and exotic landscapes had reinforced the cosmic feeling so basic to the British character. A magnificent and proud farewell to all this had sounded in the work of Rudyard Kipling: a work which, in many respects, is also an epic of national energy, imperturbable in face of hostile blows. Long-nourished on a strong and proud philosophy of force, England nevertheless proved capable of accepting those changes which slowly but inexorably demolished her certainties, uprooted her prejudices, sapped the very foundations of the mighty Victorian edifice. The world-wide criticism evoked by the Boer War constituted a heavy blow to her pride, as did the Irish problem. The trial of Oscar Wilde was a no less painful blow to her desire for respectability, not to mention her hypocrisy. Nor should it be forgotten that it was in England that infant socialism found one of its earliest cradles. The infinite richness of the English soul was such that, side by side with the imperial doctrine which had been its stay, it possessed a whole philosophy of work, of empiricism, of liberty and democracy, as well as a feeling for nature and an imaginative faculty so powerful that England had long been a privileged land of poets and novelists ranking among the most fruitful and the most original in world literature. To take her novelists only, England at this time possessed in the person of Thomas Hardy, a very great, robust and powerfully human writer. His message was a true message of life and *Tess of the d'Urbervilles* is perhaps the most terrible indictment ever made of the sin of puritanism, for it is with a fierce biblical ardour, with a true religious feeling, inspired by a religion which had at last become the religion of man and nature, that Hardy condemns the most terrible sin of all, that of a religion of sin inflicting upon the universe the indelible stain of sin. This whole epoch, one of the most flourishing periods in the history of the British genius, was, moreover, full of healthy gusts of air disturbing convention, liberating the mind and destroying sophism by dint of paradox. Let it suffice to evoke here the work of two very different but equally libertarian writers, equally heartening in their pitiless lucidity and biting humour: that of the Catholic G. K. Chesterton, and that of the socialist — or anarchist — George Bernard Shaw.

The political history of France during the same period is the history of the progress of the Third Republic and of the Republican parties. Boulangism, the Dreyfus case, the creation of undenominational State schools, the disestablishment of the Church, constitute so many tumultuous and brilliant chapters of this history. To these democratic victories must be added the struggles of syndicalism and of socialism, paralleled by those of the English Labour movement and of Belgian and German socialism. No injustice, wherever it might be perpetrated, was a matter of indifference to enlightened French opinion. This is obvious from the *Cahiers de la Quinzaine* published in 1900 by the extraordinary Charles Péguy, of whom we have already spoken, a refractory figure, issued from that popular French provincial stock which had already yielded such outstanding figures as Proudhon or Péguy's great contemporary, the modest yet sublime Charles-Louis Philippe. Loyal to his origins, at once sensuous and spiritual, generous, obstinate, indomitable to the point of occasional outbursts of blind and foolish fury, Péguy was a writer of absolute originality, creating and perfecting a highly individual form of expression. Although a socialist and a Dreyfusard, Péguy was attracted by the opposing French tradition, that of Christianity, and effected within himself, in the village of his imagination, the reconciliation of priest and schoolmaster, under the banner of Joan of Arc, his own Jeanne d'Arc, in whom, however, there survived something of the Jeanne d'Arc of Michelet. Later, in his desire to counter politics by mysticism, he leaned heavily to the other side, breaking violently with Jaurès and with his former rationalist and republican Sorbonne friends, never however, abandoning his hatred of money, his passion for revolt and justice and the repulsion he felt for the blasphemous and abstract sophisms of Maurras and l'*Action Française*. His death in the Battle of the Marne was to bring this saga to its heroic end.

The crisis traversed, during this last period, by the arbitrary and heretical conscience of Péguy is symptomatic of the currents then stirring the whole of French opinion. There appeared growing signs of a patriotism eager for the sacrifice, easily confused by superficial observers with the noisy campaigns of the *Camelots du Roy* and other symptoms of bourgeois reaction. Pan-Germanism had by now reached such a point of aggressive insolence that it was only natural that on the French side of the Rhine the old idea of 'la revanche' should be revived. From this time onward German nationalism developed along paths leading to those forms of madness with which we have since become only too well acquainted. Its doctrine sprang, however, from the same ideological and emotional sources as that of French nationalism, finding justification in the works

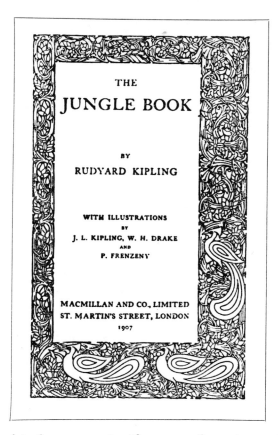

THE
JUNGLE BOOK

BY
RUDYARD KIPLING

WITH ILLUSTRATIONS
BY
J. L. KIPLING, W. H. DRAKE
AND
P. FRENZENY

MACMILLAN AND CO., LIMITED
ST. MARTIN'S STREET, LONDON
1907

of a great French writer, Gobineau, currently neglected by his own compatriots. We have already observed the analogies which can be drawn between certain German maxims and those of Maurice Barrès. Anti-semitism was mastered in France, thanks to the courageous victors of the Dreyfus case, only to scatter its poisonous seeds in Germany. Meanwhile the entire system elaborated by the *Action Française* lay ready for adoption by, and adaptation to, any other brand of European nationalism.

To complete the picture of the ideological background to French life in the years immediately preceeding the Great War, we must record a new and extraordinary outburst of pure literature and poetry and the foundation of another of those literary coteries, the happy and fertile influence of which we have already described: the brilliant and remarkable *Nouvelle Revue Française*.

During the XIXth century, Spain — from Goya to Galdos — had contributed nothing, invented nothing. Relegated to the furthest corner of Europe, fully occupied with political agitation of no real influence or significance and serving only to emphasize her impotence to assume a historic role, her impermeability to the great movements then affecting the world, her generally regressive, stagnant state. Her colonial disaster, was, however, to prove a powerful stimulus. This harsh lesson was the symbol for a whole group of writers: the generation of 1898, to open up the way for a remarkable intellectual and moral renaissance. Galdos, the isolated figure to when we have just referred was one of the great novelists of the century, worthy to rival Balzac, Dickens and the Russian masters. At the dawn of the XXth century, the ' Generation of 98 ' revealed the foolishness of despairing of the creative power of a nation which, in the ' Siglo de Oro ' had shone so brilliantly over two great continents. A whole cohort of writers, poets, essayists and professors turned back these glorious pages of Spanish history, rediscovering and revalorizing the men of genius lying at the roots of its inspiration, El Greco, Gongora, the Mystics and, of course, Cervantes, and — even more than Cervantes — Don Quixote and the whole philosophy of Spanish quixotism. Not only did they turn to these who had inspired Spanish civilization, the creators of the Spanish genius, but also the the fountainhead to which they owed their inspiration and their inalienable originality — the people itself. And more particularly, more intimately, to the people of Castille and to Castille itself, the permanent and fiery core of the genius of Spain. They reaffirmed those deeply original spiritual values which constitute the Spanish contribution to humanity. Nor was it only a spiritual renewal, but also a reawakening of Spanish consciousness : a preoccupation with Spain's re-entry into history, into Europe, and of the necessity of providing her with a political economic and social structure. These problems were studied by the great reformer Costa, and tormented the mind of another short-lived pioneer — Angel Ganivet, author of a brief but close-packed *Idearium Español*, and of a prodigious novel, equal to Don Quixote, entitled the *Works of the indefatigable creator Pio Cio*. The problems of the political regime, that of irrigation and other great practical works to be accomplished, those of regional autonomy and of federalism, and in particular the problem of Catalonia were examined and discussed anew. All this to the accompaniment of a magnificent renaissance of the Universities of Spain. A wind of reform and liberation blew over this stultified land, the eventual result of which was to be the Revolution of 14th April 1931 and the establishment of the Republic.

A great figure dominates the movement of 1898: Miguel de Unamuno. Not that he was a greater writer than certain of his contemporaries, Antonio Machado, Baroja, Azorin or Valle-Inclan, but being a universal spirit — poet, essayist, novelist, dramatist, philosopher, orator, letter writer, politician and man of action — Unamuno constitutes one of those great symbolic figures in which we may recognize, along with all his individual traits of genius, the particular genius of

Année 1909   1 FÉVRIER
N° 1.

LA NOUVELLE
REVUE FRANÇAISE

SOMMAIRE:

JEAN SCHLUMBERGER : Considérations.
LUCIEN JEAN : L'enfant Prodigue.
JEAN CROUÉ : Rivages.
MICHEL ARNAULD : L'Image de la Grèce.
ANDRÉ GIDE : La Porte Étroite (1ʳᵉ partie)
TEXTES.
NOTES :
    L'Exposition Georges Seurat (Émile Verhaeren) — Aquarelles et
        dessins de Bonnard, Cézanne, Cross etc.
    Les 'Pastorales par Mᵐᵉ Marie Dauguet. — Contre Mallarmé,
        — Francis Jammes et le sentiment de la Nature, par Edmond
        Filon. — La vie unanime, par Jules Romains. — Poèmes
        par un riche Amateur.
    Le cinquième acte des Fagts. — Le Poulailler, par M. Tristan
        Bernard.
NOTULES.

78, RUE D'ASSAS, 78
PARIS

Dépositaire général : E. DRUET, 108, Faubourg Saint Honoré.

EXEMPLAIRE DE LUXE

Cover of the first issue of ' La
Nouvelle Revue Française ' (1909)

DOUZIÈME CAHIER DE LA ONZIÈME SÉRIE

CHARLES PÉGUY

notre jeunesse

CAHIERS DE LA QUINZAINE
périodique paraissant tous les deux dimanches
PARIS
8, rue de la Sorbonne, au rez-de-chaussée

Cover of one of the ' Cahiers
de la Quinzaine '

Spain. A figure of an existential philosopher par excellence, a tragic philosopher, whose thought was interpreted in his life, in his tragic ' consciousness of life ', the first existentialist philosophy since that of Kierkegaard, his spiritual brother, at this time almost unknown in the Europe where he today enjoys so great a vogue. In order to read his works Unamuno went so far as to learn Danish! Existentialism had so far appeared only in a single German University in the work of Husserl whose ' *Ideas for a pure phenomenology and a phenomenological philosophy*' were published in 1913, exactly a year before the outbreak of the war.

This brings us to Germany, where Expressionism was not only an artistic, but also a literary movement producing works of a violent and dynamic schematism, and — to quote the title of one such work — Wedekind's famous drama — an ' *Awakening of Spring* '. Their spring was a bitter spring, heavy with erotic emanations, and with anger. For in Germany too there were chains to be thrown off, the overwhelming pressure of the Kaiser Wilhelm régime, the formidable industrial and military concentration weighing menacingly over the whole world. Yet the literary and artistic *avant-gardes*, the youth gathered in the *Sturm* and elsewhere, satirical papers like *Simplicissimus*, a whole series of vital and subversive actions, testify not only to a feeling of fury against the weight of all things German, but also to a generous desire to see that Germany, that same sombre and problematical Germany which had been the despair of Hölderlin and Nietzsche, attain to a clear free state of civilization and of humanism.

That these same values of civilization and humanism should concurrently have been cultivated in Vienna, capital city of the Empire of Franz-Joseph, and turn-table of Central Europe, will surprise no one. Vienna was at this time the meeting point of many currents, notably those of Baroque and Rococo of Germanism, of Italy and of the whole Slavonic world. Such diversity encouraged in the spirit of the Viennese a delicate intellectual courtesy, a delightful adaptability, great flexibility and irony, all qualities liable to culminate in dilettantism and aestheticism, as is shown in the rich, complex and often profound works of Hugo von Hofmannsthal. As events moved nearer to the edge of catastrophe, the feeling grew that such an artificial combination must burst asunder, scattering its elements far and wide, whence the emergence of a certain brand of tragic fatalism. In Prague, the home of Rilke, Kafka's tortured genius had begun to seek expression. As early as 1908, however, another Bohemian Austrian, the fantastic draughtsman Alfred Kubin, had been irresistibly impelled to write his novel *Die Andere Seite*: the hallucinations of this work foreshadow all the perturbations later to characterize not only the human psyche of the XXth century but also its abominable history.

To sum up, wherever our gaze lights upon the European scene, there appear forewarnings of national and social conflicts shortly to be unleashed by war. Disquiet was growing stronger, passions were approaching boiling point, tragedy was preparing its triumphal entry. Yet among youth gathered on the threshold of the future, the artists and the poets, whose mission was essentially pacific, there persisted a feeling of extraordinary optimism. The invention of original forms, the delight of surprising even themselves by such inventions, of letting themselves be swept along by the current, on occasion even outstripping it or deviating, for the purpose of spiritual creation, the accumulating potential of energy perceptible in the workings of the universe — none of this could have been undertaken without confidence, without enthusiasm. Contemporary *avant-garde* movements were, indeed, inspired with such confidence and such enthusiasm. An indefinable morning-freshness pervaded these schools, which broke with past conventions, and imposed so peremptorily those new languages the whole universe has since learned to speak. No moment in the history of culture ever presented so swift a series of revolutions as those exploding in swift succession in the ten years between 1904 and 1914. The Italian Futurists, the Central and Northern European Expressionists, the work of the poets and artists of Montmartre, Montparnasse and Moscow all echo with the feverish joy of participation in a new and unknown world, so rich in untold marvels. The epitome of all such figures is that of Guillaume Apollinaire — a true ship's figure-head — poet and commentator on the works of his artist and sculptor friends — whose outlook was directed entirely towards the future. His particular genius was prophetic — a genius vouchsafed only rarely and to a few rare beings, and which can, of course, upon occasion, also prophesy disaster. It can equally well remain in doubt as to the form of the future which it prophesies, satisfied with the emotion aroused by the immediate presence of this future and with the expectation of new and positive events, the joy of such expectation being sufficient unto itself. Things were about to happen. What exactly these things would be was not and could not yet be determined. Merely to be present on the eve of their birth, however, provoked not disquiet but a strange and jubilant emotion. So vast and ingenious a jubilation that it even went so far as to encompass the war itself.

This same war was to smite the helmet of Apollinaire, marking with a star of blood the brow which sheltered ' *une si belle Minerve* ' and wiping out so many other promising young men: Roger de la Fresnaye, Raymond Duchamp-Villon, Franz Marc, August Macke, Umberto Boccioni, Henri Gaudier-Brzeska and Antonio Sant'Elia.

An epoch is characterized not only by its historical but also by its geographical conceptions. It is known, defined and understood according to its knowledge of the planet and according to that portion of the planet to which its knowledge is restricted. We have already seen how, at the end of the last century various Universal Exhibitions had awakened in bourgeois society a certain taste for exoticism. This had not yet become a taste for travel, which was still confined to those for whom it was a professional obligation, such as naval officers. The few hours of nostalgic emotion brought back by Pierre Loti from his brief stays in distant countries was as much as was required; the rest could well be delegated to another type of traveller, the classic English globe-trotter — Phileas Fogg.

A little later, the collective consciousness of the age was enriched by the acquisition of a far less superficial kind of knowledge of what is known as *foreign*. Less conventional travellers appeared, inspired by more genuine, direct and individual curiosity, not unlike the romantic travellers of an earlier age. Such a traveller was Barrès, in whom we may observe an expansion of the field of human sensitivity. The fact that this new sensitivity discovered new continents, to whet its appetite and procure its pleasure, constitutes an important phenomenon of which we have already spoken apropos of aestheticism and of dilettantism.

I do not wish to speak here of the passion inspiring a few great solitary souls to turn their backs on the narrow world and seek in some actual or chimeric *elsewhere* a new and ideal scene, fresh springs of inspiration, the message of the primitive or of the strange: souls like Van Gogh, Gauguin, Segalen, or Claudel, whose diplomatic career led him to discover the message of Asia, or again Valéry Larbaud, a humanist curious of other literatures and languages. Nor shall I here speak of England, whose vocation has always been to hold up a mirror to adventure, offering the world such men as Stevenson and Conrad. Germany, on the other hand, provided many instances of travelling philosophers. What I wish to emphasize with Barrès is a transformation of overall contemporary taste, the beginning of the diffusion of a special kind of pleasure: no passionate or tragic quest, but simply a new and pleasurable experience. Without going to extremes, and indeed, deliberately avoiding such extremes, this new sensitivity found delight in the stimulation provided by contact with countries, cultures, one might even say spiritual harmonies, whose common bond was that of strangeness — a craving for the piquant denounced by Julien Benda under the name of the demon *Belphégor*.

This same craving, in the work of Barrès, in that of d'Annunzio with his composite and voluptuous style, and in that of so many others, outran the limits of its native frontiers, becoming ' touristic ' in the best sense of that term. For it was roused not by any surface picturesqueness but by certain entirely new modalities of soul deliciously stimulating new reactions in that of the beholder.

Thus we come to a third level in this transformation of sensitivity and taste: the example of Gauguin being here essential. We are dealing here with a fundamental transformation. It is no longer a question of tickling an epicurean palate, but a true reversal of the scale of values. The entire planet now entered our sphere of consciousness. How small, how miserable appeared not only our tiny store of emotion, but also our artistic canons, fit only to be sent to the pawn shop along with the

GUILLAUME APOLLINAIRE

LE
Poète assassiné

Guillaume
APOLLINAIRE,
*Le poète
assassiné.
Cover
by Cappiello.*
(1916)

MAURICE BARRÈS

DU SANG, DE LA VOLUPTÉ
ET DE LA MORT

UN AMATEUR D'AMES
VOYAGE EN ESPAGNE
VOYAGE EN ITALIE, etc.

PARIS
BIBLIOTHÈQUE-CHARPENTIER
G. CHARPENTIER ET E. FASQUELLE, ÉDITEURS
11, RUE DE GRENELLE, 11
1894

Maurice BARRÈS,
*Du sang,
de la volupté
et de la mort.
Title-page*
(1894)

accumulation of family furniture, Renaissance dressers and Regency chests of drawers. Gauguin's gesture of abandoning, like Rimbaud's *Bateau Ivre*, 'the ancient parapets of Europe' to join a distant, still free, pure and true humanity, capable of furnishing new prototypes of beauty.

The discovery of the so-called primitive and savage arts was an event extremely rich in consequence. The exhibition of wood sculpture from the Palau Islands and from Africa held in the Ethnographical Museum in Dresden caused a great sensation. French and German painters and poets became enamoured of negro and oceanic art. They also discovered the Douanier Rousseau, also in his own way a primitive, but a primitive living in the midst of our civilization, following no school save that of the illustrated papers, his truly popular soul remaining unpolluted, and authentically naïf. All this completely destroyed our superstitious belief in any canon of transcendental beauty, laid down once and for all by academics and tradition.

At the same time the Swiss art historian Wölfflin and his Austrian and German colleagues were engaged in a revaluation of Baroque art. This great cultural and artistic movement had dominated the world, including Spanish America, from the time of the Renaissance until well into the middle of the latter half of the XVIIIth century. All the world, that is, excepting France. And even France will bear examination. The France of Louis XIV was, however, self-proclaimedly classic, and the very concept of Baroque remained unknown in France until the present time. For Baroque was not a historical and geographical style, but an idea, an aesthetic concept indispensable to the languages of aesthetics. The differentiation of Baroque, its obvious opposition to the fundamental principles of classicism leads to the identification of two basic possibilities of creative operation as manifested at all times and in all places. Hence the appearance of a number of general philosophies of art, the most masterly being Worringer's *Abstraktion und Einfühlung*, published in 1907, the same year as Bergson's *Evolution Créatrice*. This coincidence was significant, for Worringer defined one of the two possible orientations of creative activity as intuition and abstraction, born of a sentiment of belonging to and immanence in mysterious cosmic powers. The contrary, Greco-Roman tradition, is marked by a domination of nature by intellect leading inevitably to the imitation and representation of nature. The plastic universe created by such representation is, however, a universe limited in time and space, a *relative* and not an absolute universe, as had been thought both in France and in those schools in which French dogma was perpetuated. We must consider too the wide extent of those arts developing independently of such dogma, independently of the original creative inspirations systematized in such dogma.

Paul GAUGUIN,
Noa Noa (1893-1894)

Other principles, other initial impulses, other necessities had given rise to all sorts of other arts no less worthy of consideration than those determining our Western plastic universe and elevated by us to the rank of universal rules. There is, however, no universal rule, no absolute beauty, no hierarchy of styles — only relativity of style and beauty. Justice must therefore be done to Nomadic and Barbaric art; however great, in our own eyes, is the prestige of western art, fundamentally different, but in no way ' superior '. Such realizations opened the way to the Germanic intuitional and abstract schools, providing them with the elements of scientific and philosophic justification.

At the same time they demolished the frontiers of artistic taste and knowledge, giving it an entirely new elasticity and freedom as well as a far larger field of action. Nothing was barred and nothing exempted from revision. Other poles of attraction, other links, and correlationships were revealed in the laboriously built-up image of our glorious western civilization and of its relationship with other civilizations. A shift, a transmutation of values appeared henceforth eminently possible, as did the emergence of new values. To take but one example: the discovery of El Greco. This discovery took place in Spain on the occasion of the 1902 Prado exhibition, followed by Manuel B. Cossio's important book, published in 1908, by the work of San Roman, and by the passionate admiration of the 1898 Generation. The German Meier-Graefe, in his *Spanische Reise* (1910) corroborated the importance of this discovery. In 1912, Barrès published his *Greco ou le Secret de Tolède*: never had the melodic power of fascination of this ' *amateur d'âmes* ' enriched the modern soul more generously. El Greco provided a ' *frisson nouveau* '. It must, however, be observed that the discovery of this highly original genius who, for intimate reasons of his own, carried form to such arbitrary excesses, must have corresponded to some basic intent of modern art, as well as to all the current modification of the scale of values.

One of the principal victories of this period was thus the liberation of aesthetic judgment. To this victory contributed the great expansion of our range of knowledge, due partly to the contemporary *libido sentiendi* and *libido sciendi*, as well as to the magnificent extension of human, historical, ethnological, sociological and psychological science.

There can, I think, be no more fitting way to complete this picture of an epoch than by an investigation of those arts expressing the collective consciousness of the era: the arts of public performance in face of which vast human masses share the same vision and the same emotion. Having recounted the adventures of so many individuals or isolated groups, their whole trend of action contradictory to general taste, we must now consider a sector in which general taste was directly solicited, in which general initiatives had direct impact on the masses gathered together, as they have gathered together since time immemorial, for the enjoyment of communal entertainment.

We have already seen how photography had provided the pre-eminently social pleasure of knowing and recognizing reality at the very instant of its action. Continuous technical progress led to new conquests, and, before long, also to new styles. Every Tom, Dick and Harry could experience the delights of recording images of the world for future tender reminiscence, and of becoming expert ' amateur ' photographers. Meanwhile, owing to certain contemporary influences, there appeared a number of true artists through whom photography became an art. Towards the turn of the century, in sympathy with Symbolism, this art assumed a certain vaporous style, which aroused a certain nostalgia for the honesty and overwhelming truth of portraits by Nadar or Carjat. Another tendency, such as that manifested in the work of Aget, continued the naturalistic trend. Journalism began to exploit the use of photography, and in 1903 *Le Matin* published the first photograph reproduced in half-tone. Photographic reporting became a profession of its own. In 1907 telegraphic transmission of images became possible through

Cover for the 3rd edition of ' Abstraktion und Einfühlung' by W. Worringer (1911)

the invention of Edouard Belin. In the same year, Louis Lumière perfected the autochromatic plate, thus introducing the world to photography in colours. From 1910 onwards, scientific photography made continuous strides in every field: radiography, aerial and sub-marine photography, micro-photography and astronomical photography.

Similar progress was being made in another technique for the optical conquest of the world: cinematography. This technique was to lead to the creation of a truly prodigious art of spectacle: a social art destined to touch the greatest possible number of viewers. Even after the addition of sound, the art of the cinema was to know no bounds: language proving no more than a feeble barrier to its triumphant, international appeal to crowds throughout the world.

As we have already said, this art realized almost at once the full extent of its potentialities, invading the spheres of imagination and of fantasy. Reference has already been made to Meliès, one of its earliest masters. The fact that the earliest period in the history of the cinema should be known as the Meliès period, is a matter for congratulation. On December 28th, 1895 Georges Meliès, professional conjuror and director of the *Théâtre Robert Houdin* was invited to attend the final rehearsal of a Lumière cinematographic performance at the Grand Café on the *Boulevard des Capucines*. Its staggering effect upon Meliès resulted in the introduction of conjuring, of trick photography, and of enchantment for an invention still in a period of technical development. Before long, French companies, shortly followed by English companies, began to exploit it for these very values. In America it was taken up by the trusts, and incorporated into the peepshows of travelling showmen, to whom Charles Pathé sold Edison phonographs and kinetographs, prior to launching, in 1901, some few years later, in company with Decca, and supported by a financial group, a film-producing enterprise. Neither the artistic nor the industrial and financial repercussions of the miraculous invention were, however, so far clear. In 1897, it was held responsible for the terrible fire which destroyed the Charity Bazaar in Paris and thus remained in a state of hesitation and repeated crises until the genius of Meliès, cloistered in his Montreuil studios, opened wide the path to fantasy and the impossible. This miracle was accomplished thanks to the theatre and to theatrical resources: a paradox later eliminated by the return to the Lumièrian light of day and to the direct representation of reality. The paradoxical dominion of the theatre over the cinema was to go so far as the production of *reconstituted news reels*; which, however, only goes to emphasize the basic character of the cinema as that of *art*. The cinema as an art was born in 1902, heralded by the prodigies of the *Journey on the Moon*, rivalling the imagination of Jules Verne or H.G. Wells, in a contemporary theatrical style no doubt, a spectacular *Châtelet* style, but with a poetic quality equal to that of these two highly original poetic geniuses, and with a fantasy and a humour which always has been and always will be an inexhaustible source of enchantment.

From this point onwards, large scale industrialization made it possible for the cinema, like any other form of art, to try its wings in the most diversified directions, creating its own genres, its own styles, its own actors — each of whom created in turn his individual genre and style — and, later on, its own producers, whose creative genius grew progressively like that of any other type of creative artist; painters, novelists, dramatists or poets.   Pathé, the master of the immediate post-Meliès period secured the services of Boireau and Max Linder.   Later came the birth of Gaumont and Eclair.   Meanwhile American companies were launched upon their brilliant careers, their great producer David W. Griffith marking a significant success in 1915 with the *Birth of a Nation*.   An original school originated in Denmark and another in Italy, responsible for *Cabiria* in 1914.   The cinema perfected its own techniques, in particular that of montage, and the adoption of the ' one turn, one picture ' technique by the Gaumont producer Emile Cohl was to lead in due course to the invention of the animated cartoon, destined to enjoy such an outstandingly successful future.

Little by little the wonderful and highly specialized climate of the cinema was evolved, with its own rhythm, its power of creating illusion, surprise, emotion, its tragic and its comic accents, its whole extraordinary poetry: a poetry revealed in a repertory admittedly popular in character, and containing something elementary and primitive, to be taken at its own level, which was the level of the popular serial.   Fear and horror were expressed by pathos, laughter provoked by chases, gags, changes of rhythm, and acrobatics lifted from the circus ring or from theatrical farce.   Everything was carried to an excess bordering on the fantastic, and for this very reason, the cinema became an art.   Men of good taste, and those who would like to be reputed such, are always somewhat disturbed by the emergence of a technique which, by the originality of its methods and its results, is in fact an art, a title previously reserved for more noble and more holy use.   This explains why, in France, the Academy, the Boulevard and the Comédie Française should have conjugated their efforts to produce, a number of ' art films ' of which the most famous example remains ' *L'Assassinat du Duc de Guise* ' (1908), which today appears to us faintly ridiculous.   We are, however, forced to admit, with Georges Sadoul, one of the finest experts on the history of the Cinema [1] that, in spite of its theatrical nature — which was, in fact, a regression towards the Meliès tradition, imperfectly understood — certain specifically cinematographic qualities displayed in this work place it clearly among those controversies and contradictions without which the cinema would never have become an art.   Today we are, however, more inclined to see the signs of this evolution in certain more humble, more vulgar and, at the same time, more genuinely cinematographic works.   Mack Sennet and the early Chaplin films were soon to dispell all doubt : here was a burlesque art form absolutely specific to the cinema, a form never before produced by man in any previous artistic media.

The cinema, and only the cinema, with its mime and *tempo*, its technical constraints, its specific limitations, its fantastically fertile indigence, could have engendered the kind of laughter in which every class of society could participate, from those seeking only to laugh at the slightest opportunity to those demanding the satisfaction of subtle aesthetic demands.   The absolute originality of the cinema — the ' Seventh Art ' — with its infinite potentialities, was thus abundantly clear from its very earliest and most rudimentary productions.   It must, however, be admitted, proclaimed even, that the development of cinematographic art constitutes a remarkable adventure; that the cinema is, in fact, the characteristic, the great, distinctive art form of the twentieth century.

The ancient art of the theatre, perhaps the most ancient of all the arts of man, the origins of which are bound up with religious beliefs and practices, was, however, not dethroned by its young rival.   While its prestige remained intact, it underwent certain profound modifications, following the powerful and regenerative current then carrying in its course all human forms of expression.

A fixed stage, frontal settings, sumptuous in the case of the Opera, meticulous and providing an illusion of reality for modern plays, the centring of the whole dramatic interest in the person of the actor — in the voice, gestures, presence and stature of the actor — such were the elements of theatrical art before the advent of these contemporary revolutions in other forms of human expression.   The ideas inspiring these other revolutions also affected theatrical art: arousing a desire to make stage direction an art in its own right, free of any obligation to imitate reality, subject only to its own technical requirements. Naturalism found a further defender in the meticulous, cruel and masterly art of Antoine.   Symbolism was, of course,

---

[1] *Les Pionniers du Cinéma* (1897-1909). Denoël, Paris, 1947.

La Grande Ourse

Georges MÉLIÈS, ' *The Conquest of the Pole* ' (1912)

bound to oppose its intellectual and spiritual claims to this journalistic ' slice of life ' approach, laying bare an elemental truth by insisting, in face of this materialistic fetishism, the magic power of the word. Dramatic action is created by the word: the theatre exists only because the play, and ipso facto, the author of the play, exists. A highly salutary and effective return to the purely suggestive power of text, performed with all its vital silences and accompanied by the strict minimum of gesture was brought about by the *Théâtre d'Art* of Paul Fort and the *Théâtre de l'Œuvre* of Lugné-Poë and Suzanne Després, In conformity with the contemporary trend, this restoration of theatrical autonomy, was accompanied by an appeal to the power of music. Inspired by the ideas of Schopenhauer and Nietzsche, and by the triumph of Wagner's great creations Adolphe Appia in his work on *Die Musik und die Inszenierung*, published in Munich in 1898, attributed to music, to the spirit, the inspiration, the principle of music, the predominant role in that particular creation of reality represented by dramatic development and action.

Léon Moussinac, in this little work *Traité de la mise en scène* [1] rightly remarks that Appia's ideas appeared ' at the moment when, in France, new electric organs were replacing the gas organs at the Opéra Comique and at the Chatelet '. The brilliance of Loïe Fuller ushered in a new era of light bearing no relation to the former marvels of flickering gas light so beloved by the Impressionists. In the theatre the power of electricity was to prove as important and as creative as that of music. Interest was no longer aroused by means of petty, extraneous, ornamental, anecdotal, illustrative detail, but by spiritual forces fused into the spectacle itself, becoming an essential part of its inspiration and its form.

From this point to the discipline of the *Vieux Colombier* was but a step. Jacques Copeau was consumed by a fever for discipline as powerful as any religious vocation, in complete harmony with the new critical severity of the *Nouvelle Revue Française*. The spirit of Jansenism and Reform uniting this group, this coterie — one might almost say this sect — has often been emphasized. We have already observed here the salutary effects of such a spirit and the profound influence

---

[1] Ed. Charles Massin et Cie, Paris, 1948.

exercised by those hermetic groups preoccupied with high intellectual dignity, which emerged from time to time, only to disintegrate with the advent of success. Their influence was, however, durable. Thus it was with the action of Copeau, a reformer enamoured of monastic brotherhood and order, a purifier of theatrical life as well as of the scene itself, an incomparable master in whose noble school were formed all those who were destined to be the greatest theatrical figures of French post-war history.

The stage was the site of all dramatic action: on it should appear nothing susceptible of distracting the attention of the spectator. Action sprang from the text, from the presence of the actors, from a sober and pure architecture of which the actors themselves were as integral a part as was the interplay of light and shade. Something of the same ideas of structure and of picture-object were here implied as those inspiring contemporary plastic revolutions such as Cubism. Similar ideas are also found in the work of another great reformer, Gordon Craig in his passionate quest for Style. 'Not realism, but style' was his aim, a style achieved by a rigorous discipline, cold calculation, and by insistence that each element, including the individuality of the actor, should undergo synthesis in a machine of which every detail, every proportion, every inter-relationship had been meticulously combined: an exalted type of mechanisation later to assume new from sin the work of Stanislavsky and of Meyerhold.

Il me semble que je les vois. (Page 158.)

Émile BAYARD, *Illustration for Jules Verne's 'Trip to the Moon'* (1901)

Thus the theatre, like all other modern art forms, awoke to a realization of its true — theatrical — nature. In his work '*Die Revolution des Theaters*' (Munich, 1909) Georg Fuchs has insisted on this 'theatrization' of the theatre. The masses too played a role in this purifying operation. For the spectator, too, is part of the theatre, part of the play, in which he is, indeed, the principal participant, sharing with the actor in an identical communion. Hence the attempt to annihilate the barrier separating the public from the dramatic action, to modify completely the structure of scenic presentation, to enlarge the scene, to mobilize and render it more flexible. In so doing our increasingly collective and community-minded era returned to the great theatrical tradition of the Greeks, of the Elizabethans, and of the early days of pure theatre — of the Mystery play and the itinerant farce, out of which sprang Molière himself. Here we see the explanation for the modification of the position of the stage in relation to the spectator, whether this was made to revolve as in Max Reinhardt's *Deutsches Theater* in Berlin in 1905, or to take its place in the centre of the theatre, like a circus ring, while the performers appeared from among the ranks of the spectators. Gémier's popular theatre was full of such inventions, as was, later, that of the Russians and the Germans, both imbued with the activist and socialising spirit of Expressionism.

The theatre, a community art, was to give rise to a true community of arts — the *Gesamtkunstwerk* — and in particular to solicit the co-operation of painting. Décor had previously been something extraneous to the plays itself, no particular style, no demonstration of plastic invention being required of the artist. If the décor was changed, it was because the act or play was over, or because the scene had changed from garden to throne room, from Carthage to Benares. Its intrinsic nature — its style — showed no trace of originality. Now, however, originality became the aim, and the idea arose of seeking for the provision of stage settings, if not for the construction of the scene itself, the collaboration of artists whose function

Michel LARIONOV,
Serge de Diaghilev.

was original creation. The collaboration of plastic and scenic revolutions was to be one of the events of the century. Jacques Rouché selected a team of artists, among them Drésa and Maxime Dethomas, who were to become specialists in the technique of theatrical decoration, and, moreover, in the production of certain given spectacles, an appeal was made to the collaboration of creative artists who, despite their pre-occupation with form, were ready to submit to the constraints of specific crafts and thus also to become true craftsmen. Reference must here be made to the existence among the creators of modern painting of a lively curiosity concerning various crafts: stained glass work, ceramics, tapestry, mural painting, engraving, typography, and book illustration. A similar curiosity has already been observed among the Nabis at the time of *Art Nouveau*. It was continued by the Fauves and the Cubists, as well as by the Expressionists who displayed a passionate interest in the graphic arts in which they were both creators of masterpieces and dictators of fashion. The theatre also attracted painters both during and immediately after the 1914 war.

A similar move towards a synthesis of the arts practised in the theatre, combining music, dance and painting, had already taken place much earlier, at the beginning of the century, thanks to the inspirational genius of the extraordinary impresario Serge Diaghilev and his *Ballets Russes*. Diaghilev's original intention was simply to reveal to the West the marvels of the new school of Russian music: that of 'the Five', and the charm of Russian folklore. In this enterprise he was admirably seconded by two brilliant decorators, Alexandre Benois and Léon Bakst. He soon, however, became more ambitious, and dreamed of creating a great new ensemble, a new reality introduced into a Western melting pot then already simmering with so many new and admirable inventions. He sought painters for his team in *avant-garde* Russian artistic circles discovering Natalia Gontcharova and Michel Larionov, and introduced into his repertory ballets by contemporary French musicians, Debussy, Dukas and Ravel. The first performance of *L'Après-Midi d'un Faune*, with Nijinski, in 1912, was a battle followed in 1913 by another, no less famous battle, that of *Le Sacre du Printemps*. The name of Stravinsky was henceforward inseperable from that of Diaghilev and the history of the *Ballets Russes*. European history had become Parisian history. In 1917, at the *Châtelet*, was launched the scandal of *Parade*: theme by Jean Cocteau, music by Erik Satie, curtain, décor and costumes by Picasso. The choice of these three names was significant of the determination of the great impresario to take up his position at the head of contemporary *avant-garde* creation, by combining the most audacious creations of the century. He subsequently called on Manuel de Falla, Derain, Balla, Robert and Sonia Delaunay, and Matisse. To all these *avant-gardes*, Diaghilev gave an opportunity for effective, brilliant, concrete realization, by putting them before the public.

A sociologist would certainly stress the importance of such an event, apotheosis of the action towards which so many and varied forms and types of genius had been striving during the years preceeding the 1914 war. By his intervention such genius became known to, and recognized by, society, or at least by the social *avant-garde* of fashionable society, which, through the workings of snobbery, exercises an influence so powerful that it often ends by gaining general acceptance. Opening to loud boos and closing to delirious applause, supported by the irrefutable argument of financial success, modern art had gained acceptance — the battle had been won. New ways had come to stay, and a new relationship between artistic creation and society developed. Not that this relationship was to prove always and everywhere harmonious. As we have constantly emphasized, the 1914 war opened an era of such chaos that twentieth century man can certainly claim to be living in the most chaotic period in the history of the universe. He has seen and still sees today political régimes which have considered and still consider artistic creation, and indeed also literary, philosophical, scientific and indeed any other kind of creation as their Enemy Number One. This form of divorce between intelligence and society is very different from the flat denial which bourgeois society inflicted on intelligence in the peaceful years of the 1900's: a very different, and extraordinarily stupid, systematic and vicious form. This, however, is another story. From this time onward everything is, in fact, another story.

Jean CASSOU

VIII

Oskar Kokoschka

The tragedy of man (poster)

(1908)

Fig. 32. Fig. 33. Fig. 34.

82
E. J. Marey
Chronophotographic experiments
(1887)

83
Edward Muybridge
Stand of Palo Alto, California
(1881)

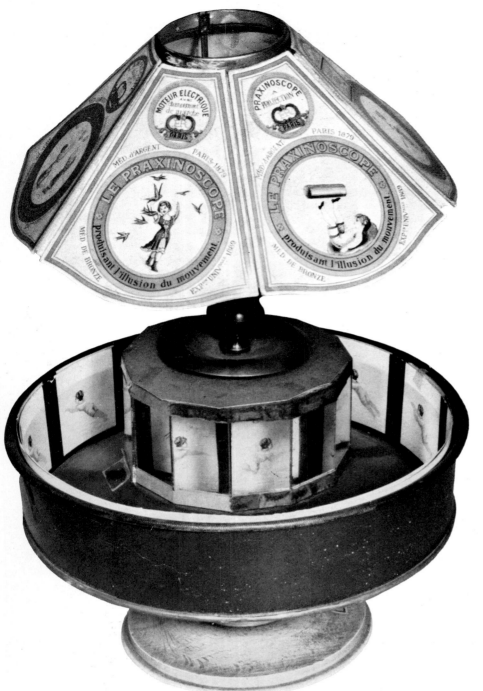

85
Lumière cine-camera
(1895)

84
Émile Reynaud's proxinoscope
(1890)

86
Thomas A. Edison in his laboratory
(1900)

THOMAS A. EDISON *dans son laboratoire; fac-similé de sa signature.*

87

E. J. Marey's photographic gun
(1882)

88

E. J. Marey's chronophotograph
(1889)

89

*Physiological centre
in the Parc des Princes
(E. J. Marey)
(1889–90)*

90

Émile COHL

Joyful microbes
(1909)

91

Men jumping for the Marey experiment
(1889)

92
André BARRÈRE
Poster for the film Nick Winter
(1910)

93
Poster for the film ' L'Arroseur arrosé '
(1895–96)

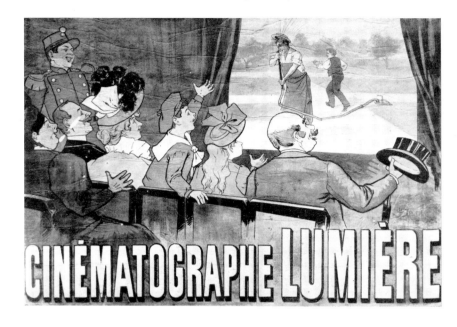

94
Georges MÉLIÈS
Still from the film ' A Trip to the Moon '
(1902)

95
LE BARGY and CALMETTES
Stills from the film
' The Assassination of the Duke of Guise '
(1908)

96
Léon Bakst
Maquette of décor for
' *Thamar* ' *by Balakirew*
(1912)

97
Alexandre Benois
Maquette for the décor of the
fair-ground scene in
' *Petrouchka* ' *by Stravinsky*
(1911)

98

Léon Bakst

Costume for a village girl,
' Daphnis and Chloe' by Ravel
(1912)

99

Nathalie Gontcharova

Design of a curtain for
' Le Coq d'or' by Rimsky-Korsakov
(1914)

100

Karl WALSER

Decor for ' Romeo and Juliet '
Production: Max Reinhardt, Berlin
(1907)

IX
Alfonso Maria MUCHA
Medea (poster)
(1898)

THE VISUAL ARTS
from 1884 to 1914

INTRODUCTION

Although the sources of modern art go back in part to pre-history and — a fact without parallel in the history of aesthetics — embrace the *Musée imaginaire* of all mankind, the authors of this book have selected as their starting-point the year 1884. There is nothing arbitrary in their choice. True, the founding of the Société des Indépendants (Seurat, Signac, Redon, etc.) and the birth of Divisionism, did not strictly create a violent breach with the recent past, but they sounded the knell of the Impressionists, who two years later ceased from all collective action. However, what began as a mutiny soon took on the form of a revolution calling everything into question: the spirit as well as the technique, the way of thinking and feeling as well as the way of painting and sculpting. The result was an attitude of rejection, a revolt of the mind and of the soul. The artist, as much as or more than the architect, decorator and technician, began working against the stream. In these years the divorce between society and living art was absolute. Confronted with an arrogant middle-class and official conventionality, the creative artist was now an outlaw. The Manet scandal became an everyday affair. But almost at once the ' *maudits* ' formed themselves into independent colonies (Montmartre, Worpswede, Dresden, Munich, Laethem-Saint-Martin, Moscow, etc.), real spiritual homes where, linked together by bonds of affinity and fruitful meetings, they created a new humanist network extending all over Europe and beyond. This tremendous efflux of ideas, feelings and forms, thought up by men like Seurat, Cézanne, van Gogh, Munch, Ensor, Gauguin, Picasso, Kandinsky, Mondrian and other independents, was to crystallise in ' isms ', whose apparent contradictions only betokened an extraordinary wealth.

Following Symbolism, which was inspired by poets and musicians and was strongly tinged with *fin-de-siècle* decadence, and Nabism, a mild endeavour to rehabilitate colour by enlisting it in the service of bourgeois cosiness, modern art after 1900 was dominated by two main streams, one of them rational, the other irrational.

The first was an Apollonian stream, heir to the art of Ancient Greece and of Piero della Francesca, Poussin, David and Ingres. It accepted the discipline of reason and displayed a love of order, balance and clarity, based upon a set of rules within which feeling was channelled. These were the systematized movements — Divisionism, Cézannism, Cubism, Futurism, Suprematism, Orphism and Neo-plasticism.

The second, the Dionysian stream issued from Baroque, Goya and Romanticism. Launched by van Gogh, Munch, Ensor and Gauguin, it gave birth to Fauvism, Expressionism (German, Scandinavian and Flemish), metaphysical art, Dada and informal abstract art.

Set in motion by a few isolated giants, this double stream gradually attracted to itself a growing number of non-conformist artists and avant-garde circles. Each of these contributed an individual note, even a new trend, but, at the end of thirty years, and despite individual, regional and national differences, there emerged two powerful international styles which constitute Modern Art and, by the inevitable process of evolution, led to the abstract arts of the present day.

In the following pages we shall attempt to recount briefly the glorious adventure of an artistic revolution without its like in human history.

SYMBOLISM

A REVOLT OF THE MIND

Of all the movements marking a break away from Naturalism and Impressionism, more or less organised and formulating a coherent theory, the earliest in date is Symbolism. Born simultaneously in France and Belgium, with more remote contributions from Anglo-Saxon countries, its character in the beginning was essentially literary. The offspring of Gérard de Nerval, Baudelaire, Lautréamont, Villiers de l'Isle Adam, Verlaine, Rimbaud, Mallarmé and J.-K. Huysmans, the movement, starting in 1886 [1], grouped together a galaxy of poets, novelists and playwrights, the brightest stars in which included Georges Rodenbach, Jean Moréas, Émile Verhaeren, Henri de Régnier, Charles Van Lerberghe, Maurice Maeterlinck, Rémy de Gourmont, André Gide, Paul Valéry, Paul Claudel and Alfred Jarry.

These men set poetry free, created new forms of versification, and endowed literature with a lofty ethic based upon a pure and individualised lyricism. The move was away from reality, from the visible, from the grossness of the workaday world, from 'tribal catchwords'. The Symbolists stood sentry around the 'fortress of the soul', enclosing within it their esoteric dreams and visions nursed on myth and legend. Escape was sought in the early Middle Ages and towards the Far East, with their gifts of sweetness, chivalry and true civilisation. This *fin-de-siècle* mentality borders upon decadence and professes a refined, an aristocratic pessimism. Yet the absence of illusion does not exclude a sincere belief that the world can be changed through the mind and the feelings. Symbolism, although it subscribes to no positive creed, is profoundly religious. In politics most of its followers behave rather as anarchists. Symbolism is a spiritualised Romanticism, the prelude to Surrealism, which was later to form the Romanticism of the magically absurd.

In the field of the visual arts, the Symbolist theory, vague and disparate, developed on a smaller scale, but with subtler shades, than in poetry. An important element in the ultimate decay of Impressionism, it did not attain — partly because of its literary aims and its looking back to the past — the level of a great revolutionary style. Although it was a violent reaction of minds against the bourgeois sensuality of a whole epoch, Symbolism did not, in the end, prove to be a XXth century *source*, but was rather the vanguard of battles not foreseen in the plan of campaign: the victory of the Nabis and the revolt of the Fauves. Its imprint was stronger upon music and drama than upon painting and sculpture.

The saying of Tristan Corbière, one of the Poètes Maudits (1845-1875), that painters must only paint what they have never seen and never will see, applies to the whole of Symbolist painting. The first of the pioneers was the patriarchal figure of Gustave Moreau (1826-1898). He was nearing sixty when he assumed charge of that legendary workshop to which rallied the most eager and gifted of the young painters: Matisse, Marquet, Evenepoel, Rouault, Manguin, Friesz, Dufy and Braque. All of them swore fanatical allegiance to the hero-teacher who guided their talent with a complete respect for their individuality. Moreau, cradled in Quattrocento art and mystico-aesthetic literature, knew everything about painting. All that he lacked was the touch of genius. His taste for the mysterious and his preference for sombre themes, the richness of his colours, solid and with the brilliance of precious stones, as well as the attention to detail in his scholarly treatment, place him at the opposite pole from the Impressionists. Even in very late works like *Orpheus mourning at the Tomb of Eurydice* (1898) (105), summarily executed though this was, he intrigues us by his self-imposed reserve, the nobility of his imagination and the brilliance of his palette, with golds and reds standing out from a ground of green and blue enamels. A providential link between Romanticism and Symbolism, Gustave Moreau presaged a movement, the theory of which was to be determined by others. To him, with his host of famous pupils, the *fin-de-siècle* school owes a great part of its pictorial knowledge.

While the influence of Gustave Moreau, apart from the impact of his personality, found its main expression in the renewal of colour, that of Puvis de Chavannes (1824-1898) was to revolutionise line and composition. A convert, like

---

[1] Jean Moréas (1856-1910), published the first Symbolist manifesto in 'Figaro' of 18 September 1886, and founded the review *Le Symboliste* in the same year.

his contemporary, from Romanticism (Delacroix taught him as much as Scheffer), he came back from Italy haunted by the spirit of monumentalism. His dream was of an art that was static, sober, ornamental and religious. He forged a style after the manner of the great Florentine fresco-painters, painting in soft colours and sharp contours, an architectural composition in which straight lines, horizontal and vertical, predominate, with beautiful empty spaces enhancing the motifs. His noble, majestic style went strangely with a mind at once dreamy and religious, intimate and familiar. The intimacy was on a monumental scale, the mystery within the grasp of all. He succeeded in imbuing the mystic themes of the Romantics with fresh sentiment which, by its sobriety and rejection of grandiloquence, sounded an authentic note. This pagan mystic treated the fair legends of France and of antiquity in the spirit of St. Francis of Assisi. He gave them back their naive and homely charm. Something in him reminds us of the mentality and linear technique of the elder Brueghel, and this explains the attraction he had for certain Northern painters, especially the Flemings (Gustave Van de Woestijne, Valerius De Saedeleer, Albert Servaes in his early days, and even the sculptor Georges Minne) before these, in 1902, rediscovered the XVth century Primitives.

In the end, the art of Puvis de Chavannes became set to some extent in an academic mould, from which the spontaneity had vanished; but a Swiss painter, Ferdinand Hodler (1853-1918), his junior by 30 years, borrowed the principles of the French master, bringing to the movement fresh blood, a Nordic, even slightly barbaric strain. With the same austere draughtsmanship and the same sober brushwork, he embarked upon a lengthy series of huge compositions, some of them historical, others allegorical, and, a very few, religious. Abandoning the realism of his early Munich years, he now aimed only at a stylised monumentalism, constructed upon a rhythm of lines, colours and masses which he called 'Parallelism' (*Eurythmie*, 1895) (59). The symbolic content of his work is of specifically Teutonic inspiration. The ancestral myth takes precedence of the golden legend. The priestly gesture gives way to the static dream,

Aubrey BEARDSLEY, *Title-page of Oscar Wilde's 'Salomé'* (1907)

Odilon REDON, *The eye, like a strange balloon, aims at the Infinite* (1882)

127

rhythmic action to contemplation. Wagnerian in the best sense of the word, Hodler's art has an intellectual strength and a restrained ecstasy which could not fail to influence the Symbolist aspirations of the Germanic and Scandinavian countries. Through him, Symbolism penetrated parts of Europe least receptive to the Latin quintessence of the movement. His art gained added popularity in Europe when the German Expressionists hailed him as one of their precursors.

Unlike those who sought to express themselves in a severe but necessarily somewhat exteriorised monumentalism, Odilon-Redon (1840-1916), a hypersensitive recluse, gave himself entirely to introspection. The waking dreams of his solitary existence — visions and hallucinations, phantasmagoria, weird nightmares — were reflected in drawings, engravings and lithography. His strange and self-enclosed art, uncomprehended until he was taken up by the Symbolists, has its roots deeply implanted in the kingdom of Nature. Like Bosch and Arcimboldo, Redon had a profound knowledge of the natural sciences, particularly botany. Still deeper was his knowledge of the dark recesses of the human soul, of what was later to be called the subconscious. A passionate lover of music (Schumann, Berlioz, Wagner) and poetry (Baudelaire, Mallarmé, Poe), his inexhaustible fancy, quite untrammelled by reason, produced works of a beautiful absurdity enveloped in a mystery that defied interpretation. In his paintings and pastels the colours leap from the canvas with the brilliance of Gustave Moreau's brush. Redon's art impresses by form as much as by content, by its matter as much as by its spirit. It eludes all the snares in the path of literary painting. A surrealist long before the school existed, he is aligned with the James Ensor of 1885-90 and proclaims the lineage of Kubin, Hill, Josephson and others.

Between 1885 and 1895, the urge of a whole generation towards rejection and escapism was so strong that Symbolism rapidly overran most of the Western art world. In the Netherlands, Central Europe and Scandinavia, it gained an acceptance which France, with its love of balance and proportion, was unable to give. Belgium, engaging in the literary upheaval from the beginning, threw into the Symbolist campaign the best among those of its artists who were not sworn to Impressionism. The groups known as 'L'Art Indépendant', 'Les Vingt' and 'La Libre Esthétique', under the leadership of Octave Maus, Edmond Picard and Émile Verhaeren, spurred painters, sculptors and engravers to the boldest flights of an intellectuality à outrance. Moreover, much of Symbolist doctrine was attuned to the mystic element in Flemish painting. Its disciples found a forerunner and teacher in Xavier Mellery (1845-1921). This native of Brussels, the friend of Charles De Coster and Camille Lemonnier, chose to translate his idealism into noble allegorical figures, in sepia on a gold ground, after the manner of Walter Crane. It is, however, by his drawings of interiors, in velvety blacks, expressing the *silence at the heart of things*, that he proclaims himself a precursor of Seurat. His best pupil, Fernand Khnopff (1858-1921), is physically and morally the perfect incarnation of a Symbolist, with his aristocratic breeding, disdainful pessimism and deep classical culture. Nurtured in the school of Gustave Moreau and the English Pre-Raphaelites, Burne-Jones and Rossetti, his painting exhales solitude, silence, reticence and languor. *A Blue Wing* (110) illustrates that 'hot-house' art in which beautiful pale ladies wander sadly among lilies and relics of the past.

A far better painter than Khnopff, Henri Evenepoel (1872-1899), although he too was one of Gustave Moreau's pupils, returned to the motifs of daily life and drew inspiration from Manet's technique. A Nabi rather than a Symbolist, his street scenes and portraits — for instance, *Lady with a White Hat* (1897) (113) — nevertheless borrow much from the undulating line of his predecessors. Another Belgian, William Degouve de Nuncques (1867-1935), an intelligent and highly cultivated artist, occupies a peculiar place in the Symbolist movement of his country. His art lay in the delicate transformation of empty, undistinguished places into scenes of supernatural magic, bathed in a mysterious twilight. He achieved poetry by the simplest of means, a very sparing brushwork and meticulously careful drawing. By his kinship with the painters of Holland, he is the connecting link between Belgian and Dutch Symbolism.

It is in fact in Holland that Symbolism, despite memories of Van Gogh, flourished with especial vigour. It permeated all the arts, deeply and for a long time. The Netherlands created a Symbolist style of their own, which was to survive in decor and in the arts of the book until the 1914-18 War. Its first exponent was a remarkable artist, Jan Toorop (1858-1928), who was born in Java and studied in Amsterdam, Brussels and London, becoming the friend of James Ensor and William Morris. Of an inquiring and impassioned mind, with an ardent sense of social justice, and deeply

X

Henri ROUSSEAU, dit le Douanier

La charmeuse de serpents
(1907)

religious, he experimented with all the new techniques and every art trend of his time. Into Dutch art he introduced a permanent state of religious ecstasy, impregnated with the spirit of Java and with Indian fatalism. His elaborate draughtsmanship, all idly undulating arabesques, has the delicacy of filigree; his composition, often overcrowded, aims at a monumental symmetry (*The Three Fiancées*, 1893) (109). The last twenty years of his life were spent entirely in a glorification of the Christian faith. His compatriot, Jan Thorn Prikker (1868-1932), has more of the Teutonic, Wagnerian and epic spirit. His religious and allegorical paintings are more severe and easier to interpret, but, on the other hand, overladen with ornament. (*The Betrothed*, 1893) (108). After 1900, Prikker came under Van Gogh's influence and turned to more abstract painting. His influence, like that of Toorop and his fellow-disciples, A. J. der Kenderen and Roland Holst, was especially felt among craftsmen and in the decorative arts (posters, typography, bookbinding and furniture). In Germany and Austria, Symbolism is practically synonymous with the *Jugendstil* [1] and with the Munich (1893) and Vienna (1898) *Secessions*. These movements, here, as everywhere else, coloured by Japanese art, present a mixture of Oriental mystagogy, Slav nostalgia and Wagnerian grandiosity. Less refined, but more virile than their Latin brethren, the Germanic artists retained a taste for the sumptuous and the sentimental, only slightly tempered by *fin-de-siècle morbidezza*. All these features are found in the work of the Viennese Gustav Klimt (1862-1918), whose innumerable decorative paintings formed the spiritual and plastic link between Symbolist decor and modern architecture. His portrait of *Madame Fritza Riedler* (1906) (112), and his famous mosaic (*The Kiss*, 1909) (LII), in the dining-room of the Palais Stoclet in Brussels [2] reveal an unerring mastery of his craft and a perfect feeling for the monumental. Treated as a rule in broken up colours, these works nevertheless glow with the rich reds of their ornamentation, the enamels gleaming like jewels. Klimt's art is an eclectic blend of distinction and barbarism, of austerity and charm, of life and petrifaction. The Leipzig painter Max Klinger (1857-1920), less happy than Klimt in his choice of media, failed to achieve international stature. With more talent than inspiration, he sought to bring a new element into sculpture by the use of coloured marble, a praiseworthy endeavour but one with no future.

Italy, in the last quarter of the nineteenth century, seems to have abandoned Naturalism with reluctance and to have found delight almost exclusively in the plastic research started by Impressionism. Only one Italian artist, Giovanni Segantini (1858-1899), the simple robust painter of mountain landscapes, really responded to the charms of Symbolism. Riveted, however, like Millet, to nature, he was less at his ease in the few allegories he executed in the last years of his short life (*Love at the Source of Life*, 1896) (106). Despite a moving lyricism and a brilliant technique, he is not master of his subject. With him, Nature prevails over the artist's dream and, fortunately, forms the greater part of his œuvre.

By way of conclusion, Symbolism may be said to be a movement which did much to free the arts from their academic bondage and from Impressionist sensuality. Never before was there so close an interpenetration of all the arts, poetry, drama, music, painting, architecture and decoration. In painting, however, Symbolism posed the problem in false terms. By extolling the primacy of the mind, it paralysed the artist's visual sense and robbed colour of its magic. Through the rigidity of its principles, it gave birth, especially in painting, to an *unauthentic* art, from which genuine plastic emotion is missing. Already we look upon its history as upon a phenomenon long past. Happily, the Nabis were soon to set matters right.

THE NABIS LIBERATE COLOUR

While the Symbolists were steeping themselves in literature and music to the point of forgetting the very essence of painting, namely colour, a new group emerged under the name of Nabis [3]. It did not declare war upon Symbolism, to

---

[1] A name taken from the German review *Die Jugend*, launched by Otto Eekmann in 1896, ten years after the Symbolist Manifesto in France.
[2] The work of Josef Hoffmann (1870-1956), architect, founder of the *Wiener Werkstätte* and a pioneer in modern architecture. This unique and perfect example of Jugendstil aestheticism was built between 1905 and 1911.
[3] The rather ambiguous term *Nabi* is derived from the Hebrew, meaning prophet or visionary; it was invented by the poet Cazalis. The group held its first exhibition in 1891.

which it was largely the sequel, but it broke away with the conviction that the real problem lay elsewhere and that painting could not be liberated either by the mind or by feeling, but by colour itself, by painting that was painting simply and solely. In place of the high-flown aristocratic ideas of their fellows-artists, the Nabis substituted the pleasure in life of a bourgeoisie with no past either historic or histrionic. Instead of the archaic allegories of nostalgic legend, they preached the real and poetic charms of family happiness, made up of the thousand small amenities of daily life. The weary and disillusioned hero gave way to the common man, civilized and agreeable, noting with kindly eye his friends and associates within the home or in the subdued light of quiet and comfortable drawing-rooms. In the same way Beatrice and Ophelia were banished by nude little girls taking their baths before the enraptured gaze of a painter intoxicated by form and colour.

Never was the bourgeoisie endowed with so much splendour by the best among its children. Never moreover, since Vermeer, was a social atmosphere evoked so accurately and so poetically by the mere miracle of colour. Nabi colouring, common to all with no dependence upon a particular theory, was a programme in itself, a credo. Colour was to be liberated by the harmony of blended shades, warm or cool, pure and neutral, without recourse to line, violent contrasts or *trompe-l'œil*; the meretricious sheen of oil painting was to be mitigated by the use of absorbent priming or by distemper; a velvety flat painting was to create plastic space without gaps in the picture and at the same time without recourse to modelling.

These homely painters lacked neither boldness nor grandeur. They found their spokesman in Maurice Denis (1870-1943), who left us bulky writings on the aims of the new movement. His painting however was not at the level of his thought. More deeply influenced than his friends by Symbolism — of which he might have been the Cervantes — he spent too long over literary and religious subjects, loosely treated in wishy-washy colours and in forms surrounded by fanciful ornamental arabesques (*Soir trinitaire*, 1891) (164). The whole career of this artist, with his very lucid ideas, consisted of hesitations and reversions to tradition. His masterpiece, *Homage to Cézanne* (1900) (66), is no example of Nabi theories, but remains a moving document in which we see, grouped around a still-life by Cézanne, Redon, Vuillard, Vollard, Denis, Sérusier, Bonnard and other artists of the *Revue Blanche* gathered in Ambroise Vollard's gallery [1].

The group was formed in 1888 at the Académie Julian in Paris around a senior, Paul Sérusier (1863-1927), whose gifts were later to be wasted in theorizings about the golden number and other sacred proportions. But although his art suffered the same fate as that of Maurice Denis, it had the great merit of infusing Nabism with the spirit of Gauguin. Obsessed by the Master of Pont-Aven, he created under his influence that astonishing landscape, at the same time shapeless and synthetic, aptly called *The Talisman* (1888) (167), painted in pure strokes of violet, blue, green and crimson, the whole art of Nabi counterpoint.

The sensitivity and pictorial splendour of Nabism are embodied in the work of Pierre Bonnard (1867-1947). This painter, nicknamed by his friends *Nabi-japonard*, achieved at the age of twenty-five a synthesis between the Japanese print (fine rhythmical draughtsmanship, flat colours, overhead perspective, delicate poetry) and the art of Gauguin (flat surfaces, pure separated colours, free harmonies, expressive lines, all in the service of an essentially pictorial feeling, free of bondage to literature, gay and spontaneous, and with a grand simplicity). No one in his day struck with such facility and resonance the chromatic chords of neutral colours, grave harmonies, bold gradations (*La Loge*, 1908) (XVII). With a mastery of light equal to that of the best Impressionists, he metamorphosed the humblest objects and figures by the mystery of his particular lighting and chiaroscuro, in which golds shimmer among blacks, greys and browns. He exceeded the very goal of Nabism and carried colour into the realm of abstraction. His worship of the female form — the model seen against the light, caressed by irridescent illumination — rehabilitated the nude, which Degas had made look too much like pretty squatting toads.

The work of Edouard Vuillard (1868-1940) was very close in its early stages to that of Bonnard, his friend and rival:

---

[1] The famous *Revue Blanche*, started in 1891 by the Natanson brothers, united all the most talented young painters of the day and lent its authority to the defence of Toulouse-Lautrec and the Nabis. At about this time, Ambroise Vollard, the shrewdest of picture dealers, was showing and selling in his cellar in the Rue Laffite the works of the artists most representative of the moment: Cézanne, the Nabis, Vlaminck, Gauguin and, later, Picasso, Rouault and Chagall.

Félix VALLOTTON, *The Execution. Wood-cut* (1894)

the same liking for intimacy, the same poetic charm and the same technique, refined yet seemingly simple: rough brush-work in broken-up and subdued colours, flat surfaces against a neutral ground, the whole painting constructed around attractive areas of soft black. His was an extremely serious art despite its everyday, intimate and cosy appearance. Fifteen years were to pass before we meet in the Cubists such skilfully constructed painting. Furthermore, some of Vuillard's pictures in which he juxtaposes pinks, oranges and blues in pure unbroken colours (*Mother and Child*, 1899) (XVI) foreshadow the Fauvism of 1905 and many other twentieth-century achievements. Bonnard and Vuillard also revived decorative painting in line with the great tradition, but without imitating their predecessors. At the same time, Vuillard, although essentially a master of the small picture, had the advantage over his friend of an architectural discipline of a most intelligent spontaneity.

A Parisian of Swiss origin, Félix Vallotton (1865-1925), was to contribute to Nabism the touch of irony and self-criticism it lacked. With a warm temperament and a caustic wit, he drew from life all sorts of everyday incidents, some of them with biting humour. His paintings, like his lithographs and woodcuts, surprise us by their incisive and synthetic draughts-manship. However, this genial sceptic remains at heart a naturalist who found himself by breaking with the Nabis to create a rather dry style, a hard design in crude colours, which made him a forerunner of the *Neue Sachlichkeit* (*Woman combing her hair*, 1900) (114). We find the same cold palette and the same firmness of line, without charm but also without weaknesses, in Suzanne Valadon (1867-1938), a former model of Renoir and Degas, though there is no question of any direct influence. This material heaviness and these acid colours are found later in some of the German Expressionists, such as Adolf Erbslöh and Ernst Ludwig Kirchner.

Although his links with the group are very loose, we may associate Aristide Maillol (1861-1944) with Nabism, at any rate in the first fifteen years of his long career, before he devoted himself exclusively to sculpture. His tapestries, drawings and early paintings, very much *Art Nouveau*, align him with the artists of the *Revue Blanche* by their tempered colour-ing and static monumentalism (*Woman with a Parasol*, 1896, Musée National d'Art Moderne, Paris). But despite

131

the magnificence of his graphic work and craftsmanship, his fame lies in his capacity to produce from the spirit of Nabism — essentially anti-sculptural — sculptural monuments which figure among the finest examples of contemporary art. Maillol was among the very first to abandon the Impressionist manner and emotional dynamism of Rodin. At the age of forty he joined up with the pre-classical art of Greece and Rome and forged that sturdy, virile style, majestic in its ease, static and flexible, with generous curved volumes, smooth taut surfaces, constituting a miraculous balance between the sensual and the serene. His monument to Blanqui [1], *L'Action enchaînée* (1906) (119), despite something theatrical about it was a culminating point in his *œuvre*, itself a main turning-point in the sculpture of the Latin countries in the early part of the present century [2]. Georges Minne and Wilhelm Lehmbruck, the one before and the other after, were to play the same role in the Northern countries and Central Europe.

The spread of Nabism beyond the French frontier followed after some lapse of time and coincided with the Symbolist and Pointillist experiments of other countries. In Belgium, Georges Morren and Georges Lemmen were post-Impressionists whose work was tinged with a certain Nabi spirit, as was that of Evenepoel at the end of his short life. Many works of Léon Spilliaert (1881-1946), especially his pastels and water-colours, are bathed in an atmosphere akin to that of Bonnard and Vuillard, in spite of his Symbolist arabesques after the style of Munch. His, however, was of so mysterious and unusual a nature that he stands quite as close to the Expressionists (*The Pink Hat*, 1904) (169). Great Britain was inevitably drawn to the Nabis by their distinguished colour sense and natural facility. Philip Wilson Steer (1860-1942) came under their influence, although he retained his freedom of design and his Impressionist manner (*Southwold*, 1892) (104) which explains his ultimate return to Constable. There are also reminders of Nabism in the music-hall scenes, interiors and nudes of Walter Richard Sickert (1860-1942), particularly in his groundwork and distribution of light. His sense of line, his excitable temperament and breadth of treatment led him in the end towards a modified Fauvism (*The Dutchwoman*, 1905) (168). Among all the Nordic painters, there is only the sweet and gentle Helena Schjerfbeck (1862-1946), who, trained in Paris, was to introduce first into Finland and then into the other Scandinavian countries the new ideas of simplified composition and independent colouring through an art which has the sensitiveness of a wounded bird. Nabism ended without founding any school. None of its masters trained any pupils. Yet it was more than a fashion: its influence was felt after the lapse of time and in some depth. To it the twentieth century owes the release of colour, a capital phenomenon upon which the future was to be built. Itself involuntarily affected by a certain *fin-de-siècle* sentiment, it lacked perhaps that soupçon of bad taste — which becomes, in the end, taste itself — and which left a strong mark upon the achievements of the Fauves.

APOLLO OR DIONYSUS

The passage of nearly fifty years affords us a gradual view of all the major, essential and international currents which determined the great adventure of the plastic arts between 1884 and 1914. Disregarding minor movements which proved stillborn — Symbolism and Nabism — we find that during these thirty and more years the real battle was fought simultaneously on two fronts. Nor was there at the outset any clearly defined strategy. Moreover, with very few exceptions these theories were not evolved by the artists themselves. At the whim of a round half-dozen painters of genius [3], independents, visionaries, solitaries and *peintres maudits*, the art of half a century was to experience the most profound revolution in history. Before 1900 their names were Gauguin, Toulouse-Lautrec, Van Gogh, Ensor, Munch and Seurat, followed later by Picasso, Kandinsky and Malevitch. All of them assimilated rapidly what their age had to give and prodigally squandered the heritage of their forebears. For psychological, moral and social reasons they adopted from the outset an attitude of rejection. They wanted to be themselves, to speak with their own tongue and to

---

[1] Louis-Auguste Blanqui (1805-1881), tribune and revolutionary, spent 37 years in prison.
[2] Even Renoir (1841-1919), twenty years Maillol's senior, was under the latter's influence when in 1915 he created his *Venus Victrix*. Yet Maillol owes much to Renoir's painting.
[3] Gauguin: ' There are only imitators or revolutionaries. '

bring fresh testimony to beauty in its thousand facets. They knew by instinct what must never be done any m[c]
had no ready-made style to hand. The long and gradual conquest of that style — some sacrificed to it life or
— is a spiritual and a material drama, for in art there can be no spiritual revolution without a total reappraisal of
technique. In order to adopt a new position towards creation or express new pictorial emotions, the artist must invent
other compositions, fresh harmonies, new lines, even colours that have never been seen. He is aware that a work of
art can hold its own by its mere plastic *existence*, independently of any other significance [1].

Making a clean break with Impressionism and Naturalism, Classicism and the Renaissance, art at the end of the nineteenth century had only two means of escaping from sensory intoxication and mythological story-telling: namely, to
imbue colour with Reason or Instinct, that is, with one of the vital elements which were lacking in the painting and
sculpture of the time. After 1884 two main currents dominated modern art, until our own day. One of these
cherished the rule which corrects emotion [2], the other, the emotion that breaks every rule.

Paraphrasing Nietzschean terminology [3], the first current may be called *Apollonian*, so directed is it by the desire for
order, clarity and harmony. The second, on the other hand, is given up wholly to exaltation of instinct, spontaneous
impulse, even the raptures of the tormented soul: it is *Dionysiac*. The former submits to the discipline of a system,
the second rejects all method based on principles. Classicism is an element of the former, Baroque (in the best sense
of the term) of the latter. For this reason, the connections of Poussin and Ingres with the Cubists are as evident as
the links of Rubens, Delacroix and Van Gogh with the Expressionists. Both streams were absolutist in their
tendencies and pursued their investigations to the extreme limit of their goal, arriving in 1914 at *abstraction*, geometrical
on the part of the Apollonians, anti-formal on the part of the Dionysiacs. We shall try to explain this twofold development first, through the systematized movements of Divisionism, Futurism, Cubism and constructional abstract art, and then
by analysing the Dionysiac current made up of Fauvism, Expressionism, Surrealism and *informel* abstract art.

THE FIRST APOLLONIAN STREAM :

SEURAT, CONSTRUCTOR OF COLOUR

The question was how to break away from Impressionism without abandoning its hard-won conquests, how to evade
its fugitive and sensory essence. How could a painting be *organized* otherwise than by fixing instantaneously a moment
of emotion, the fleeting impression of a hypersensitive retina? How to rediscover the flat perspective of the ancients
without recourse to the atmospheric depth of bluish and misty horizons? In a word, how was Impressionism to be turned
into something *solid and durable*, to use the language of Cézanne?

With fewer than fifty paintings, a certain young intellectual, a solitary eccentric, Georges Seurat (1859-1891), who died
at thirty-two, was to shatter the whole luminist edifice. He was not a product of the school. His preferences
went back to Ingres. His most distinguished co-painters excluded him from their cotérie. All alone, seeking refuge
in nature, he made use of scientific works in order to devise a revolutionary technique — neo-Impressionism. He
abandoned the traditional method of mixing pigments on the palette and placed upon the canvas a quantity of little
dots in pure colours (Pointillism) which, by the laws of optics, furnished the tint. The latter was broken down,
divided into its constituent elements (Divisionism). The artist compelled the viewer to take a physical part in the
creation of the work, a creation made under and through his own eyes. Although based upon a theory of physics,
Seurat's art did not lapse into intellectualism. Science was the handmaid of inspiration, the solution remained plastic.
Seurat worked geometrically upon landscapes and figures through a rigorous and static composition, a balanced

---

[1] Did not Gustave Flaubert dream of writing a novel about *nothing* which would exist by its *style* alone?

[2] The words are those of Georges Braque.

[3] Nietzsche's *Birth of Tragedy* defines as *Apollonian* all art in which the classical element of order and harmony predominates, contrasted with *Dionysian* art, where ecstasy and the demoniac prevail. Sculpture is essentially Apollonian; music, still according to Nietzsche, is fundamentally Dionysian.

play of surfaces cutting each other at right angles and a severe linear rhythm suggested rather than traced (*Asylum and Lighthouse, Honfleur*, 1886) (123). This born painter was the only neo-Impressionist to perform the miracle of a synthesis between a cerebral system and infinitely poetic visual sensitivity. All his followers were analytical in their approach, even the best of them, Paul Signac (1863-1935), the zealous theorist of the movement [1].

Since the days of the Romantics, no style spread throughout the West so rapidly as Divisionism. In a few years it reached the Mediterranean and most countries of Western Europe. This meteoric triumph it owed to its formula rather than to its spirit. For that reason it managed to survive through Fauvism and Futurism into the days of abstract art. Kupka's fugues (*Nocturne*, 1910) (153) and their bold contrasts of colour unconsciously betray a Divisionism carried to the point of the non-figurative.

Even in France, Cross, Van Gogh, Pissarro and Gauguin borrowed elements of their technique from Divisionism, adapting it to the needs of their temperament. Van Gogh, in the days of his first collapse in Paris, stuck firmly to it and found in it a temporary salvation. Ensor, like Renoir and Degas, rejected it contemptuously, but another Belgian, Théo Van Rysselberghe (1862-1926), completely surrendered to it with a conviction equal to his talent and an unshakable fidelity. Although his work derives psychologically from the Symbolists by a strain of Nordic melancholy, his technique shares the Nabi liking for subdued harmonies. His great merit lies in the extraordinary skill with which he applied the Divisionist formula to portrait-painting. His group *The Reading* (1903) (65) is a model of the genre and also a moving historical document. Influenced by Van Rysselberghe, Henri van de Velde (1863-1957), before launching his valiant crusade for the revival of architecture and handicrafts, sought refuge in neo-Impressionist painting, finding in it that Apollonian discipline which characterizes his aesthetic life and his architectural work.

In the Netherlands, Jan Toorop, freed from his Symbolist attachments, was to popularize Divisionist painting in the early years of this century. H. P. Bremmer, P. Hart-Nibbring, Floris Verster, Dirk Nijland, Jan Sluyters and Leo Gestel followed hard upon his heels, but did not carry the experiment beyond a detailed and analytical naturalism. The Cubist and Expressionist wave was soon to submerge an initiative which had attracted the Dutch more by its spiritual essence than by its revolutionary technique.

Italian painting in the nineteenth century was confined within an out-of-date realism which, in spite of spurts of warm humanity, remained provincial. In the end neo-Impressionism offered to a few of the most advanced painters a way out, a release and an international platform. We have already seen how Segantini tried to marry Symbolism to Pointillist technique. Others — good painters, too — Gaetano Previati (1852-1920) and Giuseppe Pelizza (1868-1907), at the Milan Triennale of 1891, were to lend their authority to stamping Divisionism upon a whole generation of young revolutionary minds. Pelizza became the leader of the school and is to be credited with a number of important works marking his period, among them his famous *Sun* (1906) and his *Linen in the Sun* (1905) (124). His more mystical predecessor, Previati, remained faithful to a decorative Symbolism. For Italy and, more particularly, for Milan's bohemia, the important thing was to have discovered around 1905 a revolutionary style which, by exorcism, as it were, delivered artists from the stifling and paralysing spell of the past. The hour had struck. Some were to exploit the technique to the full, to the very limits of Divisionist potentialities, and it was their extreme facility which really killed the movement. Others broadened the style, broke out from the static constraints of composition and — heretically — introduced Dynamism into their work, the age-long dream of *movement painting*. From that moment, Italian Divisionism was ripe for Futurism.

For a long while the importance of Divisionism to twentieth-century art was underestimated. The term ' neo-Impressionism ' did it great harm. It sowed confusion, for Seurat and his followers were not Impressionists of any ' neo ' kind. Their style fertilized *Art Nouveau* and gave birth to the Futurist technique. Carried to its ultimate conclusions, it led to figurative decomposition and became abstract. That is not the least of Divisionism's claims to fame.

---

[1] Signac wrote a treatise on painting *From Eugène Delacroix to neo-Impressionism*, published in 1899.

FUTURISM
VITALITY AND DYNAMISM

Although Cubism was born two years before the Manifesto of Marinetti and his Italian friends [1], Futurism must be linked closely with Divisionism by its technical debt to the latter. (Cubism has altogether different sources.) *Complementarism is a first essential*, declared the Futurist painters with one voice. But 'complementarism' is an axiom of the law of the simultaneous contrast of colours, the very basis of Seurat's aesthetics.

Can Futurism be regarded as an Apollonian movement? By its *system*, it certainly can, less so by its spirit. For Futurist painting contains as many contradictions as the programme it claimed to defend. An extreme manifestation of apolitical, social and ideological stand-point, it aimed at being violently anti-traditional, anti-rationalist and anti-academic. It was fundamentally anarchic — Here's to the act which kills! — and glorified militarism and war. Anti-capitalist, it sang the praises of industrialization by which the middle classes grew rich. Anti-traditionalist, it preached the primacy of Italian genius. Positivist, it generated a *new fever, scientific discovery*, and at the same time exalted the lyrical value of the *free gesture* in the best Romantic manner. Nevertheless, the movement, brimful of emotion, action (even destructive action), speed and dynamism, concealed a profound disorder, an inverted pessimism, a nihilism not a little exhibitionist. Confusing the idea of *life* with that of *movement*, the Futurist believed that he was performing acts that were revolutionary — warm and heartfelt acts no doubt — but which were only subversive by reason of the nonconformist *gesture* accompanying them. The Futurist ideal was to find its heir in Italian fascism.

In painting and sculpture, Futurism earned fame by a system that was half-sensory, half-cerebral, and, on the whole, Apollonian. In its passion for dynamism it snatched at the *vibratory* element in Divisionism and added to it *lines of force*, that other discovery of kinetic science.

The most talented among the Futurists, Umberto Boccioni, born in 1882, met his death in that war of 1914-18 he hymned so enthusiastically. An ardent propagandist and able exponent of theory, he was also a genuine plastic artist with a fertile imagination and proven skill. After studying Impressionism in France and taking part in the first Cubist manifestations, he signed the Futurist charter in Milan with Marinetti, Carrà, Russolo, Balla and Severini. His early works are a skillful combination of Fauvist and Symbolist elements, but before long, with the aid of his dazzling Divisionist technique, he painted *Road waking up*, a programmatic work proclaiming his Futurist creed: a mobile rhythm of curved lines, simultaneity of impressions, superimposed motifs, the whole inspired by an exalted lyricism. The system became quickly established with increasing severity. Straight lines took the place of spirals; the lines and planes of

---

NOUS DÉCLARONS:

1.° Qu' il faut mépriser toutes les formes d'imitation et glorifier toutes les formes d'originalité;
2.° Qu' il faut se révolter contre la tyrannie des mots "harmonie" et "bon goût", expressions trop élastiques avec lesquelles on peut facilement démolir les œuvres de Rembrandt, de Goya et de Rodin;
3.° Que les critiques d'art sont inutiles ou nuisibles;
4.° Qu' il faut balayer tous les sujets déjà usés, pour exprimer notre tourbillonnante vie d'acier, d'orgueil, de fièvre et de vitesse;
5.° Qu'il faut considérer comme un titre d'honneur l'appellation de "fous" avec laquelle on s'efforce de bâillonner les novateurs;
6.° Que le complémentarisme inné est une nécessité absolue en peinture, comme le vers libre en poésie et la polyphonie en musique;
7.° Que le dynamisme universel doit être donné en peinture comme sensation dynamique;
8.° Que dans la façon de rendre la nature il faut avant tout de la sincérité et de la virginité;
9.° Que le mouvement et la lumière détruisent la matérialité des corps.

NOUS COMBATTONS:

1.° Contre les teintes bitumineuses par lesquelles on s'efforce d'obtenir la patine du temps sur des tableaux modernes;
2.° Contre l'archaïsme superficiel et élémentaire fondé sur les teintes plates, et qui en imitant la facture linéaire des Egyptiens réduit la peinture à une impuissante synthèse puérile et grotesque;
3.° Contre le faux avenirisme des sécessionistes et des indépendants, qui ont instauré de nouvelles académies aussi poncives et routinières que les précédentes;
4.° Contre le Nu en peinture, aussi nauséeux et assommant que l'adultère en littérature.

Expliquons ce dernier point. Il n'y a rien d'*immoral* à nos yeux; c'est la monotonie du Nu que nous combattons. On nous déclare que le sujet n'est rien et que tout est dans la façon de le traiter. D'accord. Nous l'admettons aussi. Mais cette vérité inattaquable et absolue il y a cinquante ans, ne l'est plus aujourd'hui, quant au nu, du moment que les peintres, obsédés par le besoin d'exhiber le corps de leurs maîtresses, ont transformé les Salons en autant de foires aux jambons pourris! *Nous exigeons, pour dix ans, la suppression totale du Nu en peinture!*

UMBERTO BOCCIONI *peintre* (Milan)
CARLO D. CARRÀ *peintre* (Milan)
LUIGI RUSSOLO *peintre* (Milan)
GINO SEVERINI *peintre* (Paris)
GIACOMO BALLA *peintre* (Rome)

MILAN, le 11 Avril 1910.
"POESIA" - 2, rue Senato - MILAN.

POLIGRAFIA ITALIANA - MILANO - 5465

The Futurist Manifesto (1910)

---

[1] Born in Milan a few days earlier, Futurism launched its famous Manifesto on 20 February 1909 in the Paris *Figaro*. *The Manifesto of the Futurist Painters* followed a year later.

force imparted to the composition a powerful rectilinear movement in no way injurious to the monumentalism of the work. Electric light — a source of inspiration on a par with the motor-car and aeroplane — pierced the dark blue night with its orange darts (*Strength of the Road*, 1911). On the eve of the war, Boccioni discarded the last remnants of realism. His *Dynamism of a Cyclist* (1913) (XXIII) is simply the sublimated expression of a body moving through space: the forms, colours and atmosphere illustrate speed in the abstract. This painting, non-figurative before the term existed, embodied the quintessence of Futurism better than any empty theoretical verbiage. Boccioni was the only one who tried with any success to apply the axioms of Futurism to sculpture, a fundamentally anti-dynamic art. At the same time, he adopted a nihilistic attitude by demolishing the charms of traditional sculpture (*Unflattering Portrait*, 1913) (145), and a constructive one by breaking down a form in space, rather in the manner of the Cubists. In his finest work — only five of his sculptures have survived — *Dynamism at the Human Body* (1913) (144), also known as *Unique forms of continuity in space*, the artist attempted to fix, not the instantaneity of a moving body, but all all the simultaneous forms engendered in space by the movement itself.

Next after Boccioni, mention must be made, among the signatories of the Manifesto, of Carlo Carrà, painter, critic and propagandist [1]. At first attracted by Seurat, he accepted the rules of Divisionism, a discipline which served him in good stead when at the age of thirty he threw himself into the Futurist melée. A powerful colourist, with a profound gift for composition, he brought to the movement an ardent temperament, ripe experience and a craftsmanship versed in all the new techniques including the Cubist. His eclecticism and intellectual restlessness led him to break with Futurism after five or six years, but not until he had given it masterpieces portraying simultaneous impressions (optical and psychological) and frenetic action (cinescopic vision of objects moving through space, light vibrations, the clash of contrasting colours). The whole of Carrà and the whole of Futurism, social and artistic alike, are to be found in his *Funeral of the Anarchist Galli* (1911) (77), ' that bubble and swirl of forms and lights giving forth not only their sounds but their very odours ', in the artist's own words. After 1915, Carrà passed through a phase of *concrete forms*, until he fell in with De Chirico, who converted him to a fervent adept of metaphysical painting. The other important Futurist painters of Italy, each in his manner, treated a specific aspect of the Manifesto. However, Giacomo Balla (1871-1958) proved to be the most independent of them, though their senior and guide. Zestfully applying Seurat's great lesson, he espoused the Futurist theses to create a kind of Divisionism in movement, with broad, light-coloured brushwork, producing an effect not unlike that of time-stop photography (*Young Girl running on a Balcony*, 1912) (146). Immediately after, he turned to plastic movement in the abstract: the Apollonian idea corrects the optical process, the moving object is obscured behind the lines of force, the graphic design dominates the colouring, the whole aim being to purge the work of its concrete elements. *Abstract Speed*, painted in 1913, sums up in its title and content this artist's ideal. In the same year, a Frenchman, Jacques Villon (born 1875), likewise preoccupied with the expression of movement, attained via analytical Cubism an art approaching that of Balla (*Marching Soldiers*, 1913) (150). Luigo Russolo (1885-1947) and Gino Severini (born in 1883) are also among the early adherents of Futurism. The former's painting is not always on a level with his writings, but Severini, thanks to his period in Paris and close contacts with Picasso, Braque and Léger, achieved an art in which Cubism and Futurism merge harmoniously. Less orthodox than his Milanese fellow-artists and more elegant in style, his dance-hall scenes in particular represent a form of mobile, kaleidoscopic Cubism, the decorative charm of which tends towards abstraction. It is his merit to have introduced Futurist works into France [2], an event which had immediate repercussion on Marcel Duchamp, Raymond Duchamp-Villon, Casimir Malevitch, Francis Picabia and Robert Delaunay. The last-named was to transmit the message to the Germans Franz Marc and Lyonel Feininger. The Futurist example, far more than Cubist experimentation, underlies the Apollonian character which distinguishes some of the *Brücke* and *Blaue Reiter* painters from their Expressionist confrères in Germany. See *Deer in the Forest* (1913) by Marc and *The Bridge* (1913) (149) by Feininger.

---

[1] Born in 1881, Carlo Carrà, like Boccioni and several of his confrères, published several theoretical works on Futurism. All the painters in this group combined militant criticism with their painting.

[2] Fénéon (65 and 125), influenced by Severini, organized the first Futurist exhibition in Paris at the Gallery Bernheim Jeune on 5 February 1912. This is a very important date in the development of the Paris School.

XI
Georges Rouault
Olympia
(1906–1907)

The last important Italian painter to join the group of Boccioni-Balla-Severini was Mario Sironi (1885-1961), but by that time the movement was already near its end. On this account, Sironi presents us with a personality notably free from theories of Dynamism. His *Self-Portrait* of 1913 (148), though revealing centrifugal movement, belongs by its structure, contrasting geometrical planes and austere colouring to the Cubist order. The same tendency is seen in Roberto Melli (1885-1958), both in his sculpture and in his painting, each of which is highly personal.

Futurism failed to survive the First World War. The death of Boccioni and the desertion of Carrà, Russolo and Severini dealt it a death blow. Politically, its furious vitality bore fruit in war and Fascism [1]; artistically, it was to spread for a decade or so across the Alps, but belatedly and transported there to some extent by Cubism. It was thus that most painters of Northern and Central Europe sustained the shock of Futurism and Cubism together. Hence that heteroclite style which between 1913 and 1920 prevails in certain Belgian, Dutch and German paintings. Rik Wouters came under its influence for a short time, but less so than Felix De Boeck and Prosper De Troyer in Flanders. The Dutch painters Jan Sluyters (*Portrait of a Woman*, 1914) (141) and Leo Gestel (1881-1941) (*Woman Standing*, 1913) (140), brought to it bravura. Expressionism was not immune from it either in Belgium or in Germany, even after 1917 [2]. Paradoxically, in the case of a movement founded upon worship of life itself, Futurism failed on the side of vitality, being empty and superficial. In art it survived by the Apollonian doctrine it imposed upon its adepts and their followers. All its attempts at psychological externalization were in vain.

THE SECOND APOLLONIAN STREAM:

CUBISM FROM CÉZANNE TO PICASSO

We have seen that a third, at least, of all Apollonian art in the XXth century derives directly, or indirectly, from Seurat. The remainder — the most important and fertile part — comes in direct line of descent from Cézanne.

This great painter, born in Aix in 1839, is clearly the doyen of all those artists who have left their mark upon the painting of our period. And yet the full significance of his extraordinary mission does not make itself felt until after 1900 — that is only shortly before his death [3]. For a long time he remained faithful to the romantic technique of laying on great thicknesses of sombre colour. But when he eventually abandoned this manner in favour of Impressionism, it was already late enough in the day for him to evaluate it in its true light and to distinguish in it all the elements of haziness, fluidity, sensuality and inconsistency that offended his sense of precision and order. From the very outset he attempted to insinuate into the Impressionist landscape and subsequently also the human figure a firmer basic *structure*: a *structural process* using surfaces and volumes, a *synthesis* of physical solidity with the changeless constructions of geometry. It was like attempting the marriage of fire and water. Where others saw nothing but vibrating light, atmospheric variations, series of reflections and radiations, Cézanne was conscious of a fundamental prevailing order. The Impressionist technique was unsuited to this kind of study. Cézanne therefore concentrated on a more rigorous treatment applying the paint with close-set, rectilinear and rhythmic brush-strokes. By outlining the individual object he robs it of all the nebulous ambiguity imparted to it by refracting light. In order to achieve *representation of volume by colour* and not by light, he makes use of the latter only when, reflecting off flat planes, it accentuates the three-dimensional quality of form; but he does not allow it to eat into the volume. He restricts his palette to a limited scale of brownish-orange (the cubists' *café-au-lait*), dark green, grey and ultramarine, but each colour is taken to its maximum of intensity. He eventually came to see landscape purely in terms of its architectural structure. With almost Cartesian lucidity he invested it with the elements of a subtle, but rigorous geometrical disposition: ' *nature*

---

[1] The Futurist artists as a whole refused to join the Fascist movement. Marinetti's influence over Mussolini explains how it was that they retained a relative freedom of expression in Italy throughout the regime, at least insofar as the visual arts are concerned.

[2] This Futurism tinged with Cubism infected Permeke at Chardstock in 1916 and, in the same year, Gustave de Smet, exiled in Amsterdam. Even the extreme Dadaism of George Grosz employed the Futurist technique in the *Burial of the Poet Oskar Panizza*, 1917.

[3] *Homage to Cézanne* by Maurice Denis (66) was composed in 1900, that is five years after Cézanne's first big exhibition at the home of Ambroise Vollard. Cézanne died in 1906. His first retrospective exhibition was in 1907.

treated in terms of the cylinder, the cone and the sphere'. This mathematical process nevertheless attains the heights of real poetry by virtue of the immense visual sensibility of this artist of genius, who with slow, laborious perseverence, achieved his work without losing, after innumerable sittings, his original confidence and enthusiasm. A kind of carefully fostered spontaneity painstakingly kept in check lends an eternal quality to all that Cézanne creates. Working on his own, and belaboured by moral anxiety, misunderstood by his friends and derided by his opponents, he succeeded in establishing the premises of a new aesthetic outlook which was to bring about the first radical revolution in the position of the artist vis-à-vis Creation since the Renaissance: nature was henceforth to provide man with the material necessary for a completely autonomous work of an entirely new order. This 'poetic geometry' was to create a 'nature' apart, in no way compromising with the visual world, a *cosa mentale* — a thing of the intellect. Whichever of his landscapes one picks upon — his *Montagne Sainte-Victoire* (1904) (128), for example, there is evidence, notwithstanding the compact unity of the whole, of such painstaking attention to detail in the composition that in the last analysis a fragment the size of a pocket handkerchief may reveal the whole gamut run by Cubism and Apollonian abstract art.

Quite apart from all that the generation of Picasso and Braque founded on his art, Cézanne exercised a vast and direct influence over a multitude of European artists; this all the more so because the sudden notoriety of his work met — outside France — a real need for a guide who would act as something more than simply the best of the Impressionists, Symbolists or even Divisionists. The cult of Cézanne reached most countries almost at the same time as Fauvism, and gave birth to a form of painting half-Apollonian, half-Dionysiac, less disciplined and rich in colour; Rik Wouters in Belgium, Vaclav Spala in Czechoslovakia, the early periods of Paula Modersohn-Becker and Ernst Ludwig Kirchner in Germany are among the best examples.

Most painters, while captivated by the aesthetics of Cézanne, only find there a source of general directives which help them to look again at their position vis-à-vis nature, to readjust it, and to subject their workmanship and palette to a new discipline. But one man, Picasso, goes to the heart of the problem: the creation of a pictorial statement of the *imagination* whose justification and only reality are drawn from its sense of plastic form. In its absolute sense, this means a re-invention of painting in an abstract idiom [1], by way of knowledge, whether intuitive or rational. *One must paint things as one knows they are, not as one sees them* (Picasso).

Picasso was formed in Spain, by personal contact with his unsophisticated contemporaries in Barcelona, far more than by the École des Beaux-Arts. When, at the age of 22, he arrived in Paris, he was untamed, rather contemptuous, satirical and generous-hearted. His first day in France coincided with the visit of his friend Isidro Nonell (1873-1911), whose debut in Paris had been marked by his figures of tramps and gypsies, freely executed in a muted scale of grays, greens and 'broken' reds. (*The Embrace*, 1903 (166) by Picasso and *The Two Gypsies*, 1903 (165) by Nonell.) This dwelling on misery and wretchedness, full of sad and resentful compassion, with a symbolist flavour and reminiscent of Steinlen and Toulouse-Lautrec, dominates all Picasso's work for five or six years, and he remains faithful to his wandering performers and beggers, women ironing, absinthe drinkers, and rickety girls throughout his Fauve period and his *Blue* and *Pink* periods. He has no one style, he has all styles. The colours range from dramatic shade to Fauvist brilliance, returning to an intensely refined scheme of monochromes. His drawing is by turn hieratic like the symbolists, sinuous like the Nabis, and contorted like the Expressionists. He finds rather than searches, interprets rather than assimilates. His striving for the absolute at last breaks out in *Les Demoiselles d'Avignon* (XIX) whose date of completion in 1907 marks a turning-point in the history of XXth-century painting. Although this cardinal work sums up most of the young Picasso's preoccupations and betrays the rapidly awakening interest in the primitive arts and negro sculpture it constitutes not the final solution of his previous work but a break with it, a new point of departure. He applies the essence of Cézanne with unsparing force; forms are recreated in terms of a monumental, schematic geometry, hewn like statues with wide, shadowless polychromatic planes. Varying degrees of tone form the relief; there is no resort to the classic trick of the third dimension. An imaginary space replaces the traditional perspective, and the angular lines accentuate the

---

[1] Abstraction does not mean, above all in the case of Picasso, the absence of all memory of objects. It is a question rather of the removal of the personal form from an object — but the object remains.

concise composition. Yet this picture presents a sort of upheaval in the design and organisation which places it on the very fringe of Apollonian art. If the term had any meaning, we would call Picasso a 'spasmodic Apollonian' — his art strives continuously to break the rules of its own innate discipline. For this reason many of his works have a frankly Expressionist quality.

Picasso as a Cubist, and Georges Braque at his best, must be sought among the l'Estaque landscapes, the still lifes and portraits of 1908-14. In the miraculous year of 1908 both painters, soon to be joined by Raoul Dufy (1877-1953), contrived a series of works of a rare severity, balance and distinction. They start (if it is possible to say so) from a sort of distillation of Cézanne, strip their predecessor's palette to the best of their advantage, toning down his greens and ochres, and exploit his structuralism with great insistence, but always with a view to realising the ideal of a geometric beauty founded on purely plastic characteristics. At this period, despite some slight differences in temperament, there is such an affinity and even similarity between the canvases of Picasso, Braque and Dufy that it is possible to speak of a collective style. It is enough to compare Braque's *Nude* (1907-08) (132) with one of the *Demoiselles d'Avignon*; *The Reservoir* (1909) (129) by Picasso with *The House behind the Tree* (1908) (130) by Braque, and all of them with Cézanne's *House on the Bank of the Marne* (1888-90) (127). Cubism has taken shape and will flower magnificently, even though its doctrine may never be clearly defined [1].

Having freed themselves, the Cubists set about analysing the mental universe which they had created. The problem which rears its head is not simply the question of colour (for a long time their palette is rigorously limited to green, grey and *café-au-lait*) but a battle against the remembrance of traditional form and of the object within everyone's mental scope. Even the most beautiful object of Cézanne must be analysed, broken down and scrutinised from all angles at once [2]. The geometrical facets of each motif are unfolded and displayed within the scheme of the picture. The century-old search for the third-dimension is abandoned, and the art of differentiating the degrees of tone, with no logical sequence, creates a new form of relief, an ingenious geometry in space. The *Portrait of Ambroise Vollard* (1909-10) (133) is a striking example of this style, known as analytical Cubism, as noble as the art of the fugue. In order to see the distance covered in ten years, despite identical aims, compare it with the *Portrait of Ambroise Vollard* (1896) (126) by Cézanne.

Braque, in the same way as Picasso, but with greater serenity, developed this aesthetic to the verge of abstraction. The object is broken up into fragments that are no more than *signs* (the scroll of a violin, strings of a guitar, a music stand, etc.) and is then incorporated, on the flat, into a two-dimensional composition. (*The Mandola*, 1910) (131). The rejection of depth is sometimes emphasised by the presence of a realistic element, such as a nail, painted as a piece of *trompe-l'œil*. This breaking-up into small prisms later gives way to a wider, simpler and more vividly-coloured layout. The metaphors are more easily deciphered and the whole gains in unity. *Girl with a guitar* (1913) (XX) remains the master-piece of Synthetic Cubism [3]. It is on this basis that Braque founded the whole of his astonishing career. His style, of course, achieved a more supple grace and the reverberating brilliance of the colours of his Fauve period returned to his palette, but he always remained faithful to the principles that made him the great master of Cubism.

A late arrival on the Cubist scene, Juan Gris (1887-1927), tried to bring about a complete reversal of the data of the problem. Instead of imposing an architectural structure upon the disorder of the visible world, his composition is based on geometric abstractions which then become objects in their own right. *I take architecture as a point of departure*, he said, and, *from a cylinder I make a bottle*. The application of this principle imbues his art with a certain spiritual calm, both noble and a little frigid, but of great distinction. His harmonies in grey are amongst the most subtle of this period.

---

[1] The term Cubism, which was originally the joke of an art critic (sometimes attributed to Matisse) on the paintings of Braque in the *Salon d'Automne* in 1908, has become a glorious title, and been given an added brilliancce by the writings of Guillaume Apollinaire. The doctrine of Cubism — so admirably realised in the painting itself — still remains vague, and the theories of Picasso, Braque and Juan Gris are often contradictory.

[2] Here Cubism almost coincides with the *simultanéité* dear to the Italian Futurists. Moreover, the object loses its opaque appearance and so allows the other elements of the composition to show through: 'continuity in space'.

[3] Synthetic Cubism enables Picasso, Braque, Juan Gris and the Futurists to introduce non-painted elements of attractive colour and matter into some of their works, by means of *découpage* and *collage*. Later 'sticking' becomes a autonomous form of expression masterfully exploited by the Dadaists.

(*Still-life with Fruit Dish*, 1914) (139). In the meanwhile, at Puteaux, the group known as the *Section d'Or* had formed around Jacques Villon, the brother of Marcel Duchamp and Raymond Duchamp-Villon. Although mainly composed of Cubists, the group tried to direct the movement towards a more lyrical and dynamic style and, taken all in all, less based on imaginative values. The artists of this group were not attempting a reaction against Cubism, from which they had sprung, but did on the other hand oppose the ascetic orthodoxy of Picasso and Braque. The resultant rather hybrid style of painting is often more a more schematisation of nature than a transfiguration operated by the intellect. Jacques Villon, whose connections with Futurism have already been described, Louis Marcoussis (1878-1941) in his rather poetic vein (*Still-life with a Chequer-board*, 1912) (136), Albert Gleizes (1881-1953), Othon Friesz (1879-1949), Jean Metzinger (1883) and André Lhote (1885) — all ingenious theoreticians as well as masters of pictorial composition — tended to encourage the return of Cubism to colour, light and representation; but their influence did not become apparent until after 1914. Roger de la Fresnaye (1885-1925), mathematician and artist, stands out as more independent and personal. He made use of the principles of Cubism in the creation of his strongly stylised compositions, in which material reality is treated in a series of large coloured surfaces set in close equilibrium one against the other (*Seated Man*, 1914) (137).

The only painter who at that period can be considered on a par with Picasso and Braque [1] is Fernand Léger (1881-1951). His training as an architectural draughtsman, his ephemeral connections with the Fauves, his admiration for Cézanne, his friendship with the Douanier Rousseau, his contacts with the Cubists and the 'Golden Section' group, could have made him infinitely susceptible to all kinds of temptations. This was however not to be the case, and before the year 1910 he already showed himself to be the unique individual that he remained the whole of his life. He owes little to the influence of others and in his *Nudes in the Forest* (1908-1910) (134) he already demonstrates that he is preoccupied with problems peripheral to Cubism: the problem of volume — not analytically to break it down into its component parts as his colleagues attempted to, but to *construct* by means of three-dimensional round or cylindrical shapes. He creates as much by intuition as by positive intention — *Constructivism*. This obsession with volume is at first detrimental to colour which is reduced to tones of grey, purple and green, but once Léger has achieved mastery of form his palette grows lighter, at first in soft harmonies (*The Wedding*, 1910-11) (XXI), then subsequently and permanently in strong discords to obtain *the maximum expressive effect*, as he himself put it. This colour scheme composed of contrasts of unadulterated red, blue and yellow blends perfectly with the dynamically controlled structure of the composition. Léger's constructivism is based on a ponderous and concentric spherical geometry (*Contrast in Forms*, 1913) (135). Seldom does he make a clean break with nature; his tendency is rather to draw nearer to it over the course of the years and to achieve in the end a kind of *social realism* in art worthy of this name.

It will be remembered that, during the course of its expansion outside Paris and beyond the frontiers of France, Cubism met with, and in its turn helped to fertilize, the Futurist movement. Carlo Carrà, Gino Severini and Giorgio Morandi (*Still-life*, 1914) (138) drew inspiration from this aesthetic outlook that lay so close to their own. Carrà and Severini even went as far as to adopt the *collage* technique. In Holland the new style was interpreted by Jan Sluyters and Léo Gestel on lines dictated by their respective temperaments [2]. All over the Western World Cubism forced a great many painters to come to grips with the principles that it advocated; but its effects made itself felt in an appreciable manner only after the First World War. The direct influence exerted by Cubism on the German artists of the *Neue Künstlervereinigung* and the *Blaue Reiter* group in Munich was of a quite different nature. In that milieu, through exhibitions, meetings and lectures, the art so fervently promulgated by Apollinaire made itself deeply felt in the painting of Franz Marc (1880-1916) and August Macke (1887-1914). Expressionism in its dionysiac frenzy was also somewhat curbed by Cubism, but German art gained in a certain spiritual dignity and clarity of composition that disappeared on the death of its two great colourists. It was principally Macke who, encouraged by Delaunay, based his endeavour on Cubist structural

---

[1] Not to mention Marcel Duchamp, Picabia, Delaunay and Herbin who however soon turned their backs on Cubism and the 'Golden Section' to concentrate instead of the development of their art in other directions.

[2] The arrival of the French Cubist Henri Le Fauconnier (1881-1946) in the Netherlands in 1914 exercised an important influence on the artists of the Bergen group and even on the first Flemish Expressionists: Gustave de Smet and Frits van den Berghe, exiled in Holland.

arrangements in order to satisfy his dream, in which the interplay of form and the reverberation of colour symbolise the rhythm of nature (*Brightly-lit shop windows*, 1912) (151). Shortly after this he joined forces with Klee in a purely abstract form of art.

Cubist sculpture developed alongside Cubist painting but at first it experienced much more difficulty in shaking off the influence of Impressionism. Sculpture had no such figure as Cézanne, and the work of Maillol was unable to attract a large following. Besides there are several fundamental principles of Cubism that cannot apply to sculpture — the rejection of the third-dimension, for instance. The whole artistic activity of the Cubist ' sculptors ' was concentrated on achieving a compromise: high-relief treated on a basis of sharp angular planes. In Lipchitz, Laurens, Gargallo and Gonzalez the result is a kind of painting in the round to which Archipenko adds colour. This was the beginning of the polychromatic sculpture of our own time. Raymond Duchamp-Villon (1876-1918) opposed this hybrid art with a conception in terms of space, *The Horse* (142), a purely intellectual development which stands as a perfect example of the ultimate logical consequence of Cubist theory, the abstraction of form. Henri Gaudier-Brzeska (1891-1915) and Constantin Brancusi (1876-1957) retaliated with *The Imp* (1914) (202) and *The Sleeping Muse* (1909) (203). Neither of them ever gave himself up to the purely mental process of geometric abstraction. The smooth purity of their delicately surfaced form expresses a powerful lyricism as symbolic and eternal as the most ancient creations of Mediterranean civilisation.

RAYONISM — SUPREMATISM — NEO-PLASTICISM — ORPHISM

Of all systematised movements only Cubism has given rise to currents which, with astonishing logic and audacity, have ventured to draw the inevitable conclusions from the teachings of Cézanne. While most of the other Apollonian styles faded out or degenerated into mannerisms, the art of Picasso, Braque and Gris opened up perspectives so vast that two generations of painters have still not exhausted their ultimate potentialities. After 1910 synthetic Cubism introduced into painting a purely intellectual element, that *rule which corrects emotion* (Braque), that kind of intuitive geometry which has nothing to do with the subtle speculations of Humanist theorising or with the scholarly dictates of Poussin. Space in depth yielded place to the two-dimensional surface, modified at most by a slight displacement of absolutely parallel planes. The object, broken into fragments, no longer signified reality; it ended by disappearing altogether. The simplest anecdote was banished because it disturbed the purity of the pictorial fact. This last was self-sufficient, like the concrete image of an insubstantial emotion, an inner feeling, a spiritual music in colour, excluding all recourse to external reality.

The progress of Cubism towards non-figurative Apollonian art was so rapid that all its stages may be said to have been accomplished by 1914. In less than four years men like Larionov, Delaunay, Malevitch, Mondrian and Wyndham Lewis were producing works which went far beyond the experimental phase and were true prototypes of an art, the continual extensions of which occupy an important place in contemporary painting.

The pioneer [1] of this non-representational world, to use Malevitch's term, appears to have been the Russian, Michel Larionov (born near Odessa in 1881) who, after a few Cubist experiments, launched in Moscow the movement known as Rayonism, an aesthetic system according to which the content of the work of art has no connection with time or place. Containing in fact no subject-matter, the Rayonist picture consists of a large number of beams of light in contrasted colours, projected diagonally accross the canvas in parallel movements without beginning or end (XXII). Obviously inspired by Futurism and its dynamism and lines of force, Rayonism, like Futurism, extended to the farthest bounds of the Apollonian universe, to which however it belonged by the primacy it accorded to mind over instinct. Larionov's wife, Nathalie Gontcharova (born 1881), was to prove his most successful follower, though without sacrificing her own personality, which found expression in figurative painting glorifying machinery and electricity with the faith of the Futurists, and using the same methods.

---

[1] Larionov's first deliberately non-figurative pictures date from the same year (1910) in which Kandinsky is supposed to have painted his first water-colour heralding abstract Dionysian art.

Rayonism proved short-lived, although another Russian, of Polish-Ukrainian origin, Casimir Malevitch (1878-1935), was to extract from it an art as uncompromising as it was lasting. Influenced in turn by Impressionism and Fauvism, he made contact with Kandinsky in Munich and with the Cubists in Paris. The example of Fernand Leger seems to have been responsible for his constructivist period. His collaboration with Larionov and Gontcharova determined his move towards Rayonism, which he soon left behind in order to launch in Moscow at the end of 1913, Suprematism — abstract art with an almost ascetic conception, based upon the supremacy of pure sensitivity [1]. Abandoning the fluent mobility of Rayonist painting, he created static compositions in which diagonal and oblique lines played a subordinate part, though more important than in the work of his *alter ego* Mondrian. Malevich's style, free of all artifice, is extremely simple: a neutral ground with a few geometrical forms harmoniously spaced and in high colours, arranged as a rule on a cruciform axis (*Supreme*, before 1915) (152). The artist, though this is not certain, is said to have exhibited in 1913 a *Black square on a white ground*, which established with some finality the goal he aimed at. In any case his art developed year by year up to 1922-23 with a severity approaching monochrome painting, tone being added to tone in white and grey. Malevitch's influence outside Russia grew from that date, particularly in Holland with De Stijl and in Germany through the Bauhaus. Those two groups espoused Suprematist principles and the theories of Piet Mondrian with equal fervour. For this reason the art and mystique of Malevitch, which had no influence in the Soviet Union [2], contributed indirectly to the success of modern functional architecture and furniture.

Although the term Neo-plasticism was not invented until 1917, a date incidentally which coincides with the founding in the Netherlands of the De Stijl group and review, mention must be made of the movement at this point because it found its complete embodiment in the person of Piet Mondrian (1872-1944). The artist was forty when he arrived in Paris armed with an assortment of Naturalist, Divisionist and Fauvist ideas. In contact with the Cubists, he moderated the brilliance of his palette and began to distill the essence of the Naturalist motifs dear to him: trees, still-lives, architectural monuments. This he did not in obedience to Cézanne's geometrical rules but by a fluid and harmonious design, a kind of linear choreography, sometimes found in a less abstract form in Juan Gris (*Apple Tree in Blossom*, 1912) (154). This led him inevitably to analytical Cubism. In less than two years he exhausted its utmost possibilities and created oval, austere, grave compositions like those of Picasso and Braque, but with no echo of realism. Later, while Cubism was moving towards synthesis, Mondrian abandoned his fluid drawing and his tonal range of browns and greys in favour of the earliest examples of 'constructed' abstract art: a world of the mind built up from pure geometrical features, horizontal and vertical lines, right angles and primary colours, to form a balance of absolute calm and serenity. No more diagonal lines, and therefore no more movement. Malevitch's dream crystallized in the work of Mondrian with a static exactitude (*Composition*, 1914) (XXIV). Apollonian painting was approaching its apogee. Mondrian reached this point in 1917, soon after his return to Holland, and adhered to the style to the end of his life. His single-mindedness, his unshakable determination and the startlingly novel solutions he found for his plastic problems make him the undisputed master of intellectualised non-figurative art. Strongly supported and developed by painters, architects and sculptors such as Theo Van Doesburg, G. Vantongerloo, B. van der Leck, G. Rietveld, J.P. Oud and others, Dutch Neo-plasticism asserted itself in various forms throughout the western world. It still survives in the art of many first-rate painters.

In contrast with the non-material severity of Mondrian, we find the intuitive art of Robert Delaunay (1885-1941), to which Guillaume Apollinaire gave the name of Orphism. Unlike analytical Cubism, this style of painting, again proceeding from Cézanne and Picasso, retained all the expressive power of colour. In addition, it made a brilliant analysis of form decomposed by light. These fragmented forms, according to Delaunay, created planes of colour. These planes form the pictorial structure, and nature, ceasing to be the subject of description, becomes only a pretext. His first abstract paintings date from 1912, for example, *The Window*, immortalised by the author of *Calligrammes*. Before long the coloured

---

[1] The Suprematist Manifesto, drafted by Malevitch with the help of the poet Maiakowski, was not actually published until 1915, but the painter applied its principles in his work from 1913 onwards. For quite a while his Cubist-constructivist and his Suprematist pictures overlapped. It is difficult to fix the date of the latter with certainty.

[2] Around 1917 Poland, more receptive, produced an *avant-garde* group, the Formalists, who derived from Malevitch as well as from the Cubists and Futurists. Vladislav Strzeminski and Henryk Berlevi were its founders. Under their leadership it formed in 1924 in Warsaw a Cubist-Constructivist-Suprematist group.

planes became circular, like large luminous stars projecting their contrasted brilliance into space (*Circular forms, Sun, Tower,* 1913) (156). Delaunay's art, like that of his wife, Sonia Delaunay-Terck, is as much musical counterpoint as pictorial lyricism. Although a cosmic breath blew through this painting, it was still controlled by a mind. Amidst so many movements that abjure light-colour, Delaunay's great merit is to have extolled it — for him it was both form and subject-matter.

Every variety of the Apollonian non-figurative style, whether we call it constructed art, formal art or concrete art — studio jargon, wrongly, speaks even of the ' cold abstract ' — is to be found between Mondrian and Delaunay, extending from Magnelli, Kupka, Wyndham Lewis and Moholy-Nagy to Herbin, Adam, Servranckx, Nicholson, Mortensen, Baumeister, Soulages and Vasarely. For a long time abstract art concentrated upon the discipline of Reason, representing the urgent need for spiritual harmony and balance in a chaotic world. Meanwhile the opposite pole, the Dionysian and Expressionnist pole, was offering painters diametrically opposed pictorial solutions which were no less attractive. Here came Kandinsky's work.

The years preceding the war of 1914-18 saw a movement in England not unlike the new movements in Russia, Holland and France. Named Vorticism [1] by its founder, Wyndham Lewis (1882-1957), this English movement was strongly Futurist in character, although its art was entirely abstract (*Composition,* 1913) (157). Among Wyndham Lewis's associates should be mentioned the painter-architect Frederick Etchells (1886) and the sculptor Jacob Epstein (1880-1959). Vorticism failed to survive the first world war. Among German artists, Adolf Hölzel (1853-1934) stands more or less alone. Painter, lithographer and theorist, he was already in 1905 painting geometrical works of a strict simplicity, and this makes him a precursor of the movement. His ascendancy as a teacher exceeded his influence as an artist.

Sculpture, which logically should have profited most from the trend abstract of painting between 1908 and 1914, remained preoccupied with the formal problems of Cubism, even with an insipid post-impressionism after the style of Medardo Rosso (*The Bookmaker,* 1894) (58) [2]. Some of the best sculptors of our time, the Spaniards, Julio Gonzalez (1876-1942) and Pablo Gargallo (1881-1934), the Russian, Alexander Archipenko (1887) and the Franco-Lithuanian, Jacques Lipchitz (1891) work in a heterogeneous style made up of archaic and Cubist elements in an attempt to vie with painting (*Sailor with a Guitar,* 1914) (143). There was still no trace of a deliberate trend towards the abstract, if we except the plastic genius, Constantin Brancusi (1876-1957), who in 1908 — that *annus mirabilis* — entered upon his gradual and triumphant conquest of pure volume, self-contained, smooth and polished, highly stylised yet extremely sensitive (*The Sleeping Muse,* 1909) (203). The only sculpture of this period which can stand beside the work of Brancusi is *The Horse* (1914) (142) of Raymond Duchamp-Villon (1876-1918), brother of Jacques Villon and Marcel Duchamp. This masterpiece, which became the manifesto of Cubist sculpture, though greatly influenced by Futurist ' spatial developments ', reveals a perfection of plastic feeling: restrained movement, reflex curves, interlocking forms, an anti-naturalistic synthesis, inner tension, life and volume.

Despite the notable case of Brancusi — though he was never an out-and-out advocate of the abstract — abstract sculpture developed very slowly and only belatedly took its place in modern art, thanks to the imagination, intelligence and patient endeavour of such artists as Antoine Pevsner, Naum Gabo, Barbara Hepworth, Robert Jacobsen, Max Bill and other inventors of ' rational ' beauty.

THE DIONYSIAN STREAM
ITS FOUNDERS:
VAN GOGH, GAUGUIN, ENSOR, MUNCH

While Apollonian painting, as exemplified by Seurat and Cézanne, swept away the remains of academic Realism and made good the deficiencies of Impressionism by means of systematisation, another current set in which attacked the same

---

[1] The Vorticist Manifesto was published in June 1914 under the title ' Blast '.

[2] Whether Medardo Rosso or Rodin originated an Impressionist sculpture of self-contained contours, so characteristic of the former's *Bookmaker* and of the latter's *Balzac,* is fiercely disputed. But Rosso's creation preceded Rodin's by three years.

problems by completely different methods. The Dionysian current, even when nourished by minds of extreme lucidity, refused to be controlled by reason and relied entirely on spiritual impulse.

Apollonian art before all else sought a style, that is, a plastic solution to a given problem by means of an appropriate technique. Its ideal lay always in the direction of a pure plasticity, as untroubled as possible by uncontrollable flashes of instinct. Man himself — in the full sense of the word — became the object in a world of objects. This objectivity, compounded of nobility and serenity, often attained the sublime, when the artist dominated the formula. But there was always a formula. While of equal merit, a picture by Braque is a state of mind, a van Gogh canvas a state of the soul.

Dionysian art, on the contrary, is not a style: it is a conception of life, a vision of the world ' discovered from within '. It is a projection of the soul on to nature, on to life and man himself. Chagall described it admirably when he said, *I am concerned with psychic space. Other artists look at nature. I have it within me.* The psychic image replaces the optical impression or memory. Everything is reconsidered and recreated, activated and brought to life in accordance with the artist's hidden will in a movement that is direct, spontaneous, impetuous, impassioned — and sometimes contorted with ecstasy. Colour and line exteriorise with maximum intensity, arbitrarily and quite without a system, the intense and profound, violent and unexpected emotions of the conscious, the sub-conscious, and even of primitive instinct. Free of all constraint, Dionysian art excludes no expression of human feeling. Its universe extends from the idyllic to the perverse, the divine to the demoniacal, from the metaphysical to the neurotic. Every Dionysian painting — still-life, figure or landscape — is primarily a confession and a psychological portrait of the artist himself.

The Dionysian artist par excellence is Vincent van Gogh (1853-1890), who was sincere to the point of self-destruction. The drama of his work and his tragic life were superimposed on each other with terrifying fidelity. He took up his painting after more than one spiritual and emotional crisis, and immediately following the bitter failure of his sojourn at the Borinage.

Arriving in Paris in 1886 he abandoned the sombre colouring and muted harmonies of his Dutch period, without however foregoing his desperate search for intensity of expression. Through contact with Seurat, Signac, Gauguin and Lautrec, he discovered the light tones, the Divisionist touch and a rare serenity which imparted to his first masterpieces, portraits and landscapes a luminous cheerfulness only slightly tempered by a certain nervous strain in the quick, staccato brush strokes — a technique which he used admirably without it ever becoming a mannerism. Two years later, when he was alone in the Camargue, he achieved in his *View of La Crau with blue cart* (1888) a sublime moment of classical balance, a single instant of Apollonian harmony. Immediately afterwards anxiety beset him, and with it came the struggle between the desire for order and the brain-storms of a noble mind tottering to its fall. He recovered himself with staggering lucidity. *One must never give in*, he wrote to his brother. Despite anguish and terror, despite the drama with Gauguin, he joined battle with the Angel. His way pointed him towards sunshine, the intoxication of colour, the flamboyance of line. Everything in nature, sunflowers, cypresses, mountains, clouds and stars, things and people, shared in this state of extreme tension, which was not madness but a kind of hyperacuteness of perception (*Starry night*, 1889) (XXVI). There was nothing apocalyptic about this cosmic vision of all Creation. His mental disorder never affected his art, and even in moments of delirium he retained his mastery as a painter. No one has shown such exactitude in exaggeration. Witness the *Portrait of Dr. Gachet* (1890) (160), bursting with life and expression, where every feature and every colour is full of conscious purpose. A month later came the end that we know, but the world had been enriched by a new language of colour.

Following in van Gogh's steps, Paul Gauguin's wandering life (1848-1903) was also a grim struggle against fate, the fate of the maladjusted man who, once emancipated, went adrift on his way to the Lost Paradise. A sailor at heart he launched into painting, sought escape in it as an amateur — but an amateur with individuality and genius. Under Pissarro's guidance he produced good Impressionist work, then settled at Pont-Aven, where in the harsh landscape of Brittany he rid himself of facile formulae and — like Cézanne — tried to impose a plastic synthesis on nature's image. But he did not resort to geometry; intuitively he felt that the problem of simultaneously simplifying and intensifying should be solved by qualities of line and colour. With encouragement from Emile Bernard (1869-1941) he created *Synthétisme* or *Cloison-*

XII
Alexej von Jawlensky
Woman with a fringe
(1913)

nisme [1], an appellation with a purely technical meaning, the technique consisting in perceiving the object through its contour, accentuating the graphic design, producing a fluid composition from those lines and filling in the encircled portions with flat areas of lively colour, without disturbing the even surface of the canvas.

Gauguin transferred his ideas and his style to Arles where he stayed with Van Gogh, who was so struck by them that for two months he used the technique of ' *The Alyscamps* ' (1888) (102), a work he saw born before his eyes. After the drama of the *Man with his ear cut off* Gauguin went back to Pont-Aven and there founded a small colony of Cloisonnistes, at the same time setting his seal upon the Paris Symbolists, although these proved incapable of grasping the whole span of his genius. Then came the escape into exoticism, the plunge into the primitive life of Tahiti and the Marquesas, where death awaited him. There he attained the summit of his achievement, an art in which his love for simple people, magic beliefs and a natural fairyland was expressed in a paean of bright colours and rare harmonies (*Ta Matete* or *The Market*, 1892) (XV). His influence — immediate upon the Symbolists and indirect on many other painters of his period — was considerable. He had freed colour from manner. The expressive and synthetic linear quality of the wood engravings he produced between 1891 and 1893 inspired Edward Munch and the first German Expressionists.

The other two masters of Dionysiac art in the 19th century came from the north: the Belgian, James Ensor (1860-1949) and the Norwegian, Edward Munch (1863-1944), isolated cases but of great importance. Ensor, who was immensely talented, at a very early age joined the *avant-garde* movements in his country and quickly produced his first *intimist* masterpieces, entirely in muted tones, using an *impasto* technique. He was already leaving behind him the bourgeois cosiness and mildly melancholy climate of the Nabis. Then, turning suddenly from that sombre phase, he reverted to the early themes painted in vibrant colours, outdoing the boldest Impressionism, finally attaining the freest, most Dionysiac pictorial lyricism. At that time Turner seems to have been his God. His friends and fellow-painters were baffled, and they expelled him from *Les Vingt*. From then on, alone in his Ostend studio, looking out on to his beloved North Sea, he produced visionary works, passionately felt, scintillating with colour and with a Goya-like imagination (*Defeat of the Rebel Angels*, 1889) (XXV). Ensor admits us to a fantastic world where the most hallucinatory and droll creations of fancy are juxtaposed in a mixture of the macabre and the grotesque, of masquerade and tragedy, love and hate, hope and despair, persiflage and spiritual grandeur — the whole dominated by the spectre of Death, which intrudes at all points, to be confronted by the artist with the same cynicism with which Brueghel manhandled the devil (*Skeletons warming themselves*, 1889) (158). Ensor founded no school and his importance was not fully recognised until his genius was on the decline. But his art and technique were the prelude to all the Dionysiac movements of our day — Fauvism, Expressionism, even Surrealism (*The Entry of Christ into Brussels*, 1888) (73).

Edward Munch, who was much more closely associated than Ensor with the revolutionary movements in Paris, Munich, Berlin and Oslo, first tried to adapt the Naturalism of his young days to the style of Bonnard and Gauguin, but his extremely emotional Nordic temperament, with its morbid pessimism nourished on the plays of Ibsen and Strindberg, could only find utterance in a violence profoundly opposed to the Latin spirit. He became, in his way, Van Gogh's rival. Using intense, sometimes acid, colours boldly contrasted, always heavy with psychological meaning and arranged in long fluid curves, he depicted with the courage of despair and the lucidity of a madman the disturbing fresco of a life without happiness or escape (*Little girls on the bridge*, 1899) (XXVII). His world was peopled with anguished, morbid beings, bearing mental and physical hereditary taints, under the spell of some unending drama that darkened their whole existence, demoralising men and women alike and corrupting love (*Evening in Karl-Johan Street*, 1892) (159). His paintings and engravings have such power of suggestion that in the end their ultra-realism is sublimated into dreams of black and menacing magic. Munch, who reached his artistic peak in 1900, knew fame in his lifetime. To some degree he took Van Gogh's place and, more than a precursor, personally inspired the young artists of *Die Brücke*; he was thus the first to blaze the Expressionist trail in Central Europe. Long before this Munch had brought new vigour to the graphic quality of the Symbolists by his etchings, lithographs and wood engravings. Alone among the French, Albert

---

[1] Emile Bernard, who adopted *Cloisonnisme* for only a few years, claimed that it was his, and not Gauguin's invention. And, indeed, his first canvases in the *Synthétique* manner appear to date from 1887 when Gauguin was in Martinique.

Marquet (1875-1947), that other solitary figure, attained in his portraits (*Portrait of André Rouveyre*, 1904) (170) the monumental and arresting fluency of Munch.

The last of the great precursors of 20th century art was a man who, like Hokusaï, loved drawing beyond all else, Henri de Toulouse-Lautrec (1864-1901). To be sure, he owed much to Degas, still more to the masters of the Japanese print, then in vogue among the Symbolists and the Nabis; but he succeeded in obtaining more personal, spontaneous and expressive effects from line than did any of his contemporaries. His rapid, firm, straightforward draughtsmanship, without afterthoughts, fluid or mordant, tender or cynical, merciless but without cruelty, was undeniably Dionysiac in essence, yet free from the exaggerations of Expressionist distortion. Without being a neuropath, Lautrec, like Van Gogh and Munch, opened the way for a new style of psychological portrait which went far beyond the aims of caricature (Picasso, Nolde, Kokoschka). For a long time Lautrec's renown suffered from the picturesque quality of his subjects and even form the legend of his short and lamentable life. He was more than an illustrator and a painter of 'atmosphere'. His little world of race-courses, music-halls and brothels was a slice of life lived with intensity and immortalised in all its tawdry splendour. Others after him took the same scenes, just as they took what is best in their style, from his palette and his drawing. Picasso, Rouault, Matisse and all the Fauves were in the beginning influenced by his outlook and technique. Lautrec takes his place with Gauguin among the sources of modern French art (XIV).

THE FAUVES :
THE POLYPHONY OF PURE COLOUR

Soon after 1900 the noble line of great precursors came to an end, either by death or by the gradual extinction of its creative genius. But there was no reversing the victories of the *maudits*, the rebels and the suicides of the *belle époque*, and their succession was assured. Paris and Dresden, simultaneously sharing the heritage of Van Gogh, Gauguin, Ensor and Munch, shifted the centre of gravity of western painting and placed it for a whole period near to the Dionysiac pole. And that was before the birth of Cubism. In France the movement was called Fauvism [1]; in Germany it crystallised round the group known as *Die Brücke* [2].

The Fauves painted according to the instinctive feeling they had for life and nature. Their intoxication with 'living in colour' was based on no other philosophy or ethic than the creation of happy and joyous symphonies of pure colour aided by the clash of brilliantly orchestrated contrasts. This lyricism of free colour was expressed with a fanaticism unknown even to Van Gogh in his creative paroxysms, and led to Derain being told that he dipped his brush in dynamite Yet Fauvism is all lightness, clarity, strength and grandeur. It derives its explosive quality from the intensity of its colour and light. The light came from nowhere; it shone through the colour with pure, steady brilliance [3].

No system or theory directs the composition. The disposition of the picture depends broadly on contrasts of colour. The line is rhythmic and the contour voluptuous, but the effect remains sober and strong. The drawing and the colouring chant in unison, but the one is often released from the other, and an arabesque may appear in a spot of colour that does not correspond with its form. Fauvism is an essentially aesthetic revolutionary movement with an anarchic purpose behind its postures. It remained opposed to any psychological or ethical intention. Its weakness lay in that excess of sensuality with which it reproached the Impressionists, but to it our century owes some of the purest masterpieces of Dionysian lyricism.

The German Fauves of *Die Brücke*, while painting in a manner astonishingly close to that of their French contemporaries, looked towards Munch rather than Gauguin. As belated Romantics their temperament was opposed to the sensory

---

[1] The Fauves owed their nickname to the art critics of the period, who applied it to the young painters whose works created a scandal at the Paris Autumn Salon of 1905 — Matisse, Marquet, Van Dongen, Derain, Vlaminck, Rouault, Friesz, etc.

[2] The year 1905 also saw the group *Die Brücke* formed in Dresden with the purpose of bridging the revolutionary trends of the day in Germany. Among its founders were Kirchner, Hechel, Schmidt-Rottluff and Bleyl. Nolde, Amiet, Pechstein and Müller joined it later. It was dissolved in 1913.

[3] Picasso once epitomised his admiration for Matisse in the words 'He has a sun in his belly'.

optimism of the Paris school; the repressed anxieties and torments of a young generation shaking off the yoke of a bourgeois inheritance founded on mediocrity and provincialism, combined a pseudo-grandeur with something pitifully small.   Strongly tinged with Messianic Judaïsm, the Bridge movement called on painting not only to find a new solution to the eternal plastic problem, but also to express all the psychological, moral and religious anxieties of a strange and isolated group.   Unlike the French Fauves, they sought a solution not in their paint-box but in minds obsessed by an unhappy and highly dramatic nostalgia.   Their line was abrupt and hachured, their colour acid, the subject exacerbated to the point of violence.   At last German art was awakening from a century of medieval slumber, which the brave endeavours of Lovis Corinth (1858-1925) had scarcely ruffled.

One of the originators of Fauvism was Henri Matisse (1869-1954), that Frenchman from the north who raped the southern sun.   Cultured and intelligent, a Latin to his finger-tips, nourished on Cézanne and Seurat and gifted with a prodigious colour-sense and an exemplary craftsman's conscience, of unrivalled audacity, but with self-restraint, reckless yet well-balanced, he embodied in his own person more than a programme — a style.   The man who dreamed of *Luxe, calme et volupté* (1904-05) (XXX) and wanted painting to be a rest for the mind and a joy for the eye — that armchair tiger was a revolutionary who knew how far he could exceed the limit.   Along among the Fauves he pursued his aesthetic theory to its logical end, painting the same picture ten times over, never finished, never jaded, ever more dazzling in its purity. Sometimes, in his determination to recreate the model in higher tones, Matisse became an Expressionist, as in *The Gipsy* (1906) (174).   At other times he would reduce the motif to its bare elements, tending towards a certain abstract quality (*Lane in the Woods at Clamart*, 1912) (178), which went back to the Orphism of Delaunay.   As a sculptor Matisse was the only Fauve who tried to apply a basically pictorial aesthetic to volume.   The experiment was inconclusive (*La Serpentine*, 1909) (175) and did not go beyond the sculptural Impressionism which Rodin carried to the length of virtuosity (*Nijinski*) (176).

More Dionysian than Matisse, but no lesser a colourist, Maurice de Vlaminck (1870-1958), painter, musician, writer and racing cyclist, incarnated the rebel, the rough diamond, the anarchist of Fauvism.   Of Flemish origin he ranked as a kind of barbarian from the north.   Poor and bohemian, he created a self-taught impassioned style of his own, inspired with true grandeur.   He was a born painter with an infallible instinct, whose brilliant palette matched the violence of his virile temperament.   His bold colouring verged on the brutal, yet from a debauch of crude colours he produced a powerful symphony built upon a miracle of intuitive knowledge (*The outing in the country*, 1905) (172).   After the 1914-1918 war Vlaminck became a dynamic and headstrong Impressionist.   His fate had been written in the works of his Fauvist years.

His friend and comrade-in-arms, André Derain (1880-1954), a man of refinement and education, cautious and eclectic, also threw himself into the Fauvist fray around 1905.   At once he proved himself a master with an admirable command of the tonal chords first struck by Matisse.   His manner was broad and supple, his design ample and free, his palette blended and dissonant by turns, the composition light and skilful, ordered rather than impulsive.   Obsessed by Van Gogh, he nevertheless tried to get near to Gauguin and once achieved a marvellous compromise between two manners (*Westminster Bridge*, 1906) (XXVIII).   He leaned increasingly towards an art of the golden mean which well matched his hesitant, over-cultivated mind.   After a return to Cézanne he discovered Negro art, Cubism, Byzantinism (*The Billiard players*, 1913) (177), finally settling down to traditional painting, whose warmth and subtlety were in tune with his real temperament.

Georges Braque painted only a few Fauvist canvases, as rare as they are beautiful, and already revealing the wish to build up a landscape by other means than a harmony of crude colours.   Othon Friesz (1879-1949) concentrated on the problem of light with a passionate zeal and a virtuosity more technical than emotional.   Albert Marquet (1875-1947), on the other hand, endowed Fauvism with a quality it had sadly lacked: the human presence, not in the sense of a pictorial abstraction but in the form of something that had life, dynamism and psychic meaning.   Among the Fauves he plays the same part as Vallotton among the Nabis.   Witty, caustic, sensitive and warm-hearted, he painted excellent portraits with a sure and virile touch (*Rouveyre*, 1904) (170).   Though undaunted by any of his companions' audacities, he sought a harmony beyond the turbulence of violent contrasts.   He found his medium in blacks and greys, which in his street scenes and harbour views he combined with poetic refinement and rare distinction. As a colourist he is the Juan Gris of Fauvism.

Marquet was not alone in accusing the Fauves, and Matisse in particular, of being inhuman. The Dutchman, Kees Van Dongen (1877), who from direct poverty became the most fashionable painter in Paris, specialised in the human face with passion, sarcasm and insight, admirably supported by a powerful, forthright and expressive technique (*Anita*, 1905) (173). Later his art veered towards a wilful virtuosity and was led into raffish formulas which appealed to a certain eccentric clientele.

Raoul Dufy's (1877-1953) Fauvism, at first extravagant — see his *Paved Street* of 1907 (XXIX) — after a brief but fertile Cubist period acquired a highly individual charm. He tempered his tonal exuberance without in any way abandoning his sumptuous colouring or the conciseness of his drawing. Dufy always began with colour; he would put it on in broad layers of shimmering and contrasting hues. Into this colour-synthesis, much more imagined than seen, he afterwards introduced a hurried design, brief and independent, of astounding lightness, full of graceful movement. This painter of paddocks, regattas and studio nudes cared little for the human drama, although he did excellent portraits. He was Apollonian in his contentedness and *joie de vivre*: a natural charmer in whom one divined a young and healthy vitality. Rarely has an artist expressed himself with such earnestness in painting that is so spontaneously optimistic and lucid.

Altogether different was Georges Rouault (1871-1958), who came to painting after starting — much to his benefit — with stained glass. Trained by Gustave Moreau, who settled his palette for life, and initiated by Léon Bloy into his own bitter and defiant Catholicism, he joined the Fauves in 1904 and brought to them his passion for justice, his love for the unfortunate and his fanatical faith, all attributes which were unusual, not to say alien to the preoccupations of his companions. He undertook Daumier's mission, accusing, mocking and flaying, and all for love of his fellow-men — himself the numbed and unconscious victim (*Monsieur and Madame Poulot*, 1905) (179) [1]. The only member of the group to resist the spell of Fauvist polyphony, Rouault returned to Goya's tragic tones — grey, brown and black — against which the brick-reds and brilliant blues ring out like bugle-calls (*Red nude, Olympia*, 1906-07) (XI). As much of an Expressionist as any Latin could be, Rouault stood alone in contemporary French painting [2]. His biting line and muted colouring developed with his growing mysticism; what they lost in tortured and dramatic savagery they gained in lyricism and richness.

In France many other artists were inspired by Fauvism (Henri Manguin, Maurice Marinot, Jean Puy, Louis Valtat and other painters of merit, relegated somewhat to the background by the fame of the great ones. Shortly before 1914 the movement showed the first signs of disintegration as the aesthetic of a group. Yet its influence abroad was rapid and widespread, through meetings between artists as much as through exhibitions. But other influences were at work at the same time, and it is often difficult to decide how much Fauvist technique contributed to the work of the Swiss painters, Giovanni Giacometti and Cuno Amiet; to the Flemings, Rik Wouters (*The red curtains*, 1913) (XXI), Jan Brusselmans, Ferdinand Schirren [3]; to the Dutchmen, Jan Sluyters and Leo Gestel; to the Italians, Gino Rossi and Felice Casorati, not to mention the *Brücke* artists, particularly Kirchner and Heckel, who from 1908 adopted Fauvist colouring, to be put to purposes quite alien to French genius.

---

[1] This picture actually shows Léon Bloy and a poor woman. The author of *La femme pauvre* failed to understand Rouault's artistic purpose and, reproaching his friend for being 'dizzy with ugliness', withdrew his friendship with rather un-Christian scorn.

[2] Marcel Gromaire, born 20 years later, was one of the few painters whom French Expressionism could, with due allowance, class with Rouault. Of Flemish origin he belongs rather to the Nordic school, despite his constructivism. His main work was subsequent to 1914.
Henri Le Fauconnier (1881-1945), who came from the Pas-de-Calais, broke with Cubism in 1913 to plunge into Expressionism. During his exile in the Netherlands he contributed much to the spread of this style among Dutch and Flemish painters. But his Expressionism did not derive from Fauvism.

[3] Ferdinand Schirren and Rik Wouters started painting in the Fauvist manner in Belgium and from 1910-1914 inspired a few artists whose work in Brabant caused them to be classed together as 'Fauvisme brabançon'.

DIE BRÜCKE:
A TORMENTED FAUVISM

Despite appearances there is a vital difference between the Latin Fauves and their companions of *Die Brücke*: Ernst-Ludwig Kirchner, Erich Heckel, Karl Schmidt-Rottluff, Fritz Bleyl, Emil Nolde, Max Pechstein, Otto Müller and the Swiss, Cuno Amiet. Although they had a sincere and loyal admiration for each other, a common technique and a similar palette, the French were separated from the Germans by a mental gulf — the importance which the latter gave to problems of the soul. What was a plastic solution, an end-in-itself, for the French was for the Germans merely an eloquent means of expressing an ethic, vague and at the same time complex. In a perpetual state of fusion this ethic was an amalgam of northern pessimism, Jewish *angst*, Slav exaltation and every Germanic obsession. The artist readily abandoned himself to the most violent and unexpected urges of his instincts; all sense of proportion was lost; nature and life seemed to be dominated by tumultuous, disunited forces, often calamitous and always dramatic. The spirit of Nietzsche and the shadow of Dostoevski haunted this art, its impetuous vitality consumed by a tortured and barren nostalgia. Dionysian *par excellence*, the painters of *Die Brücke* created the mental climate in which five years later German Expressionism was to be born.

Emil NOLDE, *Prophet. Woodcut* (1912)

Although the members of *Die Brücke* recognized only Munch, Ensor, Van Gogh and Gauguin as their forerunners, their art had its roots no less in the romantic, symbolic or mystical work of Arnold Böcklin, Anselm Feuerbach, Hans von Marées and Max Klinger, who in the second half of the 19th century raised German painting out of the rut of Classicism and Naturalism. This non-conformist movement accompanied a great social awakening in which poets, dramatists and artists of talent all shared, moved by a revolutionary anti-bourgeois spirit, anarchic but profoundly humanitarian. No one illustrates better than Käthe Kollwitz (1867-1945) the artist's 'engagement' in the sociological conflict of his time. Caring little for the formalistic problems of the graphic arts, she created a highly personal style which gives her etchings, lithographs and wood engravings a rare explosive dynamism and persuasive power. Her work developed from romantic Naturalism (*Unemployed*, 1909) (185) to an Expressionism that was monumental, meditative, and terrifyingly accusatory. Never in art did a woman's heart beat with so much rebellious love and generosity, without fear or hatred. In subject-matter and style her art is related to that of her friend, the sculptor, poet and artist, Ernst Barlach (1870-1938). After studying in Paris and all the main German centres Barlach found himself during a visit to Russia where, coming into contact with folk art, he produced his first statuettes of peasants and beggars (*Russian beggar with a cup*, 1906) (188), which show a highly expressive plastic density of form. Sincerely religious and with a profound feeling for humanity he carved figures — mainly from wood — in piteous attitudes and in an austere and concentrated style deriving from folklore as much as from Gothic art (*The Vandal*, 1910) (187). His pictures are bathed in an emotional climate of hallucination and *angst* and, like his sculpture, belong to German Expressionism at its most characteristic.

Neither Kollwitz nor Barlach was a member of *Die Brücke*, any more than was that other independent artist, Paula Modersohn-Becker (1876-1907), who died at the age of thirty-one, having enriched the art of her country with a series of works much in advance of their time. Her figures of women and children, solidly constructed, with the colours broken up into lovely harmonies, combined the robust simplicity of folk pictures with the skilled synthetic composition of a Gauguin. Her *Portrait of Rainer Maria Rilke* (circa 1906) (75) in its boldness of form and colour recalls Ensor's expressive and mysterious masks.

The moving spirit of *Die Brücke* proper, which was founded in Dresden in 1905, was Ernst-Ludwig Kirchner (1880-1938), who came to painting from architecture. With an enquiring, cultured and restless mind, nourished on Goethe and Helmholtz, open to every influence, yet with a strong personality, he wanted before all else to revive the art of coloured wood engraving with large, simplified forms and pure colouring. Deriving from Munch and Lautrec, enriched by the contributions of African art and urged on by a feverish imagination and incredible industry, in no time he laid the foundations of that Expressionist style which was to make the fame of German artists for a quarter of a century. Dominated at first by his research into engraving and strongly influenced by the Fauvist palette, his painting later evolved towards quick, nervous and diagrammatic notation, highly expressive, executed with hachured and oblique brush-strokes in tones of green and sepia (*Berlin Street Scene*, 1913) (189). Obsessed by the human drama, ill and lonely, he worked with a bitter intensity on an enormous output of harrowing works. Until his suicide he remained alone faithful to the Expressionism of the heroic period.

His companion in the struggle, Karl Schmidt-Rottluff, born in 1884, and also architect, produced paintings wholly free of any mental obsession. He was the most *fauve* of all the artists of *Die Brücke*. In closer touch with reality he concentrated on transposing it pictorially in broad constructive, monumental syntheses, with massive figures, their contours emphatically delineated in a manner deriving both from Cubism and Negro sculpture. His Expressionism lies more in plastic distortion and his startling palette than in the exteriorisation of spiritual torment (*Norwegian landscape*, 1911) (XXXIV). Erich Heckel (1883), on the other hand, surrendered himself to a dreamy, melancholy lyricism. Self-taught and also coming to painting by way of architecture, he remained under Fauvist influence until 1910. He broke from it in his wood engravings with their angular, incisive and expressive lines. After this his feeling for colour declined and he showed a preference for cold blends of blue, sepia, yellow and black, which suited his ascetic, sad and mysterious themes (*Two Men at Table* 1912) (192). It is difficult to place the art of Otto Müller (1874-1930) in the Expressionist context of *Die Brücke*. He spent nearly all his time on the female nude, though a few of his pictures (the gipsy series) strike an undeniable social and human note. His figures of women move against a tropical background in a climate of troubled and listless eroticism. His sober palette often seeks luminous effects which detract from the monumental quality of the figures. Müller introduced into German Expressionism the exotic flavour dear to Gauguin, and Max Pechstein (1881-1955) followed him along this path, but in a rougher, more hasty and violent style.

Of all the German artists of this period Emil Nolde (1867-1956), the eldest of them, was undoubtedly the finest painter. He also personified the Expressionist spirit *in excelsis*. For this reason members of *Die Brücke* and *Der Blaue Reiter* welcomed in their respective groups as their master and example one who refused allegiance to any aesthetic whatever. He began as a sculptor and draughtsman, and shook off the influence of Böcklin and Hodler after meeting Ensor and Munch who determined his course. No one used colour with the delirious passion of this elemental mystic (*The Last Supper*, 1909) (191). Dauntlessly he unburdened his conscious and subconscious mind in pictures of virulent colour and bold line which bordered on ecstasy (*The Legend of Maria Aegyptiaca*, 1912) (190). Combining bad taste with sublimity, the divine with the Satanic, grotesque and sacred, his work is the prototype of Dionysiac art carried to a paroxysm of pictorial and psychic exaltation (*Slovenes*, 1911) (XXXIII).

Die Brücke fell apart in 1913 but a whole generation of German and foreign artists was to experience the strange fascination of its forms, its colours and its spirit: in Germany, Cesar Klein, Conrad Felix Müller and Lasar Segall; in Paris, the Lithuanian, Chaim Soutine; later, in Holland, Jan Sluyters and Henk Chabot; and, in Flanders, Constant Permeke, Gustave De Smet and Frits Van den Berghe.

DER BLAUE REITER:
FROM EXPRESSIONISM TO THE ABSTRACT

Two years before *Die Brücke* broke up in 1913 a new group of artists came into being in Munich, centred on *Der Blaue*

Wassily KANDINSKY, *Der Blaue Reiter Almanach. Title-page* (1912)

Reiter (*The blue rider*) [1], a review founded by Kandinsky and Marc. They were painters and engravers who had known one another for some years, had fought together as dissidents from the *Neue Künstlervereinigung* and made common cause with the Fauves and Cubists in Paris [2]. They called themselves Expressionists.

Although the aspirations of both groups, *Die Brücke* and *Der Blaue Reiter*, were at first more or less identical, the problem of form assumed different aspects in Munich and Dresden. The course followed by Kirchner and his companions was and remained basically Germanic in its origins, forerunners, programme and spirit. Despite the diversity of its members the *Brücke* formed a monolithic group working in a single style. The *Blaue Reiter* movement, on the other hand, was not only led by two Russians, Kandinsky and Jawlensky, but was profoundly influenced by Latin currents such as Fauvism, Cubism and even Futurism. Hence the incongruity of the *Blaue Reiter* style, which on the whole was less Expressionist — in the narrower sense — than that of *Die Brücke*.

We have already seen what Franz Marc, August Macke and Lyonel Feininger, for a long time hampered by the *Jugendstil*, owed to the French Cubists in general and to Delaunay's Orphism in particular. This lent to a large part of their work a specifically Apollonian character. It is thus by their 'spiritualised' colour and psychological interpretation of nature, rather than by their technique, that these artists belong to the Expressionists.

Franz Marc (1880-1916), after wavering between theology and painting, won fame by paintings high in tone and admirable in composition in which he gave infinitely poetic expression to his religious pantheism. Everything in his art was symbolic; his burning desire was to be one with all creation, animals especially, which he represented in their unchanging attitudes in the midst of cosmic landscapes pervaded by a melancholy and crystalline poesy (*Tyrol*, 1913-14) (XXXV). His friend, August Macke (1887-1914), with his limpid compositions in shimmering colours and sensitively drawn, remained more attached to visual impressions. But his figures move in an unreal world and towards the end of his short life he composed some abstract landscapes, very much on the lines of Paul Klee's experiments at that time (*Arab town*, 1914) (XXXI). The premature death of Marc and Macke, both killed at the beginning of the 1914 war, dealt a hard blow to the *Blaue Reiter*, already shaken by the tragic events of that year.

The real inspiration behind the group, its propagandist and its best painter, was Vassily Kandinsky, who was born in Moscow in 1886 and died in Paris at the age of fifty-eight. Though long settled in Munich and involved with all the

[1] This review was really an art almanac, produced in 1911 but published in 1912. Its name was taken from the title of a picture by Kandinsky.

[2] The *Blaue Reiter* group introduced to Germany the work of Redon, Picasso, Braque, Rouault, Derain, Van Dongen, Le Fauconnier and, later, of Delaunay, Henri Rousseau, Arp, Vlaminck, de la Fresnaye and Malevitch.

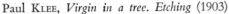

Paul KLEE, *Virgin in a tree. Etching* (1903)

A. KUBIN, *Illustration for his novel ' Die Andere Seite '.*

avant-garde movements, his painting was impregnated with memories of his youth: popular imagery, gaudy fabrics, ikons and Russo-Byzantine art all mingled with the impressions he received from the Baroque architecture and sculpture of Bavaria. He painted his pictures in the sonorous tones of the Fauves, with even more daring dissonances and a graphic dynamism which made much use of black outlines (*Study for Improvisation no. 8*, 1910) (194). He was already attributing a spiritual mission to painting and increasingly tried to divorce it from the factual and the objective (*Lyrism*, 1911) (195). Gradually his animated landscapes, waving forests and galloping horsemen became quasi-musical improvisations on a theme perceived until the day when the theme, the source of visual impressions and therefore linked with matter, was banished as inimical to the purity of the conception. Abstract painting had been born [1]. After 1912 Kandinsky produced only compositions in which colour and line, alone and autonomous, expressed by their intensity and arrangement, their harmony or contrast, rhythm and combination, all the artist's emotions (*The black arch*, 1912) (VI). There was a mobile, spontaneous, almost Baroque interplay of colour, form and drawing, which bordered on automatism. The lyricism of this abstract art was impulsive, spasmodic and at moments delirious [2]. Forty years ago the genius of Kandinsky, an Apollonian artist *par excellence*, opened up unsuspected paths to the glorious adventure of modern art. The creator of abstract Expressionism, he was the pioneer of many of today's most fruitful movements from non-formal art to tachism and action painting.

Among the artists of the *Blaue Reiter* Alexej von Jawlensky (1864-1941), Kandinsky's friend and compatriot, was distinguished for the vigour of his Fauvist palette, with its brilliant colours and shrill contrasts, all extremely Slav. He remained faithful to objectivity, although his paintings are charged with psychological and religious meaning. His composition, perfectly controlled, is based on a spacious design which delineates the contours with a thick line. He aimed at monumental serenity and intensity of expression at the same time (*Woman with fringe*, 1913) (XXII). The human face figures prominently in his art and gave him the opportunity to go a long way in his search for an abstract art which should be both intellectual and emotional.

When Paul Klee (1879-1940) joined the *Blaue Reiter* group, he was already over thirty and had experimented in many directions. A musician with a learned and subtle mind, sensitive and delicate, he was drawn in turn towards the *Jugendstil*, early Christian art, Redon, Blake, and then Goya. He was first distinguished for his caustic etchings; grotesque and cynical,

---

[1] Kandinsky summarised his theory in a book published in 1912 under the title of *Ueber das Geistige in der Kunst* (The Spiritual in Art).

[2] Later Kandinsky, while teaching at the Dessau Bauhaus, produced lyrical art of a much more orderly and geometrical nature. The constructivist and rationalist theories of this celebrated school of architecture and applied art played an important part in it.

152

XIII

Marcel DUCHAMP

Nude descending a staircase, No. 2
(1912)

they resembled Kubin's engravings. From 1906 to 1912 his painting steered a course between Munch and Ensor, between Cézanne and Matisse. Delaunay greatly impressed him, and so did Douanier Rousseau. And all the while he was trying to rid himself of his poetic personality and, in his own words, invented *something unpretentious, quite small, with no thought of technique*. But the repetition of these small gestures created a strangely original world, childlike, unreal, a paradise of happiness, purity and light. His finest work was done after 1914 but even earlier, on a visit to North Africa, he painted those delightful water-colours, luminous, delicate and fantastic, a prelude to the most spiritual abstract art of our age (VII).

Heinrich Campendonck (1889-1957) played the part of a Douanier Rousseau in the *Blaue Reiter* group, using an Expressionist palette to depict naive poetic scenes in the spirit of folklore. His painting and wood engravings influenced the first Dutch and Flemish Expressionnists. The engravings of the Austrian, Alfred Kubin (1877-1958), despite a graphic method borrowed from Goya, Doré and Redon, fit perfectly into the atmosphere of German Expressionism, so much was his hallucinated fancy consumed by *Angst* and despair. This defiant romantic would, however, have been more at home with *Die Brücke* than with the *Blaue Reiter* group.

INDEPENDENT EXPRESSIONISTS :
FROM KOKOSCHKA TO CHAGALL

The Austrian, Oskar Kokoschka, novelist, polemic, painter and engraver, summed up in himself most aspects of Expressionism. He more than anyone commanded world attention and admiration for that style. Fiercely independent, he joined no group, but frequented them all. If he came under certain influences — Klimt, Munch, van Gogh — they were only transitory and affected his outlook rather than his technique. By and large he owed more to Viennese Baroque and the art of the Far East and Polynesia than to any of his contemporaries. An uncompromising and complex character with a lively and searching mind, capable of cruel penetration and as relentlessly honest with himself as with others, he produced the most striking portraits of our age in which he laid bare the sitter's soul (*Herwarth Walden*, 1910) (XXXVII), painting with a nervous, taut hand, and engraving incisive outlines in symbolic layers of colour, turbid and stormy. Full of complexes, this admirable painter exteriorised all the repressions of his inner life, all his private conflicts, in works of tragic lyricism — imposing and sometimes prophetic (*The Bride of the Wind* 1914) (200). His innumerable landscapes are filled with a strong cosmic afflatus — almost apocalyptic. Kokoschka had no disciples although Ludwig Meidner's (1884) emotional painting seems very close to his. After 1918 his influence, particularly as an engraver, left its mark on the revolutionary art of the *Veristes*, Georges Grosz and Otto Dix.

Although at this period Sigmund Freud, Gustav Mahler and Arnold Schönberg [1] were living there, Vienna had little sympathy for the Expressionist movement. The *Jugendstil* and Klimt continued to lay down the law for the best artists there, even for Egon Schiele (1890-1918), a latecomer who died young; he was a true virtuoso of drawing and painting whose Expressionist zeal bordered on psychosis, but was held in check by certain out-of-date Symbolist formulae (*Portrait of the Artist*, 1911) (XXXVIII). The very restricted work of Richard Gerstl (he died in 1908 at the age of 25), produced under the influence of Schönberg's music, disclosed an artist's soul in the throes of mental disorder. His subtle palette and very free treatment owed much to Goya and Manet (*Two Sisters*, 1906) (197).

Among the independent Expressionists of distinction one isolated patriarchal figure, Christian Rohlfs (1849-1938), should be mentioned. He was well into his fifties when, after meeting Munch, Henry Van de Velde and Nolde, he at last gave free rein to an imagination brimming over with visionary mysticism. In his landscapes, brilliantly coloured and rhythmically composed, he carried synthesis to the furthest limit of spontaneous abstraction (*Red roofs*, 1913) (196). His work, long despised, occupies a place apart in the great Germanic movement to dematerialize painting.

---

[1] Arnold Schönberg (1874-1951), whose atonal music is unquestionably Expressionist, lived in close touch with the *Blaue Reiter* group. Excited by the relationship between his friends' pictorial theories and his own musical aims, he painted a number of symbolical and intuitive pictures between 1907 and 1910.

Outside Germany and Austria Expressionism did not appear until after 1914, except in Flanders and more especially at Laethem-Saint-Martin, where even before 1900 the Symbolist and Neo-primitive *avant-garde* — Gustave Van de Woestijne, Valerius De Saedeleer and Albert Servaes — were grouped around the sculptor Georges Minne and the poet Karel Van de Woestijne. For a long time the colony lived in a confined atmosphere of meditation, melancholy and mysticism dear to Maeterlinck, and which inspired Minne's immortal *The Relics-bearer* (1897) (181). (This ascetic piece of sculpture made a strong impression on Wilhelm Lehmbruck before he conceived his *Kneeling figure* and his *Adolescent standing* (1913) (182), both hailed as ' symbols of Expressionism '). But after 1910 Albert Servaes left the group and broke away from Minne's influence. Following the example of Jacob Smits and using the same technique, he introduced into his scenes of peasant life and the New Testament an intense, dramatic element of primitive and strained religiosity (*The Raising of Lazarus*, 1911) (198). Later his style became so extreme in its Expressionism that his *Way of the Cross* (1919), a monument of devotional pathos, drew upon him the Church's vehement disapproval. Constant Permeke (1880-1952), the undisputed master of Flemish Expressionism, owed much to Servaes at the start, but quickly shifted the problem to the plane of pure plasticity. His *Moonlight* (1913) (199) shows the violent reaction against the Impressionism of his youth and a stern determination to escape from it through a simplified, spiritualised, yet sombre and mysterious style. Flemish Expressionism was tonal in quality, while the German trend was primarily colourist. The Laethem-Saint-Martin colony was dispersed by the first world war and paradoxically it was in exile that Permeke, Gustave de Smet and Fritz Van den Berghe — the first in England and the others in Holland — developed this typically Flemish style.

It remains to speak of an independent painter who with Matisse might well be the greatest colourist of modern times — Marc Chagall. He is not Expressionist in the orthodox sense, but his emotional art perfectly incarnates the Apollonian spirit, whimsical and magical. With him all is poesy, love, emotion and fantasy. He has all reality within him but has turned his back on the world and only uses it according to the whim of his imagination and the unforeseeable needs of his palette. He arrived in Paris in 1910, much richer in memories of the Vitebsk ghetto than in those of his days at the St. Petersburg Academy. From Gauguin, the Fauves, the Cubists and Delaunay he borrowed no more than was needed to renew his palette and his idea of space (*Homage to Apollinaire, Walden, Cendrars and Canudo*, 1911-12) (180) [1]. For the rest he shut himself up happily, with his tenderness and his Chaplinesque touch of irony, in a little imaginary world of rabbis, moujiks, musicians, strolling players, cows, hens, angels, devils, synagogues and farmyards. He reconstructed from memory a fairy world, more real than reality, in unreal colours of unequalled brilliance. His vivid palette, bold distortion and novel composition far surpassed the extraordinary feats of *Die Brücke* and the *Blaue Reiter* (*To Russia, asses and others*, 1911) (XXXII). Never had the meeting between Jewish mysticism and Slav sensibility produced an infant prodigy of such pure genius, both as man and artist.

Amedeo Modigliani's painting (1884-1920), poetic, sensuous and melancholy, in warm tones and pre-raphaelite arabesques, attained its highest flights after 1914, and then it destroyed him in six years. But in 1913 he had already produced seven pieces of sculpture, such as the *Head* (201) in which Tuscan, Negro and Cubist influences were assimilated and left behind. The noble stylised form and its serenity of spirit imparted to this work a transcendental character typical also of Brancusi's sculpture (*Sleeping muse*, 1909) (203). It is for this that Modigliani as sculptor has his place on the confines of Dionysiac art while his painting is completely impregnated with it.

METAPHYSICAL ART

The art which the historians have called metaphysical was the creation of one man, an Italian born in Greece, Giorgio De Chirico (1888). He too went to study in Munich but kept aloof from the revolutionary movement, so fascinated was he by the romantic and mythological painting of Arnold Böcklin with its theatrical mystery and shrill, harsh colours. This overrated Swiss painter awakened a poet of singular originality in the boy of twenty, a kind of Rimbaud of painting.

---

[1] Herwarth Walden, art critic and painter, who also organised exhibitions, did most to encourage Expressionism in Germany and outside it from 1910 to 1913. His Berlin gallery and his review, *Der Sturm*, defended and publicised the art of the *Blaue Reiter* as well as of the Fauves, Cubists and Futurists. (See his portrait by Kokoschka pl. XXXVII).

On his return to Italy Chirico began a series of landscapes that are pure mystery: the enigma of time, the enigma of an autumn evening, the enigma of a morning departure. All is uncertainty, melancholy, a dream world. Each object is real and tangible, yet elusive. Reality dissolves in an atmosphere of desolation, anguish and somnambulism, from which man is absent. Italy's empty squares, heavy with solitude, are transported to another planet, illuminated by the slanting rays of an obscured sun (*The Enigma of the Hour*, 1911) (204). Inside deserted palaces with their delicate vistas wander headless statues, disturbing muses, blind heroes and figures constructed higgledy-piggledy. Through some kind of sudden illumination Chirico removed painting ' completely from human limitations: it lacks all common sense and logic '. Now at last the pattern was traced of what tomorrow was to be Surrealism.

Chirico's friends, Carrà, Morandi and Severini, extended the range of his images and *trouvailles* and under his guidance founded *Pittura metafisica*. But none of these former Futurists ever equalled their master in imagination, treatment or colouring. All they really looked for was a haven of rest and meditation after the noisy conflicts of their early days. From this viewpoint metaphysical painting helped to liquidate Futurism. Chirico's message remained a single, shining example with no immediate echo.

THE BEGINNINGS OF DADA :
MARCEL DUCHAMP AND PICABIA

While Chirico in Italy was inventing ' the logic of the absurd ' (Baudelaire), something similar but much more radical was happening in Paris. Strangely enough it was from the Puteaux group, obsessed with the ' Golden Section ' and other geometrical formulae, that the prodigy of anti-rational art, Marcel Duchamp (1887), brother of the sculptor Raymond Duchamp-Villon and of the painter Jacques Villon, broke away. Intellectually at home in many disciplines, a chess champion with a practical mind, Duchamp, after a period under Cezanne's influence, embarked on plastic experiments inspired by time-stop photography and towards 1911 produced the *Nude descending stairs*, a synthesis of movement in space carried to the limit of the abstract. Despite appearances this work was not Futurist; it espoused neither the vitalist theory nor the dynamic revolt of the Italians. It was the plastic interpretation of an imagined fact, poetic and unreal, as is evidenced by the fact that this picture, with a few alterations, was repeated in *Le passage de la vierge à la mariée*. Duchamp fell out with the mathematicians of the Golden Section shortly before the Armory Show in New York in 1912 [1] where his pictures created a sensation. The following year he produced his first ' ready-mades ', domestic objects of painful banality transformed into strange creatures, mystifying figures, puzzles and rebuses with freakish titles (*Cocoa grinder*, 1914) (208). The shock of ludicrous juxtapositions in Chirico's manner, was a thing of the past and became the expression of the artist's deliberate attitude in defiance of the conventional, the commonplace, even the modern. Beauty was created at random, by accident. The images and subjects of painting were set free; anti-painting was produced like anti-logic, and a new Apollonian poetry was invented, animistic, disconcerting and surrealist, on which the Dadaists later imposed a mission of destruction.

The art of Francis Picabia (1878-1953) until 1909 presented a mixture of Cubism and Orphism, with a very strong leaning towards the abstract. Indeed his water-colour, *Rubber*, dated 1909, (207), could well be one of the first examples of abstract art. But it was only after he had come into touch with the Golden Section group and Marcel Duchamp in Jacques Villon's studio that he produced his most important works which are real foretastes of Dada (*Udnie*, 1913) (XXXIX). His inventive genius and diverse talents made him the most exciting and provocative of the little circle in the United States during the war who grouped themselves round Marcel Duchamp, Man Ray, Arensberg and the art-dealer Stieglitz. By their writings no less than by their paintings they challenged the art world with their furious anti-conformism, and their attitude found an echo in Zurich where Tristan Tzara and Hans Arp had just then founded Dada.

---

[1] This exhibition, arranged by a group of New York artists and financed by Arthur B. Davies, was held in February 1913 in the armoury of the 69th Regiment (hence its name). The Americans, bewildered and shocked, saw there for the first time Cézanne and Matisse as well as Duchamp, Kandinsky, Brancusi and Picabia. Despite the scandal the Armory Show was a turning-point in the art life of the United States.

Braque's *collages* and, even more, Picasso's (*The student with the pipe*, 1913-14) (205) undoubtedly prepared the way for the birth of the Dada style. But for Duchamp and his companions that did not mean introducing a new plastic element into painting, but a destructive foreign body made up of everyday materials, anti-artistic by nature. The first to compose such an ' object-picture ' deliberatedly seems to have been the Italian, Enrico Prampolini (1894-1956), who in 1914 introduced the idea of entirely replacing painted reality by the reality of the ' material objects '. His *Béguinage* (206) was thus the source of that admirable series of works by Kurt Schwitters, Man Ray, Max Ernst, Miro, Tanguy and others who rehabilitated the meanest of materials by incorporating it in beauty of a another kind, formed of slight disgust and abundant lyricism. The jewellery of Gustave Moreau had no other signifiance.

CONCLUSION

The outbreak of the 1914 war snapped the ties of mutual friendship, understanding and admiration uniting numberless artists across the frontiers of Europe, that old world which had just created the newest art of all time. Four years of slaughter thinned the ranks of the pioneers. Boccioni, Marc, Macke, de la Fresnaye, Wouters, Duchamp-Villon and many other young men fell in battle. Others stagnated in uniform. All work was done under chaotic conditions. Artists' colonies were dispersed. Malevitch and Chagall went back to Russia. Those who were driven into exile took their nostalgia with them or there fomented revolt (Dada). Futurism, overtaken by events, faded out. It seemed that everything was to be challenged.

When reassessment followed after the war, Apollonian art stood secure, out of the way of the general disruption. This was in the nature of things. At most there was some relaxation of the rules of Cubism, but this was counterbalanced by a stiffening in the attitude of non-figurative painters. The movement towards abstraction was precipitated by a compelling need, after chaos, for an earnestly spiritual moral order, pure and austere (Mondrian). This ultra-orthodox attitude was in turn tempered by the introduction into abstract painting of mechanistic elements (Léger).

The effect of the war and its aftermath on Dionysiac art was to hurl it into a vortex of violence, fury and despair, especially in the defeated countries. Expressionism fell at once into the depths of the abyss, where the demoniacal, the erotic and every primitive instinct shrieked in a blaze of acid colours, venomous and malefic. To this witches' sabbath was added Dada's sarcastic, nihilistic farandole, driven by the spectre of self-destruction, until the day when Surrealism gave direction and a meaning to this torrent. Here again reaction soon set in with a return to subject and object: the *Neue Sachlichkeit*, dry and objective, ushered in a period of magical realism that led back by devious paths to Chirico's mysterious poetry. The cult of the Douanier Rousseau put the primitives, those masters of popular reality, back in their place of honour. But towering above this blossoming of Dionysiac styles, the great example of Kandinsky was to lead abstract Expressionism to its ultimate conclusions.

Thus, as we look back at it from our present distance — pending proof of the contrary — the art of this half-century seems still to rest entirely upon the discoveries of the two generations — penniless and despised, exultant and desperate, strong in their faith and beset by doubts, who, between 1884 and 1914, amassed that splendid heritage — *the sources of 20th century art*.

Emile LANGUI

156

XIV
Henri de Toulouse-Lautrec
La Goulue au Moulin Rouge
(1891)

101

Auguste RENOIR

Madame Renoir

(about 1885)

Paul Gauguin
The ' Alyscampes ' at Arles
(1888)

XV
Paul Gauguin
Ta Matete
(1892)

103
Edgar DEGAS
The Milliners
(1898)

104
Philip Wilson STEER
Southwold
(1892)

105
Gustave MOREAU
Orpheus
(1897-98)

106

Giovanni SEGANTINI

Love at the Source of Life
(1896)

107

Pierre PUVIS DE CHAVANNES

Geneviève keeping watch over the sleeping city
(1898)

108
Johan THORN PRIKKER
The Betrothed
(1893)

109
Jan TOOROP
The Three Fiancées
(1893)

XVI
Édouard VUILLARD
Mother and child
(about 1899)

111
Ejnar NIELSEN
Blind Girl
(1896–1898)

110
Fernand KHNOPFF
A Blue Wing
(1896–1898)

112
Gustav KLIMT
Madame Fritza Riedler
(1906)

XVII
Pierre BONNARD
La Loge
(1908)

113
Henri EVENEPOEL
Lady with a white hat
(1897)

114
Félix VALLOTTON
Woman combing her hair
(1900)

115

Henri ROUSSEAU,
le Douanier

The chair factory
(1897)

116

Maurice UTRILLO
Berlioz' house
(1907)

117
Auguste RODIN
Balzac
(1897–1898)

118
Edgar DEGAS
Grande arabesque (second study)
(1882–1891)

119
Aristide MAILLOL
L'Action enchaînée
(1906)

120
Aristide MAILLOL
Night
(1902)

121
Antoine BOURDELLE
Herakles the archer (detail)
(1910)

XVIII

Paul CÉZANNE

Les grandes baigneuses
(1900–1905)

124
Guiseppe Pelizza
da Volpedo
Linen in the Sun
(1905)

125
Paul Signac
Portrait of Fénéon
(1890)

XIX

Pablo Picasso

Les demoiselles d'Avignon

(1907)

126
Paul Cézanne
Portrait of Ambroise Vollard
(1896–1899)

127
Paul Cézanne
House on the bank of the Marne
(1888–1890)

128
Paul CÉZANNE
La Montagne Sainte-Victoire
(1904)

129
Pablo PICASSO
The reservoir
(1909)

130
Georges BRAQUE
The house behind the tree
(1908)

131
Georges BRAQUE
The Mandola
(1910)

132
Georges BRAQUE
Nude
(1907–1908)

XX
Georges BRAQUE
Jeune fille à la guitare
(1913)

133
Pablo Picasso
Portrait of Ambroise Vollard
(1909–1910)

134
Fernand LÉGER
Nudes in the forest
(1908–1910)

135
Fernand LÉGER
Contrast in forms
(1913)

XXI

Fernand LÉGER

La Noce

(1910–1911)

136
Louis MARCOUSSIS
Still-life with a chequer-board
(1912)

137
Roger DE LA FRESNAYE
Seated man
(1914)

138

Giorgio MORANDI

Still-life
(1914)

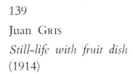

139

Juan GRIS

Still-life with fruit dish
(1914)

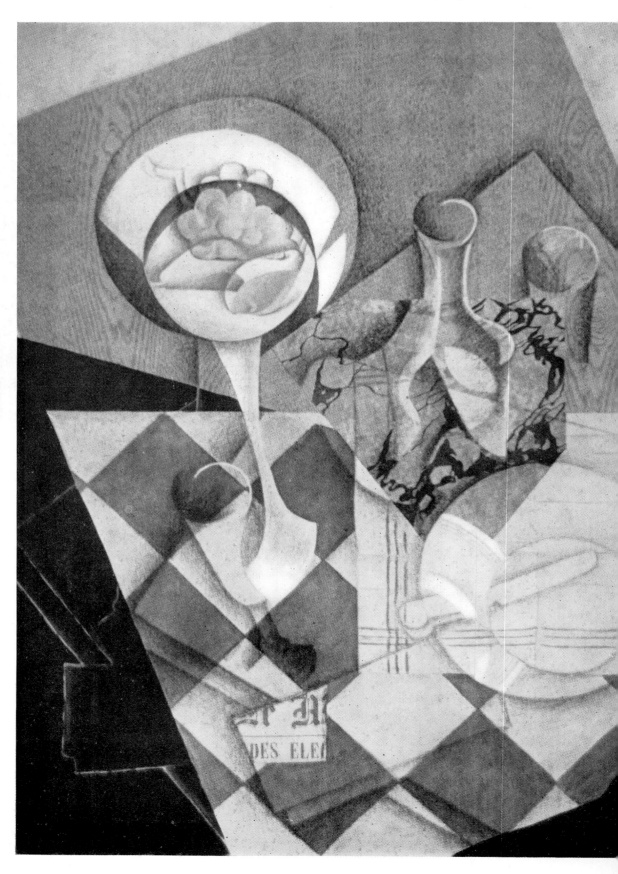

XXII
Michel LARIONOV
Rayonism
(1911)

140
Leo GESTEL
Woman Standing (Cubist figure)
(1913)

141
Jan SLUYTERS
Cubist portrait of a woman
(1914)

142
Raymond Duchamp-Villon
The Horse
(1914)

143
Jacques Lipchitz
Sailor with a Guitar
(1914)

144

Umberto Boccioni

Unique Forms of Continuity in Space
(1913)

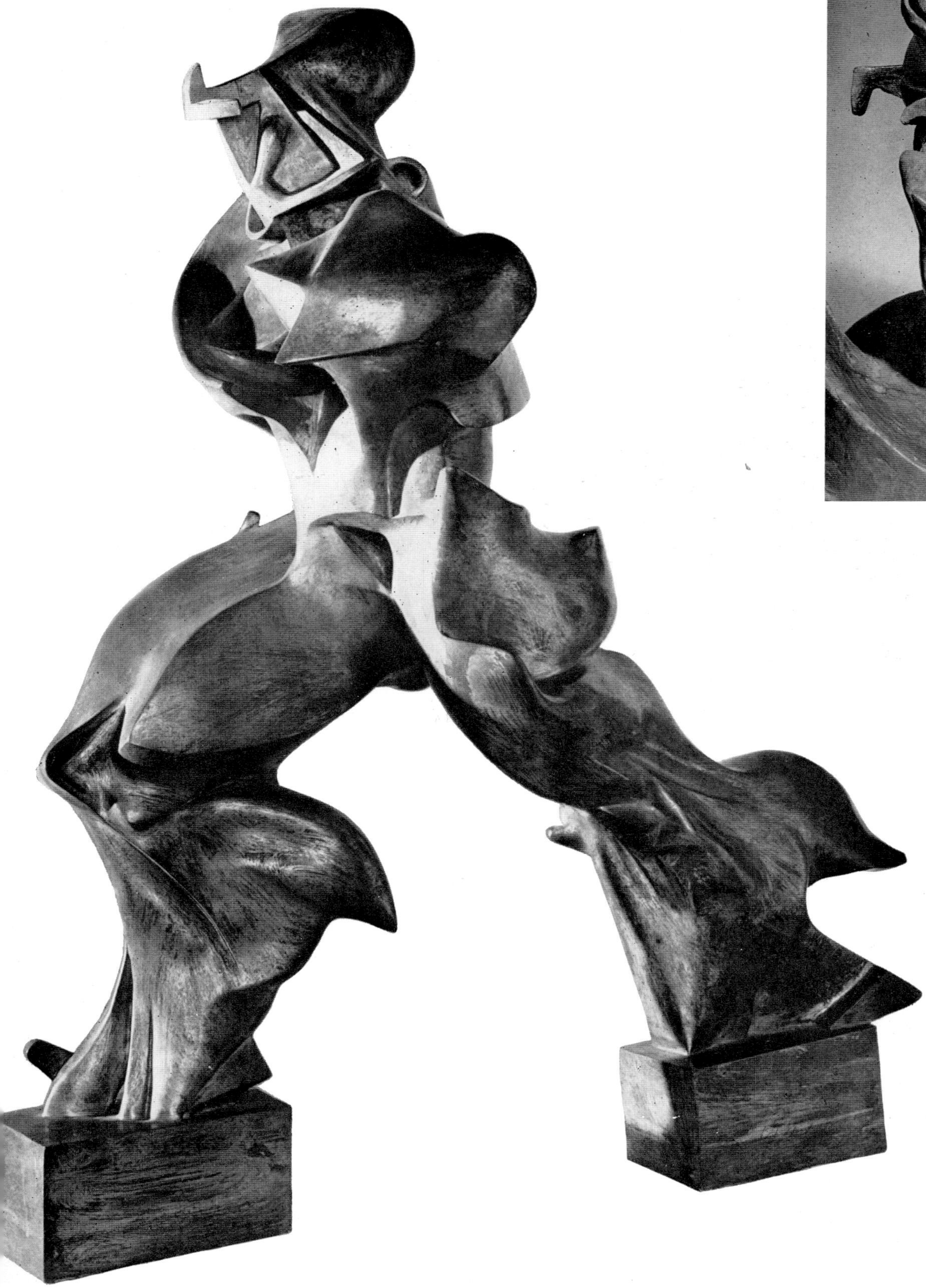

145

Umberto Boccioni

Unflattering portrait
(1913)

146
Giacomo BALLA
Young Girl running on a balcony
(1912)

XXIII

Umberto Boccioni

Dynamism of a cyclist
(1913)

147

Jean METZINGER

Study for the portrait of Apollinaire
(1910)

148

Mario SIRONI

Portrait of the artist
(1913)

149
Lyonel FEININGER
The Bridge
(1913)

150
Jacques VILLON
Marching Soldiers
(1913)

151
August MACKE
Brightly-lit shop windows
(1912)

152
Casimir MALEVITCH
Supreme
(before 1915)

153
Frantisèk KUPKA
Nocturne
(1910)

XXIV

Piet MONDRIAN

Composition

(1914)

154
Piet MONDRIAN
Apple Tree in Blossom
(1912)

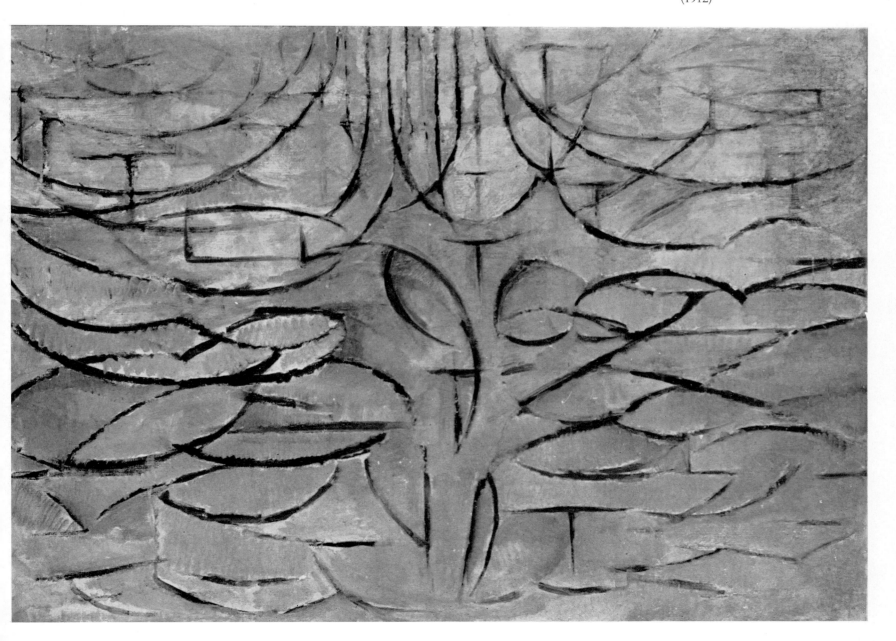

155
Paul KLEE
Abstraction: coloured circles joined by bands of colour
(1914)

156
Robert DELAUNAY
Circular Forms, Sun, Tower
(1913)

157
Percy Wyndham LEWIS
Composition
(1913)

158
James ENSOR
Skeletons Warming Themselves
(1889)

XXV

James ENSOR

Fall of the rebel angels
(1889)

159
Edvard MUNCH
Spring evening in Karl-Johan Street in Oslo
(1892)

Vincent VAN GOGH

Doctor Gachet

(1890)

XXVI
Vincent VAN GOGH
Starry night
(1889)

161
Odilon REDON
The Cyclops
(1895-1900)

162
Jens Ferdinand WILLUMSEN
After the storm
(1905)

163
Ernst JOSEPHSON
At the sea-shore
(1894)

XXVII
Edvard MUNCH
Girls on the bridge
(1901)

164
Maurice DENIS
Soir Trinitaire
(1891)

165
Isidro Nonell y Monturiol
Two Gypsies
(1903)

166
Pablo Picasso
The Embrace
(1903)

167
Paul Sérusier
The Talisman
(1888)

XXVIII
André DERAIN
Westminster Bridge
(1906)

168
Walter Richard SICKERT
The Dutchwoman
(1905)

169
Léon SPILLIAERT
The pink hat
(1904)

170

Albert MARQUET

Portrait of André Rouveyre
(1904)

XXIX
Raoul DUFY
La rue pavoisée
(1906)

XXX

Henri Matisse

Luxe, calme et volupté
(1904–1905)

171
Georges BRAQUE
The Port of Antwerp
(1906)

172

Maurice DE VLAMINCK
The outing in the country
(1905)

173
Kees Van Dongen
Anita
(1905)

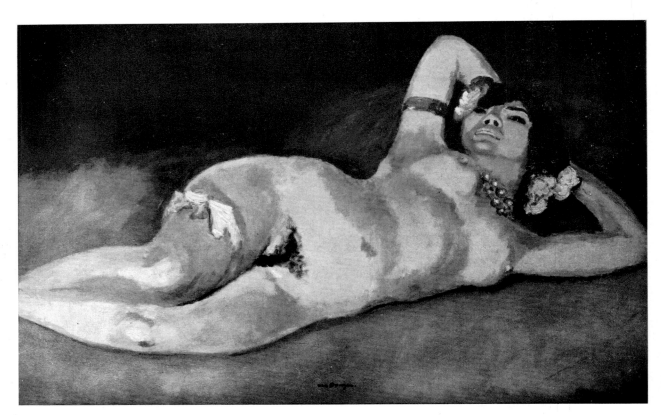

174
Henri Matisse
The Gipsy
(1906)

XXXI
Rik WOUTERS
Red curtains
(1913)

175
Henri MATISSE
La Serpentine
(1909)

176
Auguste RODIN
Study from Nijinski
(about 1911)

177
André DERAIN
The Billiard players
(1913)

178
Henri MATISSE
Lane in the woods at Clamart
(1912)

180

Marc CHAGALL

Homage to Apollinaire, Walden, Cendrars and Canudo
(1911-1912)

XXXII
Marc CHAGALL
To Russia, asses and others
(1911)

181
Georges MINNE
The Relics-bearer
(1897)

182
Wilhelm LEHMBRUCK
Adolescent standing
(1913)

183
Antoine BOURDELLE
Penelope
(1915, first version 1903)

184
Rik WOUTERS
Domestic cares
(1913)

XXXIII
Emil NOLDE
Slovenes
(1911)

185
Käthe KOLLWITZ
Unemployed
(1909)

186
Paula MODERSOHN-BECKER
Self-portrait with amber necklace
(1906)

187
Ernst Barlach
The Vandal
(1910)

188
Ernst Barlach
Russian beggar with a cup
(1906)

XXXIV

Karl SCHMIDT-ROTTLUFF

Norwegian landscape (Skrygedal)
(1911)

189
Ernst Ludwig KIRCHNER
Berlin street scene
(1913)

193
Otto MÜLLER
Three girls before a mirror
(c. 1912)

XXXV
August MACKE

Kairuan I
(1914)

194
Wassily Kandinsky
Study for Improvisation No. 8
(1910)

195
Wassily KANDINSKY
Lyrism (Horseman)
(1911)

XXXVI
Franz MARC
Tyrol
(1913–1914)

196
Christian ROHLFS
Red Roofs
(1913)

197
Richard GERSTL
Two Sisters
(c. 1905)

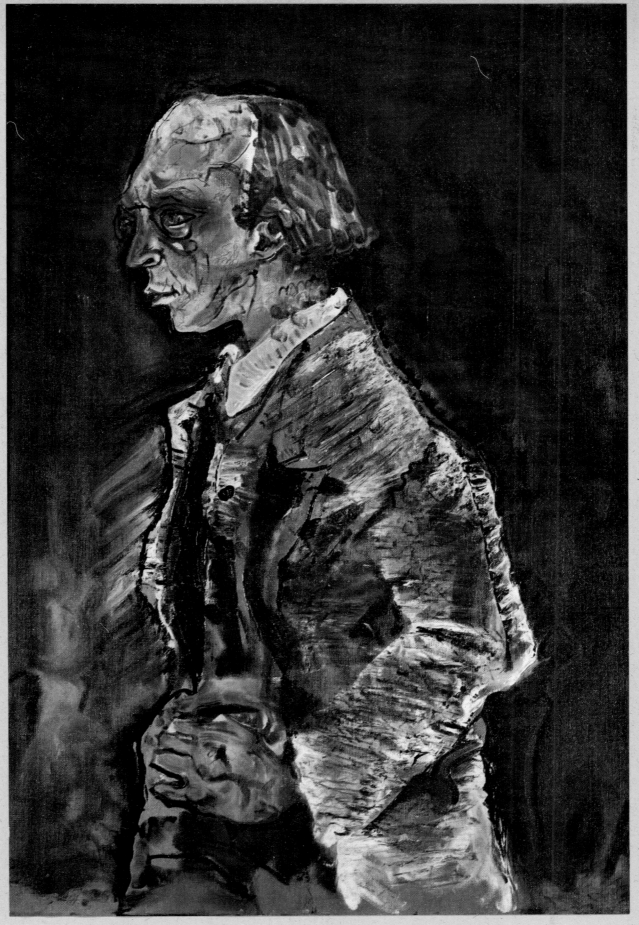

XXXVII
Oskar KOKOSCHKA
Portrait of Herwarth Walden
(1910)

198
Albert SERVAES
The Raising of Lazarus
(1911)

199
Constant PERMEKE
Moonlight
(1913)

200

Oskar Kokoschka

The Bride of the Wind (The Tempest)
(1914)

201
Amedeo MODIGLIANI
Head
(1913)

202
Henri GAUDIER-BRZESKA
The Imp
(1914)

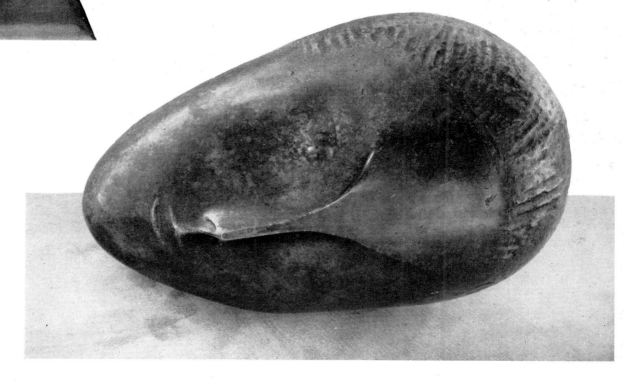

203
Constantin BRANCUSI
The Sleeping Muse
(1909)

204
Giorgio de Chirico
The Enigma of the Hour
(1911)

XXXVIII
Egon SCHIELE
Self-portrait
(1911)

205
Pablo Picasso
The student with the pipe
(1913-1914)

206
Enrico Prampolini
Beguinage
(1914)

207
Francis PICABIA
Rubber
(1909)

208
Marcel DUCHAMP
Cocoa grinder
(1914)

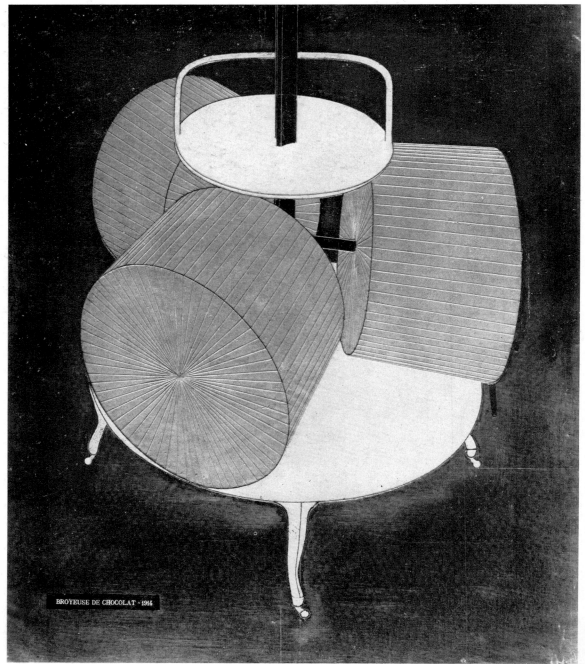

BROYEUSE DE CHOCOLAT - 1914

XXXIX

Francis PICABIA

Udnie (American girl, or The Dance)
(1913)

ARCHITECTURE
AND THE APPLIED ARTS

Where lie the sources of the twentieth century? To speak of sources there must issue from them a stream, then a river, and finally, in our particular case here, the ocean of the International Style of the 1930s. Do Prometheus and the unknown inventor of the wheel stand by the source as the *genii fontis*? No; because there are breaks, and our civilization is not connected with that distant past by a continous flow. But even if we admit that civilizations ' rise and fall, crumble, are extended, Are renewed, destroyed', even if we keep within Western civilization, are the sources of the twentieth century then the invention of clocks with wheels and weights and of printing with movable type? They are; for without printing and clocking-in there could be no twentieth century. Mass communication and mass production are among the things distinguishing ours from all preceding centuries. However, it is only the quantitative exploitation which belongs exclusively to us, not the invention itself. And that is indeed a phenomenon to rank high in force among the sources of the twentieth century. The twentieth century is the century of the masses: mass education, mass entertainment, mass transport, universities with twenty thousand students, comprehensive schools for two thousand children, hospitals with two thousand beds, stadia with a hundred thousand seats. That is one aspect; the other is speed of locomotion, every citizen being an express-train driver on his own, and some pilots travelling faster than sound. Both are only expressions of the technological fanaticism of the age, and technology is only an application of science.

Science, technology, mass locomotion, mass production and consumption, mass communication — in the field of the visual arts which is our field in this book, that means the predominance of architecture and design over the *beaux-arts*, it means the predominance of the city over the small town and the country, and it means the concentration on architecture and design for the masses and on what new materials and new techniques can do for them.

If this is accepted as a diagram of the twentieth century, so far as we can observe and analyse it, where do its sources lie then? We can now endeavour to list and consider them in their order of time.

Architecture and design for the masses must be functional, in the sense that they must be acceptable to all and that their well-functioning is the primary necessity. A chair can be uncomfortable and a work of art, but only the occasional connoisseur can be expected to prefer its aesthetic to its utilitarian qualities. The plea for functionalism is the first of our sources. Augustus Welby Northmore Pugin, born in 1812, the English son of a French father, wrote on the first page of his most important book: ' There should be no features about a building which are not necessary for convenience, construction, or propriety... The smallest detail should... serve a purpose, and construction itself should vary with the material employed ' [1]. That was written in 1841, but it was not new then. It is the direct continuation of the prin-

---

[1] *The true Principles of Pointed or Christian Architecture*, 1841, p. 1.

ciple of French seventeenth and eighteenth century rationalism. Architecture, writes Batteux [1] ' n'est pas un spectacle... mais un service ', and ' sûreté, convenance, commodité, bienséance ' are all familiar from Cordemoy to Boffrand and the younger Blondel. To quote two less familiar passages, both not French: Hogarth called the first chapter of his *Analysis of Beauty*, ' Of Fitness ', starting thus: ' Fitness of the parts to the design for which every individual thing is form'd... is of the greatest consequence to the beauty of the whole... In ship-building the dimensions of every part are confin'd and regulated by fitness for sailing. When a vessel sails well, the sailors call her a beauty; the two ideas have such a connection ' [2]. And the Abbate Lodoli, not uninfluenced perhaps by Hogarth, referred in his stimulating conversations to the Venetian gondola as a piece of rational design and stipulated that nothing ought to appear in a building which is not ' veramente in funzione ', has not ' il proprio suo uffizio ' and is not ' parte integrale della fabbrica ' and designed in a logical relation ' alla natura della materia ' [3].

The fact that Pugin, who came first in this string of quotations, called the book which he started with this clarion call *The True Principles of Pointed or Christian Architecture*, the fact that his principal purpose was not a plea for functionalism but for the Gothic Revival as the expression of a Catholic Revival, even the fact that he argued extremely intelligently the functional aspect of the Gothic style, of buttresses, of rib-vaults and so on, all these facts do not concern us at present. He was read by the Gothicists, but he was also read by the Functionalists. For such existed among the mid-nineteenth century writers and thinkers. Gottfried Semper in Germany, with his explanation of the applied or decorative arts conditioned by materials and techniques, was one of them. He had lived in London as a refugee in the years 1851-55, and must have been in contact with the small group of architects, artists and administrators responsible for the preparation, the success and the ruthless criticism of the Great Exhibition of 1851: Henry Cole in the first place, Owen Jones, Matthew Digby Wyatt, Richard Redgrave in the second. These men, even before the exhibition, had issued a small journal called the *Journal of Design and Manufactures* and in this had applied the principles of Pugin, as Semper was going to do later, to matters of craft and industrial art. Pugin had objected to carpets where one walks ' upon highly relieved foliage ' [4], the *Journal* now insisted that carpets should keep to ' a level or low plane ' [5], that wallpapers should convey ' the proper impression of flatness ' [6] and in a more general way, that ' the first consideration of the designer should be perfect adaptation to intended use ' [7] and that every object ' to afford perfect pleasure must be fit for the purpose and true in its construction ' [8].

No wonder that these men, when the Crystal Palace had gone up and been filled with the proudest products of all nations, were appalled at the standard of taste displayed. ' The absence of any fixed principle in ornamental design is most apparent ', they wrote, and ' the taste of the producers is uneducated ' [9]. No wonder either that they admired the Crystal Palace itself.

The Crystal Palace (209) is the mid-nineteenth century touchstone, if one wishes to discover what belongs wholly to the nineteenth century and what points forward into the twentieth. The Crystal Palace was entirely of iron and glass, it was designed by a non-architect, and it was designed for industrial quantity production of its parts. It is a source in one sense, but it also had its sources, and they take us back once again to the eighteenth century. The use of iron in architecture starts in France in the 1780s with Soufflot and Victor Louis, who were especially concerned with making theatres fireproof, and in England in the 1790s with manufacturers who, acting as their own designers, attempted to make their factories fireproof. In both cases the iron was an expedient of high utilitarian but of no aesthetic significance. It came into the open, as it were, playfully and only internally, in some romantic buildings such as Nash's Royal Pavilion at Brighton in 1815-20, and seriously and externally in the great bridges of the same years. The earliest iron bridge was in fact erected as early as 1777 — the Coalbrookdale Bridge in England (210). It has a span of 100 feet. It was

---

[1] *Les Beaux-Arts réduits à un même principe*, 1747, p. 47.

[2] *The Analysis of Beauty*, edited by Joseph Burke, Oxford 1955, pp. 32-33.

[3] A. MEMMI, *Elementi dell'Architettura Lodoliana*, Rome 1786, Vol. I, p. 62.

[4] *True Principles*, p. 26.

[5] *J. of Des. and Manuf.*, IV, 1850, p. 175.

[6] *J. of Des. and Manuf.*, I, 1849, p. 80

[7] REDGRAVE, *Supplementary Report on Design*, in *Report by the Juries...*, 1852, p. 720.

[8] OWEN JONES, *The True and the False in the Decorative Arts*, 1863 (lectures given in 1852), p. 14.

[9] *J. of Des. and Manuf.*, Vol. V, p. 158 and *Supplementary Report on Design*, p. 708.

at once surpassed by the bridge at Sunderland which in 1793-96 spanned 206 feet, and this by James Finley's Schuylkill Bridge of 1809, with 306 feet. The two English bridges had been iron arches, the Schuylkill Bridge was a suspension bridge, and the suspension principle gave us the finest of the early nineteenth century bridges such as Thomas Telford's Menai Bridge of 1820-26 with a main span of 579 feet (211).

Some architects later in the nineteenth century — Matthew Digby Wyatt among them — were ready to count them among the finest structures of the century. But they were not the work of architects. The architects, as we have seen, had been ready to use iron in a minor way, where necessity arose, but otherwise at best they only played with it. Now this is what Wyatt wrote in 1850-51, apropos the bridges, these 'wonders of the world': 'From such beginnings what glories may be in reserve... we may trust ourselves to dream, but we dare not predict [1].' This was the year of the Crystal Palace. Pugin called it the 'glass monster' [2], Ruskin a 'cucumber frame' [3], but Wyatt wrote 'that the building is likely to accelerate the 'consummation devoutly to be wished' and that the novelty of its form and details... will exercise a powerful influence upon national taste' [4]. A little later he even foretold from the union of iron and glass 'a new era in architecture' [5]. This was still in 1851.

But by then, a few of the most adventurous architects of repute had begun to take notice of iron, and Labrouste's Bibliothèque Ste-Geneviève in Paris of 1843-50 (212) and Bunning's Coal Exchange in London (213) of 1846-49 remain as the earliest buildings whose aesthetic character is determined by iron. Labrouste's has the greater elegance and ornamental restraint, as Labrouste was indeed doubtless the better architect of the two. That comes out even more clearly in the exteriors: Bunning's of an unprincipled jollity which was accepted at the time in England as belonging to the Free or Mixed Renaissance; Labrouste's also of the Renaissance and also a free Renaissance, but treated nobly, with discipline and economy of decoration. And both architects, it must be remembered, hid their display of iron behind solid stone.

Wyatt appreciated Bunning, a greater man appreciated Labrouste and was guided by him: Emanuel Viollet-le-Duc (1814-79). When Labrouste stopped teaching, his pupils induced Viollet-le-Duc to take over, and he taught for a short time. In connection with this he began to deliver his *Entretiens* in 1858, published the first volume in 1863 and the more important second in 1872. His approach to architecture is the functionalist's. He demands the 'alliance de la forme avec les besoins' and 'avec les moyens de la construction' [6]. He demands truth: that 'la pierre paraisse bien être de la pierre; le fer du fer; le bois du bois' [7], that no 'apparences monumentales ne cachent des habitudes bourgeoises' [8]. And consequently he insists on the necessity of a style for the nineteenth century. Today, he says, 'on possède des ressources immenses fournies par l'industrie et la facilité des transports' [9]. Architecture belongs 'presque autant à la science qu'à l'art' [10]. Architects must cease to be interested only in whether their façades are to be Roman, Gothic or Renaissance. From that attitude 'il ne peut rien sortir de neuf, de vivant' [11]. The engineers who have invented the locomotive 'n'ont pas songé à copier un attelage de diligence' [12]. If architects want to prevent their profession from becoming obsolete, they must become 'des constructeurs habiles, prêts à profiter de toutes les ressources que fournit notre état social' [13]. And so he arrives at iron, praises iron, proposes iron even for ribs in vaults (as Boileau had already shown it in Paris churches) and even for externally visible framing.

Bold words indeed, but what were the deeds? Viollet-le-Duc was the great restorer of French cathedrals, the great scholar of Gothic architecture — though admittedly with a keen sense of structure. Like Pugin before him, he did not perform what he preached. His opposite number in England was Sir George Gilbert Scott, also a self-confident restorer, also a scholar of Gothic architecture of no mean achievement, and also a man who could write: 'An iron arched bridge may always be made beautiful, and it would be difficult to make a suspension bridge anything else' and 'It is self-evident that... modern metallic construction opens out a perfectly new field for architectural development' [14].

---

[1] *J. of Des. and Manuf.*, IV, pp. 10 etc. and 74 etc.
[2] So Mrs Stanton tells me, quoting from one of the many unpublished letters which will go into her monograph on Pugin.
[3] Library Edition, vol. xxxv, p. 47.
[4] *J. of Des. and Manuf.*, IV, as before.
[5] *J. of Des. and Manuf.*, VI, p. 16.

[6] *Entretiens*, I, 451. [7] *Entretiens*, I, 472. [8] *Entretiens*, II, 289.
[9] *Entretiens*, I, 388. [10] *Entretiens*, I, 321. [11] *Entretiens*, II, 114.
[12] *Entretiens*, II, 67. [13] *Entretiens*, II, 55.
[14] *Remarks on Secular and Domestic Architecture, Present and Future*, 1858, pp. 224 and 109.

But it was not his field, as it was not Viollet-le-Duc's. When he was asked to design a hotel in connection with the new St. Pancras Station in London, he provided a towering Gothic pile hiding entirely the magnificent metallic construction which the engineer William H. Barlow had erected behind it as a train-shed and which, with its span of 243 feet, was the largest span ever, until then, achieved by man. It remained the largest for twenty-five years, until it was finally vastly surpassed by Dutert and Contamin's splendid *Halle des Machines* at the Paris Exhibition of 1889, with its 362 feet span (214).

But while iron and glass, and the new aesthetic vocabulary which its extensive use entailed, went on in exhibition buildings and train-sheds and also in factories and office buildings, where much light and a cellular structure were demanded, the architect continued to keep away from the new materials and to be satisfied with the trappings of Gothic, Renaissance and — more and more — Baroque. Neither the aesthetic possibilities of defeating the limitation of past styles by means of the new possibilities of skeletal construction nor the social possibilities of mass-produced parts were taken seriously by the profession.

The great impetus in the fields of aesthetic and social renewal came from England and centres in the larger-than-life figure of William Morris, poet, pamphleteer, reformer, designer — trained a little at university, a little in architecture, a little in painting — and ending by being a manufacturer and shopkeeper, though a very special one. Morris's firm was started in 1861, in collaboration with his close friends, the architect Philip Webb and the painters Ford Madox Brown, Rossetti and Burne-Jones. Morris's theories, as he lived them from when he was twenty-five and as he expounded them in impetuous lectures from when he was over forty, are familiar. They derive from Ruskin who had hated the Crystal Palace, gone out of his way to say that a railway station could never be architecture and denied with frantic fanaticism the necessity for his age to search for a style of its own: ' A day never passes without our... architects called upon to be original and to invent a new style... We want no new style of architecture... It does not matter one marble splinter whether we have an old or new architecture... The forms of architecture already known to us are good enough for us, and far better than any of us ' [1]. Morris was wiser. He refuted the current historicism, the ' masquerading in other people's cast-off clothes ' [2], but he too recommended to ' study the ancient work directly and to learn to understand it ' [3]. He was not a revolutionary; he loved the Middle Ages and loved nature and the open country, and he hated the big cities. His hatred was visual at first, but turned social almost at once. London to him was not only ' a whole county covered with hideous hovels ' [4], but also a ' beastly congregation of smoke-dried swindlers and their slaves ' [5]. The Middle Ages were not only pleasing to his eyes, they were also — as they had been to Ruskin — right in their social structure, or what he believed to have been their social structure. In the Middle Ages, he said, art was not ' divided among great men, lesser men, and little men ' [6], artists were not, as they are now, ' highly cultivated men whose education enables them, in the contemplation of the past glories of the world, to shut out from their view the every-day squalors that most of men live in ' [7]. Artists were plain workmen, ' common fellows ' who worked away ' on the anvil ' or ' about the oak beam ' with ' many a grin of pleasure ' [8]. The things which are museum pieces now ' were common things in their own day ' [9]. And the reason why that was so, is that in the Middle Ages ' daily labour was sweetened by the daily creation of Art ' [10]. And so Morris arrived at his definition of art as ' the expression by man of his pleasure in labour ' [11]. He arrived at the demand that art should become this again: ' A happiness for the maker and the user '. For while the average man can have no interest in the ' conscious ' of the isolated artist, he can enjoy what the craftsman does for him. So art should not be ' by the people ' but also ' for the people ' [12]. ' I do not want art for a few, any more than I want education for a few, or freedom for a few ' [13].

It is a strange system of theory to be guided by for a man in the mid-nineteenth century. It can only be understood as a demonstration of opposition against the standard and the taste of design as exhibited at the Great Exhibition of London

[1] *The Seven Lamps of Architecture* The Lamp of Obedience, par. IV and V.

[2] *Collected Works*, xxii, 315.   [3] *Collected Works*, xxii, 15.

[4] *Collected Works*, xxii, 11.

[5] J. W. MACKAIL, *The Life of William Morris*, World's Classics, II, 15.

[6] *Collected Works*, xxii, 9.   [7] *Collected Works*, xxii, 25.

[8] *Collected Works*, xxii, 40 and 42.   [9] *Collected Works*, xxii, 40.

[10] *Collected Works*, xxii, 33.   [11] *Collected Works*, xxii, 42.

[12] *Collected Works*, xxii, 46.   [13] *Collected Works*, xxii, 26.

Signet of the William Morris firm

in 1851, Paris in 1855, London again in 1862 and Paris again in 1867. Looking at the goods, especially the domestic goods, illustrated in the catalogues of these exhibitions, one can appreciate Morris's outbreaks. In the Middle Ages 'everything which was made by man's hand was more or less beautiful', today 'almost all wares that are made by civilized man are shabbily and pretentiously ugly'[1]. What is offered and sold is 'hurtful to the buyer, more hurtful to the seller, if he only knew'[2]. Our houses are filled with 'tons upon tons of unutterable rubbish', and the only acceptable things are usually in the kitchen[3]. The reason is that they alone are honest and simple, and 'the two virtues most needed in modern life (are) honesty and simplicity'[4].

Morris in his own day was no doubt right in blaming industry. 'As a condition of life, production by machinery is altogether an evil'[5]. But if you refuse to accept the machine, you cannot produce cheaply. Morris maintains that a bonfire ought to be made of nine tenths of all that is in wealthy people's houses[6]. But even so, what Morris's firm made was bound to be expensive, and could not be 'for the people'. Nor was it strictly speaking 'by the people'; for Morris and his friends designed their chintzes and wall-papers, their furniture and stained glass, and it was made, admittedly by hand (though not always), but it was not really creative craft. Yet, in spite of such inconsistencies, Morris succeeded in what he had set out to achieve. He made young painters and architects in all countries turn to craft or design, i.e. to help people in their everyday lives.

Why he succeeded, where Henry Cole and his friends had not, is easily seen. For one thing he did (up to a point) as he preached. He was a fanatic craftsman himself, trying his hand at wood-carving and illumination as early as 1856, and furnishing his first rooms in London with self-designed and carpenter-made 'intensely medieval furniture... as firm and as heavy as a rock'[7]. Two years later he got married, and yet one year later, in 1860, he moved into Red House, a house at Bexley Heath outside London, designed for him by his friend Philip Webb and furnished to Webb's and Morris's own designs. The house was daring in many ways, in exposing its red brick without a coat of stucco, in planning from inside out, i. e. without consideration of façades, and in frankly showing the construction inside. In fact, such a detail as the fireplace (215) is of a truly revolutionary character, completely devoid of any period allusions and completely functional in displaying its brick courses horizontally where the logs are laid and vertically where the smoke goes up. It is an exception in its own day and more prophetic of the coming twentieth century than anything in the field of domestic design in any country for thirty years to come. Most of the firm's early furniture is much more backward-looking, though to the simplicity of the cottage and never to the displays of the rich man's house. Yet even among the furniture sold by the firm, one can find occasional pieces of remarkably independent design. A chair e.g. designed by the Pre-Raphaelite painter Ford Madox Brown about 1860, though also clearly a simple cottage chair, shows originality in the slender elongation of the rails of the back (216).

Simplicity and directness unite this chair, Webb's fireplace, and the very fine designs in the flat of Morris and his firm, such as his famous *Daisy* wallpaper designed in 1862 and Webb's *Swan* tiles designed in the same year (217). It was the absence of simplicity and directness from the goods one could buy in the existing shops and stores which led to the creation of the firm. And there again Morris directed development both as a craftsman and a designer. When he decided that the firm should turn to the printing of textiles, and when he saw that bad dyeing was one of the chief trou-

---

[1] *Collected Works*, xxiii, 145-146   [2] *Collected Works*, xxii, 22.   [5] *Collected Works*, xxii, 335.   [6] *Collected Works*, xxii, 48.
[3] *Collected Works*, xxii, 23-24.   [4] *Collected Works*, xxii, 47.   [7] J.W. MACKAIL, *l.c.*, I, 116.

bles, he learned to dye himself. And later, when the firm turned to tapestry weaving, he spent 516 hours in four months at the loom. But Morris's success was not only grounded in the example of craftsmanship he set, it was even more due to his genius as a designer. The designs of the Cole circle are dry and doctrinaire, Morris's are brimful of life. That is one memorable thing about them, the others are these. His designs are always crisp. There is no 'slobbering and messing about' in them [1]. Secondly, he succeeded better than anyone before or after him in achieving a balance between nature and style, between the plainness recommended for textiles etc., by Pugin and the Cole circle, and the richness and abundance of flower and leaf as he had studied it so well in his childhood and youth. Moreover, his designs — in terms of design, not of imitation — possess the equivalent of the closeness and density of nature observed. Finally — and this matters most in our particular context — the designs, especially those of before 1876, are not in any way closely dependent on the past. They may be inspired to a certain extent by Elizabethan and Jacobean embroidery, but they are essentially original (218, 219).

Just as Morris knew that to re-establish values in the things of one's every-day use was a matter of social conscience before it could ever become a matter of design, so he also knew — and in this he proved just as much a prophet — that the revival of sound architecture must precede the revival of sound design. 'Unless you are resolved', he said in 1880, 'to have good and rational architecture, it is … useless your thinking about art at all' [2]. 'The great architect' of his own day, he knew, lived a life carefully 'guarded from the common troubles of common men' [3]. What he was referring to here is the fact that the leading architects of the nineteenth century spent their lucrative working hours designing churches, public buildings and country houses and villas for the rich. This attitude changed only gradually, and it will be one of our tasks to watch the change. Its first stage is what became known as the English Domestic Revival, a turn of some architects of Morris's generation to the domestic field entirely or almost entirely and at the same time to a smaller scale and a greater delicacy of detail.

The two most important names are that of Morris's friend Philip Webb and that of Richard Norman Shaw. We have already met Webb more than once. An early work of his maturity is Joldwyns in Surrey of 1873. Its chief merits are a combination of boldness and straightforwardness, a refusal to do anything for show, and a great faith in local building materials. Webb, like Morris, was not a revolutionary. He loved old building in the country and used its methods and motifs. He was never afraid of mixing styles and he relished unexpected solecisms such as the long chimneys of Joldwyns, or the far-projecting five gables in a row at Standen, a house of 1892 (220).

Shaw was a different character, more the artist, where Webb was the builder, more fanciful and elegant and perhaps also more sensitive. He also never departed far from the past at least in his individual motifs, and he also mixed them with delight. The oversailing upper floors of Swan House (223), Chelsea, of 1876, are in the tradition of timber-framed building. The oriel windows on the first floor are a favourite English motif of about 1675, the excessively slender windows above are Queen Anne — but the delicate, even *piquant* ensemble is Shaw and no one else and had a great deal of influence in England and America. Shaw even introduced this novel idiom into the City of London. New Zealand Chambers (222) of 1872, unfortunately destroyed in the Second World War, is just as dainty and domestic. The oriel windows on the ground floor are specially remarkable. There is no period motif here; they are simply introduced to allow a maximum of daylight to enter the offices. Shaw's country houses are nearer Webb's, although they also can perhaps be called more lighthearted (221).

There is one more respect in which Shaw's work concerns us here. At Bedford Park, not far from London, though at the time still not engulfed in the town, he built from 1875 the first garden suburb ever. The idea was not his, but he made it come to life, in terms of streets of modest houses and of old trees preserved in the gardens and new trees planted in the streets (224).

Again the design of the houses is not specially original. Their source is Tudor England and Stuart England, though again not the England of the 'prodigy houses' but of the manor house of the size of William Morris's own at Kelmscott in Oxfordshire. Webb and Shaw had established the middle-class house as the progressive architect's chief preserve. Morris had

---

[1] J.W. MACKAIL, l.c., II, 24.   [2] *Collected Works*, xxii, 73.   [3] *Collected Works*, xxii, 41.

re-established the aesthetic importance of our closest everyday surroundings. But neither he nor Webb nor Shaw had felt as strongly about the necessity of an original style of the nineteenth century, i.e. about forms not taken over from the past, as Viollet-le-Duc had done. It made little difference; for Viollet-le-Duc, when it came to designing, was if anything more period-bound than Webb and Shaw. No one in Europe could get away from historicism before the 1880s.

And Europe does in fact not cover the world situation any longer at this juncture. The defeat of historicism was the work of Americans as much as Europeans, though their front of attack was significantly broader than that of the English. In the field of the private house, H.H. Richardson and Stanford White of McKim, Mead and White showed as mush fresh enterprise as Shaw, though admittedly not without knowing of his earlier houses. Occasionally, such as in the house for W.G. Low at Bristol, Rhode Island (225), of 1887, White displayed a radicalism beyond Shaw's and explicable no doubt out of the pioneer background of building in a young nation. The same radicalism was applied with even greater independence in commercial architecture. It is here that America about 1890 established international leadership.

The fact that America now reached this crucial moment is one of the most memorable facts of the century. The United States had been colonial in their reaction to European styles. They had become provincial, i.e., part of a common front of progress, but an outlying part. Now all at once they left everyone else behind. They did this in first developing the skyscraper and then in finding a new style for it. In 1875 in New York the Tribune Building by Hunt rose to 260 feet, in 1890 the Pulitzer (World) Building by Post to 375 feet.

These early skyscrapers are simply high houses, not even specially characterized as office buildings. It would have been possible to do that; for English office buildings had evolved a style as early as the 1840s in which the façade was reduced to a grid of stone piers and large windows (226). Chicago, a newer city than New York, and one in which traditions could not possibly matter, took up this novel and logical treatment and made it the standard of its skyscrapers. Moreover, Chicago added of its own the equally logical and most far-reaching innovation of applying the system of the iron frame, originally a system used for factories, to the high office building. This was first done by William Le Baron Jenney in the Home Insurance Building in 1883-85. It was an untidy and fussy building, but the tidying up was done only five or six years later by a few more talented architects: Burnham & Root, Holabird & Roche and Louis Sullivan. Holabird & Roche's Tacoma Building dates from 1887-89, Burnham & Root's Monadnock Building (not a frame structure) from 1889-91, Sullivan's Wainwright Building at St Louis from 1891. In the following years appearances were rapidly even further purified. Holabird & Roche's classic moment is the Marquette Building of 1894, Sullivan's the Guaranty Building of 1895 at Buffalo (227).

The importance of the School of Chicago is threefold. The job of the office building was here approached with a perfectly open mind and the functionally best solution found. An untraditional building technique offered itself to fullfil the needs of the job and was at once accepted. And it was now at last architects who took the necessary action and no longer engineers or other outsiders. Sullivan in particular knew clearly what he was doing. In his *Ornament in Architecture*, an article of 1892, he had written: ' It would be greatly for our aesthetic good, if we should refrain entirely from the use of ornament for a period of years, in order that our thought might concentrate... upon the production of buildings... comely in the nude ' [1]. Yet Sullivan himself loved ornament, though he used it externally only in a few judiciously chosen places. It is a very personal feathery foliage ornament, inspired probably by the Morris Movement but much freer, wilder and more entangled. It has been called Art Nouveau or Proto-Art Nouveau, and whether such a term is justifiable cannot be decided until Art Nouveau has been closely examined.

This is in fact our task now; for Art Nouveau was the other campaign to drive out historicism. This is its primary significance in European design and architecture, whatever other delights and aberrations it may harbour. Among the sources of the twentieth century it is still the most controversial. Today's architecture and design having taken a turn away from rationalism and towards fancy, Art Nouveau has suddenly become topical, and the very qualities of it which in this narrative will appear its historically most dubious are hailed. Books and exhibitions have vied with

---

[1] *Kindergarten Chats*, edition of 1947, 187.

each other to present its fascination. All the more important must it be to attempt an analysis — aesthetic as well as historical.

The term Art Nouveau comes from a shop in Paris opened in December 1895, the corresponding German term Jugendstil from a journal which began to appear in 1896. But the style is older. Traditionally it is supposed to have started fully mature in Victor Horta's house, No. 6 rue Paul-Émile Janson in Brussels, and that house was designed in 1892 and built in 1893. But it marks no more than the transfer of the style from the small to a large scale and from design to architecture.

The *incunabula* of Art Nouveau belong to the years 1883-88. They are the following. Arthur H. Mackmurdo, wealthy young architect and designer, in 1883 wrote a book on Sir Christopher Wren's churches in the City of London — not a subject that seems to call for Art Nouveau — and gave it a title-page fully Art Nouveau. What justifies this judgment? The area inside the frame is filled by a non-repeating, asymmetrical pattern of tulips, stylized vigorously into flaming shapes. To the left and right sharply cut short by the frame are two cockerells, pulled out to an excessive thinness and length. The characteristics which we shall see recur whenever we speak of Art Nouveau are the asymmetrical flaming shape derived from nature, and handled with a certain wilfulness or bravado and the refusal to accept any ties with the past. Of course Mackmurdo's design is not without ancestors, but they are not to be found among the hallowed period styles.

He must have looked at Morris and, like Morris, at the Pre-Raphaelites. He must have known William Blake, as the Pre-Raphaelites did, but he was also familiar — socially too — with Whistler, and although Whistler was an Impressionist in his formative years, he soon found an aim of his own, the aim to blend the light, soft, hazy tones of Impressionism with the creation of *piquant* decorative patterns, sometimes almost abstract, sometimes linear as in the celebrated Peacock Room of 1876-77. His equally celebrated signet, the butterfly, is an example of the latter. Companions of it are Morris's early signet of his firm and Mackmurdo's of the Century Guild which he started in 1882. The three signets sum up a story of nature and abstraction in which Morris, Whistler and Mackmurdo are of equal importance. It need hardly be added that the idea of calling a firm a guild was a bow to the Ruskin and Morris circle. It was to convey connotations of the Middle Ages and of co-operation instead of exploitation or competition. Mackmurdo's guild brought out a journal *The Hobby Horse*, and the title-page and typography of this also is worth remembering. It preceded by six years Morris's more famous venture into typography and book-making, the Kelmscott Press. Mackmurdo designed textiles for his guild in 1884 (33, 228) too, and they possess much of the originality and the swagger of the Wren title. It is difficult to assess the effects of the Century Guild. The eighties were the years of Morris's wide success as a designer. His by then much more staid, symmetrical, as it were classic designs for textiles were the principal influence in England. But Mackmurdo's daring also found an echo here and there. Heywood Sumner, who was indeed for a while associated with the Guild, worked in its style. The cover of the translation of Fouqué's *Undine* (1888) is a masterpiece in its own right (229). The world of sprites or fairies of the water was bound to appeal to Art Nouveau sensibility. Hair and waves and sea-weeds were as alluring as such elemental creatures themselves, not guided by reason but by instinct. For order enforced by intellect is one of the things against which Art Nouveau was in opposition, and the conscious selection of styles of the past to be imitated represented that principle of enforced order.

Mackmurdo's exploration was one in two dimensions, as indeed Morris's had been. But efforts at breaking the shackles of historicism in the crafts, expressing themselves in the shaping not the decorating of objects, were not entirely lacking either. Pride of place here goes to France. Émile Gallé of Nancy was five years older than Mackmurdo. His glass vessels of 1884 (34, XLII) and after are as alien to nineteenth century conventions as Mackmurdo's book and textile designs, with their soft, subtle colours and the mystery of their naturalistically represented flowers emerging out of cloudy grounds. Nor was Gallé alone, even in these earliest years. Eugène Rousseau, for instance, a much older craftsman in Paris of whom too little is known, turned to a new style at the same time. The Musée des Arts Décoratifs bought certain pieces from him in 1885, and among them is a *jardinière* in imitation of jade and a tall vase of clear glass, both strikingly independent and courageous (230, 231). The scratched-in pattern of the tall vase is particularly bold — Klee rather than Morris. E.B. Leveillé, a pupil of Rousseau, showed glass at the Paris Exhibition of 1889, wholly in the same spirit, e.g. a vase of

236

Arthur H. MACKMURDO,
Signet of the Century Guild (1884)

James McNeil WHISTLER,
Butterfly signature

Arthur H. MACKMURDO, *Title-page
for 'Wren's City Churches'* (1883)

craquelé glass marbled in green and red. In ceramics there is only one parallel to Rousseau, and that takes us to the most influential of all outsiders, to Gauguin.

Gauguin is the only one of the leading painters who not only influenced design by his forms but experimented with crafts himself. In 1881, before he had given up his job at the bank to devote himself to art, he decorated a cupboard in his dining-room with carved wooden panels in decidedly exotic shapes and painted red, green, yellow and brown (232). Primitivism starts from here, and a primitivism very different from Philip Webb's. Webb went back to the English countryside, Gauguin already here to barbarity. Then, in 1886 he turned to pottery. The jug here illustrated is as original and as ruthlessly crude (234). The épergne with the bathing girl of 1888 is a little less uncompromising (233). In fact, the introduction of the female figure into objects for use was both in the nineteenth century tradition and to the liking of Art Nouveau. Where Gauguin comes closet to the Mackmurdo-Sumner endeavours is in his work in two dimensions, i.e. as a painter and a graphic artist. The poster for the Café Volpini exhibition of 1889 is violently primitive again, a painting such as The Man with the Axe (235) has the vermiculating lines which became a hall-mark of Art Nouveau. Their influence was brief but wide, and not only on painters such as Munch. Gauguin conveyed his concern with craft as well as his style to his friends of Pont-Aven, and so we find Émile Bernard in 1888 doing wood-carving as well as an appliqué wall-hanging (236), and J.F. Willumsen in 1890 turning to ceramics very much of the Gauguin kind (237). Willumsen stayed in France and then returned to Denmark. There, however, while he had been away, a parallel development had begun in ceramics, independent, it seems of Pont-Aven. Thorvald Bindesbøll, two years older than Gauguin, and an architect by training, the son in fact of the most original Danish architect of the neo-Greek movement, had in the 1880s begun to work in ceramics. The plate of 1891 (238) with its crudely drawn tulips asymmetrically and indeed casually arranged still links up with Gauguin and Art Nouveau; his later plates stand entirely on their own in the whole of Europe (XLIV).

One is tempted to see in them a parallel to the Kandinsky moment in art; but they antedate it by nearly twenty years. One might also — and more justly — look in the direction of Gaudí, but even then Bindesbøll seems to retain priority. Bindesbøll's impact remains, and what ties him into our particular context here, is the attitude of the architect turning potter and indeed craftsman in general.

No radicalism of Bindesbøll's force can be found anywhere else. The nearest to it in England is certain half-concealed elements in the highly successful monuments of Alfred Gilbert. Gilbert was a sculptor in metals, precious metals on a small scale, bronze in his large works, monuments as a rule (239). Their figures are embedded in a gristly, crustaceous substance, some of it seemingly in a heavy flow like lava, some arrested in grotesques shapes (240). There was only one man in another country as ready and perhaps readier to force metal into such violent expression: Antoni Gaudí whom we shall meet more prominently soon. The material of his first challenges was iron. His father was a copper-smith; and he grew up day in day out seeing metal molten and shaped. Inspiration to experiment with iron for decorative purposes will also have come from Viollet-le-Duc's *Entretiens* which show in the details of spandrels between iron arches how medievalizing foliage trails can be made of iron. Gaudí's first house, the Casa Vicens at Barcelona, of 1878-80, is medievalizing too, though in a fantastical semi-Moorish way, and fantastical also are the spiky palm-fronds or stars of the iron fence. In the Palau Güell of 1885-89, his first major job, the forms are less aggressive and more ingratiating, and the parabolic shape of the portal is as unexpected and free from references to the past as are the undulations of the iron. The ease of bending of wrought iron and its ductility, which allow for the most delicate stalk-like filaments, made iron a favourite material of Art Nouveau.

It came into its own at once with Horta's house of 1892-3 already referred to. The famous staircase of No. 6 rue Paul-Émile Janson, too often illustrated to be shown yet once more here, has a slender iron column left exposed, an iron handrail of thin tendril-like curves and in addition, not of iron, applied wall, floor and ceiling decoration of the same curves. One can hardly believe that this should have been designed without influence from the England of Mackmurdo. Indirect influence from Pont-Aven is more easily proved, as we shall see presently. Although we are dealing with architecture here, the job on the staircase was essentially one of decorating, just as Gaudí's at the entrance to the Palau Güell. We are not sufficiently prepared yet for the architecture proper of both buildings and their designers.

Art Nouveau is indeed very largely a matter of decoration — so much so that some have denied its validity as an architectural style — and it is furthermore largely a matter of surface decoration. We must now follow it through the years of its conquest and international success — a short-lived success; for it began about 1893, and it was faced with a formidable opposition from about 1900 onwards. After 1905 it held out only in a few countries, and mostly in commercial work in which no creative impetus was left, if there ever had been any.

As textiles and the art of the book initiated the movement, they may be considered first. Henri van de Velde, Belgian painter, influenced by the *pointillistes* and by Gauguin, turned to design about 1890, the first such case of conversion by Morris which we can watch closely. The tapestry or rather *appliqué* wall hanging, called *Engelswache* (241), of 1891, can only be understood as an echo of the work of Bernard. It interests us because the disposition of the forms and the all-pervading undulations make it so thoroughly Art Nouveau. The trees are stylized more rigorously than the figures. One or two years later Hermann Obrist did that curious piece of embroidery which is inspired by tulips with their roots (242). It is a *tour de force*, and if one compares it with the best work in the field of textiles in England during the same years, the

Paul GAUGUIN, *Aux Roches Noires* (*Catalogue of the Café Volpini Exhibition*) (1889)

238

Georges LEMMEN, *Catalogue for 'Les Vingt'*
(1891)

Henri VAN DE VELDE,
Title-page for 'Dominical' (1892)

work of Charles F. Annesley Voysey, a first impression is obtained of the restraint and the sanity of England during those years. Excesses of Art Nouveau are all but absent. One exception to this rule has already been named: Alfred Gilbert, the other — Scottish and not English — will be commented on later. Voysey's textiles (XLV, 243, 244) of about 1890 are clearly influenced by Mackmurdo's, but they are milder in their rhythms and a little more accommodating. Less than ten years later Voysey was to abandon this style altogether and turn to another, more original but less Art Nouveau.

In typography Belgium again held a key position. *Les Vingt*, that adventurous club of artists whose exhibitions were perhaps the most courageous in Europe — they had shown Gauguin in 1889, Van Gogh in 1890, books and works of the artist-craftsmen in 1892 — had as the title-page of its catalogue in 1891 a design by Georges Lemmen reflecting Gauguin at his most Art Nouveau. The year after van de Velde went into book decoration. His title-page to Max Elskamp's *Dominical* is uncannily close to the Gauguin of the Man with the Axe, painted in Tahiti the year before. Of 1896 are the initials made for *Van nu en straks*, delightful play with the typical swelling and tapering curves of Gauguin as well as the English book artists in the Mackmurdo succession. Here again the contrast to the staid splendour of the Kelmscott Press is great and can serve as a reminder of how differently things were to go in England. Germany joined in the new Belgian style after a few years' hesitation. Otto Eckmann who died young in 1902 and Peter Behrens who soon repented these wild oats were the leading designers. Eckmann left painting for design in 1894, Behrens in 1895. Both designed type-faces of Art Nouveau character about 1900 and also book decoration, printed matter for business firms, book jackets, book bindings and so on.

A remark on book-binding itself must be appended to these remarks on the art of the book. The reason for picking out, as the one example here to be illustrated, a binding by the Nancy craftsman René Wiener (XL, XLVI) is that it introduces us to a different aspect of Art Nouveau. The asymmetric and the curving, curly shapes which were *de rigueur* could be obtained abstractly or naturalistically. Van de Velde believed as fervently in the one, as the artists of Nancy believed in the other. Neither was wholly original. Henry Cole and his friends had preached the necessity of ornament being ' rather abstractive than... imitative ' [1], the Victorian decorators themselves in all countries had wallowed in accurately portrayed roses, cabbage leaves and all the rest. Now Gallé had an inscription above the door to his studio ' Nos racines sont au fond des bois, aux bords des sources, sur les mousses ' and wrote in an article: ' Les formes fournies par les

---

[1] Quoted from a remarkably early source, the *Drawing Book of the School of Design*, by the Romantic or Nazarene painter William Dyce, published in 1842–43. The passage in question was reprinted in the *Journal of Des. and Manuf.*, VI, 1852.

végétaux s'adaptent tout naturellement aux ligneaux' [1]. *Ligneaux* is the operative word. In the mid-nineteenth century, naturalism reigned in all fields; the natural sciences were worshipped. Even in a church, otherwise imitated accurately from the style of say the thirteenth century, the foliage of the capitals was made yet more real than it had been at any moment in the Middle Ages, and the leaves of native trees and hedgerows were displayed proudly. Art Nouveau designers went to nature because they were in need of forms to express growth, not of human making, organic not crystalline forms, sensuous not intellectual forms.

So much for Nancy — and of course others in other countries. Van de Velde on the other hand insisted on the intellectual process of converting nature to make it ornament. Ornament, he said, must be ' structurel et dynamographique'. ' La moindre association naturalistique' would menace the eternal values of ornament [2]. Few were as radical as van de Velde, but as a matter of principle, Voysey, for instance, agreed: 'To go to nature is of course to go to the fountain head, but... before a living plant a man must go through an elaborate process of selection and analysis. The natural forms have to be reduced to mere symbols' [3]. The future was with the abstractionists not the naturalists, even if not the immediate future. For as soon as Art Nouveau spread and became commercially exploitable, its van de Velde version that was too exacting, and the less pure mixtures of curvaceous ornament with the curvaceous forms of plants or indeed the female body, were certain of greater success.

The years of universal success, at least on the Continent of Europe, were the ending years of the nineteenth and the very first years of the twentieth century. The catalogue of the Paris Exhibition of 1900 is a mine of Art Nouveau. The necklace and pendant by René Lalique was shown, and it illustrates, as do Lalique's pendant and brooch, the part played by nature and the part by stylization in Art Nouveau (245 to 247). From Germany came the brooch by Wilhelm von Cranach. It represents a jelly-fish strangling a butterfly, thought it can just as well be seen abstractly and is perhaps seen in that way to greater advantage. It is an exquisite display of red, green and blue enamel with baroque pearls and small precious and semi-precious stones (248). In Lalique's brooch the enamelled peacock's neck rises out of feathers of gold and moonstone (246). With jewellery we have moved from Art Nouveau in two dimensions to Art Nouveau in the round. There was no reason why the principle of eternal undulation should not be applied to three dimensions. All materials were indeed affected. In Victor Prouvé's bronze bowl *La Nuit* of 1894 (253) flowing hair takes the place of Mackmurdo's or Obrist's stalks and leaves, Lalique's feathers and Cranach's tentacles. Every time what tempted the craftsman were natural elements lending themselves to Art Nouveau sinuosity.

Ceramics and especially glass were ideal media for Art Nouveau. Georges Hoentschel's dark brown earthenware vase c.1901 (XLI) with the off-whites of its daringly accidental running-down glaze is an example of the former; the brothers Daum's bottle-shaped vase of 1893 with crocuses at the bottom and the glaze running down the high neck (249), and of course the famous Favrile glass of Louis C. Tiffany (251) are examples of the latter. Tiffany also began as a painter. He turned to decorative and stained glass, and in 1893 started a glass blowing department. The swaying, exceedingly attenuated forms of his vases and their subtle, never wholly calculated, shot colours made them a pattern for Europe as well, and Karl Koepping's glass (250) — Koepping again was a painter at first — is clearly in the first place inspired by Tiffany's.

Wood is a less tractable material, and much Art Nouveau furniture suffers from the conflict between its nature and the expressive desire of Art Nouveau. One way to avoid the conflict was to confine the decoration to curves on flat surfaces. But as a rule, and most dedicatedly in France, the material was forced to obey the style. France, in fact, is the country which in the end carried on longest in Art Nouveau. There were two centres: Paris, of course, and Nancy. That a provincial capital should vie with the national capital was an improbable thing to happen in so metropolitan a civilization as that of the rising twentieth century. However the case is matched by that of Glasgow. Nancy is the town of Gallé and of a group of other craftsmen-manufacturers all at first affected by Gallé's faith in nature as the source of ornament (34, 252).

---

[1] Both quotations are taken from S. Tschudi Madsen: *Sources of Art Nouveau*, Oslo, 1956. They appear on pages 177 and 178.
[2] *Les Formules de la Beauté architectonique moderne*, Brussels, 1923, pp. 65-66.
[3] *The Studio*, I, 1893, 236.

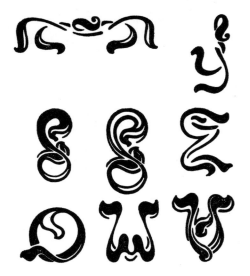

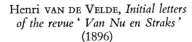

Henri VAN DE VELDE, *Initial letters
of the revue 'Van Nu en Straks'*
(1896)

Otto ECKMANN, *Cover for Ruskin's
'Seven Lamps of Architecture'*

Otto ECKMANN, *Design for a type-face*

Louis Majorelle's is the most familiar name after Gallé's. It is characteristic of the efforts needed to make Art Nouveau furniture that he used to model his pieces in clay before they were made of timber (254).

Art Nouveau like the Baroque made claims to the *Gesamtkunstwerk*. Only rarely can one do justice to an individual piece without knowing of its intended context. That alone debarred it or should have debarred it from quantity production. With the vandalism typical of sons against the generation of their fathers, most of the Art Nouveau *ensembles* have been destroyed. It is lucky that the Musée de l'École de Nancy could re-assemble, even if not without alteration and reductions, a complete dining room by Eugène Vallin (XLVII). This was begun only in 1903, at a moment when the other leading countries were moving away already from Art Nouveau. In looking at this room and trying it out as a place to live in, one can understand why. Such violent expression tires one soon. Furniture ought to be a background. Here we feel intruders. Also there is the constant clash between function and form — table legs awkwardly lumpy at the foot, doors and shelf recesses of bosomy shape. And finally one may well worry about wood made to perform ceramic or metallic curves.

One of the most daring cases is the music room by Alexandre Charpentier, a sculptor before he became a decorator. The music-stand illustrated (255) is a pure example of the three-dimensional Art Nouveau curve, spatially ingenious and functionally dubious. Charpentier belonged to the Parisian group *Les Cinq*, soon (by the accession of Plumet) to become *Les Six*. They formed one centre of the crafts revival in Paris, the other was Bing's shop *L'Art Nouveau*, a more international centre of course. Among the designers specially connected with Bing, Eugène Gaillard in his later work showed one French way out of the impasse of Art Nouveau. He said already in 1906 that furniture should express its function, that it should be in harmony with the material and that curves should be used decoratively only. His furniture is indeed a return to the principles and forms of the most refined French eighteenth century furniture, even if he never returned to imitation (256).

After these French pieces van de Velde's great desk of 1896 (257) is impressive in its radicalism and its tautness. There is neither the elephantine massiveness of Vallin's dining room nor Gaillard's half-concealed sympathy with the classic past. Van de Velde impressed Germany much when he first showed in 1897. Indeed Germany started a little later than Belgium and France, but for a short time men of strong personality joined Art Nouveau and produced outstanding work. Otto Eckmann, better known as a typographer and decorator of books, designed furniture for the Grand Duke of Hessen about 1898 (258), surprisingly structural, considering his free use of natural forms in the books he decorated. The solution of the seeming contradiction must be van de Velde. Richard Riemerschmid's chairs (259) are more English in their inspiration, and he was indeed among those who, when he turned away from Art Nouveau, did so for social as well as aesthetic reasons. The greatest ornamental originality in Germany was August Endell's, as we shall see in another context later. What is known of his furniture has a curious plastic quality — plastic in the true English sense of the word — quite different from anything so far examined. The scrolls at the ends of the arms in the chair illustrated are particularly convincing, both aesthetically and functionally.

Only one other designer of furniture did likewise, and he was neither German nor French nor English, nor indeed a furniture designer. Antoni Gaudí's chairs for the Casa Calvet of 1898-1904 (260, 261) have the same qualities as Endell's but driven to an extreme. They are Art Nouveau in that they shun the straight line, shun all relation to the past and also in that they are fanatically personal. But the bone-like formation of the elements is all Gaudí's. His most surprising furniture is that for the chapel of the Colonia Güell at Santa Coloma de Cervelló on which he worked from 1898 till 1914 (262). Here is one of the few cases of design trying to do what painting was doing at the same moment, i.e. scrapping all the agreed conventions of art. The brutality of the iron undercarriage of these benches, especially the feet, and of the seats themselves, goes indeed beyond Art Nouveau.

Gaudí's architecture poses even more urgently the problem of how far Art Nouveau as a term with an analyzable, useful meaning can be stretched. That he is first and foremost Gaudí there can be no question. The ironwork of the Casa Vicens and the portal of the Palau Güell have already demonstrated that. But that his views and those of Art Nouveau coincided in many ways is patent.

However, there is a greater problem involved here. It has been denied by more than one scholar that Art Nouveau architecture exists at all. It has been argued that Art Nouveau was no more than a decorative fashion, lasting hardly more than ten years and hence not deserving the attention it has recently been given. None of these contentions can be maintained. It might be worth looking at a number of exteriors and interiors of buildings in a systematic order culminating in Gaudí. The best start is Endell's Atelier Elvira in Munich, unfortunately not preserved (267). A flat façade is made Art Nouveau primarily, it is true, by means of a huge abstract ornament of a crustaceous kind, but surely not only by this. The asymmetrical fenestration, the tops of the windows and doorway like looped-up curtains and the glazing bars all play their part. And when you entered the house, a stair hall received you in which all forms undulated, and not only those applied to the walls. The handrail of the staircase, the newel post and the light fitting rocketing up from the post — all this is architectural, i.e. three-dimensional and articulating inner space (268). That the famous and at the time publicized staircase in Horta's house in the rue Paul-Émile Janson was the pattern is evident, and that staircase with its slender iron pillar also is genuinely architectural. Admittedly exteriors were not often up to the novelties of the interiors — as had been the case of the Atelier Elvira — but if one looks at the façade of Horta's own house of 1898-99 (272) one sees again the same spindliness of iron supports, the same play of pliable iron decoration round them and the same sense of transparency as inside.

Altogether, the role of iron in Art Nouveau is interesting enough to deserve a paragraph. Iron is a decorative as well as a structural material. Viollet-le-Duc had recognized that and suggested its use in both capacities in the same buildings. He was the fountain head. Then, and independent of him, iron and later steel externally, in conjunction with glass, became the technically most suitable material for the factory, the warehouse and the office building. The quality which recommended it was that it lent itself to the unmitigated grid. This was an argument in itself not of an aesthetic nature, though the twentieth century discovered the aesthetic possibilities of the grid. But Art Nouveau must retain the credit for the discovery of the aesthetic possibilities of iron and glass — even of qualities which have nothing to do with those of the grid. Art Nouveau adored lightness, attenuation, transparency and of course sinuosity. Iron meant thin members and ductility; iron and glass used externally produced the same transparency obtained internally by iron alone. Horta's Maison du Peuple of 1896-99 (47) is the Art Nouveau version of the American office building — both dependent on iron, but in the exactly opposite ways. In America the steel controls structure and thereby appearance, though the façades are of stone cladding the steel; in the Maison du Peuple the iron frame is visible and iron provides the music playing round the frame and embroidering on the eternal Art Nouveau theme of the curve which also is that of the façade as a whole. The rhythm of iron, glass, steel and brick is restless and the building does not read as a whole. In the great hall inside, iron is exposed everywhere and yet the effect is not utilitarian, largely again thanks to the use of curving members. The most daringly glazed commercial building of those years was Bernhard Sehring's Tietz Department Store at Berlin of 1900 (273), which consists of three broad stone bays, left, right and centre, exuberantly Baroque and not at all Art Nouveau in their details, and all the rest glass with the thinnest iron verticals and horizontals.

In France the architect with the keenest sense of the potentialities of the new materials was Victor Guimard. It was a fine show of a sense of topicality that the Paris Métro allowed him for the relatively new purpose of a metropolitan under-pavement railway to design exclusively in the new material (45, 274). The general tenor is indeed as light as befits the introduction to fast transport. But the details are bossy and bony — more similar to Alfred Gilbert's of more than ten years before than to anyone else's. However, the refusal to entertain straight lines anywhere and the sense of inventiveness all through place them firmly in Art Nouveau. Guimard's *magnum opus*, the Castel Béranger of 1897-98, on the other hand is in its façades not Art Nouveau. Its jumble of motifs is original, even forcedly so, but it is angular, static, solid and conventional in many details (275). The ironwork of the main doors on the other hand and the terracotta panels in the entrance are Art Nouveau and the latter is moreover most daring in its demonstration of pure abstraction. A rarely seen iron detail from the top of the house reminds one of another architect who ventured into pure abstraction, Endell in his Elvira ' rocaille ' (276). In fact even some of the dragon connotations are the same. Yet more amazing historically is the wall of the staircase at the back, a wall of heavy double-curved glass panels of alternating shapes whose very irregularity of surface does what in the terracotta panels had to be done by the craftsman's will (277).

Guimard's delight in materials and unexpected effects to be obtained from them and even some of Guimard's forms are the only causeway by which we can safely reach Gaudí. There are few other communications, and his originality might indeed not have become quite so extreme if it had not been for his working in the comparative isolation of Barcelona and working for a clientèle nationally disposed in favour of fantastical architecture. Indeed the extremes of Plateresque and Churrigueresque are hardly less bewildering than those of Gaudí. These he must have known, but they do not seem to have inspired him. On the other hand he must have been impressed by the Mohammedan style of Southern Spain as well as that of folk building in Morocco. And he must also have seen in the journals how Art Nouveau triumphed in France, and some of the interior details in his two blocks of flats, the Casa Batlló and the Casa Milá are indeed entirely French Art Nouveau, just as the use of concrete trees — leafless of course — in the Güell Park is a conceit of Hennebique's, the French concrete fanatic. Still, his overwhelming originality remains, but — at least in the Casa Batlló and the Casa Milá, both late works, begun in 1905 — an originality within the framework of Art Nouveau.

What after all is it that startles one in these façades as one comes upon them unprepared in the Paseo de Gracia (264, 265)? A whole façade in a slow, sluggish and somewhat menacing flow — like lava, some people have said, like washed out by the sea, say others, like the face of a long disused quarry, yet others. So here is undulation, and here is the affinity with nature ' structurized ', as van de Velde once called it. Here also — and this needs saying now at last — is that disregard for functional advantages that did such disservice to Art Nouveau in buildings and furnishings everywhere. Balcony railings which stab at you and consistently curved walls against which no one's furniture will stand satisfactorily are only two examples. What elevates these two late Gaudí buildings above those of other architects of the same moment is their restless force, their sense of masses in motion and their extraneousness. The plan of the Casa Milá to which reference has already been made is ultimate proof that Art Nouveau principles could be applied to space as well as line and volume.

The placing of Gaudí within European Art Nouveau is relatively easy as long as one confines oneself to his work after 1903. But three years earlier he had started on the Güell Park and five years earlier on the chapel of Santa Coloma de Cervelló on an an industrial estate also belonging to his patron Eusebio Güell (263). In the chapel there are no undulating lines; all is sharp, angular, aggressive. But all is also in its own idiom as unexpected as the houses in the Paseo de Gracia. If one looks for comparisons one is reminded rather of German Expressionism of the nineteen-twenties — in its wildest Dr Caligari dreams — than of Art Nouveau. As far as Art Nouveau was opposition to the past and opposition to the order of right angles, Santa Coloma of course qualifies. As far as Art Nouveau was a challenging show of individualism, it also qualifies. And that is perhaps enough. The little building, abandoned before it was completed, is in its interpenetration of outer and inner spaces bolder than anything Frank Lloyd Wright had done or was ever to do in pursuit of spatial confluence. The walls are a seemingly arbitrary zigzag, though an axiality from entrance to altar is preserved. But the approach is wholly asymmetrical, and even the round piers inside do not correspond left with right. Moreover, supports are set at raking angles, they are built up here of brick, there of stones; they are roughly shaped or frankly shapeless, and they carry ribs whose details seem to have been decided not at the office, beforehand, but on the spot, as work went on.

This is indeed true of the very similar structures connected with the Güell Park as well (44). Here also you find twisted supports set diagonally, fairly normal Doric columns but leaning, stalactite vaults, quite apart from the dead trees of concrete, and quite apart from the enchanting back of the long seat running all along the open space at the top where nannies sit and children play (XLIX, L). This back, writhing and drooping like a serpent or some antediluvian monster, is yet gay, by virtue of its delicious colours, bright, happy colours, any number of them and in haphazard relations. The seat is faced with faience and tiles, and here as well as on the roofs of his houses and indeed on the pinnacles of his great church, the *Sagrada Familia* (266), broken cups and saucers, broken floor tiles and wall tiles and chips of all kinds are used. Again Gaudí is closer to Picasso there than to the other practitioners of Art Nouveau.

The *Sagrada Familia* spans Gaudí's whole life. He dedicated his powers more and more to it and in the end to the exclusion of anything else. For Gaudí was an unquestioning Catholic. Religion was the centre of his life, and the aestheticism of much of Art Nouveau experimenting is totally absent in him. In 1887 he was put in charge of a neo-Gothic building only just begun. He continued it in that style and gradually turned freer and bolder. As one looks at the great façade of the south transept, one can watch the process of liberation. Below there are still three tall gabled portals on the French Gothic cathedral pattern, and it is only the decoration encrusting it that is transformed into rockery and naturalistic leaf-work. The towers are without precedent whatever, but they were only started in 1903. And for the pinnacles, once again, it seems impossible to believe that they are the work of craftsmen working from architect's drawings.

Gaudí was not an architect in the sense in which the profession had established itself in the nineteenth century and was going to be run in the twentieth. He was not a professional man working in an office. He was essentially still the medieval craftsman whose final decision could only be taken as he watched over the execution of what he had perhaps sketched out on paper but never made final. In him one ideal of William Morris had come true. What he built was ' by the people for the people ' and no doubt ' a joy for the maker ', i.e. the actual mason as well. It is of importance to say that; for recently Gaudí has been hailed as a pioneer of twentieth century structure, a forerunner of Nervi. But whereas, in the field of new shapes and materials he points forward indeed, his use of complicated models to experiment with strains and stresses is not that of the engineer-architect of our age at all. On the contrary, it is still that of the individualist-craftsman, the outsider, the lonely, do-it-yourself inventor.

And in this extreme individualism once again Gaudí was part of Art Nouveau. For Art Nouveau was an outbreak of of individualism first and foremost. It depended for success entirely on the personal force and sensibility of a designer or craftsman. What could be communicated of it, is what ruined it so quickly. The style of Schinkel, the style of Semper, the style of Pearson, the style of the École des Beaux-Arts could be taught and used with impunity by the rank and file. Commercialized van de Velde and Tiffany is a disaster. Commercialized Gaudí was hardly attempted. This individualism ties Art Nouveau to the century at whose end it stands. So does its insistence on craft and its antipathy against industry. So finally does its delight in the precious or at least the telling material.

But Art Nouveau straddles the boundary line between the two centuries, and its historical significance lies in those of its innovations which pointed forward. They are, as has been said in these pages more than once, its refusal to continue with the historicism of the nineteenth century, its courage in trusting its own inventiveness, and its concern with objects rather than with paintings and statues.

It is in this latter way that Art Nouveau was most decisively inspired by England. The message of William Morris was heeded everywhere. In other ways the relations between the English and the Continental developments of the 1890s are more complex. They deserve more than one close look. The situation, it must be remembered, was that in the 1880s Morris's art of design had reached its richest, most balanced maturity. A synthesis between nature and stylization was

244

XL
René WIENER
Portfolio for engravings
(1894)

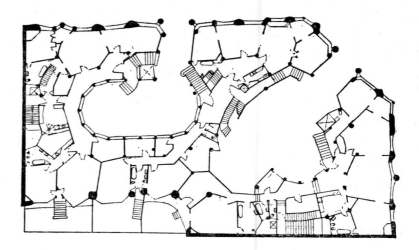

Antonio GAUDÍ, *Plan of the Casa Milá* (begun 1905)

achieved which has never been outdone. At the same time in architecture Webb and Shaw had, at least in the field of domestic building, defeated Victorian pomposity and re-introduced a human scale and sensitive or at least telling details. And already before 1890 Morris as well as Shaw and Webb had their successors. The Arts and Crafts Exhibition Society had started and the progressive architectural journals had begun to illustrate the designs of Voysey, of Ernest Newton, Ricardo and others. Meanwhile, however, this Arts and Crafts movement had also benefited from those among the young who wanted to go beyond the enlightened traditionalism of Morris and Shaw. Mackmurdo, as we have seen, was their leader, and Mackmurdo with his Wren title-page of 1883 had started Art Nouveau. The effect of the journal of his Century Guild, the *Hobby Horse*, had been great, and English book art right on to Beardsley was indebted to it. But where Continental Art Nouveau of the 1890s acknowledged this debt freely and developed its own national versions out of English precedent, England itself turned away from it and followed Morris and Shaw rather than Art Nouveau.

Indeed, and this is perhaps the most surprising aspect of Mackmurdo's situation, he himself, when it came to designing buildings and furniture did not apply the sinuosity of his book-work and textiles. The often-illustrated early chair which some regard — without sufficient evidence — as designed in 1881 [1] has, apart from ornament directly connected with that of the Wren title-page, at least a curvaceous back, but the little desk of 1886 (278) and the exhibition stand at Liverpool of the same year are entirely rational and rectangular. It is true they are in their own way as original as the proto-Art Nouveau of a few years before, but their originality is their slender square posts and the curious far-projecting hats or pieces of cornice each of them carries.

This motif in particular influenced Voysey and Mackintosh in their beginnings, and Voysey was also strongly influenced by Mackmurdo in his early textile designs. Charles F. Annesley Voysey must be regarded as the central figure in English architecture and design during the two decades around 1900. His style of domestic architecture was complete by 1890. In 1891 he built a small studio house in West Kensington (280), and there already are the low, comfortable, spreading character, the bands of unmoulded window openings and of bare wall, the big, tapering chimneystacks. There is no longer even as much of period details as there had been in Shaw and Webb, but there remains all the same a strong period flavour, a flavour of the Tudor or Stuart cottage or manor house. The house is in its own way as original as Morris's designs, but hardly more original. In the late nineties and shortly after 1900 Voysey was extremely successful as a designer of private houses of moderate size (279, 281), and for good reasons; for his plans are easy and at the same time his houses fit their setting, and their simple geometry was refreshing; they were eminently reasonable, unradical and unexacting.

Others in England at the same moment were bolder, none more so than E.S. Prior, W.R. Lethaby, and the much younger Edwin Lutyens. Prior, more distinguished as a scholar than as an architect, built a few houses (282) between about 1895 and 1905 which combine Voysey's sixteenth or seventeenth century sympathy with a fanatic use of mixed local materials.

---

[1] The only evidence is a caption in *The Studio* of 1899, and their are intrinsic reasons against too early a date.

Occasionally the bits of brick and the pebbles used in the raw are almost reminiscent of Gaudí. Lutyens was a man of brilliant talents who later turned away from the progressive developments and led the retreat into the grand manner which Shaw himself had started in his buildings after 1890. This neo-Baroque or neo-neo-Classicism need not concern us here. It reigned in official architecture nearly everywhere. Such public buildings as Nyrop's Town Hall at Copenhagen, begun in 1893, and Berlage's Exchange of Amsterdam of 1898 are highly exceptional in their free handling of traditional materials, and Nyrop at least stayed on safer ground even than Voysey. Of Lutyens' talents and his temptations into drama the finest show is Tigbourne Court of 1897 (283). At least as dramatic, but without any of Lutyens' playfulness is W.R. Lethaby's church at Brockhampton of 1900-02 (284). Lethaby, after Morris the most constructive thinker on architecture and design in England, gave up practising altogether after Brockhampton in order to teach at the London Central School of Arts and Crafts which was the most progressive school of those years anywhere. Lethaby in his writings recommended the step from craft to industrial design, a step which Voysey and others already had taken as practising designers. But only Lethaby in England saw that more was concerned than a matter of production techniques. A style for industrial design was visualized by Lethaby but it was developed in practice in other countries. As far as the style is concerned, it mattered little whether what Voysey designed was in the end made by the craftsman or the manufacturer (285, 286). The style is moderate, sensible, always graceful, whether in furniture or in textiles or in metalwork.

The same applies to other architects, designers and craftsmen. A chair such as that made by Baillie Scott for the Grand Duke of Hesse in 1898 is a good example, also in the design of the covering of the back which has abandoned the Art Nouveau's way of Mackmurdo while keeping the sense of the pretty flat pattern. Another example is the exquisite cabinets designed by Ernest Gimson. They also are in no demonstrative way novel, yet in no way imitative, and they are a triumph of revived craftsmanship. However, the cabinet illustrated (288) dates from 1908, and by then, on the Continent, had lost all topicality. Gimson was trained as an architect and designed a few houses before he turned entirely to the crafts. The combination is characteristic of Britain at this moment. On the Continent, in terms of Art Nouveau, it was the painters rather who listened to Morris. In Britain the message could be heard by the architects, because already at the Webb - Shaw stage the alliance with the Morris Movement had been established. One of the more interesting cases is that of C.R. Ashbee who designed houses of considerable originality, though obviously inspired by Shaw, and founded a Guild and School of Handicraft having learned the Morris lesson. The school operated at first in the East End of London, later in a small town in the country; for Ashbee was keenly interested in social reform too. It is worth comparing the work of his craftsmen about 1900 with Continental work at the Paris Exhibition. What appears is that in furniture and metalwork for use (287) Ashbee was entirely on the Voysey side, but in jewellery (291) he comes remarkably close to Art Nouveau — a typically English compromise.

There was no compromise across the border in Scotland, where, suddenly, at the beginning of the 1890s a group of architect-designers sprang up converting what they knew of Voysey and others in England and of work on the Continent too (for The Studio kept readers up-to-date) into an idiom entirely their own, as original as Art Nouveau, as radical too, but never so contorted. Or at least not when they had reached maturity. The leader of the group was Charles Rennie Mackintosh, eleven years younger than Voysey, seventeen years younger than Mackmurdo. In addition there were his wife and her sister — the sisters Macdonald — his brother-in-law McNair, and a few others. The diploma document of Mackintosh, datable to 1893, is contorted indeed. The nearest parallel to these lean, sombre nudes is Toorop in Holland, and their completely abstract bands of hair, their draperies and trees reduced to one leaf (or fruit) on each upward growing branch are entirely Mackintosh's. In the next few years they did other stationery, and the ladies did repoussé work as well (292). Then Mackintosh's great opportunity came. In 1896 he won the competition for a new building for the Glasgow School of Art, and the building was erected in 1897-99. In 1897 The Studio published an illustrated article on the group. In 1900 they exhibited in Vienna, in 1902 in Turin. In 1901 Mackintosh went in for a competition set by a German publisher. What Glasgow was in fact destined to find more resonance on the Continent than in England.

The front of the Glasgow School of Art (289) sets the theme for all that Mackintosh was to do in the next ten or twelve

Arthur H. MACKMURDO, *Exhibition Stand, Liverpool* (1886)

years.   Between 1900 and 1911 he had plenty of work at Glasgow, a number of private houses, a number of tea-rooms (LI), a school, and some interior work.   England however remained closed to him, and from about 1910 his star waned.   He was a fascinating but a difficult, erratic man, and he alienated clients' sympathies in the dour city of Glasgow.   For the last fifteen years of his life he had hardly any commissions.

The front of the School of Art is primarily a wall of large studio windows facing north (289).   They have the English Tudor motif of mullions and transoms, but the mullions and transoms are, like those of Voysey, completely unmoulded. The front would be a functional grid, if it were not for the entrance bay or frontispiece which is placed out of the centre and is a free, asymmetrical composition of elements of the Baroque, of the Scottish baronial past and of the Shaw-Voysey tradition.   The pediment on the first floor belongs to the first, the bare turret to the second, the little oriel windows to the third.   Moreover the functional grid and the sturdiness of the centre are relieved by delightful, very thin metalwork, the area railings, the handrail of the balcony and especially the odd hooks carrying transparent, flower-like balls in front of the upper windows.   Their practical purpose is to hold boards for window-cleaning, but their aesthetic purpose, like that of all the other metalwork is to provide a delicate screen of light and playful forms through which the stronger and sounder rest will be seen (294).   Inside the building also there are transparent screens of slender wooden posts, sudden surprises of relations between forms, especially in the board room (293), where pilasters are treated as an abstract grid of a Mondrian kind below their perfectly harmless Ionic capitals and on the roof (295), where shapes are almost as bold and abstract as Gaudí's and Le Corbusier's at Ronchamp, and there are again the most unexpected curligigs of metal.   Once again in these years did Mackintosh design a building as functional as the School of Art — the Concert Hall for the Glasgow Exhibition of 1901, designed in 1898 (296).   It was to be circular and to hold over 4000 people.   Mackintosh provided for a low building with a saucer dome on mighty buttresses.   The supports were of iron, forming a span of about 165 feet.   The organ, the artists' rooms and services were in an attachment with polygonal walls and curved parapets and roof.   The design gained no prize.

While the building was severely plain, the organ-case would have had all the finesses and surprises of Mackintosh's furniture design.   What characterizes all Mackintosh furniture can be said to be a successful synthesis of the contrasting criteria of England and the Continent.   Take, for example the two tables illustrated (298, 299), one is as square as Voysey and indeed more rigidly so — as close in its grid as a cage —, the second is oval, with two small oval set-in rose and ivory panels of abstract curves.   Moreover, the first table has a black finish, the second a glossy white one, and white and rose, white and lilac, with black, and perhaps silver and mother-of-pearl became Mackintosh's favourite colours.   These sophisticated, precious colours go to perfection with the sophistication of his slender uprights and shallow curves. But the radicalism of ornamental abstraction and the lyrical softnessof the colours also contradict each other, and it is the tension between the sensuous and the structural elements that makes Mackintosh's decoration unique.   But as one looks at some of the most remarkable chairs (297, 300) by Mackintosh, one's conviction might well be shaken that his

247

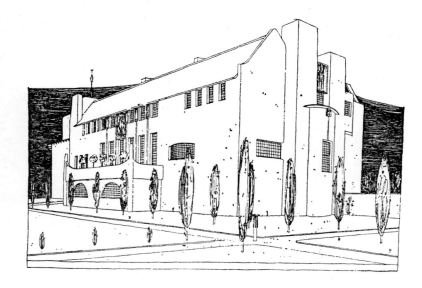

Charles Rennie MACKINTOSH, *House of an Art-Lover* (1901)

use of grids is indeed structural — in the sense of the skyscraper grids. The hard verticals and horizontals must have been an attraction to Mackintosh in themselves, an aesthetic counterpoint to his tense curves, and a safeguard for the frail blooms and feminine hues not to cloy.

Mackintosh's fame was greater on the Continent than in Britain, let alone in England. The exhibition of 1900 in Vienna, the competition of 1901 in Germany where he was placed second — Baillie Scott won first prize — and the exhibition of 1902 in Turin have already been mentioned. What made it possible for the Continent to admire him was precisely what deprived him of patronage in England. He was too Art Nouveau, and England, after the few years of her Art Nouveau *avant la lettre* had, as we have seen, turned away from everything *outré*. Indeed, when in 1900 some mostly French Art Nouveau furniture had been acquired from the Paris exhibition by a private donation for the Victoria and Albert Museum, protests were published in the press — one of them signed by E.S. Prior, saying that ' this work is neither right in principle nor does it evince a proper regard for the material employed ' [1]. Those who protested were of course right within their own terms of reference. They were also right from the point of view of the arising twentieth century. Art Nouveau can only be appreciated on purely aesthetic grounds — and its products might well be called unprincipled. But looked at on aesthetic grounds, if one were ready to do so, as they were in Austria and Germany, what a find the Glasgow group was. Vienna was particularly responsive, because Vienna in 1900 was, on her own, already on the way to a straightening out of the Art Nouveau fancies. Joseph Olbrich's building of 1898 for the Sezession, the club of young artists in opposition, proves that. While it has a wrought-iron dome the intertwined laurel-branches of which are Art Nouveau, the dome also is a pure hemisphere, and the walls are sheer. What the same Sezession then showed of Mackintosh's work was a confirmation and made converts — none more successful than Josef Hoffmann. *Quadrat*-Hoffmann became his nickname, because of his preference for squares and rectangles in his decoration. Olbrich was called to Darmstadt by the Grand Duke of Hesse in 1899. The Grand Duke, a grandson of Queen Victoria, commissioned furniture and interior decoration for his palace from Ashbee and Baillie Scott. The German publishing house which had set the competition for the house of an art lover and which published Mackintosh's design was also in Darmstadt. Looking at Mackintosh's designs one can understand why he took Germany and Austria by storm. Here was the wilfulness and irregularity of Art Nouveau handled with an exquisite finesse as yet unknown anywhere. But here was also a sense of slender, erect verticals and smooth, unbroken surfaces which might well serve as a weapon to defeat Art Nouveau. Adherents of Art Nouveau and the just-emerging opponents against it could replenish their arsenals from the *Haus eines Kunstfreundes*.

The ubiquity and intensity of English influence on the Continent during these years is evident. Its contradictory directions,

---

[1] Quoted from MADSEN, *loc. cit.* 300. The pieces are now in the Bethnal Green Museum and are as follows: by Gallé a tray, a work-table, a screen and a commode, by Majorelle three cabinets, a tea-table, an armchair and and two trays, by Gaillard a chair, by Christiansen a stool, by A. Darras three chairs, by Pérol Frères a wardrobe, a bedstead and a commode, by E. Baguès a writing-table, an armchair, a chair and a stool, by Jallot a chair, and in addition panelling and settle by the Germans J.J. Graf and Spindler and a chair designed by Eckmann for Bing.

however, require some comment. The influence started with Morris and the Domestic Revival. It stood then for a revived interest in craft, i.e., the provision of objects for use, and for an appreciation of the modest, comfortable, middle-class house as against the pomposity of the public building and the rich man's villa. Then came the influence of Morris's Kelmscott Press on the one hand — which meant again a sense of aesthetic responsibility, this time in the art of the book — and of Mackmurdo and ultimately Beardsley on the other, and this encouraged Art Nouveau rather than responsibility. Voysey again stood for reason, domestic comfort and prettiness in the design of interior furnishings; Ashbee and Baillie Scott a little more floridly for the same. Mackintosh alone, to say it once more, could be a witness for the defence and for the prosecution of Art Nouveau, for the defence and the prosecution of Anti-Art-Nouveau. Olbrich in an essay published

Josef HOFFMAN
Design for an interior
(1900)

in 1901 [1] defended Art Nouveau against England: ' It is only if one can feel both democratically and autocratically, that one can evaluate the imaginative craftsman who wants to express in decorative art more than mere utility. One may then even approach the question which no one now ventures to touch: which forces are more valuable for a nation, those which evolve rationally, consciously and intellectually good forms ... or those which create in the abundant plenitude of their inventiveness hundreds of new shapes and visions, each carrying the germs of new possibilities ... The limit to which one may advance in expressiveness without getting aesthetically objectionable becomes confused ... must lie at different levels for different natures and must affect different natures differently... Just as it is not given to the Englishman to utter such a wealth of feelings as the German soul has pronounced them in the untold variety of its music, so the English

[1] *Zweckmässig oder phantasievoll?*, quoted from H. SELING and others: *Jugendstil*, Heidelberg and Munich, 1959, pp. 417-418.

Peter BEHRENS
AEG Catalogue
(1908)

race cannot ornamentally and constructively express itself with force, violence, agitation, fantasy ».   But others, several years earlier already praised England for these very limitations.   This is what Edmond de Goncourt meant in 1896 when he called the new style Yachting Style.   This is why, in the same year, *Pan*, the lavish only just established journal for modern art and decoration in Germany, brought out an article on English Art in the House, and this is what made Adolf Loos say that ' the centre of European civilization is at present in London ' [1] and what made the Prussian Board of Trade send Hermann Muthesius to England to stay there for several years and study English architecture and design.

Vienna was first on the Continent in returning to the straight path of the straight line and the square and rectangle and, being Vienna, succeeded in preserving the elegance and the sense of precious materials of Art Nouveau.   In Germany the change is principally connected with the names of Riemerschmid and Peter Behrens, and while the change in Austria was an aesthetic one entirely, in Germany it was also social.   Riemerschmid and his brother-in-law, Karl Schmidt, the founder of the *Deutsche Werkstätte*, as early as 1899 began to tackle the problem of cheap furniture (302) and in 1905 at an exhibition showed their first machine-made furniture, designed, they said, ' from the spirit of the machine '. Behrens, who had belonged to the colony of artists at Darmstadt, abandoned the curve about 1904 and turned to cubic shapes and square decoration, as they had done in Vienna, but with greater severity.   A few years later he was given the opportunity by the A. E. G., the German electricity combine, of concentrating for a time entirely on factory architecture and industrial design.   But already in 1898 he had designed glass for quantity production (303).

In France the revolt against Art Nouveau took yet another form.   It centred on the conquest of the new materials by new architects.   The triumphs of steel architecture at the exhibition of 1889 had still been the triumphs of engineers, even if the Eiffel Tower (304) by its very height and position became at once one of the chief constituents of the architectural scene of Paris.   Being a monument and not a work of utility such as the grandest of the exhibition halls and bridges — Eiffel's own Garabit Viaduct of 1880-88 (42) with a span of 543 feet, the two Roeblings' Brooklyn Bridge of 1867-83 with a span of 1595 feet, Fowler and Baker's Firth of Forth Bridge of 1881-87 (43) with a span of 1710 feet, the first an arch bridge, the second a suspension bridge, the third a cantilever bridge — the Eiffel Tower had more chance to be looked at by layman and architect alike as a piece of design with aesthetic connotations, i.e. as architecture.   Indeed Muthesius, the Prussian architect whose studies in England have been mentioned, listed in a book of 1902, called characteristically *Stilarchitektur und Baukunst*, the Crystal Palace, the Bibliothèque Ste-Geneviève, the Halle

---

[1] *Ins Leere gesprochen*, 1897-1900, Innsbruck, 1932, p. 18.

des Machines and the Eiffel Tower as examples of the right kind of architecture for the twentieth century. In 1913 in an article he added to his list train-sheds and grain elevators [1].

Train-sheds were of steel and glass, but grain elevators were of concrete. France had led the world in the aesthetic appreciation of iron — the part played by Labrouste and Viollet-le-Duc has been discussed — she was now going to lead in that of concrete. The first concrete fanatic of many to come was François Coignet. He wrote at the time of the exhibition of 1855 that 'cement, concrete and iron' would replace stone and the year after took a patent for iron members in concrete — not the first such patent incidentally — in which they are called *tirants*, i.e. in which their tensile strength of mass concrete was appreciated. In the seventies Joseph Monier worked on posts and beams of reinforced concrete and Americans and Germans made the necessary analyses and calculations on the perform-ance of the two materials in conjunction. Finally, in the nineties François Hennebique built factories of concrete and steel reinforcements on the utilitarian grid principle. The factory illustrated here is of 1895 (306). In 1894 already Ana-tole de Baudot, a pupil first of Labrouste, then of Viollet-le-Duc, and their true follower in the sense that he followed their principles rather than their forms, decided to use concrete for his church of St-Jean de Montmartre and not to conceal it (305). There are pointed as well as round arches and rib vaults. The internal character is Gothic, the exterior only vestigi-ally medieval.

While Baudot's church was still incomplete, in 1902, Auguste Perret, thirty years younger, designed the celebrated house in the rue Fran-klin (307, 308). It has many titles to fame. It is the first private house to use concrete framing. It demonstrates this fact proudly, even if the concrete posts and beams are still clad in terracotta, it distinguishes with care between the appearance of supporting members and infilling panels — the latter are in lively Art Nou-veau leaf patterns of faience —, it opens the façade in a U-shape to avoid a backyard, and it faces its staircase entirely with glass hexa-gons, proclaiming in this its indebteness to Guimard's Castel Béran-ger. In 1905 in his garage in the rue de Ponthieu Perret exposed his concrete skeletons naked; in 1911 in the Théâtre des Champs-Élysées he intoduced the concrete skeleton into public architecture. To the end, however, he refused to test concrete for its pos-sibilities of wide cantilevers and curved surfaces in tension. This was left to others, one French by nation, the other at least by race and name.

Tony Garnier was a few years older than Perret. He won the Prix de Rome in 1899, but used most of his time there to develop the plan and the architecture of an ideal industrial town (IV). The result was sent to the academy in 1901, but at first refused. It was exhibited in 1904 and published — not without revisions — in 1917. Meanwhile, in 1905, Édouard Herriot, a socialist like Garnier, and at the time mayor of Lyons, had appointed Garnier city architect of the town. This gave him the opportunity of realising some of his ideas. What makes the *Cité Industrielle* a milestone in the history of the early twentieth century is that here for the first time a young architect took as his theme the needs of a town of today; 'car

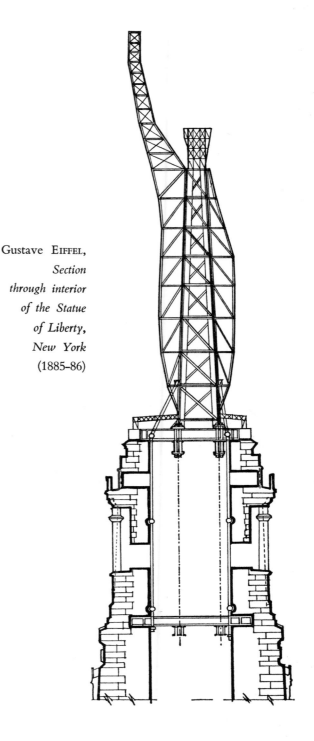

Gustave EIFFEL,
*Section
through interior
of the Statue
of Liberty,
New York
(1885-86)*

---

[1] *Stilarchitektur...*, pp. 42-43; *Jahrbuch des Deutschen Werkbundes*, 1913, p. 30.

c'est à des raisons industrielles', he stated in the Introduction, 'que la plupart des villes neuves que l'on fondera désormais, vaudront leur fondation'. The plan is developed on a possible site, somewhere, Garnier says, in the south east of France, his own homeland. The town is to have 35,000 inhabitants. The plan refuses to have anything to do with academic tenets of axiality but to work in the interests of those who would live and work in the town. Planners sixty years later may raise their objections; the plan yet remains pioneer work. The houses have no backyards. Each house has at least one bedroom window to the south. The built-over area does not exceed half the plot. The rest is public green-spaces. There are plenty of pedestrian passages. The materials used are cement for foundations, reinforced concrete for beams and ceilings. 'Tous les édifices importants sont presque exclusivement bâtis en ciment armé'. This one sees at once; the cantilevered roofs of his Municipal Offices and his station would be impossible otherwise and go far beyond what had at the time been executed. The cubic shapes of the small houses were as revolutionary. Decoration is not banished but remains « totalement indépendant de la construction ». Garnier never had an opportunity to realise anything as bold and sweeping as the *Cité Industrielle*, but in the Public Slaughterhouse at Lyons, built in 1909-13 (309), he did demonstrate dignity in industrial architecture, and he was one of the very few anywhere in the world to do so. We shall return presently to successes in this field in Germany. But first the story of reinforced concrete must be rounded off by reference to the discovery of the new combined material's structural and aesthetic advantages in the field of arcuated as well as trabeated architecture. Here the first in the field was once more an engineer: Robert Maillart, a Swiss, but a pupil of Hennebique. He first suggested and carried out improvements on the current system of warehouse or factory construction with posts and beams of concrete by making one the formerly supporting and supported parts. The mushroom principle he evolved was at the same

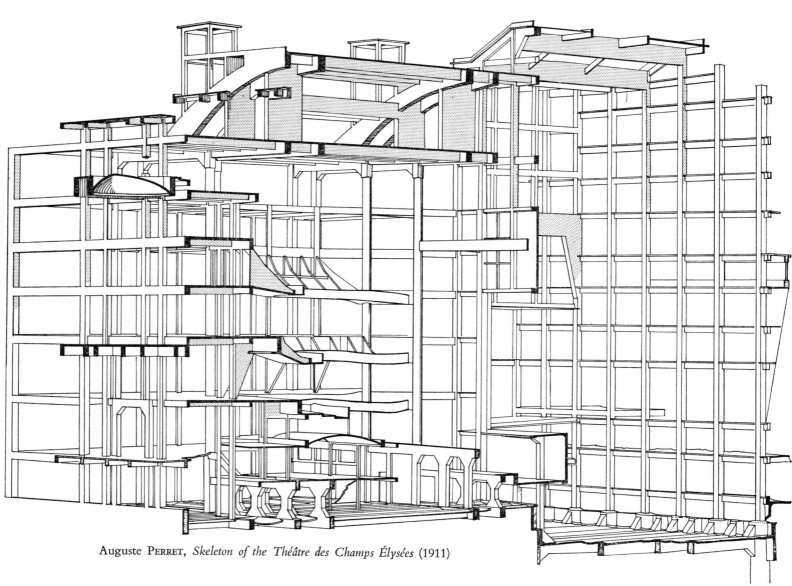

Auguste PERRET, *Skeleton of the Théâtre des Champs Élysées* (1911)

Tony GARNIER, *Industrial City* (1901-1904)

time discovered in America.   Soon after he turned to bridges (310) and again succeeded in making the arch and the road-way one.   In France at the same moment, or to be precise in 1910, Simon Boussiron, another engineer, built the roof of the railway station of Bercy near Paris of very thin parabolic concrete vaults' [1].   But the aesthetic possibil-ities of using arches combining the long sweep of steel with the solidity of stone in architecture, acknowledged by the public as such, were first recognized to the full by Max Berg in his Centenary Hall of 1913 at Breslau (311).   Max Berg is not as well known as he deserves.   This is largely due to the fact that already before 1925 he abandoned archi-tecture to devote himself to a Christian mysticism.   And who can say whether Lothar Schreyer of both *Sturm* and *Bauhaus* who tells us about this is so wrong in seeing even in the Centenary Hall ' the Cosmos opened to reveal the of the order courses of the stars and the Empyraeum ' [2].

The famous names in the Germany and Austria of Perret's, Garnier's and Maillart's generation are Josef Hoffmann and Adolf Loos in Austria, Peter Behrens in Germany.   To them must be added Otto Wagner, professor at the academy of art in Vienna, in age only seven years younger than Morris.   In his inaugural lecture, in 1894, he reiterated Viollet-le-Duc's faith in the modern age, the need to find forms to express it, and the conviction that ' nothing that is not practical can be beautiful ' [3].   His buildings of those years were less radical.   His stations of the Stadtbahn of 1894-1901 (46) are in a kind of Baroque Art Nouveau, emphatically less stimulating than Guimard's Métro which they preceeded (45), and his office buildings and flats are simple, but in their fenestration not untraditional.   The favourite facing with faience reminds one of Perret.   Only one of all Wagner's works has the prophetic character which we found for the first time in Garnier's *Cité Industrielle*: the interior of the Postal Savings Bank of 1905 (49), with its tapering metal supports and its cur-ved glass roof.

In speaking of prophetic character here, one is perhaps not quite right.   The buildings of the *Cité Industrielle* and the Postal Savings Bank are not prophetic of the twentieth century: they belong to it, i.e. they contributed to its creation, out of the new materials and their authentically integrated use, out of the anti-historicism of Art Nouveau and out of William Morris's faith in serving people's needs.   The buildings designed in the same years by Josef Hoffmann and Adolf Loos must be looked at in the same way.   Hoffmann's Palais Stoclet (312-314) in Brussels demonstrated once and for all that the new style with its reliance on unmitigated right angles was as suitable for luxury as for pure function, for leisure as for work.   The secret, if you are bent on banishing ornament, mouldings, curves altogether, is fine materials and the play of proportions.   The latter determines the varied and lively exterior of the Palais Stoclet, the former the interior with its marble facings and its large mosaics by Klimt (LII).   The mosaic is flat decoration, Klimt's scrolly trees and figures are

[1] See C.S. WHITNEY in *Journal of the Concrete Institute*, Vol. 49, 1953, p. 524.   I asked M. J.B. ACHE for documentation on this in French journals, but he knew of none.
[2] *Erinnerungen an Sturm und Bauhaus*, Munich 1956, p. 154.
[3] *Moderne Architektur*, Vienna 1896, p. 41.

exquisitely flattened, and their perfect suitability to Hoffmann's ensemble shows once more the part Art Nouveau could play in the creation of the twentieth century style.

Adolf Loos hated Hoffmann and the Wiener Werkstätte of which Hoffmann was one of the founders and which succeeded in combining the new, post-Art-Nouveau style with an inimitably Viennese daintiness and prettiness. For the initial patron of the Werkstätte, the man who had put the necessary money at the disposal of the founder, Mackintosh had designed a music room. Loos was the purist of the emerging movement. *Ornament and Crime* is the title of his most often quoted essay. This was published in 1908. The purest of his purist houses and therefore the most often illustrated is the Steiner House in Vienna of 1910 (315). Here for the first time the layman would find it hard to decide whether this might not be of 1939.

The greatest contribution of Germany during these years was the foundation of the Deutscher Werkbund in 1907, the society in which architects, craftsmen and manufacturers met and in which the new conception of industrial design was evolved, a conception whose origin in England — in spite of all the conflicts between Morris's faith in craft and the new equally enthusiastic faith in the machine — is made patent by the fact that the term *design* had in the end to be taken over by Germany — because of the absence of a German word with the same meaning. An appreciation of the machine and its possibilities was not in itself new, and a kind of aesthetic worship of the machine can be found here and there in all countries and in all decades of the nineteenth century. As early as 1835 in a parliamentary enquiry in England into the relation between qualities of design and Britain's exports the neo-classical architect T. L. Donaldson had said that he knew no ' example of a perfect machine which is not at the same time beautiful ' [1]. Redgrave, one of Henry Cole's circle, in his report on design at the 1851 exhibition, had similarly written that in objects ' where use is so paramount that ornament is repudiated ... a noble simplicity is the result' [2]. And so it goes on to Oscar Wilde, the aesthete: ' All machinery may be beautiful ... Do not seek to decorate it ' [3]. But it was still a far step from Wilde's purely aesthetic reaction and the Cole circle's recognition of the problem on paper to its final facing and solving by the Werkbund.

The Werkbund published year-books in the years 1912-15, and they contain the record of what was achieved. I illustrate at random: a tea-set (318) by Riemerschmid for the Deutsche Werkstätte — the pioneer role of this architect and this firm has already been mentioned —, linoleum by Riemerschmid for the Delmenhorst Linoleum factory (317), electric tea kettles by Behrens for the A.E.G. (320). The case of Behrens is the most significant in Europe at that moment. The Allgemeine Elektrizitätsgesellschaft or A.E.G. under its director Paul Jordan took up the new Werkbund principles in earnest and made Behrens the architect of their buildings (319), factories, as well as shops, the designer of their products (321) and even their stationery. Behrens was the first of the line that leads to the present-day American stylists or Gio Ponti and Arne Jacobsen. But his buildings seen purely as architecture are as important. What Garnier was doing at Lyons, Behrens did in Berlin, and his expression of the nobility of work is even purer, and more detached from motifs of the past, than Garnier's.

The final synthesis of all that had been developed in industrial architecture up-to-date is the Fagus factory for shoe-trees at Alfeld on the Leine (327) which was designed by the much younger Walter Gropius, pupil of Behrens, in collaboration with Adolf Meyer, in 1910, the very year of Loos's Steiner House. The two buildings have this in common: a ruthlessly cubic shape and the total absence of ornament. But Gropius dealt with a novel job, Loos with an old one, and Gropius courageously picked up the threads of the existing, utilitarian essentially anonymous architecture of glass set in a structural frame, such as they were to illustrate it in the Werkbund Year Book of 1913. And he imbued it with the nobility he had seen in Behrens' factories and a social awareness ultimately derived from the Morris Movement.

The illustrations just referred to accompanied an article by Gropius on the development of modern industrial architecture.

---

[1] *Reports from Committees*, 1836, IX, pp. 29 etc.
[2] *Supplementary Report on Design*, p. 708.
[3] *Essays and Lectures*, 4th ed., 1913, p. 178. The lecture was given in 1882.

In the Werkbund Year Books other articles were by Riemerschmid, by Behrens and also by Muthesius who more than any other was responsible for leading the Werkbund in the twentieth century direction. He had to fight his case against the opposition of van de Velde who pleaded for individual expression where Muthesius wanted to develop standards. Muthesius in the famous discussion at Cologne in 1914 said: ' Architecture and with it the whole area of activity of the Werkbund moves towards standardisation (*Typisierung*) ... Only standardisation ... can once again introduce a universally valid, self-certain taste '. Van de Velde answered : ' As long as there are artists in the Werkbund ... they are going to protest against any suggestion of a canon of standardisation. The artist, according to his innermost essence, is a fervent individualist, a free, spontaneous creator. He will never voluntarily submit to a discipline forcing on him a type, a canon '. It must have been a memorable moment — Art Nouveau at its best resisting the needs and declining the responsibilities of the new century.

In fact the victory of Muthesius was assured even before the Cologne meeting. The meeting was held apropos the first Werkbund exhibition, and this exhibition, at least in its most important buildings, actually demonstrated that victory and would have demonstrated it internationally if the outbreak of the First World War had not disrupted European unity and held up cultural progress. Among the buildings, Behren's Festival Hall was disappointingly classical, Hoffmann's Austrian pavilion equally classical outside but inside had a playfulness which was as backward-pointing as was Van de Velde's impressive theatre with its emphatic curves. The two most powerful buildings were the Glass House by Bruno Taut (316) and Gropius's *Halle des Machines* and attached offices of a fictitious factory. Taut's prismatic dome was the most original shape in the exhibition, a prophecy of geodesic domes to come. The glass wall below is in the line of descent of Guimard and Perret. Gropius at this moment was clearly influenced, not only by Behrens but even more by Frank Lloyd Wright whose work had been made known to Europe first by two publications issued in Berlin in 1910 and 1911 and then by lectures of Berlage's who had himself visited Chicago in 1911.

The Chicago to which he made his pilgrimage was however no longer that of Sullivan, though Sullivan was still alive. After the completion of the Carson, Pirie & Scott store, he received no further commissions of importance and died lonely and disappointed in 1922. When at the great Chicago Exhibition of 1893 the classicism of Beaux-Arts derivation had triumphed, he had prophesied that this would put back architecture in America by fifty years. He was nearly right. The so called School of Chicago fizzled out during the last years before the First World War, and though something equally influential took its place, it was not of the calibre of the work of the School of Chicago. What had been work in new materials and for new purposes was replaced by work — admittedly aesthetically brilliant — in the limited field of the private house.

Yet Frank Lloyd Wright's is not entirely an aesthetic achievement. What it consisted of is easily said: a new vision of the house embedded in its natural surroundings and opening towards them by means of terraces and cantilevered roofs, and a new vision of the interior of the house as freely intercommunicating spaces. As a way of life there was precedent for both these things in American domestic building before him; as an aesthetic experience they belong to him entirely and by their influence from 1910 onwards they established new ideals for Europe as well. The operative dates are these : the Charnley House of 1891, severely cubic but closed; the Winslow House of 1893 with far oversailing eaves but still closed; the Studio, Oak Park of 1895, the first with a complex interlocked plan, and so to the watershed of 1900-01 when the type was fairly established and to the maturity of the Martin House at Buffalo of 1906 (328) and the Coonley and the Robie Houses of 1907-09.

As has already been said, 1910 saw the first publication of Wright's work in Europe, 1914 Gropius's Wright-inspired office range of the exhibition factory at Cologne, 1915 Rob van't Hoff building a complete Wright house in Holland. But Holland very soon abandoned Wright's message and developed Wright's forms in a new spirit. It was the spirit of Cubism. Wright's forms were sufficiently cubic to allow for such a change of meaning. *De Stijl*, the carrier of this transformation, was started in 1917, and its achievements and repercussions are outside the bounds of this book. Its most significant architectural expression at the beginning is Oud's design for seaside housing at Scheveningen, still as simple in the block shapes of the elements as Garnier's in his industrial city. Then almost immediately unfunctional complications were introduced to indicate aesthetically the interaction of planes. Interaction of planes is also the basic aesthetic conception behind Rietveld's famous chair of 1917 (323). It is more ingenious and was more stimulating than his own earlier work, but a chair he did nine years earlier, when he was only twenty, has a *Sachlichkeit* which acquaintance with Cubism could only disturb (322).

Germany in the first years of the Werkbund was indeed not alone in seeking simplicity and functional form for objects of everyday use. The Dutch contribution started in the first decade of the twentieth century. The Danish contribution started too, and Denmark was to gather strength until some forty years later it had become one of the most important countries in the world in the field of the crafts and industrial design. The furniture and metalwork of Johan Rohde, a painter at first, acquainted with and appreciative of Gauguin, Van Gogh, Toulouse-Lautrec, the Nabis, Toorop, is of great beauty as well as functional soundness. Rohde was led in the direction of design by the Pont-Aven attitude, but realised early that the introduction of figures heavy with symbolic significance was not an answer to the problem of design. His answer is nearer Voysey's, and the cupboard illustrated is as independent of past styles as Voysey at his rare best (326). Rohde's metalwork (324) was largely designed for Georg Jensen, the silversmith and his workshop, and Jensen's own cutlery (325) of the same years shows the identity of approach of the two men.

Of the major nations of Europe only Italy has so far not been mentioned in this survey. Her role during the years here under consideration and up to 1909 has indeed been secondary, in architecture as well as painting and sculpture. Menardo Rosso, it may be argued, mattered internationally, and Sommaruga, D'Aronco, Cattaneo made their *Floreale* in their own way out of elements of the Vienna Sezession and the naturalism of French Art Nouveau. But their message was not essentially different from the message of those who had inspired them. The years 1909-14 changed all that. Futurism is one of the constituent movements of the revolution which established the twentieth century, in aesthetic thought, in painting and in architecture. Without Marinetti, Boccioni, Sant'Elia the early twentieth century cannot be described. In architecture, alas, the outbreak of the war and the premature death of Sant'Elia in 1916, prevented anything being actually built. As in the case of Garnier's *Cité Industrielle* we must go to drawings, to visions of the future. And Sant'Elia's is indeed like Garnier's, a contribution to town planning at least as much as to architecture. In architecture he was the descendant of Vienna and the *Floreale*, though other drawings prove that he was aware of the new rectangularity as well and of specific Parisian work. Henri Sauvage in 1912 in a block of flats, 26 rue Vavin (329), had conceived the idea of improved daylighting in city streets by stepped-back upper stories [1]. Sant'Elia took up the idea (or recreated it?), and later it became part of the zoning law of New York and an internationally accepted principle. It is an urban, indeed metropolitan, principle, and in this lies its importance, as the importance of Futurism to architecture lies in its adherents' passionate commitment to the city.

The city was the most urgent and the most comprehensive problem of the nineteenth century. It had been criminally neglected by the architects, and by governments as well. To cut boulevards through Paris had its traffic advantages and offered plenty of spectacular *points de vue* for the placing of monumental buildings, to open up the glacis of the fortress walls of Vienna, to create a generous ring of gardens and ideal sites for yet larger public buildings was no solution. These urban displays had their aesthetic points — and who does not get a visual thrill out of looking up the Avenue de l'Opéra or the Rue Royale? — but the real problem was the visually unpromising one of housing a population which in London (the area which in 1888 became the County of London), grew between 1801 and 1901 from under a million to nearly four and a half million, and in Manchester from about 100,000 to about 550,000. Equally unpromising visually and equally urgent was the problem of the siting of industry. If architects did not care, manufacturers cared only rarely. But Robert Owen, the socialist manufacturer, designed in 1817 a model village with factory and housing, as Ledoux had done twenty years before, and about 1850 the first manufacturers built more modest versions of such schemes, the largest and most convincing being Sir Titus Salt's Saltaire near Leeds which dates from 1850 to about 1870. The huge mill dominates the streets of the workers' houses which are laid out unimaginatively if acceptably from the purely hygienic point of view. Then came Morris and Norman Shaw, Morris with his fervent sermons of

---

[1] M. J.B. ACHE, in the Catalogue to the Exhibition *Les Sources du XXme siècle*, Paris, 1960, gives the date as 1912. My date is taken from THIEME and BECKER's *Künstlerlexikon*. M. ACHE was unable to state his reasons for preferring 1912 to 1913.

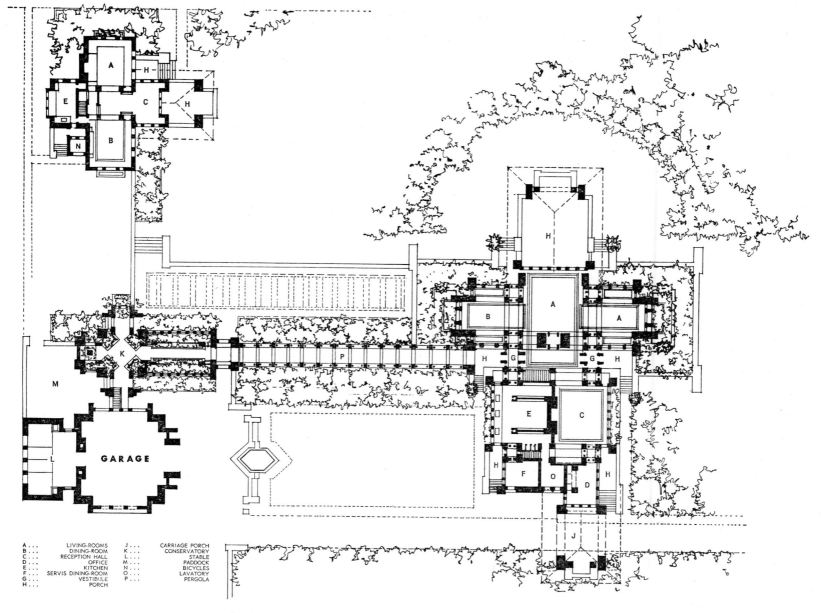

Frank Lloyd Wright, *Plan of the Martin House, Buffalo, U.S.A.* (1903)

happy labour and social duties, Norman Shaw with his pretty houses of moderate size. And so Bedford Park (see p. 234) was built just outside London in 1875 as the first garden suburb. It was for a middle-class with aesthetic leanings, not for the working-class, but its message could be adapted easily. Make your houses friendly, vary their appearance, leave trees on the site. They were all lessons learned at once, and already in 1888 Port Sunlight was begun outside Liverpool for the employees of Lever's, and in 1895, Bournville for the employees of Cadbury's. In these cases, as at Saltaire, the factory was part of the general scheme. This principle was extended and systematized in Ebenezer Howard's *Tomorrow* which came out in 1898 and again as *Garden Cities of Tomorrow* in 1899. Now the word was coined. Let us leave the old cities, vast, dirty, crammed, noisy, and build new ones, to a manageable size and a human scale, and with gardens and spacious parks.

But Howard's was a diagram, the first real garden city Parker and Unwin's Letchworth (330,331), about 35 miles north of London, was started in 1904, but yet in 1931 had no more than 15,000, inhabitants and the Hampstead Garden Suburb (333), started in 1907 and also by Parker and Unwin, was a garden suburb, not a garden city, as was a design by Riemerschmid of 1907 (332) and as was the Krupps' Margarethenhöhe outside Essen of 1912. The message was unmistakable. The garden city, or what we now call the satellite town, the *Trabantenstadt*, is possible, it is a help even, but it is not the final solution. The big city has come to stay, and we must come to terms with it. That is what Tony Garnier was the first to see. The *Cité Industrielle* is a milestone as much as Howard's *Garden Cities* because, as has already been observed, it is the fiction of a real town on a real site, and because its designer is clearly as interested in its industrial and its commercial districts as in its public buildings and houses. Howard's was a social reformer's contribution; Garnier's the potential architect-planner's employed by a government department or a city council; the Futurists' contribution was delirious enthusiasm for exactly that which Howard was running away from.

Here is Marinetti and the Futurist Manifesto of 1909: ' We declare that the splendour of the world has been enriched by a new beauty — the beauty of speed ... A roaring, racing car, rattling past like a machine gun, is more beautiful than the winged Victory of Samothrace ... We will sing of the stirring of great crowds — workers, pleasure seekers, rioters ... We will sing the midnight fervour of shipyards blazing with electric moons ... ' and so on to stations and the smoke of trains, to factories, to bridges, to steamers and finally to aeroplanes. And here is Sant'Elia's *Messaggio* published in the catalogue of his exhibition *Città Nuova* and remodelled by Marinetti to be the Manifesto of Futurist Architecture: ' We must invent and build *ex novo* our modern city like an immense and tumultuous shipyard, active, mobile and everywhere dynamic, and the modern building like a gigantic machine ... Lifts must swarm up the façades like serpents of glass and iron. The house of concrete, iron and glass, without ornament ... brutish in its mechanical simplicity ... must rise from the brink of a tumultous abyss, the street ... gathering up the traffic of the metropolis connected for necessary transfers to metal cat-walks and high-speed conveyor belts. '

Perhaps, in spite of Behrens and Gropius, the new style to win the day needed someone to grow lyrical over it. The Futurists provided that. The Expressionists after the war took it on and dreamed up their first steel and all-glass skyscrapers, and finally, only in the middle of the century, the synthesis of the garden city and the metropolitan city was achieved, and garden cities culminating in urban centres, garden estates for ten thousand, with skyscrapers carefully placed, and office buildings of various grouping and enclosing patio gardens.

With this, architecture has made a contribution to human life as great as architecture ever did. Is the contribution of painting and sculpture on the same level, and are the so-called fine arts of painting and sculpture and the so-called applied arts of architecture and design working towards the same aims, meeting with the same kind and intensity of response? Such it had been in the Middle Ages, such in the Baroque. But that mutual sympathy, that common understanding had not always been a matter of course. The Town Hall of Amsterdam and the *Conspiracy of Claudius Civilis* which Rembrandt painted for it, do not belong together. Those who praised the one would not necessarily praise the other, and if some did they would do it for opposed reasons. Holland in the seventeenth century was a middle-class republic. It was here, that the figure of the misunderstood, the neglected, the starving artist first appeared. Moreover, Holland was a Protestant country and not in need of the visual arts for worship. The second age of the art that mattered being unwelcome was the first middle-class age, the nineteenth century, or rather the nineteenth and the later eighteenth century which belongs to it. Neglect grew into active opposition; art on the other hand in Goya, in Blake, in Runge went into a secret language. If you want to understand the artist, you must entrust yourself to him and work at it; he is no longer going to work for you. Patronage in the old sense was dead; what patronage there was to be was as individual, as exposed as the artist's gospel itself. Isolation, half imposed and half self-imposed, was the fate of the painters of Barbizon, of Courbet, of the Impressionists, of the Post-Impressionists. If anything, the pitch of hostility rose. The social development of architecture was bound to be different. There never can be an architect as isolated as a painter. But while this relative security was a gratifying fact for the architect, it was not for architecture. It meant quite simply that in the nineteenth century the most ruthlessly creative minds did not choose the profession of the architect. This explains to a certain extent the phenomenon of the collapse of aesthetic values in so much of the century. It also explains why it is that the most forward-pointing work so often came from outsiders. The reason why it came from engineers is that the century was one of materialism and hence of science and technology. No century ever before had seen comparable progress in these fields. The progress was made at the expense of aesthetic sensibility of the subtle kind that would have granted acceptance to Impressionism and Post-Impressionism. The Crystal Palace met with success but so also did the horrors of decorative art displayed in it. Architects' architecture and salon or academy art went together, engineers' and altogether explorers' architecture and explorers' art did not.

But this statement is perhaps too abrupt. The roads followed by the best painters, the best craftsmen or manufacturers

258

Antonio SANT'ELIA,
Skyscraper (c. 1914)

and the best architects did occasionally meet. The earliest was the most fruitful meeting; it is that between Morris's preaching and the conversion to craft and design of young painters and young architects. Otherwise meetings were mostly much less significant. One might perhaps just say that the turn to intimacy, the turn away from bombast was of a similar nature in the English Domestic Revival and in Impressionism in painting of the same years. One can perhaps also say that the elegance of façade detail which replaced the grossness and bluster of the High Victorian architects corresponds to the elegance of Impressionist painting as against Courbet's. But that does not take us very far.

It is different with Art Nouveau. Here indeed certain painters were in full accord with the craftsmen-designers. If Art Nouveau is characterized by radical innovation, and by the incantation of the curve, than Gauguin certainly belongs to it — as one of the illustrations to this survey has already demonstrated — and so do the Northerners Munch and Toorop and Hodler, and to a more limited degree Maurice Denis, Vallotton, the Seurat of *Le Cirque*, the Signac of the Fénéon Portrait. But after that moment, the short years about 1900, what happened? Architecture went the way of Garnier and Perret, of Loos and Hoffmann, of Behrens and Berg, and design the way of the Werkbund, but painting went the way to Fauvism and Cubism, to the Brücke and the Blaue Reiter, to Futurism and Kandinsky. It is easy to see the similarities of approach and result in Bindesbøll's plates, Gaudí's pinnacles of the Sagrada Familia and Picasso's pottery, but the dates will not match. It is also easy to see as one cubist paintings of the geometrical kind and cubic architecture of the nineteen-twenties — after all Le Corbusier produced both — or Léger's machine men and the machine-worshippers among the architects. But these comparisons are superficial. They do not concern the essential change which is that architects and designers once more accepted social responsibilities, that architecture and design consequently became a service and buildings and objects of daily use were designed not only to satisfy the aesthetic wishes of their designers but also to fullfil their practical purposes fully and enthusiastically. Painters and sculptors moved in exactly the opposite direction. They had been cut off from their public already in the nineteenth century. Now they were cut off beyond redemption. Courbet shocked his public because of his message, but that message, as M. Cassou has pointed out, was perfectly plain to everybody. The Impressionists were attacked for their paintings not being recognizable. But that proved a matter of visual habits. Their aesthetic aims were still those of Titian and Velasquez. Only they had no other than aesthetic aims and that deprived them of the sympathy which the public could extend as long as the spiritual content of a work of art concerned it. To recover these lost spiritual contacts was the most important effort of Gauguin, Van Gogh, the Symbolists, Munch, Hodler — all of them. But they failed, and while from Van Gogh's longing for being accepted by simple people like the broadsheets they read, there might have been a bridge to the architects' and designers' endeavours towards a style for all, there was none from cubism and the dynamic abstract art of Kandinsky.

Gropius hoped there might be, and the Bauhaus made the noble effort of inviting Klee and other abstractionists under its roof. No successful effort has been made since. To offer an abstract artist a wall in a building or an abstract sculptor a place in a courtyard is no substitute. To force the artist into direct social service against his better aesthetic conviction, as is the principle of Socialist Realism and was that of National-Socialist Realism, is even less of a help. In fact there is no help. The gulf between Jackson Pollock and Mies Van der Rohe or even Nervi is beyond bridging. This book is not the place to suggest remedies or foretell the future. Here it must be enough to state that what is most disastrous in the visual arts of the twentieth century and what is most hopeful was fully in existence by the time the Age of the World Wars dawned.

209
Joseph PAXTON
Crystal Palace, London
(1851)

210
Abraham DARBY
Iron Bridge at Coalbrookdale, Salop
(1777)

211
Thomas TELFORD
Menai Suspension Bridge
(1815)

213
J. B. BUNNING
Coal Exchange, London
(1846–1849)

DUTERT and CONTAMIN
Hall des Machines
Paris International Exhibition
(1889)

215
Philip WEBB
Fireplace, Red House,
Bexley Heath, Kent
(1860)

216
Madox BROWN
Chair
(about 1860)

217
Philip WEBB
Faïence tile
(1862)

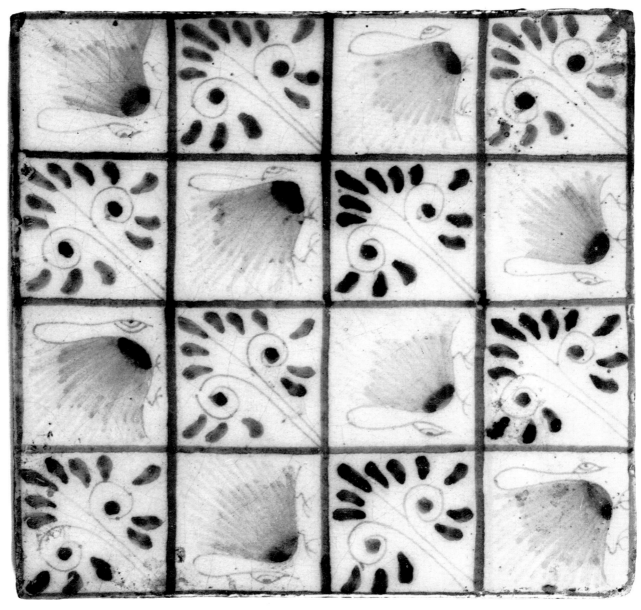

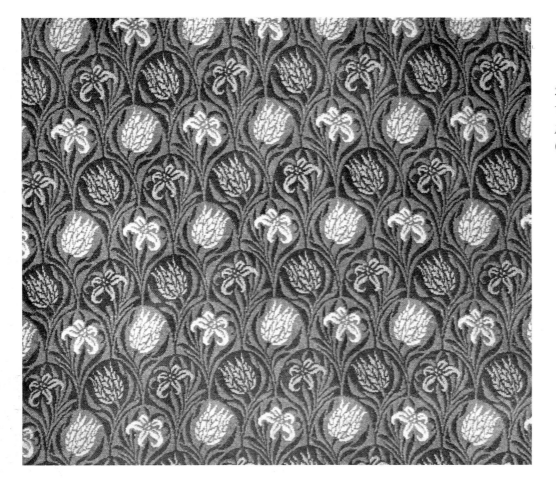

218
William MORRIS
Lily carpeting
(1877)

219
William MORRIS
Tulip chinz
(1875)

220
Philip WEBB
Standen, East Grinstead, Sussex
(1892)

221
Richard Norman SHAW
Banstead, Surrey
(1884)

222
Richard Norman SHAW
New Zealand Chambers, London
(1872)

223
Richard Norman SHAW
Old Swan House, Chelsea, London
(1876)

224
Richard Norman SHAW
Bedford Park, near London
(1876)

225
Stanford WHITE
W. G. Low House, Bristol, Rhode Island
(1887)

226
5-9 *Aldermanbury, London*
(about 1840)

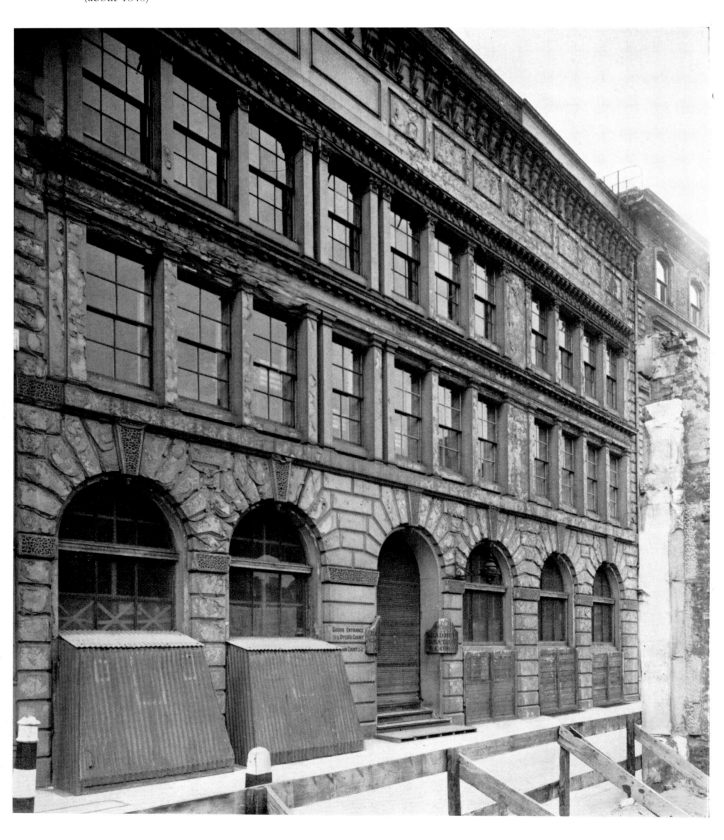

XLI
Georges HOENTSCHEL

Vase
(1902)

XLII
Émile GALLÉ

Vase
(1887)

XLIII
Ernest Baptiste LEVEILLÉ

Goblet
(c. 1889)

235
Paul GAUGUIN
Man with an axe
(1891)

236
Émile BERNARD
Wall-hanging, Woman picking pears
(1888)

237
Jens Ferdinand WILLUMSEN
Ceramic
(1890)

XLIV
Thorvald BINDESBØLL
Dish
(1889)

238
Thorvald BINDESBØLL
Plate
(1891)

239
Alfred GILBERT
Table centre-piece
(1887)

240
Alfred GILBERT
Eros (detail of base)
(1892)

241

Henri VAN DE VELDE

'*Engelswache*' *tapestry*
(1891)

242

Hermann OBRIST

'*Peitschenschlag*' *embroidery*
(1892)

XLV
Charles F. Annesley VOYSEY
Nympheas
(1888)

Charles F. Annesley VOYSEY

243
Charles Annesley VOYSEY
'*Water-snake*', *textile design*
(about 1890)

244
Charles Annesley VOYSEY
Flowers and leaves
(about 1890)

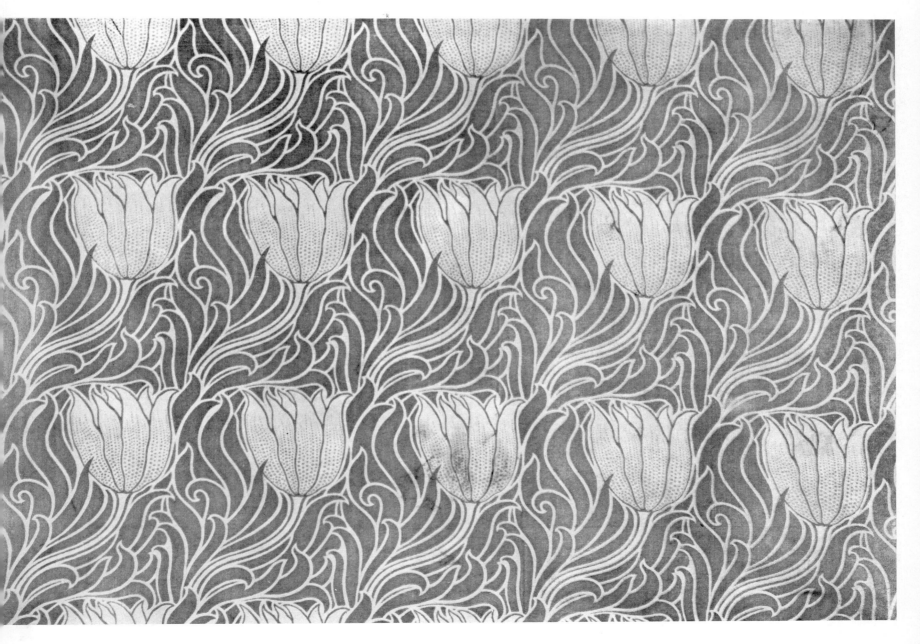

245
René LALIQUE
Pendant
(1900)

246
René LALIQUE
Brooch
(1899)

247
René LALIQUE
Necklace
(1900)

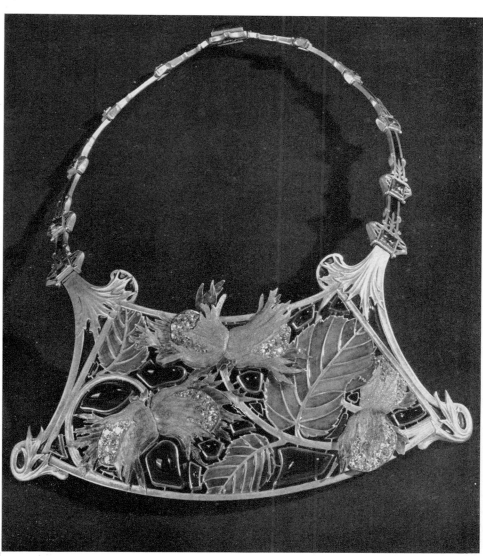

248
Wilhelm Lucas von CRANACH
Brooch
(1900)

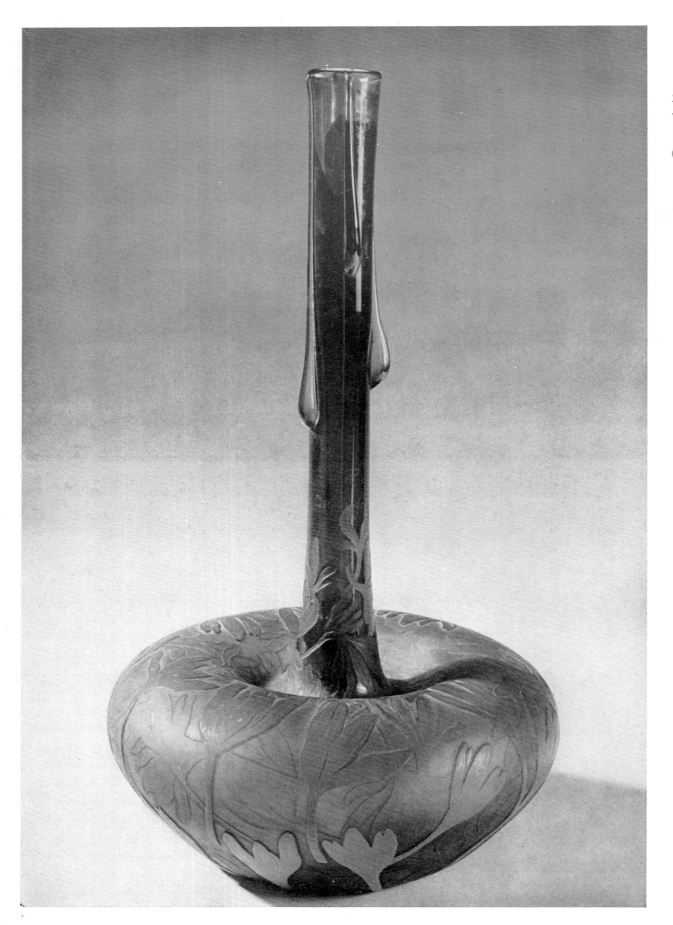

249
The Brothers DAUM
Vase
(1893)

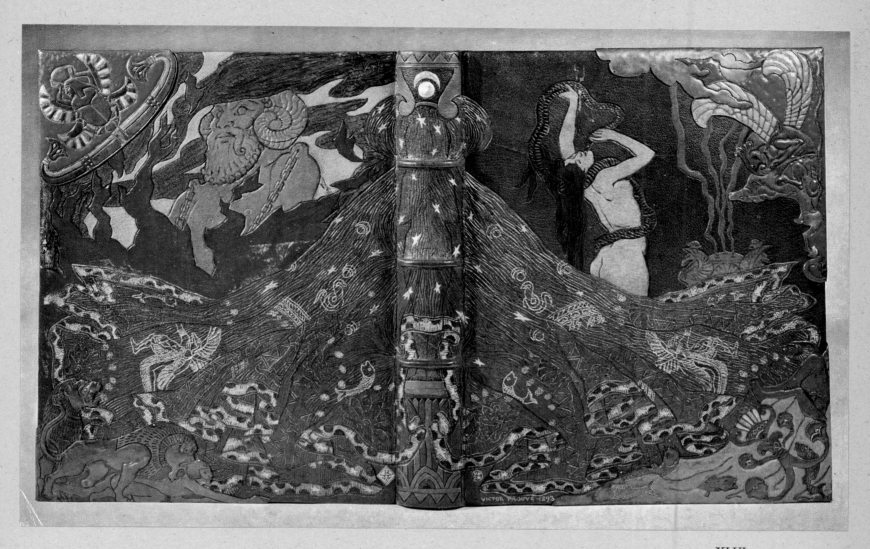

XLVI
René WIENER
Book-binding
(1893)

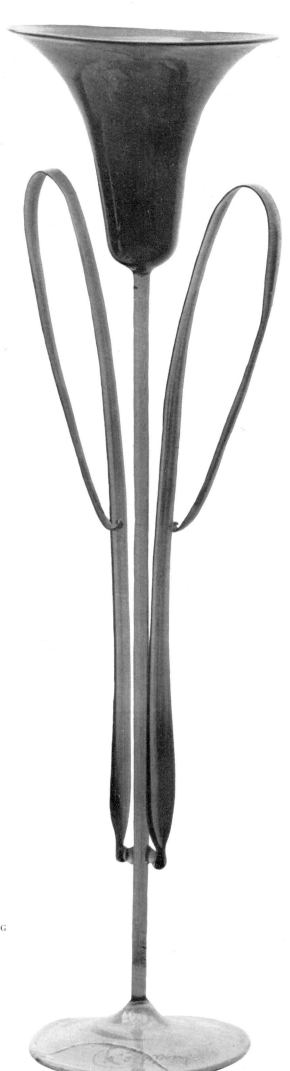

250
Karl KOEPPING
Glass

251
Louis Comfort TIFFANY
Glass vase
(1900)

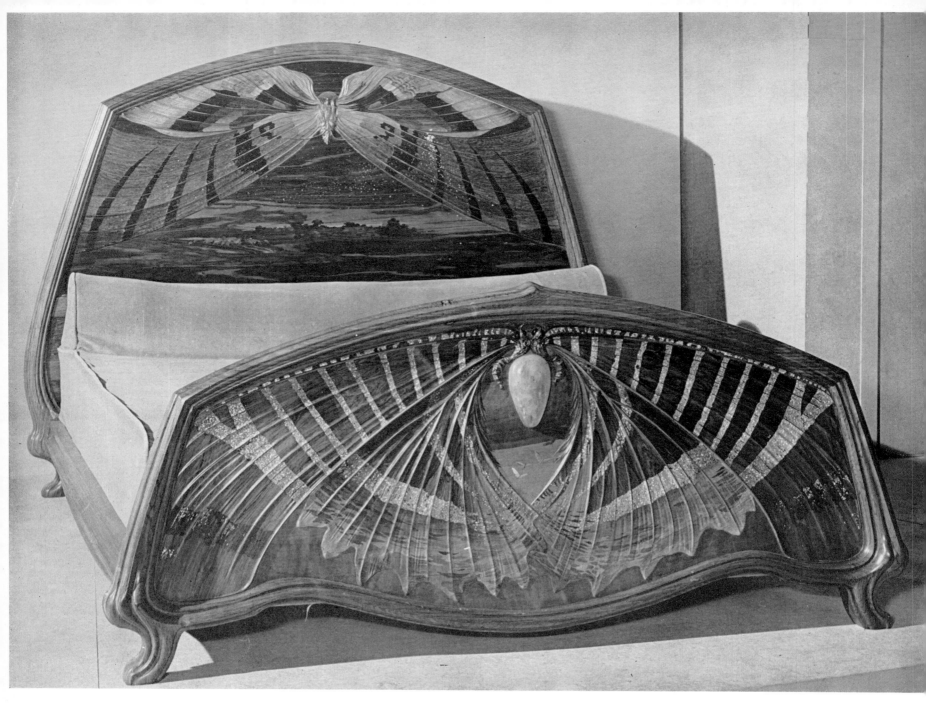

252
Émile GALLÉ
Bed
(1904)

253
Victor PROUVÉ
Bowl: Night
(1894)

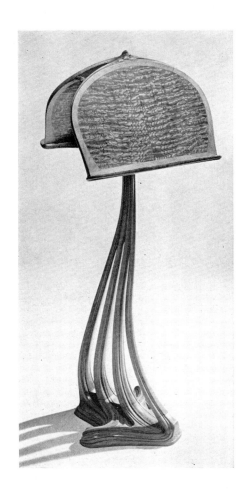

255
Alexandre CHARPENTIER
Music-stand
(1901)

254
Louis MAJORELLE
Table
(1902)

256
Eugène GAILLARD
Double-seat
(1911)

257
Henri Van de Velde
Desk
(1896)

XLVII
Eugène VALLIN
Dining room
(1903–1906)

258
Otto ECKMANN
Armchair
(about 1900)

259
Richard RIEMERSCHMID
Armchair
(1903)

260–261
Antoni GAUDÍ
Armchair from Casa Calvet
(1898–1904)

262
Antoni GAUDÍ
Bench from Santa Coloma de Cervello
(1898–1914)

XLVIII
Antoni Gaudí
Crypt of Santa Coloma de Cervello
(1898–1914)

263
Antoni Gaudí
Crypt of Santa Coloma de Cervello
(1898–1914)

264
Antoni GAUDÍ
Casa Milá
(1905–1910)

265
Antoni GAUDÍ
Casa Batlló
(1905–1907)

266
Antoni GAUDÍ
Church of the Sagrada Familia, Pinnacle
(about 1924)

XLIX-L

Antoni Gaudí

Details from the Güell Park

(1900-1914)

267
August ENDELL
Atelier Elvira, Munich
(1896)

268
August ENDELL
Atelier Elvira, Munich : staircase
(1896)

269
Victor HORTA
House, formerly the Hotel A. Solvay, Brussels
(1895–1900)

270

Victor HORTA

Staircase from house, formerly Hotel A. Solvay, Brussels
(1895-1900)

271

Victor HORTA

Window from house, formerly Hotel A. Solvay, Brussels
(1895-1900)

272
Victor HORTA
House, formerly Hotel Horta
(1898–1899)

273
Bernhard SEHRING
Tietz Department Store, Berlin
(1900)

274
Hector GUIMARD
Entrance to a Paris Metro Station
(1899–1904)

275

Hector GUIMARD

Entrance, Castel Beranger (detail)
(1897–1898)

276

Hector GUIMARD

Ironwork, Castel Beranger
(1897–1898)

277

Hector GUIMARD

Glass wall, Castel Beranger
(1897–1898)

285
Charles Annesley VOYSEY
Clock
(1906)

286
Charles Annesley VOYSEY
Teapot
(about 1896)

LI
Charles Rennie MACKINTOSH
Pair of doors
(1904)

287
Charles Robert AsHBEE
Bowl with lid
(1899–1900)

288
Ernest William GIMSON
Cabinet
(1908)

289
Charles Rennie MACKINTOSH
Glasgow Art School
(1897–1899)

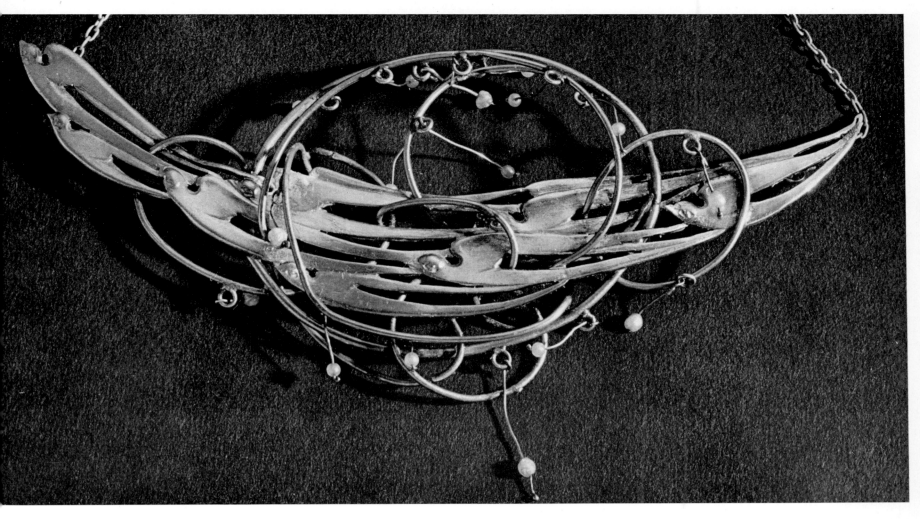

290
Charles Rennie MACKINTOSH
Pendant
(1902)

91
Charles Robert ASHBEE
Pendant
(1900)

292
Sisters M. and F. MACDONALD
Mirror frame, ' Honesty '
(about 1896)

293
Charles Rennie MACKINTOSH
Glasgow Art School, pilaster
(1906–1909)

294
Charles Rennie MACKINTOSH
Glasgow Art School,
wrought–iron emblem on staircase
(1906–1909)

295
Charles Rennie MACKINTOSH
Glasgow Art School, arch on the roof
(1906-1909)

296
Charles Rennie MACKINTOSH
Project for a concert hall
(1898)

297
Charles Rennie MACKINTOSH
Chair
(1902)

298
Charles Rennie MACKINTOSH
Table from Hill House
(1902)

299
Charles Rennie MACKINTOSH
Table
(about 1900)

300
Charles Rennie MACKINTOSH
Armchair
(about 1902)

301
Richard RIEMERSCHMID
Glass
(1912)

302
Richard RIEMERSCHMID
Chair
(1899)

303
Peter BEHRENS
Bottles
(1898)

304

Gustave EIFFEL

The Eiffel Tower, Paris
(1887–1889)

305
Anatole DE BAUDOT
Saint-Jean de Montmartre
(1894–1902)

306
François HENNEBIQUE
Factory at Tourcoing
(1895)

307
Auguste PERRET
Block of flats, 25bis Rue Franklin, Paris
(1902)

308
Auguste PERRET
Block of flats, 25bis Rue Franklin, Paris
(1902)

309
Tony GARNIER
Slaughterhouse at Lyons
(1909-1913)

310
Robert MAILLART
Tavanesa Bridge
(1905)

311
Max BERG
Centenary Hall, Breslau
(1913)

312
Josef HOFFMANN
Palais Stoclet, Brussels
(1905-1911)

313
Josef HOFFMANN
Palais Stoclet, Brussels, hall
(1905–1911)

314
Josef HOFFMANN
*Palais Stoclet, Brussels,
dining room*
(1905–1911)

315
Adolf Loos
Steiner House, Vienna
(1910)

LII
Gustav KLIMT
The Kiss
(1909)

316
Bruno Taut
Glass House, Cologne
(1914)

317
Richard RIEMERSCHMID
Linoleum
(1912)

318
Richard RIEMERSCHMID
Tea-set
(1914)

320
Peter BEHRENS
Two teapots
(1912)

321
Peter BEHRENS
Two ventilators
(1912)

322
Gerrit Thomas RIETVELD
Armchair
(1908)

323
Gerrit Thomas RIETVELD
Armchair
(1917)

324
Johan ROHDE
Teapot
(about 1906)

325
Georg JENSEN
Cutlery
(1908)

326
Johan ROHDE
Cupboard
(1897)

327
Walter GROPIUS
Fagus factory at Alfeld-on-the-Leine
(1911–1914)

328
Frank Lloyd WRIGHT
Martin House, Oakpark, Buffalo
(1906)

329
Henri SAUVAGE
Flats at 26 Rue Vavin, Paris
(1912)

333
Raymond Unwin and Barry Parker
Hampstead Garden Suburb
(begun 1907)

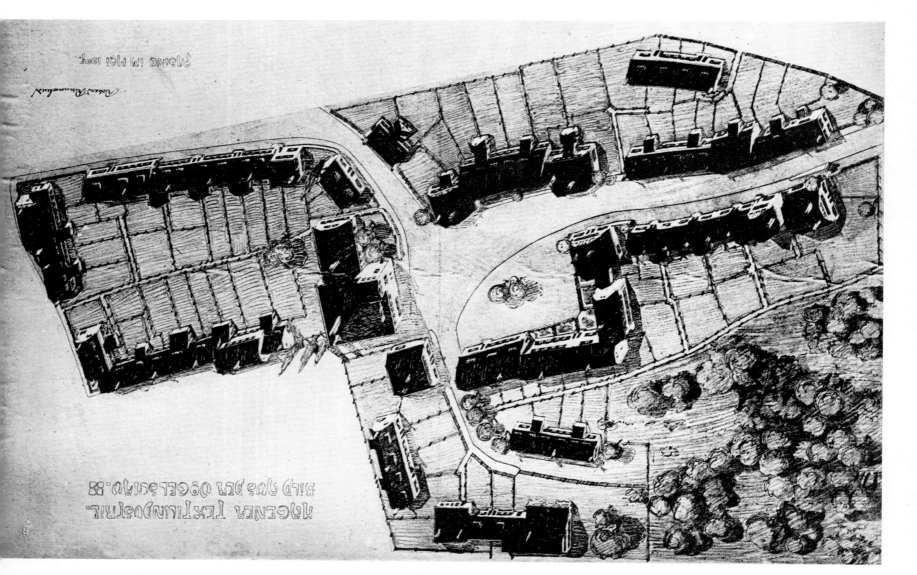

332
Richard Riemerschmid
Industrial City at Hagen
(1907)

SOURCES OF ILLUSTRATIONS

COLOUR PLATES :

Amigos de Gaudí, Barcelona: XLVIII, XLIX, L. — Paul Bijtebier, Brussels: XXXI. — Jacqueline Hyde, Paris: I, II, VI, VIII, IX, X, XI, XII, XIII, XV, XVI, XVII, XX, XXI, XXII, XXIV, XXV, XXVII, XXVIII, XXIX, XXXII, XXXIII, XXXIV, XXXV, XXXVI, XXXVII, XXXIX, XLIV, LI, LII. — Benno Keysselitz, Munich: III, XLI, XLII, XLIII, XLV, XLVI, XLVII, XL. — Il Milione, Milan: XXIII. — Mayer, Vienna : XXXVIII. — Statens Museum for Kunst, Copenhagen: XXX. — La Photothèque, Paris: XVIII. — Thames and Hudson, London: V, XIV, XIX, XXVI.

BLACK AND WHITE PLATES :

A.C.L., Brussels: 65, 73, 110, 113, 198, 199. — Victor Amato, Washington: 122. — Amigos de Gaudí, Barcelona: 44, 263, 266. — Wayne Andrews: 225. — Annan, Glasgow: 289. — Architectural Press: 229. — Archives Photographiques, Paris: 26, 57, 114, 173, 212. — Aron, Frères, Paris: 42. — Arts Council of Great Britain, London: 216. — Bedford Lemere Ltd, Croydon: 223. — Bernés Maronteau et Cie: 56. — Paul Bijtebier, Brussels: 74, 158, 169, 171. — Bildarchiv der Oesterreichischen Nationalbibliothek, Vienna: 49. — Walter Binder (Kunstgewerbemuseum), Zurich: 241. — Ets. Braun, Mulhouse: 18. — British Council, Paris: 33, 104, 168, 221, 228, 279, 280, 281, 282, 283, 293, 294, (Michael Witchmann): 295, 296. — L.-G. Buchheim, Feldafing: 193.— Camponogara, Lyon: 60. — Ludovico Cartotti (coll.), Milan: 124. — Cauvin, Paris: 236. — Centre Culturel Américain, Paris: 50, 54, 55, 227. — Chevalier, Ivry: 164. — Chevojon, Paris: 214, 304, 329. — Cinémathèque française, Paris: 85, 88, 89, 90, 91, 92, 93, 94, 95. — Conservatoire National des Arts et Métiers, Paris: 272, 309. — Cosmopress, Geneva: 155. — Country Life, London: 213. — Courtesy Museum of Modern Art, New York: 12. — Jean Desmarteau, Paris: 1, 2, 3, 4, 5, 6, 7, 8, 9, 10, 11, 13, 14, 16, 21, 22, 36, 37, 38, 39, 40, 41, 45, 61, 62, 83, 84, 86, 87, 275, 277. — Walter Dräyer: 194. — Durand-Ruel, Paris: 71. — Est-Ouest, Brussels: 185.— R.B. Fleming Ltd, London: 132. — Foto Mas, Barcelona: 264, 265. — Foto-Sammlung der Oesterreichischen Galerie, Vienna: 197. — Fototecnica, Bologna: 138. — John B. Freeman, London: 209, 232, 233, 234, 237, 306, 311, 317, 318, 319, 320, 321, 328. — Frequin, A., The Hague: 195. — Galleria d'Arte Moderna, Milan: 146, 148. — Galerie Louis Carré, Paris: 150, 153, 156. — Galerie Louise Leiris, Paris: 129, 130, 139, 205. — Gemeentemuseum, The Hague: 154. — Giraudon, Paris: 23, 28, 31, 66, 68, 69, 103, 107, 115, 126, 135, 136, 160, 179. — Graphic Art Color s.r.l., Milan: 106. — Jacqueline Hyde, Paris: 29, 30, 32, 62, 64, 81, 127, 131, 147, 166, 207, 239. — Institute of British Photographs, London: 210. — Benno Keysselitz, Munich: 34, 35, 58, 117, 118, 119, 121, 125, 145, 172, 174, 175, 176, 181, 182, 184, 187, 188, 201, 203, 230, 231, 243, 245, 246, 247, 248, 249, 252, 253, 254, 255, 256, 258, 259, 260, 261, 262, 278, 285, 286, 287, 288, 290, 291, 292, 297, 298, 299, 300, 303, 322, 324, 325, 326. — Kleinhempel, Hamburg: 190, 191, 192. — Kunstgewerbemuseum, Zurich: 257. — Kunstmuseum, Berne: 59, 142, 143, 144. — Lewyt Corporation, New York: 235. — Eric de Maré, London: 43, 224, 240, 284, 333. — Gianni Mari, Milan: 204. — Günther Mehling, Munich: 242, 301. — André Meyer, Paris: 63. — Kunstindustrimuseet, Copenhagen: 238, 250. — Musée Gustave Moreau, Paris: 105. — Musées Nationaux, Paris: 120, 167. — Museum of Modern Art, New York: 302. — Museo de Arte Moderno, Barcelona: 165. — National Buildings Record, London: 215, 220, 222, 226. — Nasjonalgalleriet, Oslo: 162. — National Gallery, London: 123. — Nationalmuseum, Stockholm: 76, 163. — Niedersächsische Landesgalerie, Hanover: 151. — Oeffentliche Kunstsammlung, Bâle: 200. — Oesterreichische Galerie, Vienna: 112. — Pierre d'Otreppe, Brussels: 269, 270, 271. — Philadelphia Museum of Art: 101, 208. — Philips Collection, Washington: 122. — Studio Piaget, St-Louis: 149. — Reifenstein, Vienna: 315. — Rijksmuseum Kröller-Müller, Otterlo: 108, 109, 134, 161. — Oscar Savio: 206. — Robert Schnitzler, Zurich: 251. — Walter Scott, Bradford: 211. — Emmanuel Sougez, Paris: 183. — Staatliche Galerien, Munich: 24, 25. — Staatsgalerie, Stuttgart: 189. — Staatliche Kunsthalle, Karlsruhe: 196. — Stedelijk Museum, Amsterdam: 140, 141, 152, 186, 323. Dr Franz Stoedtner, Düsseldorf: 267, 268, 316, 327, 332. — Studio Minders, Genk: 312, 313, 314. — Soichi Sunami (Museum of Modern Art), New York: 77. — The Tate Gallery, London: 70, 157, 202. — Theaterwissenschaftliches Institut, Berlin-Dahlem: 100. — O. Vaering, Oslo: 72, 159. — Victoria and Albert Museum, London: 218, 219, 244. — Pierre Vorms, Belvès: 96, 97, 98, 99. — Whitney Museum of American Art, New York: 51, 52, 53.

NOTES ON THE PLATES

I DELAUNAY, ROBERT - Paris 1885 - Montpellier 1941 - Delaunay made a start in an atelier for decoration, but in 1904 he came into contact with the Pont-Aven school, and decided to devote himself henceforth to painting. After a Neo-Impressionist period he became a pioneer of Cubism. In 1911 he was invited to exhibit with the *Blaue Reiter* group in Munich. This period saw his first abstract works, to which Apollinaire gave the name of ' Orphism '. In 1913 he exhibited with the *Sturm* group in Berlin. This was the beginning of the circular form period. Delaunay had a great influence on Klee and Kandinsky, and he greatly contributed to the development of abstract art. — See 156.

THE CARDIFF TEAM (1912-1913) - Figurative themes still persist in this work, but soon afterwards they disappeared completely from Delaunay's work in favour of pure abstraction. This picture was shown at the Rétrospective des Indépendants in 1906. Canvas 196,5×130 cm.

Eindhoven, Stedelijk van Abbe Museum

1 FLYING MEN - Front cover of *L'Illustration* of November 2nd 1907. Henri Farman (1874-1958) aviator and aeroplane builder. In the following year he was to win the prize for flying a kilometre in a closed circle with the Voisin machine. Robert Esnault-Pelterie (1881-1957), launched the theory of inter-planetary navigation by means of the jet-driven rocket. Elected member of the Académie des Sciences in 1936.

Paris, Bibliothèque Nationale

2 BLÉRIOT'S AIRCRAFT (1908) - Louis Blériot, aviator and aeroplane builder (1872-1936). Blériot was the first man to fly the Channel in an aeroplane (July 25th 1909).

Paris, Musée des Arts et Métiers

3 ' LA FUSÉE ' - Electric locomotive. Heilmann system (1894).

Paris, Musée des Arts et Métiers

4 A RENAULT AUTOMOBILE (1908).

Paris, Union centrale des Arts décoratifs,
' *Maciet* ' *Collection*

5 A FORD MODEL ' T ' (1908) - The model ' T ' was a great success, and eighteen million were sold. Manufacture stopped only just after the 1914-18 war.

Paris, Musée des Arts et Métiers

6 A DION-BOUTON AUTOMOBILE (1898).

Paris, Union centrale des Arts décoratifs,
' *Maciet* ' *Collection*

7 FIRST SERIES OF 34 DÉCAUVILLE RAILWAY POSTERS - Exhibited at the Universal Exhibition in 1889. The posters appeal to the general public to take care — in all languages. Paul Décauville (1846-1922) designed the equipment for the narrow guage railways with which his name has remained connected.

Paris, Union centrale des Arts décoratifs,
' *Maciet* ' *Collection*

8 PARIS UNIVERSAL EXHIBITION 1889 - The central dome and the Coutan fountain.

Paris, Union centrale des Arts décoratifs,
' *Maciet* ' *Collection*

9 PARIS UNIVERSAL EXHIBITION 1900 - Foreign pavilions on the Quai des Nations.

Paris, Union centrale des Arts décoratifs,
' *Maciet* ' *Collection*

10 PARIS UNIVERSAL EXHIBITION 1900 - The water-tower on the Champ de Mars. Decoration of the top of the supporting towers and lower part of the roof. Sketch after the mock-up of the architect E. Paulin.

Paris, Musée des Arts décoratifs. Library.
' *Maciet* ' *Collection*

11 TITLE-PAGE OF THE ' ENCYCLOPÉDIE DU SIÈCLE' for the number devoted to the Paris Universal Exhibition 1900. Designed by the painter Luigi Loir (1845-1916).

Paris, Bibliothèque Nationale

12 CHICAGO UNIVERSAL EXHIBITION 1893 - The Golden Gate, designed by Louis Sullivan (1850-1924).

New York, Museum of Modern Art

13 PARIS UNIVERSAL EXHIBITION 1900 - The entrance - Cover of the ' Encyclopédie du Siècle '. The entrance was designed by the architect R. Binet (1866-1911).

Paris, Bibliothèque Nationale

14 CARPEZAT, M.
DÉCOR FOR ' SALAMMBÔ ' by Reyer - Act IV. Scene I. Hall in the Palace of Omphale. One of the best works of the composer Ernest Reyer (1823-1909). Taken from Flaubert's book of the same title (libretto by Camille de Locle) and presented for the first time at the Paris Opera House in 1890.

Paris, Bibliothèque de l'Arsenal

15 ROLLER, ALFRED - Brünn 1864 - Vienna 1935 - Painter and draughtsman. Studied at the Vienna Academy. Teacher at the School of Applied Arts.
DÉCOR FOR ' DER ROSENKAVALIER ' by Richard Strauss (1911) - Light opera, libretto by Hugo von Hofmannsthal. This décor was used for the first night in Dresden in January 1911, and for the Vienna performance in April of the same year.

Vienna, Institut für Theaterwissenschaft

16 ' LE POINT ' - Page from No. 37, dated April 1949 devoted to official art. In this number Francis Jourdain published a violent diatribe against Academism.

17 GÉRÔME, JEAN-LÉON - Vesoul 1824 - Paris 1904 - Genre and historical painter, sculptor and engraver, Gérôme worked in Paris in the atelier of Delaroche. He taught at the École des Beaux-Arts and was a member of both the Académie des Beaux-Arts (1865) and of the Institut. — See 26.
SARAH BERNHARDT.

18 ROCHEGROSSE, GEORGES - Versailles 1859-1938 - Historical painter, his complex art combines the talent of an archaeologist with the ability of a Flaubert to re-create the past.
THE FALL OF BABYLON - This picture illustrates in particular the artist's pictorial and archaeological sense.

19 ' MÜNCHENER BILDERBOGEN ' (1895) - A page taken from No. 1126, " The world in pictures ". Scenes from German East Africa. Above: A caravan surprised by a rhineceros. Centre: Native boats, and disembarking at a German trading-post. Below: Maize plantation; Iraq cave-dwellers; Arab caravan; Phoenix palms.

Munich, Braun and Schneider Verlag

20 ' MÜNCHENER BILDERBOGEN ' (1898) - A page taken from No. 1182. ' The Street in 1900 ', as seen in anticipation by Schmiedhammer.

Munich, Braun and Schneider Verlag

21-22 CHRISTOPHE (pseudonym for GEORGES COLOMB) - 1856-1945 - Professor of Mathematics at the Sorbonne, developed the idea of drawing strips and accompanying each illustration with a humourous text. *La Famille Fenouillard*, which lightheartedly described the travels and adventures of an average French family, was received with delight by both old and young. *La Famille Fenouillard* was first published in *Le Petit Français illustré* (1889-1893), and was then issued in one volume in 1893. Armand Colin published a new edition quite recently.

23 FRIANT, ÉMILE - Dieuze (Alsace) 1863 - Paris 1932 - Genre painter, taking his subjects from contemporary life. Responsible for numerous portraits and portrait sketches. An outstanding figure of the Nancy school.
ALL-SAINTS DAY (1888) - Signed and dated in the bottom left-hand corner: E. Friant 1888.

Paris, Musée du Luxembourg

24 LEIBL, WILHELM - Cologne 1844 - Würzburg 1900 - A realist painter with a great power of expression. Under the influence of Courbet, whom he admired profoundly.
PEASANT INTERIOR (1890) - Painted on wooden panel 30×38 cm. Signed in the top left-hand corner: W. Leibl.

Munich, Neue Pinakothek

25 THOMA, HANS - Bernau 1839 - Karlsruhe 1924 - Portrait genre and landscape artist.
TAUNUS LANDSCAPE (1891) - Canvas 78×106 cm.

Munich, Elise Hirth Collection

26 GÉRÔME, JEAN-LÉON (biography see 17).
DANCING DERVISHES.

27 GAUGUIN, PAUL - Paris 1848 - Atuana (Marquesas Islands) 1903 - Grandson of Flora Tristan. At first a sailor and then a foreign-exchange clerk, he gave up his job to devote himself wholly to painting. He contributed to the last Impressionist shows. In 1886 he made his first stay at Pont-Aven. Anxious to get away from modern civilization he left for Martinique in 1887. After a second stay at Pont-Aven during which with Émile Bernard and other friends he developed his synthetic style, and his famous stay at Arles with Van Gogh (1888), he worked in Paris and then returned once again to Pont-Aven and Toulon. In 1891 he eventually left for Tahiti. A last return visit to France (August 1893-February 1895) preceded his final stay in Tahiti which he left only for the even greater solitude of the Marquesas Islands where he died. — See 68, 102, XV, 232, 233, 234, 235.
THE KING'S WIFE (1896) - ' Te Arii Vahiro '. This picture is also called ' Woman with mangoes '.

Canvas 97×130 cm. Signed in the bottom right-hand corner: P. Gauguin 1896.

Moscow, Pushkin Museum

28 DAMPT, JEAN - Venarey 1853 - Dijon 1945 - Genre sculptor and portraitist. Studied at the École des Beaux-Arts in Dijon, and then in Paris. His work was awarded a Gold Medal at the Universal Exhibition of 1889. He was a member of the Academie des Beaux-Arts.
GRANDMOTHER'S KISS (1892) - This sculptor also produced numerous statuettes in precious stone.

29 LAVERY, SIR JOHN - Belfast 1856 - London 1941 - Studied in Paris under Bouguereau and Meissonier, and also in Glasgow and London. Painter of portraits and interiors, notable for warmth of colouring. Was influenced by the Scottish tradition of painting and by the French romantics. Was particularly indebted to Whistler.
SPRING - Canvas 190×123 cm. Signed in the bottom left-hand corner: J. Lavery.

Paris, Musée National d'Art Moderne

30 BOLDINI, GIOVANNI - Ferrara 1853 - Paris 1931 - Boldini studied at the Florence Academy of Arts. From there he went to London and to Paris, where he went in for genre painting and in particular portraits elegantly mannered in a vigourous and brilliant style with skilful harmonies in which black predominated.
PORTRAIT OF ROBERT DE MONTESQUIOU-FEZENSAC (1897) - Canvas 200×100 cm. Signed and dated in the bottom right-hand corner: Boldini 1897.

Paris, Musée National d'Art Moderne

II CHÉRET, JULES - Paris 1836 - Nice 1932 - A poster designer and painter decorator, Chéret carried out bold decorations in the style of the fêtes galantes of the eighteenth for the Hôtel de Ville in Paris, the Prefecture of Police in Nice and the Gobelins Manufactory in Paris.
PANTOMIMES LUMINEUSES AU MUSÉE GRÉVIN (poster) (1892) - One of the first posters for the *Théâtre Optique*, by means of which Reynaud showed the first long public performances of animated cartoons, starting in 1892 and going on for nearly ten years, in the Musée Grévin in Paris. Signed in the bottom left-hand corner : Chéret.

Nice, Musée Chéret

31 TOULOUSE-LAUTREC, HENRI DE - Albi 1864 - Château de Malromé 1901 - A dwarf from adolescence on, a series of accidents which impeded his physical growth gave him a passion for drawing. He studied at Bonnat's atelier, and then at that of Cormon. His first works were primarily concerned with horses, but in 1882 he went to live in Montmartre where he drew and painted scenes of Parisian life, observed with a pitiless eye. The famous Moulin Rouge, its artists, and brothel interiors were amongst his favourite subjects. His art owes a great deal to Degas and to the Japanese print, and he achieved effects which were welcomed enthusiastically by the younger artists at the beginning of the century. — See 67, XIV.
MISIA NATANSON (1895) - Poster for the *Revue Blanche* (1895). The model is the well-known Misia Natanson, the first wife of Thadée Natanson and one of the dominating figures of the *Revue Blanche*. From 1893 on the Natansons often 100×93 cm.

Paris, Union centrale des Arts décoratifs, Library.

32 BONNARD, PIERRE - Fontenay-aux-Roses 1867 - Le Cannet 1947 - Intended for the law, Bonnard entered the Beaux-Arts in 1880, attended the Académie Julian, and attached himself to the *Nabis*. His first work owed a good deal to Gauguin, and, even more, to Japanese prints. His best lithographs, scenes of Parisian and domestic life, are closely related to Vuillard. Around 1900 he turned to landscape and to themes dominated by the female form. By its composition and its colour — half way between Impressionism and Fauvism — his work nevertheless belongs to the twentieth century.
FRANCE-CHAMPAGNE (poster) (1892) - One of Bonnard's first posters. Afterwards he collaborated regularly with the Natansons on the *Revue Blanche*. Signed in the top right-hand corner: P.B.

Paris, Union centrale des Arts décoratifs, ' Maciet ' Collection

33 MACKMURDO, ARTHUR HEYGATE - London 1851 - Wickham Bishops (Essex) 1942 - Architect and designer, Mackmurdo travelled with Ruskin to Italy and worked with William Morris. In 1882 he founded the *Century Guild*, and two years later he also founded the review *The Hobby Horse*. He designed furniture, wallpaper, material and metalwork. In 1904 he abandoned architecture in order to devote himself completely to his social theories. — See 228, 278.
DESIGN FOR PRINTED COTTON (c. 1884) - ' Single Flower ' printed by Simpson & Godlec of Manchester for the *Century Guild*. Block-printed cotton 68,5×81,3 cm.

London, Victoria and Albert Museum

34 GALLÉ, ÉMILE - Nancy 1846-1904 - After brilliantly pursuing classical studies he worked in the pottery and glass works of his father. He completed his training during stays in Weimar, London and Italy. He took part in the Exhibition of 1878, at which his technical mastery and originality were underlined. His work was soon imitated both in Germany and in the United States. The Exhibition of 1889 was a triumph for him, and to the end of his life he never ceased to pursue technical research and decorative invention. — See XLII, 252.
BOWL (1884) - Decorative design of flowers and tadpoles. Cased glass mottled opal and green. Height 9 cm. Monogramme: E.G. and Cross of Lorraine.

Paris, Musée des Arts décoratifs

35 ENDELL, AUGUST - Berlin 1871-1925 - He studied philosophy and as an artist he was self- of Obrist. In 1896 he built the Atelier Elvira, Munich. Returned to Berlin and became Director of the Breslau Academy. — See 267, 268.
ARMCHAIR (1899) - Elm: 106 (height of seat:45)×48 ×52 cm.

Munich, Dr Kurt Martin

36 POWER HAMMER (c. 1860) F. Bonhomme. Reproduction.

Paris, Musée des Arts et Métiers

37 ' HAMMOND ' TYPEWRITER (1887) - Model No. 12. Three letters per key. Invented in 1774 and improved during the 19th century. The typewriter came into practical use from 1874 onwards.

Paris, Musée des Arts et Métiers

38 EDISON, THOMAS A. - 1847-1931 - A physicist, Edison was the inventor of numerous modern electrical devices. He also built the first phonograph, whose principle had been first laid down by Charles Cros. Edison was also responsible for one of the decisive stages of cinematograph development with the invention of the modern 35 mm film. — See 86.
EDISON PHONOGRAPH WITH CYLINDER (c. 1900) - Edison built his first phonograph in 1878, but it was a Frenchman, Charles Cros, who established the principle, which was explained in detail in a lecture to the Academy of Sciences in 1877.
Paris, Musée des Arts et Métiers

39 THE FIRST DIESEL ENGINE (1897) - 1:10 model. built by the Maschinenfabrik Augsburg in 1896-97. The engine worked for the first time in the spring of 1897. (Bore 250 mm, Stroke 40 mm, Power 20 h.p. at 172 Tr/mn.)
Paris, Musée des Arts et Métiers

40 TWO ELECTRIC RADIATORS - Exhibited by the *Compagnie de chauffage par l'électricité* at the Paris Universal Exhibition in 1900.
Paris, Bibliothèque Nationale

41 SOLAR MACHINE MADE BY MOUCHOT AND PIFRE (c. 1880) - 1:10 reproduction of the model demonstrated in the courtyard of the Arts et Métiers in Paris in 1880.
Paris, Musée des Arts et Métiers

42 EIFFEL, GUSTAVE - Dijon 1832 - Paris 1923 - An engineer, Eiffel is above all famous for the use of steel, whose technical resources he used to carry out his architectural works. Thanks to a combination of precise calculations and a keen feeling for function, Eiffel's work is in the main line of rationalist architectural development in France. — See 304.
GARABIT VIADUCT (1880-1884) - Erected near Saint-Flour in the Cantal this bridge is a real piece of precision engineering. It was built without the aid of scaffolding. The main arch has an open span of 165 metres with a rise of 52 metres.

43 BAKER, SIR BENJAMIN - 1840-1907 - English engineer. Born in Frome and apprenticed at Neath Abbey ironworks. He began his long association with John Fowler in 1891. They were jointly responsible for the London Metropolitan Railway, and various stations and bridges. Their greatest work was the Forth Bridge; both were knighted at its opening in 1890. Baker was elected to the Royal Society. He also did much engineering work in Egypt, being consulting engineer for the Aswan Dam and designing the vessel in which Cleopatra's Needle was brought to London.

43 FOWLER, SIR JOHN - 1817-1898 - English engineer, best known for his work on railways. Set up his own business in 1844, and became engineer to the London Metropolitan Railway, the first underground railway. He designed and constructed a special type of locomotive known as 'Fowler's Ghost'. In 1865 he became president of the Institute of Civil Engineers — its youngest ever. He opposed the Channel Tunnel scheme. Worked with Baker on the Forth Bridge, completed in 1890. From 1871 he was general engineering adviser to the Khedive Ismail of Egypt.

FIRTH OF FORTH BRIDGE (1881-1887) - Cantilever bridge with a span of nearly one third of a mile between the piers. Rise 45,72 metres.

44 GAUDÍ Y CORNET, ANTONIO - Reus 1852 - Barcelona 1926 - Gaudí worked as an architect from 1876 on. His work is a personal interpretation of various styles, and in particular functional logic and for the clever use of ceramics and wrought iron. Thanks to their colour and movement they achieve a great expressive force and are amongst the finest examples of fin de siècle art in Catalonia. — See 260, 261, 262, XLVIII, 263, 264, 265, 266, XLIX, L.
ENTRANCE TO GÜELL PARK, Barcelona (1900-1914) - This municipal Park was originally conceived by Don Eusebio Güell as a garden-city. All that remains of it is two striking pavilions at the entrance to the enclosure.

45 GUIMARD, HECTOR - Lyon 1867 - New York 1942 - Guimard adopted the ideas of Art Nouveau, of which he was one of the chief representatives in France. He was both an architect and a decorator and was responsible for the famous entrances to the Métro in Paris. He applied his principles to street design. — See 274, 275, 276, 277.
ENTRANCE TO A MÉTRO STATION IN PARIS (1889-1904) - One of the stations built according to the plans of Guimard and executed in cast iron. Age caused the materials to deteriorate and made the entrances dangerous, and they were progressively replaced by simple balustrades.

46 WAGNER, OTTO - 1841-1918 - Appointed Professor at the Vienna Academy in 1894. Wagner was already well known as an architect inspired by the Italian Renaissance. His book *Moderne Architektur* written as a text-book for his students, became a classic of the architectural revolution. His first buildings were inspired by the new aesthetics, but he soon abandoned unnecessary ornament and achieved a pure expression in his Savings Bank, built in 1904-06. — See 49.
KARLSPLATZ STATION on the suburban line in Vienna (1899-1901) - The station building is an example of the new aesthetics, but even so it is not completely shorn of superfluous ornaments. Guided by his structural sense, Wagner was soon to abandon them altogether.

III GRASSET, EUGÈNE - Lausanne 1841-1917 - Architect, illustrator and ornamentalist. Studied architecture in his native town. After a stay in Egypt in 1869 he established himself in Paris in 1871 where he studied under Viollet-le-Duc. He interested himself in all forms of applied art. In his numerous writings he insisted on a proper respect for the materials used and for the functional utility of the object concerned.
SPRING, stained-glass window. Made by the Félix Gaudin workshop. Height 294 cm, total length 132 cm. Signed and dated bottom right: G. Grasset del, F. Gaudin pinx, Paris 1884.
Paris, Musée des Arts décoratifs

47 HORTA, VICTOR - Ghent 1861 - Brussels 1947 - After studying at Ghent, Paris and Brussels, Horta built his first houses in 1886. Three years later he used steel in architectural construction, which permitted him to introduce the curved line into both his interior and exterior plans. After a stay in the United States he returned to classicism and

linear architectural construction. A combination of good-quality work and good-quality materials, his achievements were amongst the most important of his day. — See 269, 270, 271, 272.
LA MAISON DU PEUPLE AT BRUSSELS (1896-1899) - One of the most important buildings of the period.

48 BERLAGE, HENDRICUS PETRUS - Amsterdam 1856 - The Hague 1934 - Berlage was the greatest Dutch architect of his time and he designed and carried out a great number of important buildings, including the Amsterdam Stock Exchange in 1898, which is executed in a very plain and simple style. In 1907-08 he was commissioned to draw up a plan for the enlargement of The Hague, and in 1913 for Amsterdam.
INTERIOR OF THE STOCK EXCHANGE IN AMSTERDAM (1898-1903) - Built in a very pure style without superfluous ornamentation this building became famous as the first example of modern construction in Holland, and made the reputation of the architect.

49 WAGNER, OTTO (biography see 46).
INTERIOR OF THE SAVINGS-BANK BUILDING AT VIENNA (1904-1908) - As indicated above, Wagner has excised all ornamentation here, and the style is extremely sober.

50 STIEGLITZ, ALFRED - Hobaker (U.S.A.) 1864-1946 - Stieglitz went to Berlin to study as an engineer, but he developed a passion for photography which he regarded promptly as an art in itself. He returned to America and in New York he founded the *Photo Secession*, and published a review *Camera Work* in 1903. From 1913 on he included paintings in his photographic exhibitions. He organized the first exhibition of the works of Matisse in the United States, and it caused such a scandal that many photographers left the *Photo Secession*. But Stieglitz persisted, and despite public hostility and the opposition of the leading newpapers he imposed modern art on the United States.
THE TERMINUS (photograph) (1892) - Stieglitz was a famous photographer in his day and the founder of an art gallery in New York. He was also one of the first and most enthusiastic supporters of modern art in the United States.

51 PRENDERGAST, MAURICE - Boston 1861 - New York 1924 - Self-taught painter. Went to Paris in 1891-92 and stayed there for four years. Thanks to the support given to him by his brother he was able to devote himself entirely to painting. Worked at the Académie Julian and was an habitué of the *Chat Blanc* at Montparnasse. Exhibited at the *Armory Show* in 1913. From 1900 on he attained a certain notoriety in the United States, where he was was one of *The Eight*.
CENTRAL PARK (1901) - Water-colour 30,8 × 47,0 cm. Signed and dated in the bottom right-hand corner: Maurice Prendergast 1901.
New York, Whitney Museum of American Art

52 MARIN, JOHN - Rutherford (New Jersey) 1870 - Cape Split (Maine) 1953 - One of America's leading contemporary water-colourists. Studied in Paris for five years, and then went to Maine. Exhibited at the *Armory Show* in 1913. After making his debut as an Impressionist he developed a style of his own based on a very free technique. He took his subjects from the sea and from the pulsating life of New York City.

SUNSET (1914) - Marin is one of the pioneers of avant-garde painting in the United States. The Venice Biennale in 1900 gave his works a place of honour. Water-colour 35,8×42 cm. Signed in the bottom left-hand corner: Marin.

New York, Whitney Museum of American Art

53 WEBER, MAX - Byalystok (Ukraine) 1881 - His family emigrated to the United States. In 1905 he went to Paris to study painting, and there he made the acquaintance of Douanier Rousseau and organized the latter's first exhibition in the United States. He took lessons from Matisse and in 1907 he made the acquaintance of Picasso. In the following year he returned to New York thoroughly acquainted with all the problems of modern art. He practised Expressionism with cubist means, and a certain amount of humour. CHINESE RESTAURANT (1915) - Canvas 88×105,6 cm. Signed and dated in the centre below: Max Weber 1915.

New York, Whitney Museum of American Art

54 BURNHAM, DAVID HUDSON - 1846-1912 - Born at Henderson, Jefferson County, New York, and educated at Chicago and Waltham, Mass. In 1871 he joined John W. Root in architectural practice in Chicago. The firm of Burnham and Root had many important comissions including the general superintendence of the World's Columbian Exposition of 1893. They were leaders in the development of steel-frame buildings, which made skyscrapers possible. Their works, beside the Monadnock Building, include the Rand-McNally Building and Mesonic Temple in Chicago and the famous Flatiron Building in New York. Also town-planning in Manila (Philippines), San Francisco, Baltimore and Chicago. Burnham became president of the American Institute of Architects in 1894. He died at Heidelberg.

54 BURNHAM and ROOT
MONADNOCK BUILDING, Chicago (1889-1891) - Traditional construction carried out in brickwork.

55 BURNHAM, D.H. & Co (biography see 54).
RELIANCE BUILDING, CHICAGO (1895) - Above a ground floor of dark stone rise fifteen stories of glass and glazed white tiles. This building has been described as the swan song of the Chicago school.

IV GARNIER, TONY - Lyon 1869 - La Bédoule 1948 - Garnier won the Rome Prize in 1899. He drafted a project for a *cité industrielle*, but it was turned down by the Academy in 1901. He was subsequently appointed architect of the town of Lyon, and he carried out a great deal of work there which was directly inspired by his original project for the *cité industrielle* in 1898. — See 309.
INDUSTRIAL CITY (1904-1917) - Garnier's designs for the Industrial City were not reproduced and published in an album until 1917. The plan originated in 1901. If Garnier made any corrections there was no change at all by comparison with the general plan dated 1901. It is indisputable to-day that Garnier's ideas with regard to a modern industrial city have had a great deal of influence both in France and in other countries. However, that did not prevent the Academy from turning him down in 1901. Sketch carried out in wash on paper 42,3×62,4 cm. Signed and dated : Tony Garnier 1917.

Lyon, Musée des Beaux-Arts

56 RODIN, AUGUSTE - Paris 1840 - Meudon 1917 - At the age or fourteen Rodin entered the École des Arts décoratifs, where he studied under Carpeaux. Refused entrance to the École des Beaux-Arts on three occasions he worked for Barye and Carrier-Belleuse. From 1870 to 1877 he worked in Brussels, where he met Constantin Meunier. His most famous works caused a scandal on their first presentation to the public, and they were rejected. It was not until around 1900 that he obtained an international reputation. His romantic inspiration was ably served by a feeling for volume and by a sense of the monumental, and together they produced work which ranks amongst the major manifestations of sculpture in the nineteenth century. — See 117, 176.
THE GATE OF HELL (begun in 1880) - Rodin was commissioned to carry out this work for the future Musée des Arts décoratifs in Paris, and he began working in plaster. Thereafter he continued working on it all his life without ever regarding it as completed. After his death in 1917 it was left for a while, still incomplete, and then in 1936 it was cast in bronze, and in 1938 it was installed at the Musée Rodin. Height: 6 m 35; width: 4 m; depth: 0 m 85.

Paris, Musée Rodin

57 CARRIÈRE, EUGÈNE - Gournay-sur-Marne 1849 - Paris 1906 - At the age of twenty he studied at the École des Beaux-Arts in Paris under Cabanel. His austere art with its nebulous palette and his liking for chiaroscuro had a great influence on his contemporaries, amongst whom he had both fervent admirers and detractors.
MATERNITY - Carrière was associated with all the great writers of his day, and he painted warm and remarkable portraits of them. He also did numerous paintings on the theme of motherhood, sometimes serene, and sometimes disquieting. It could be said of Carrière that his whole art was was placed in the service of a humanitarian idea, which he sought to express in intimate domestic scenes.

Bayonne, Former Collection Personnaz

58 ROSSO, MENARDO - Turin 1858 - Milan 1928 - Debarred from the Brera, where he had studied sculpture, he exhibited from 1882 onward, first in Milan and then in Rome. In 1884 he stayed in Paris for a while, living in great poverty, then he went to Vienna. In 1889 he returned to Paris where he became outstandingly successful amongst avant-garde circles. His important work dates from these years. His polemic with Rodin on the priority of Impressionism in sculpture attracted a good deal of attention. Finally he returned to Milan where in his closing years his renown was firmly established.
THE BOOKMAKER (1894) - Bronze 43 cm.

Milan, Galleria Nazionale d'Arte Moderna

59 HODLER, FERDINAND - Berne 1853 - Geneva 1918 - Hodler joined the École des Beaux-Arts in Geneva in 1871 and studied under Menn, who was a pupil of Ingres and a friend of Corot. In 1876 Hodler won a certain notoriety with his famous ' Tir fédéral '. From then on he painted historic and symbolic scenes in the grand style, at once both monumental and linear. The landscapes which he painted towards the end of his life were of a clearer tonality and a greater warmth of colour. Under both French and German

influence, his art made a European impact and he can be regarded as a pioneer.
EURYTHMICS (1895) - From 1895 on the artist showed an inclination for historical and mythological subjects, which he represented in a firm and somewhat angular style. His last works have a greater warmth. Canvas 167×245 cm. Signed and dated in the bottom right-hand corner: Ferd. Hodler, 1895.

Berne, Kunstmuseum

60 PUVIS DE CHAVANNES, PIERRE - Lyon 1824 - Paris 1898 - Descendant of an old legal family, Puvis de Chavannes studied successively in the ateliers of Scheffer, Couture and Delacroix, and his art was influenced in particular by two years he spent in Italy. His art, which was one of the first manifestations of Symbolism, was at first not understood. From the year 1861 onwards he was commissioned to paint a series of great murals, which won him the admiration of the Parnassians for the discipline of his style and its antique inspiration. — See 107.
SACRED GROVE FREQUENTED BY THE ARTS AND THE MUSES (1884) - In France the allegorical paintings of this artist have had no real influence. Canvas 5 m 50×10 m 41.

Lyon, Musée des Beaux-Arts

61 DEBUSSY, CLAUDE - Saint-Germain-en-Laye 1862 - Paris 1918 - In 1884 he won the Prix de Rome, when he already had a reputation as a musical revolutionary. His opera *Pelléas et Mélisande* marks a turning point in the musical world of the theatre, though it met with vehement opposition at the time of its first production in 1902. Debussy was at this time a friend of the Symbolists and more especially of Pierre Louys whose *Chansons de Bilitis* he set to music. His artistic genius excelled equally in melody, piano (*Preludes, Images,* etc.), chamber music (*Quatuor*) and symphony (*L'Après-midi d'un faune, La Mer*). His last great masterpiece was *Le Martyre de Saint-Sébastien* accompanied by D'Annunzio's text. Finally, an admirable short piece *Le Noël des enfants qui n'ont plus de maison* bears witness to the great sorrow felt by Debussy at the events of the 1914-18 war.
' PELLÉAS ET MÉLISANDE ' (1902) - First page of the original score.

Paris, Bibliothèque du Conservatoire de Musique

62 SCHÖNBERG, ARNOLD - Vienna 1874 - Los Angeles 1951 - From 1899 onwards Schönberg's music intoduced daring innovations. In 1908 he abandoned tonal music for a melody of pure timbre like the original cry of the Expressionists. His *Pierrot Lunaire* came out in the same year as the *Blaue Reiter*. He was the founder member of an important school of innovators that can pride itself with names such as Webern and Alban Berg. He died as a refugee in the U.S.A.
' PIERROT LUNAIRE ' (1912) - A page of the original score. Signed in the bottom right-hand corner: Arnold Schönberg.

Vienna, Universal Editions A.G.

63 STRAVINSKY, IGOR FEDOROVITCH - Oranienbaum 1882 - Lives in the U.S.A. - A doctor at law, Stravinsky took music lessons from Rimsky-Korsakov, but studied harmony and counter-point on his own. His meeting with Diaghilev and his contact with the Russian ballet was decisive for his musical future. The ' Fire Bird ' in 1910 won him

international fame. His *Sacre du Printemps* provoked a memorable scandal in 1913. His Russian period ended with the 1914-18 war. He subsequently set himself to search for a means of expression more cold and abstract than before. His restless evolution as an artist is landmarked by a spasmodic series of masterpieces. Of a breathtaking and self-assertive nature, they are always of a great originality.

' SACRE DU PRINTEMPS ' (1913) - First page of the original score. Page of the manuscript introduction. Signed and dated in the top right-hand corner: Igor Stravinsky, 1912-13.

Paris, A. Meyer Collection

64 VALADON, SUZANNE - Bessines 1867 - Paris 1938 - Went to Paris whilst still very young, and there she was a dressmaker, an acrobat and a model. Encouraged by both Lautrec and Degas she began to draw. In 1909 she gave up drawing and devoted herself exclusively to painting. Her work has great expressive force. She was the mother of Maurice Utrillo.

ERIK SATIE (1893) - Portrait of the composer of *Parade* (1866-1925). Style influenced by Lautrec. Canvas 41,5 × 22 cm.

Paris, Private Collection

65 RIJSSELBERGHE, THÉO VAN - Ghent 1862 - Saint-Clair (France) 1926 - Studied at the Ghent and Brussels Academies. A visit to Spain and Morocco greatly influenced and vivified his colouration. The *Grande-Jatte* of Seurat helped him to discover his own particular line. He became the only artist to adapt the neo-impressionist technique to portraiture. He was one of the founders of the *Groupe des XX* and then of the *Libre Esthétique*. Around the yeat 1895 he took part in the crusade of Van de Velde for the renewal of the decorative arts.

THE READING (1903) - Together in E. Verhaeren's study are (from left to right) Verhaeren, Vielé-Griffin, C.-Ch. Cross, Fénéon, Gide and Maeterlinck. Canvas 181 × 240 cm. Signed and dated in the bottom right-hand corner: 19 U.R. 03. Also dated on the back: 19 mai 1903.

Ghent, Musée des Beaux-Arts

66 DENIS, MAURICE - Granville 1870 - Paris 1943 - Joined the *Nabis* group, whose aesthetics he presented in an article in *Art et Critique* in 1890. With and affinity to Gauguin and working close to spirit of Symbolism his art was also related to Art Nouveau. After some time spent in Italy his art developed in the direction of an amply proportioned and serene classicism. He played a leading didactical and critical role in his day and is the originator of an important revival of religious art. — See 164.

HOMAGE TO CÉZANNE (1900) - The aim of the artist here is to express the admiration of a generation for the Master of Aix, and around a still-life which once belonged to Gauguin by Cézanne he has gathered the chief artists of the day and his wife in the company of their other master, Odilon Redon. From left to right: Odilon Redon, Vuillard, Mellerio, Vollard, Denis, Sérusier, Ranson, Roussel, Bonnard and Mme Maurice Denis. Canvas 160 × 240 cm. Signed and dated in the bottom left-hand corner: Maurice Denis 1900.

Paris, Musée National d'Art Moderne

V SEURAT, GEORGES - Paris 1859-1891 - Seurat's move from the École des Beaux-Arts to the atelier of Lehmann, a student of Ingres, gave him a taste for drawing. A study of the works of the doctor Chevreul on the laws of simultaneous contrast in colour led him to work out his own technique of the division of colours, which he then put into effect in his *Baignade à Asnières*, which was refused by the 1884 Salon. Young artists using the same technique, which became known as Neo-Impressionism or Pointillism, and marked the first reaction from the sensualism of Impressionism, now gathered round him. — See 123.

LA GRANDE-JATTE (1884) - Seurat's chef-d'œuvre was exhibited at the eighth exhibition of the Impressionnists in 1886, and was the result of a great many studies. Canvas, height 200 cm; lenght 300 cm.

Chicago, The Art Institute

67 TOULOUSE-LAUTREC, HENRI DE (biography see 31).

AU SALON (1894) - This canvas is the most important of all the series Lautrec devoted to the ' Maison ' in the rue des Moulins. All these works are marked by pitiless cruelty which is still further underlined by the sharpness of line and the violence of the colours. Signed in the bottom left-hand corner with the monogram: TL. Canvas 112 132 cm.

Albi, Museum

68 GAUGUIN, PAUL (biography see 27).

CALVARY (1889) - On a scrap of paper that has come down to us Gauguin has noted down the ideas which led to the theme of this picture. Everything proceeds from the word ' calvaire ', on to the idea of stones, Brittany, local costumes and the landscape of Brittany, concluding with the idea of poverty. Canvas 92 × 73 cm. Signed and dated in the bottom left-hand corner: P. Gauguin 89.

Brussels, Musées royaux des Beaux-Arts de Belgique

69 VAN GOGH, VINCENT - Groot Zundert 1853 - Auvers-sur-Oise 1898 - Son of a pastor, Van Gogh worked in an art gallery and subsequently felt drawn to the religious vocation. In 1877 he entered the ministry, but after eight months of evangelical training in the Borinage he began to draw and in this way found his real vocation. He left for Paris in 1886 where he worked in touch with the Impressionists and the Pointillists, but after two years he left for Arles, where he joined Gauguin. A brain storm obliged Van Gogh to let himself be put away in an asylum. After three such attacks he settled down in Auvers with Doctor Gachet, and there, before long, he committed suicide. He sought desperately for spiritual equilibrium in his work, and this gave it a more and more impressive grandeur. He was practically unknown during his lifetime, but his work will continue to affect most profoundly those generations of artists who regard him as a precursor. — See 70, 160, XXVI.

FLOWERS IN A GARDEN (1888) - In this picture the artist has set out to express horizontal coloured zones in a vertical frame. Canvas 95 × 73 cm.

Zürich, Private Collection

70 VAN GOGH, VINCENT (biography see 69).

VIEW AT AUVERS (1890) - The artist painted a number of pictures on the same theme. Canvas 50 × 100 cm.

London, Tate Gallery

71 DEGAS, EDGAR - Paris 1834-1917 - Born in good circumstances and trained at the École des Beaux-Arts, Degas adopted a traditional form of painting greatly under the influence of Ingres, but his portraiture reveals a keen psychological understanding, and by their presentation his compositions outdo the techniques of modern photography. He remained independent of the Impressionists. Towards 1884 trouble with his sight made his technique more pictorial and less rigorous in design. His themes are connected with domestic life, but above all with the life of the theatre and the ballet. His wax statuettes of dancers, which are so full of life and movement, date from this period. In 1909 blindness put an end to his creative work. — See 103, 118.

INTERIOR OR RAPE (1874) - Canvas 81 × 116 cm.

Philadelphia, Henry McIlhenny Collection

72 MUNCH, EDVARD - Lösten (Norway) 1863 - Ekely (Oslo) 1944 - After studying in Oslo Munch remained twenty years outside his own country. In Paris he was a student of Bonnat, after which he worked alone. In 1908 after a period of severe nervous depression he returned to Norway for good, and worked completely on his own there. His work is of a psychological and literary character dominated by the idea of love and death. The problem of form for him is always subordinate to the emotional factor. His influence was felt above all in Germany, where he was one of the precursors of Expressionism. — See 159, XXVII.

THE ROOM OF THE DEAD (1896) - Black and white version of a picture painted in 1895 (Oslo, National Museum). As a child Munch suffered three successive losses by death, and the theme of a room with mourners occurrs often in his work. Lithograph on paper 40 × 54 cm.

Oslo, Municipal Collection

73 ENSOR, JAMES - Ostend 1860-1949 - Son of an English father and a Flemish mother, he grew up in the home of his grandmother, who kept a shellfish and souvenir shop at Ostend. At first a painter of middle-class interiors, Ensor later developed in terms of a lighter palette, and his particular talent turned to the interpretation of new themes: masks, skeletons, religious subjects treated in a critical spirit, which made him a precursor of Fauvism and Expressionism, if not even Surrealism. His best work was done between the years 1879 and 1898, but he did not achieve fame until after the turn of the century. His work as an engraver and a draughtsman is also important. — See 158, XXV.

ENTRY OF CHRIST INTO BRUSSELS (detail) (1888) - This picture is one of Ensor's major works. It was so strongly marked by his anti-conformism that it shocked, and was refused by the *Groupe des XX* in 1888. Canvas 250 × 434 cm. Signed and dated in the bottom right-hand corner: J. Ensor 1888.

London, Louis Franck

74 ROUAULT, GEORGES - Paris 1871-1958 - Rouault began his career with a stained-glass artist, and from 1891 onwards he worked in the atelier of Gustave Moreau, whose work he was always to regard with fervent enthusiasm. He tried on two occasions for the Prix de Rome, but failed each time. In 1902 he came into contact with Fauvism, and in the Salon d'Automne he showed the first series of pictures representing girls, clowns

and acrobats. They have a streak of cruelty and are related to Expressionism. In 1913 Vollard took over his atelier and became his dealer, commissioning him to illustrate literary works. From then on Rouault's inspiration turned more and more to religious subjects. — See XI, 179.

THE HOLY FACE (1912) - Gouache 56 × 42 cm.

Winterthur, Hahnloser Collection

75 MODERSOHN-BECKER, PAULA - Dresden 1876 - Worpswede 1907 - The first woman painter in Northern Germany, Paula Modersohn-Becker was one of the colony of artists whose centre was in the little village of Worpswede. Under the influence of Cézanne, whom she got to know during the course of numerous visits to Paris, she simplified her plastic language. In her efforts to express the essence of things she was, despite her short life, one of the founders of German Expressionism. — See 186.

PORTRAIT OF RAINER MARIA RILKE (c. 1906) - Cardboard 34 × 26 cm. Signed in the bottom left-hand corner with the monogram: PMB.

Bremen, Ludwig Roselius Collection

76 STRINDBERG, AUGUST - Stockholm 1849-1912 - Strindberg, better known as a dramatist, made his first pictorial efforts in and around 1873 and then again in 1892. His most important work was done from 1900 to 1907 at the time when he was writing his symbolist dramas. He painted in a colour scale of greys, and his technique was tachist. His essay on the role of chance in artistic production, written in French, in 1894, retains its topicality down to the present day.

THE TOWN (1900-1907) - Canvas 94,5 × 53,2 cm.

Stockholm, National Museum

VI KANDINSKY, WASSILY - Moscow 1866 - Paris 1944 - After studying law in the beginning, he turned at the age of thirty to art. He left for Munich, and together with Jawlensky he studied at von Aszbe's school and at the Academy of Art under Franz von Stuck. In 1909 he founded the *Neue Künstlervereinigung*. He was a member of the *Blaue Reiter* group and took part in the first exhibition of its work. At the declaration of war in 1914 he returned to Russia, but was back in Germany in 1921 to join the teaching staff of the *Bauhaus* first in Weimar and subsequently in Dessau. After the break-up of the *Bauhaus*, he was compelled to leave Germany and in 1933 finally settled down in Neuilly. — See 194, 195.

WITH THE BLACK ARCH (1912) - ' Painting is a shock jarring different worlds which are destined to create still further worlds — and this is the work of art — by and in their struggle with each other ', said Kandinsky. Canvas 188 × 196 cm. Signed and dated in the bottom left-hand corner : Kandinsky 1912.

Neuilly, Mme Nnina Kandinsky

77 CARRÀ, CARLO - Quargneto (Piedmont) 1881 - Bologna 1961 - Carrà was one of the five first signatories to the Futurist Manifesto, and he continued to take part in the activity of the group until 1915. In 1912 he was a member of the *Novecento* Group, and then of the Metaphysical Group. He published various polemical writings.

THE FUNERAL OF THE ANARCHIST GALLI (1911) - The artist said himself (in 1913) that he had tried to convey on canvas ' the upheaval and the whirl of light and form, sonorous, blaring and odorous '

which he had felt in himself at the time. Canvas 198,7 × 259,1 cm. Signed and dated in the bottom left-hand corner: C D Carrà.

New York, Museum of Modern Art

78 SEVERINI, GINO - Cortona 1883 - Lives in Paris - Made his first pictorial efforts with Boccioni and Balla. At the age of twenty-two he settled in Paris where he took part in the Cubist movement. He signed the Futurist Manifesto and in 1912 he organized the famous exhibition at Bernheim's. From 1916 to 1921 he produced works demonstrating the theories of Cubism and Futurism. In a study published in 1921 and entitled *From Cubism to Classicism* he sought to justify his return to the ' métier des classiques '.

BAL TABARIN (1912) - Canvas 161,5 × 156 cm. Signed on the back: Gino Severini Le Bal Tabarin.

New York, Museum of Modern Art

79 GONTCHAROVA, NATHALIE - Ladygino (Russia) 1881 - Lives in Paris - Gontcharova studied painting at the École des Beaux-Arts in Moscow. In 1910, together with her husband, Larionov, she created Rayonnism, then in 1912 she did theatre décor for Diaghilev. — See 99.

ELECTRIC LAMPS (c. 1912) - Canvas 105 × 81 cm. Signed on the back: Gontcharova.

Paris, Mme Nathalie Gontcharova

80 MALEVITCH, CASIMIR - Kiev 1878 - Leningrad 1935 - In 1908 he was a Fauvist painter. In 1911 in Paris he adopted a constructivist style close to that of Léger, then his art developed towards the abstract, and in 1913 he exhibited a canvas in Moscow which consisted of a black square on a white ground. He was the creator of Suprematism, which he expounded in a manifesto drawn up together with Maïakovsky and published in 1915. His book *The Unobjective World* (Die gegenstandslose Welt) came out at the *Bauhaus* in 1925. But for several years he had already been the victim of the general persecution of *avant-garde* artists under the Soviet regime and was not allowed to exhibit. — See 152.

CUBIST ROSE (1912).

Amsterdam, Stedelijk Museum

81 KUPKA, FRANÇOIS - Opocno (Bohemia) 1871 - Paris 1957 - Studied at the Beaux-Arts in Prague then at the Beaux-Arts in Vienna. He went to Paris in 1894 where he produced comic drawings for a living. In 1910 he painted his first abstract works. It was then that he began his experiments ' to liberate colour from form ' and continued them in all possible abstract forms.

AMORPHA (1912) - The artist exhibited two paintings in the Salon d'Automne of 1912 entitled *Fugue à deux couleurs* and *Chromatique chaude*, which were preceded by the term *Amorpha*, which underlined the urge to abstraction already indicated in the titles. Canvas 66 × 66,5 cm. Signed and dated in the bottom right-hand corner: Kupka 21-12.

Paris, Musée National d'Art Moderne

VII KLEE, PAUL - Münchenbuchsee (Switzerland) 1879 - Locarno 1940 - In 1898 Klee studied painting in Munich. He made the acquaintance of Kandinsky and came strongly under his influence. He also became a friend of Marc and Delaunay. He was a member of the *Blaue Reiter* group. In 1912 he went to Paris for the first time where he studied the work of the Cubists. His visit to Tunisia with

Macke and Molliet in 1914 crowned his endeavours to emancipate colour from reality. A new world was born from the summary of his experiences on the edge of the abstract and the figurative. Mingling reality and the fantasy of dreams he created an imaginary world which has become a source of inspiration for modern art. He was on the teaching staff of the *Bauhaus*, but left Germany to settle in Berne when the Nazis came to power. — See 155.

THE CARPET OF MEMORY (1914) - Oil on canvas mounted on cardboard : 40 × 51,5 cm. Signed and dated in the bottom left-hand corner : Klee 1914/193. 1914 on the cardboard.

Berne, Kunstmeseum

VIII KOKOSCHKA, OSCAR - Pöchlarn (Austria) 1886 - Lives in Villeneuve (Switzerland) - Kokoschka first studied at the school for decorative arts in Vienna, where he came under the influence of the *Jugendstil*. In 1907 he collaborated with the *Wiener Werkstätte* founded by Hoffmann and in 1910 with the *Sturm* group. In 1913 he visited Italy. In Vienna he made the acquaintance of Rilke and Hofmannsthal. From 1925 to 1933 he was professor at the Dresden Academy. He has made numerous trips abroad and long stays in Prague and London. — See 200, XXXVII.

THE TRAGEDY OF MAN (poster) (1908) - Poster for the summer theatrical season at the art exhibition in Vienna (1908). Lithograph in colour. 118 × 76 cm. Signed in the bottom right-hand corner: O.K.

Munich, Wolfgang Gurlitt

82 MAREY, JULES G. - Beaune 1830 - Paris 1904 - Doctor and physiologist, Marey patiently investigated the movement of animals by means of a graphic process of his own invention. Then he turned to photography, and after having invented or developed various kinds of apparatus for the purpose he presented the first film takes at the Académie des Sciences in 1888. He is credited with the first modern use of the camera. — See 87, 88, 89, 91.

CHRONOPHOTOGRAPHIC EXPERIMENTS (1887) - Marey studied movement by means of a photographic apparatus he had invented, and which was, in fact, the forerunner of the film camera. The pictures he obtained deeply impressed certain artists by their plastic beauty. Marcel Duchamp was one of those who was inspired by them.

83 MUYBRIDGE, EDWARD JAMES - Kingston-on-Thames 1830-1904 - An English photographer who emigrated to the United States. He published a number of books on photography, of which the most important was *Animal Locomotion* (11 vols, 781 photographs, 1897). He developed the so-called zoopraxiscope, an apparatus for throwing moving pictures on to a screen. He returned to England in 1900.

APPARATUS CONTAINING TWENTY-FOUR PHOTOGRAPHIC CABINS at Palo Alto, California (1881) - Stand at the stud-farm of Palo Alto in California (1872). An extremely rich — and somewhat eccentric — Californian had made a bet on the positions adopted by horses when galloping, as described by Marey in 1868. In order that the English photographer Muybridge could check the statements of the French scientist a rather extraordinary device was built: ' Along the track on which the horses were to gallop twenty-four photographic cabins were erected. They were twenty-four dark-rooms in which twenty-four assistants prepared twenty-four wet collodion plates at the blast of a whistle... As soon as the twenty-four cameras were ready, the horses were made to gallop along the track, photographing themselves as they passed by breaking cotton lines spread from each cabin over the track. ' It took from 1872 to 1878 to get the whole apparatus ready.

84 REYNAUD, ÉMILE - Montreuil 1844 - Ivry 1918 - After having constructed a so-called praxinoscope in 1877, Reynaud developed this apparatus and introduced the 'théâtre d'optique' with the use of perforated strips. From 1888 onwards he showed the first long presentations of animated cartoons at the Musée Grévin.
THE PRAXINOSCOPE (1890) - This device consisted of a prism each facet of which was covered by a mirror which sent successive images to the eye of the beholder from a tape revolving in front of this apparatus. The inventor himself drew and coloured the tapes.

85 LUMIÈRE, LOUIS - 1864-1948 - An industrialist and analytical chemist, Lumière invented the French cinematograph together with his brother Auguste (1862-1954). From 1895 on he produced a number of films, the first of which, entitled *La Sortie des usines*, may be considered as the forerunner of the documentary film. Later on he made a series of comic films: *L'Arroseur arrosé*, *L'Arrivée d'un train* and *Le Photographe*. He made his own scenarios, and the various roles were played by his friends and relatives and by the workmen of his factory. In 1896 he engaged and trained operators and produced the first documentaries, news records, and so on. But this formula led Lumière into an impasse. The public soon tired of simple moving pictures with no dramatic relationship between them, and in the end the Société Lumière practically abandoned production, and confined itself to the sale of its film apparatus.
LUMIÈRE CINEMA CAMERA (1895) - With this apparatus it was possible to obtain in the same photograph a uniformly clear focus on any object from three feet to infinity thanks to the very great focal length of the object lens.

86 EDISON, THOMAS A. (biography see 38).
THE INVENTOR IN HIS LABORATORY (1900) - Photograph bearing the facsimile signature of Edison and taken from the *Encyclopédie du Siècle* devoted to the Universal Exhibition of 1900.
Paris, Bibliothèque Nationale

87 MAREY, JULES G. (biography see 82).
MAREY'S PHOTOGRAPHIC GUN (1889) - Marey invented this apparatus to improve on the 'photographic revolver' invented by the astronomer Janssen in 1876.
Paris, Musée des Arts et Métiers

88 MAREY, JULES G. (biography see 82).
MAREY'S CHRONOPHOTOGRAPH (1889) - This apparatus was invented in order to analyse movement. From the year 1882 Marey had been working on the chronophotograph with fixed plates, which subsequently became, thanks to the use of reels of film, the chronophotograph with moving plates.

89 MAREY, JULES G. (biography see 82).
PHYSIOLOGICAL CENTRE IN THE PARC DES PRINCES (1889-1890) - For a good many years the physiologist had been conducting experiments into the movements of animals by means of graphic devices of his own invention. After Muybridge's visit to Europe, Marey employed photographic methods, during the course of which he improved or invented certain apparatus. In 1888 he showed the first shots on film to the Acadméie des Sciences.

90 COHL, ÉMILE (pseudonym for ÉMILE COURTET) - Paris 1857 - Villejuif 1938 - Cohl was an inventor and he was responsible for the first animated cartoons, which he showed in Paris in 1908 at the *Théâtre du Gymnase*. ' He produced animated cartoons of such humour and inventiveness that they have retained their freshness down to the present day ' (H. Agel). His chief productions were *Fantasmagorie* (1909), *Les Joyeux Microbes* (1911), and *Le Retapeur de cervelles* (1911).
JOYFUL MICROBES (1909) - Still from the animated cartoon of the same name. MacLaren, ' the famous mythologist of the animated cartoon' has been greatly influenced by Cohl.

91 MAREY, JULES G. (biography see 82).
MEN JUMPING FOR A MAREY EXPERIMENT (1889).

92 BARRÈRE, ADRIEN - 1877-1931 - Lithographer and poster designer, Barrère did the ' têtes de turc ' in *Fantasio* from 1902 onwards. He also did a series of blocks on the professors of the Faculty of Medicine, and designed posters for the theatre, and in particular for the *Grand Guignol*.
POSTER FOR THE FILM ' NICK WINTER ' (1910) - Lithograph in colour 148×111 cm. Signed in the bottom left-hand corner: A. Barrère.

93 DUCHAMP, M.
POSTER FOR ' L'ARROSEUR ARROSÉ ' (1895-1896) - Comic film by Louis Lumière. It can be said to contain the germ of important future developments. The story is feeble but the film was very successful and was often imitated. Signed in the bottom right-hand corner: M. Duchamp.

94 MÉLIÈS, GEORGES - Paris 1861-1931 - Méliès wanted to enter the École des Beaux-Arts, but his father opposed his intention and forced him to go into the family business: the manufacture of machinery. Méliès developed a great flair for mechanical things. He was keenly interested in prestidigitation and he illustrated a satirical journal *La Griffe*. He bought the Robert Houdin theatre, and he constructed the apparatus for many illusionist tricks. He was also much taken by the advent of the cinema, and in 1895 he wanted to buy one of Lumière's apparatus to instal in his theatre, but Lumière wished his invention to be used solely in the interests of science, and refused to sell an apparatus to Méliès, who then replied by constructing the first cinematograph studio (1896). He then produced a series of cinematic spectacles in a great variety of genres: historical representations, fairy stories, phantasmagoria, and so on. An actor himself, he met with great success, and yet he ultimately died in a condition verging on poverty.
STILL TAKEN FROM THE FILM ' A TRIP TO THE MOON ' (1902) - First ' long reel ' (280 metres) a triumph of film production. This picture depicts the ramming home of the shell in which the travellers for the trip to the moon have taken their places.

95 LE BARGY, CHARLES - 1858-1936 - A well-known actor and a member of the Comédie Française, he was one of the first ' stars ' to produce a film and play a role in it himself. Together with A. Calmettes he produced the film *The Assassination of the Duke of Guise*. Le Bargy gave a great deal of thought to the requirements of the new acting medium, and he made up for the lack of words by a carefully studied miming without the use of excessive gesticulation. His theories were adopted with some success in other countries.

95 CALMETTES, ANDRÉ - Paris 1861-1942 - Prizeman of the Ghent Conservatory, Calmettes made his début at the *Théâtre de l'Odéon* in Paris in *Don Juan*, and he acted there for six years with Porel. Afterwards he went to the Grand Théâtre. He also played at *L'Ambigu*, the *Gymnase* and the *Vaudeville*. He created the role of Pascal in *Les Amoureuses* at the Théâtre Sarah Bernhardt. He became Le Bargy's assistant in the production of films for Lafitte brothers. The film *The Assassination of the Duke of Guise* was first shown on November 17th 1908 in Paris. Henri Lavedan wrote the scenario, and Saint-Saëns composed the incidental music.
STILLS FROM THE FILM ' THE ASSASSINATION OF THE DUKE OF GUISE ' - Produced by Le Bargy and Henri Calmettes; scenario by Henri Lavedan; music by Camille Saint-Saëns. Acted by Le Bargy, A. Lambert, Gabrielle Robinne and Berthe Bovy. The film was first shown in the Salle Chanas at the première of the ' Film d'Art ' and met with considerable success.

96 BAKST, LÉON - Petersburg 1866 - Paris 1924 - Bakst was the pseudonym adopted by Léon Nicolaievitch Rosenberg, a Russian painter and stage designer who became famous chiefly on account of his décors for the Russian ballet. He was the founder of the *Mir Izkonstva* (World of Art) Group. He went to Paris with the Ballets Russes in 1910 and did theatrical decor, designed costumes and posters for the ballet.
MAQUETTE FOR THE DÉCOR of ' Thamar ', ballet by Balakirev (1912).
Paris, Musée des Arts décoratifs

97 BENOIS, ALEXANDRE - Petersburg 1870 - Paris 1960 - Painter and writer on art. Collaborated with Diaghilev.
MAQUETTE FOR THE DÉCOR of the fair-ground scene in *Petrushka* by Stravinsky (1911).
Wadsworth Atheneum, Hartford, Conn. (U.S.A.)

98 BAKST, LÉON (biography see 96).
COSTUME DESIGN for a village girl in *Daphnis et Chloé* (1912) - Choreographic symphony by Maurice Ravel after a scenario by Fokine.

99 GONTCHAROVA, NATHALIE (biography see 79).
DESIGN FOR THE STAGE CURTAIN for Rimsky-Korsakov's *Coq d'Or* (1914) - Russian Ballet staged by Diaghilev. The same artist did the décor for this ballet, but the curtain design — a fragment of which is shown here — was never executed.
Paris, Mlle Evelyn Cournand

100 WALSER, KARL - Teufen, Canton Appenzell (Switzerland) 1877 - Berne 1943 - Painter, engraver, book illustrator and theatrical designer. After having made his mark as an engraver and a designer Walser devoted himself entirely to painting.

He is well-known for his frescoes in the Council Hall of the Berne Town Hall and on the staircase of the Oscar Reinhardt Museum in Winterthur. In 1907 he did the décor for the Max Reinhardt production of 'Romeo and Juliet'.

100 REINHARDT, MAX - Baden (near Vienna) 1873 - New York 1943 - In 1894 Reinhardt was working at the *Deutsches Theater* in Berlin under Otto Brahm. He staged his first productions in the cabaret *Schall und Rauch* in 1901. He was the Artistic Director of the *Deutsches Theater* from 1905 to 1920, and again in 1924. He also occupied the same post at the *Kammerspiele*. Reinhardt revolutionised theatrical production, and abandoned the 'naturalist' method in favour of more colourful and lively representations. He was compelled to leave Germany in 1933.
DESIGN for the décor of Max Reinhardt's production of 'Romeo and Juliet' by Shakespeare in Berlin (1907).

IX MUCHA, ALFONSO MARIA - 1869-1939 - Decorator and poster designer of Czech origin, Mucha studied at Munich, Vienna and Paris. He began to design and execute posters for Sarah Bernhardt in 1894. He was also a contributor to *La Plume*.
SARAH BERNHARDT AS MEDEA (poster) (1898) - Poster for Mme Sarah Bernhardt in 'Médée' at the Théâtre de la Renaissance (1898). Lithograph 208×77 cm. Signed in the bottom left-hand corner: Mucha
Paris, Union centrale des Arts décoratifs, Bibliothèque

X ROUSSEAU, HENRI, known as THE DOUANIER - Laval 1844 - Paris 1910 - After having taken part in the Mexican campaign as an Army Bandsman, Rousseau was employed by the customs and excise in Paris. He retired in 1884 and turned to painting. His ideal was Bouguereau. From 1886 on he began to exhibit his work with the Independants. He was adopted by the Symbolists who were much taken by the spontaneity of his art and its ingenuous poetry. Alfred Jarry made him known to the avant-garde painters who organized a banquet for him at Picasso's which was afterwards to become famous. Beginning with 'naive' landscapes he later turned to exotic subjects and to dreams and visions. — See 115.
THE SNAKE-CHARMER (1907) - Exhibited at the Salon d'Automne in 1907, this painting is credited with having inspired the verses composed by Apollinaire at the famous banquet given to the artist in 1908 in Picasso's atelier. Amongst others present were Braque, Max Jacob, and André Salmon. 'Rousseau, you can remember the Aztec landscape and the forests where the mango and the pineapple grow.' Canvas 165×180 cm. Signed and dated in the bottom right-hand corner: Henri Julien Rousseau 1907.
Paris, Musée du Louvre

XI ROUAULT, GEORGES (biography see 74).
OLYMPIA (1906-1907) - Rouault often took girls as the theme of his compositions. The best-known example is in the Bangerter collection at Montreux. This work seems to indicate a softening of the artist's style, which was often sharp and cruel. Mounted paper 62×46 cm. Signed in the top right-hand corner: G. Rouault.
Hem, Philippe Leclercq

XII JAWLENSKY, ALEXEY VON - Torschalk (Russia) 1864 - Wiesbaden 1941 - An officer in the Imperial Guard, Jawlensky studied at the Petersburg Academy of Art and in the atelier of Repin. In 1896 he went to Munich, where he met Kandinsky. Subsequently he lived in France, where he came under the influence of Cézanne, Van Gogh and Matisse. He was one of the founders together with Kandinsky of the *Neue Künstlervereinigung* in 1909. The extreme Fauvism of his colouration is reminiscent of ikons and Russian folk art. His favourite subject is the human form and face expressing a profound inner life.
WOMAN WITH FRINGE (1913) - The model was Mme Langenhahn-Hirzel, a pianist. The human form begins to play a bigger and bigger role in the artist's work. By their close contours and the striking harmony of colouring, the faces with wide open eyes suggest the coming deep religious movement of the artist. Cardboard 68×50 cm. Signed and dated in the bottom left-hand corner: A. Jawlensky 13.
Wiesbaden, Stadtmuseum

XIII DUCHAMP, MARCEL - Blainville (France) 1887 - Lives in New York - Brother of Jacques Villon and of Raymond Duchamp-Villon, he studied first to be a librarian and then he went to the Académie Julian. He did his first work under the influence of analytical Cubism. In 1913 he exhibited his *Nu descendant un escalier* at the Armory Show in New York. In the following year he created his 'ready-made' mechanical objects exhibited works of art. With Picabia and Man Ray he founded a movement which previsaged Dadaism. — See 208.
NUDE DESCENDING A STAIRCASE NO. 2 (ca. 1911) - Preceded by a study and taken up again in a later water-colour this work is the first in which the artist seeks to translate movement. Although he uses the breaking-down techniques introduced by Cubism he is also inspired by the chronophotography of Marey. Canvas 147,5×89 cm. Signed and dated lower centre: Marcel Duchamp 1912. Title in the left-hand corner: Nu descendant un escalier. Also signed and dated on the verso: Marcel Duchamp, 1912.
Philadelphia, Museum of Art, Louise and Walter Arensberg Collection

XIV TOULOUSE-LAUTREC, HENRI DE (biography see 31).
LA GOULUE AU MOULIN ROUGE (poster) (1891) - La Goulue, the woman who inspired numerous drawings and paintings, and in particular the famous poster for the Moulin Rouge, represents one of the artist's most powerful creations. Canvas 0,80×0,60 cm. Signed in the bottom left-hand corner: Lautrec.
Bernheim de Villers Collection

101 RENOIR, AUGUSTE - Limoges 1841 - Cagnes 1919 - Painting at first in a traditional style, towards the year 1868 Renoir adopted a lighter palette and began to interest himself in landscape. He came into contact with the Impressionists and began to paint subjects from Parisian life. Two visits to Algeria and a stay in Italy in 1881 opened his eyes to the world of colour. After a period spent under the influence of Ingres, colour took on an ever greater intensity and warmth in his work. Towards the end of his life he turned to sculpture, and his best work in this art form was done between the year 1914 and his death.

PORTRAIT OF MME RENOIR (about 1885) - Probably executed in 1885, when the artist was working under Cézanne's influence. Pierre Renoir, eldest son of the painter, was born the same year. Canvas 65.5×54 cm. Signed top left.
Philadelphia, Museum of Art

102 GAUGUIN, PAUL (biography see 27).
THE 'ALYSCAMPS' AT ARLES (1888) - Painted by Gauguin during his stay at Arles with Van Gogh. Canvas 73×91,5 cm. Signed and dated, bottom left: Gauguin 88.
Paris, Musée du Louvre

XV GAUGUIN, PAUL (biography, see 27).
TA MATETE (THE MARKET) (1892) - It has often been stressed that this composition, executed during Gauguin's first stay in Tahiti, seems influenced by reminiscences of Egyptian art. Canvas 73×97,5 cm. Signed in the bottom right-hand corner: P. Gauguin 92.
Basle, Musée des Beaux-Arts

103 DEGAS, EDGAR (biography see 71).
THE MILLINERS (1898) - Variation on a theme which had been a favourite of Degas since 1880. It shows the simplified technique practised by Degas in his later years. Canvas 76×82 cm.
Paris, Private Collection

104 STEER, PHILIP WILSON - Birkenhead 1860-1942 - Son of a portraitist, Steer studied in Gloucester and in Paris between 1882 and 1885. However, he soon lost touch with artistic circles on the continent and towards the end of his life he came deeply under the influence of Constable, and his last works were conservative in style.
SOUTHWOLD (1892) - The name under which this picture was sold at the Steer sale (1942) is dubious, as well as the supposed date (1887). It is probable that it was painted at Cowes in 1892 and exhibited under another title at the Steer Exhibition of 1894. Canvas 51×61 cm.
London, Tate Gallery

105 MOREAU, GUSTAVE - Paris 1826-1898 - A visit to Italy in 1857 brought him the acquaintance of the masters of the Quattrocento. Influenced by literary reminiscences his work is one of the first manifestations of Symbolism. He became a Professor at the École des Beaux-Arts in 1880, and amongst his students there were Rouault, Matisse, Marquet and Evenepoel, to whom he taught painting but without imposing his own aesthetics on them. His predilection for rare and precious materials, and his taste for the strange and exotic were to act as a great attraction in the eyes of Huysman's character *Des Esseintes*. His experimental work foreshadowed Surrealism.
ORPHEUS MOURNING AT THE TOMB OF EURYDICE (1897-98) - One of the last works of the artist. Canvas 174×128 cm. Signed bottom left: Gustave Moreau.
Paris, Musée Gustave Moreau

106 SEGANTINI, GIOVANNI - Arco (Trento) 1858 - Schafberg (Engadine) 1899 - After studying at the Brera in Milan, Segantini retired to the solitude of the mountains to devote himself to painting. He came under the influence of the twilight lyricism of Cremona, and was half-converted to Divisionism. But essentially rebellious, his art tended above all towards an ideal communion between man and nature.

LOVE AT THE SOURCE OF LIFE. - (1896) Canvas 72×100 cm.

Milan, Civica Galleria d'Arte Moderna

107 PUVIS DE CHAVANNES, PIERRE (biography see 60).
GENEVIEVE KEEPING WATCH OVER THE SLEEPING CITY (1898) - Mural on canvas. Signed and dated, bottom left: Puvis de Chavannes 1898.

Paris, Panthéon

108 THORN PRIKKER, JOHAN - The Hague 1868 - Cologne 1932 - After studying in The Hague, where he came under the influence of Divisionism and of Van Gogh, he left for Germany in 1904, where he was gradually attracted to Symbolism. His art is profoundly religious, severe and of a monumental nature.
THE BETROTHED (1893) - Canvas 146×86 cm. Signed bottom right: J. Thorn Prikker.

Otterlo, Rijksmuseum Kröller-Müller

109 TOOROP, JOHANNES THEODORUS, known as JAN POEWOREDJO - Java 1858-1928 - After studying in Amsterdam, in his youth he experimented in the new tendencies of his day. Trying his hand at Impressionism he developed towards Neo-Impressionism and Divisionism. He became a Catholic and thereafter his art reflected his religious faith. He became one of the dominant figures of artistic life in the Netherlands.
THE THREE FIANCÉES (1893) - The most remarkable of the artist's symbolist pictures. Drawing 78×98 cm. Signed bottom right: J. Th. Toorop.

Otterlo, Rijksmuseum Kröller-Müller

XVI VUILLARD, ÉDOUARD - Cuiseaux 1868 - La Baule 1949 - With Roussel he abandoned the École des Beaux-Arts in 1886 for the Académie Julian. It was there that the *Nabis* were grouped around Sérusier. Around the year 1891 he was inspired by Synthetism, but the soon adopted a finer colouration, and worked with small dab-like brush-strokes in small panels of domestic life. After 1900 he returned to a more traditional conception, always retaining his delicacy of colour and a sense of filtered light.
MOTHER AND CHILD (ca. 1899) - In his 'Nabi' period the artist often painted domestic scenes, and even afterwards he always retained a delicate sense of colour and a liking for the diffused light of interiors. Cardboard 50,8×58,5 cm. Signed in the bottom right-hand corner: Vuillard.

Glasgow, Art Gallery and Museum

110 KHNOPFF, FERNAND - Château de Grimbergen - lez-Termonde 1858 - Brussels 1921 - Son of a minor judge Khnopff himself studied law, but then he studied art under Mellery at the Brussels Academy. Going to Paris in 1879 he became a pupil of G. Moreau. He also came under the influence of the Pre-Raphaelites. He worked chiefly in water colours, pastel, *rehaussé* design and engraving rather than in oils. He was a fashionable painter, and his delicate work with its literary character relates him to the Symbolists.
THE BLUE WING (1896-98) - Drawing mounted on canvas, high-lighted with crayon. 30×90 cm.

Brussels, Musées royaux des Beaux-Arts

111 NIELSEN, EJNAR - Copenhagen 1872-1956 - During his stay in Paris in 1901 Nielsen's style was dominated very definitely by the art of Puvis de Chavannes. His work expresses the theme of resignation and death in a truly profound fashion.
BLIND GIRL (1896-1898) - One of the most powerful of Danish symbolist painting. Canvas 130×77 cm. Signed and dated bottom right: Ejnar Nielsen, Giern, 1896-98.

Copenhagen, Hirschprung Collection

112 KLIMT, GUSTAV - Vienna 1862-1918 - After studying at the School of Decorative Art in Vienna he collaborated with his brother and with Matsch in producing decorative painting for various public buildings in Vienna and in the provinces. After the death of his brother he stopped painting for six years. When in 1899 he began to paint again his style was completely new. He took an active part in the Vienna Secession, and became its President. The relationship between decoration and architecture remained one of his major preoccupations and his influence on the decorative arts in Austria was considerable. — See LII.
MADAME FRITZA RIEDLER (1906) - Canvas 152×133 cm. Signed and dated bottom left: Gustav Klimt, 1906.

Vienna, Österreichische Galerie

XVII BONNARD, PIERRE (biography see 32).
LA LOGE (1908) - Josse and Gaston Bernheim, with whom Bonnard had been in contractual relationship since 1899, are shown here with their wives. The forthnightness of the representation recalls Japanese art whose influence persisted with the artist despite his technical evolution since his 'Nabist' days. Canvas 91×120 cm. Signed in the bottom left-hand corner : Bonnard.

Paris, Bernheim Jeune Collection

113 EVENEPOEL, HENRI - Nice 1872 - Paris 1899 - Born of Belgian parents Evenepoel was brought up in Brussels. By 1892 he was in Paris where he studied under G. Moreau, though he hardly pursued what was taught him. He soon discovered Manet. His favourite subjects were sought amongst the people and in landscapes. A journey to North Africa gave his paintings great richness of colour. It was soon after his return from North Africa that he died. In his short artistic career he painted over 250 pictures, and amongst them his portraits, scenes and landscapes put him amongst the best painters of the end of the nineteenth century.
LADY WITH A WHITE HAT (1897) - The artist's cousin, whom he was in love with and who inspired some of his best works. Canvas 57×46 cm. Signed and dated middle left: Evenepoel 97.

London, Louis Franck

114 VALLOTTON, FÉLIX - Lausanne 1865 - Paris 1925 - Settling in Paris in 1882, Vallotton studied at the Académie Julian, where he soon came into contact with the Nabis. His sense of bitter realism and a certain rigid delineation particularly noticeable in his landscapes tend to associate his art with the period presided over by the Nabis and the *Revue Blanche*. His art bore the stamp of his origin, and the discipline of his colours was in the general tradition of Swiss painting.
WOMAN COMBING HER HAIR (1900) - Canvas. Signed bottom right: F. Vallotton.

Paris, Musée national d'Art moderne

115 ROUSSEAU, HENRI, known as LE DOUANIER (biography see X).
THE CHAIR FACTORY (1897) - The site is a Paris suburb. Canvas 46×38 cm. Signed bottom right: Henri Rousseau.

Paris, Mme Jean Walter

116 UTRILLO, MAURICE - Paris 1883-1955 - Thanks to his mother Suzanne Valadon, Utrillo grew up in artistic circles, which favoured the development of his talents. He began drawing and painting at a very early age. His tragic and chaotic life never affected his creative powers. He loved Montmartre and the neighbourhood of Paris, whose scenes he presented with a simplicity and directness which created poetry from the most ordinary of subjects. Influenced by Impressionism he developed a very personal style in his ' white period ', to which, in fact, his best works belong.
BERLIOZ' HOUSE (1907) - Canvas. Signed bottom right: Maurice Utrillo. V.

Paris, Musée du Petit Palais

117 RODIN, AUGUSTE (biography see 56).
BALZAC (1897-98) - Commissioned by the Société des Gens de Lettres, but rejected in 1897. When Rodin exhibited the plaster model at the Nationale des Beaux-Arts, in 1898, this representation of the great writer caused a scandal. Bronze 280 ×124×124 cm. Signed.

Meudon, Musée Rodin

118 DEGAS, EDGAR (biography see 71).
GRANDE ARABESQUE (second model) (1882-1891) - Degas' sculpture, known amongst his friends during his lifetime, was not shown in public until after his death. Twenty-two versions of each one were cast by Hébrard and were exhibited in 1921. Bronze, height 40 cm.

Paris, Musée du Louvre

119 MAILLOL, ARISTIDE - Banyuls 1861-1944 - Maillol studied sculpture and painting at the École des Beaux-Arts in Paris. In 1886 he founded a tapestry atelier in Banyuls. After this he came into contact with the Nabis. Losing his sight for a period of six months, he then took up sculpture. He turned to the inspiration of classical Hellenism, particularly after a visit to Greece. He became the great exponent of the female form in art, and his work is informed with an earthy power and grandeur. — See 120.
L'ACTION ENCHAÎNÉE (1906) - Commissioned for the monument put up to Blanqui in his home town of Puget-Théniers. Bronze 212×77×96 cm.

Paris, Musée National d'Art Moderne

120 MAILLOL, ARISTIDE (biography see 119).
NIGHT (1902) - Plaster 105×56×104 cm.

Paris-Malakoff, E. Rudier Collection

121 BOURDELLE, ANTOINE - Montauban 1861 - Le Vésinet 1929 - After studying in Toulon, Bourdelle went to Paris where he worked in the atelier of Falguière. From 1896 onwards he worked as an assistant to Rodin, under whose influence he came, but he freed himself from it by the great variety of his own sources of inspiration and, above all, by the deliberate discipline and construction of his form. — See 183.
HERCULES THE ARCHER (detail) (1910) - This work still shows the influence of Rodin, but the stylization is inspired by archaic Greek sculpture. It emphasizes the grandeur and monumentality characteristic of Bourdelle. Bronze gilt, 248×236×116 cm.

Paris, Musée National d'Art Moderne

122 PICASSO, PABLO RUIZ - Malaga 1881 - After studying at Barcelona Picasso settled in Paris in 1904. Having come under the influence of Lautrec, his art went through a blue and then a pink period. He became acquainted with Negro art and the work of Cézanne. *Les Demoiselles d'Avignon* opened up his Cubist period, during which he worked in close collaboration with Braque, establishing *analytical* Cubism, which was then followed by *synthetic* Cubism. A protean genius, an inventor of forms and, above all, of means of expression, Picasso subsequently passed through other periods. In every one of them he pursued his original intention right through to its logical and extreme limit. The Spanish civil war caused him deep distress and provided the inspiration for one of his most bizarre masterpieces, *Guernica*. Picasso is one of the men who have had the most profound impact upon our century. — See XIX, 129, 133, 166, 205.
THE MADMAN (1905) - Bronze, height 41 cm.

Washington D.C., The Phillips Memorial Gallery

XVIII CÉZANNE, PAUL - Aix-en-Provence 1839 - Paris 1906 - Born of a family in good circumstances, Cézanne went to the Académie Suisse in Paris, where he met Pissarro and Guillaumin, but until 1872 his art remained romantic and the treatment bogged down in a sombre tonality. Under the influence of Pissarro he tried his hand at landscapes using an Impressionist technique but with a solid construction. Around the year 1882 he definitely turned away from Impressionism to rediscover classical values in his interpretation of landscape. In his endeavour to interpret reality faithfully, Cézanne outdid the current Verism. After 1900 he found himself greatly admired by the younger painters, who regarded him as their master. Most of the pictorial movements of the twentieth century go back to his inspiration. — See 126, 127, 128.
LES GRANDES BAIGNEUSES (1900-1905) - Towards the end of his life the artist returned to this subject of bathing women, one he had often treated, but this time in an unusual format. There are three versions of this picture, which is amongst the most perfect of his work, including those in which he has succeeded in uniting all the elements in the same linear and plastic rhythm. Canvas 130×195 cm.

Paris, Private Collection

123 SEURAT, GEORGES (biography see V).
ASYLUM AND LIGHTHOUSE, HONFLEUR (1886) - Canvas noted by Huysmans at the Salon des Indépendants in 1887. One of the most important of Seurat's works, done during his second stay by the sea. At his premature death the artist left only about fifty completed canvases. Canvas 65×81,5 cm. Signed bottom left : Seurat.

London, Private Collection

124 PELIZZA DA VOLPEDO, GIUSEPPE - Tortona 1868 - Milan 1907 - Studied at Bergamo and at the Brera in Milan. Between 1893 and 1895 he abandoned his original verist style and adopted Divisionism. His work *La Grange* exhibited in 1898 gave rise to a lively polemic. Towards the end of his life he returned to Impressionism.
LINEN IN THE SUN (1905) - In its composition and technique this work reminds us of Seurat. Canvas 87×131 cm. Signed and dated bottom right: G. Pelizza 1905.

Lessona (Biella), Ludovico Cartotti

125 SIGNAC, PAUL - Paris 1863-1935 - A meeting with Seurat in 1882 was decisive for Signac's subsequent career, but in and around 1896 he abandoned Pointillism, although his technique remained dominated by the division of tones. After the war he turned towards water colours. In 1989 he published an essay entitled *D'Eugène Delacroix au Néo-Impressionnisme*, which became practically the manifesto of the latter movement.
PORTRAIT OF FÉNÉON (1890) - ' On the enamel of a rhythmic background of measures and angles, portrait of M. Félix Fénéon ' — thus the artist described his picture. Canvas 74×93 cm. Signed and dated bottom right: P. Signac 90. Numbered bottom left: op. 217.

New York, Mr and Mrs Joshua Logan

XIX PICASSO, PABLO (biography see 122).
LES DEMOISELLES D'AVIGNON (1907) - Chef-d'œuvre which is the result of numerous studies made in the winter of 1906-07. Note has properly been taken of the difference in style between the three figures to the left, which are strongly under the influence of Iberian sculpture, and those on the right whose strangely carved faces are reminiscent of Negro art, which had just come to Picasso as a revelation. But the inspiration for this composition was the strong impression made upon Picasso by *Les grandes baigneuses*. Canvas 244×233 cm.

New York, The Museum of Modern Art

126 CÉZANNE, PAUL (biography see XVIII).
PORTRAIT OF AMBROISE VOLLARD (1896-1899) - This portrait took a hundred and fifteen sittings and then Cézanne gave it up, saying to Vollard — ' I am fairly satisfied with the shirt-front. ' Canvas 100×81 cm.

Paris, Musée du Petit Palais

127 CÉZANNE, PAUL (biography see XVIII).
HOUSE ON THE BANK OF THE MARNE (1888-90) - Many works of this period show water in the foreground, parallel with the edge of the canvas. Canvas 91×73,5 cm.

Washington, United States Government

128 CÉZANNE, PAUL (biography see XVIII).
LA MONTAGNE SAINTE-VICTOIRE (1904) - Canvas 54×65 cm.

Amsterdam, Stedelijk Museum

129 PICASSO, PABLO RUIZ (biography see 122).
THE RESERVOIR (1909) - Picasso's palette during his stay at Horta de San Juan was limited to ochres and reddish tones. He pursued his researches into the Cubist interpretation of forms. Canvas 60×50 cm.

Paris, Private Collection

130 BRAQUE, GEORGES - Argenteuil sur Seine 1882 - Braque settled down in Paris in 1900 where, four years later, he adopted the technique of the Fauves. In 1907 he came under the influence of Cézanne and of Negro art. Together with Picasso he became one of the most outstanding of the Cubists. His contribution to the creation of synthetic Cubism and *papiers collés* would seem to have been decisive. Up to 1914 he carried on his work in close collaboration with Picasso. After the war, during which he was seriously wounded, he returned to his work and devoted himself to evolving a strenuously classical form of Cubism. It may be said that Braque was continuing the proud traditions of the essential genius of France in so far as this is both actively and specifically expressed in his work. — See 131, 132, XX, 171.
HOUSE BEHIND THE TREE (1908) - At the Salon d'Automne of 1908, Braque showed several works painted during that year, notably two landscapes with houses surrounded by trees. They were rejected by the Jury and Matisse himself declared that they were painted ' in little cubes '. They were exhibited in November at Kahnweiler's gallery, and in his review Louis Vauxcelles took up Matisse's phrase and christened the new movement ' Cubism '. Canvas 40,5×30,5 cm.

France, Private collection

131 BRAQUE, GEORGES (biography see 130).
THE MANDOLA (1910) - By his analysis into tiny juxtaposed areas of paint, Braque here goes further in the systematic break-down of forms. It is the birth of analytic Cubism. Canvas 73×60 cm. Signed on the back: Braque.

London, Roland Penrose

132 BRAQUE, GEORGES (biography see 130).
NUDE (1907-1908) - The most ambitious of Braque's compositions up to that date. It was inspired by Picasso's *Demoiselles d'Avignon*, which had first of all shocked Braque and of which he had said to the artist: ' In spite of your explanations, this picture... it's as if you wanted us to eat sand and drink diesel oil '. Braque's canvas, however, is marked by his sense of proportion, the deepest characteristic of his art, which distinguishes it from Picasso's extremism. Canvas 141×101 cm. Signed on the back: G. Braque.

Paris, Private collection

XX BRAQUE, GEORGES (biography see 130).
JEUNE FILLE A LA GUITARE (1913) - One of the two great paintings of the human figure carried out by the artist during his synthetic Cubism period. Canvas 130×74 cm. Signed on the back: Braque.
Paris, Musée national d'Art moderne

133 PICASSO, PABLO RUIZ (biography see 122).
PORTRAIT OF AMBROISE VOLLARD (1909-10) - Canvas 92×65 cm.

Moscow, Pushkin Museum

134 LÉGER, FERNAND - Argentan 1881 - Gif-sur-Yvette 1955 - After studying architecture, Léger became a free-lance student at the École des Arts Décoratifs and at the Académie Julian. He came under the influence of Cézanne and Matisse. In 1910 he met Picasso and Braque, and his constructive art developed towards the disintegration of form into coloured planes. Profoundly impressed by the 1914-18 war he discovered the world of the machine and of things, and he became the lyrical interpreter of a mechanised civilization. His energetic art aimed principally at the people developed mainly in the mural genre. See 135, XXI.
NUDES IN THE FOREST (1908-1910) - ' I put two years into my battle with volume in Nudes in the forest ', said Léger, and added: ' For me there is nothing but the battle with volume. I always felt that I couldn't make the most of colour. Volume was enough. ' Canvas 120×70 cm. Signed bottom left: F. Léger.

Otterlo, Rijksmuseum Kröller-Müller

135 LÉGER, FERNAND (biography see 134).
CONTRAST IN FORMS (1913) - ' Contrasts=dissonances, and therefore the maximum effect of expression... but the painter must choose, the use of contrasts not being simultaneous ', wrote Léger. Around 1913 he did a series of works that he called simply ' contrasts in forms ', thus defining the aim of his researches.   Canvas 93×73 cm.   Signed bottom left: F. Léger 1913.

Paris, Galerie Louis Carré

XXI LÉGER, FERNAND (biography see 134).
LA NOCE (1910-1911) - ' The people at this wedding hide one behind the other. Just another little attempt to get rid of perspective, that inverted fourth dimension, the perspective of inevitably making everything smaller. ' (Guillaume Apollinaire). Canvas 257×206 cm. Signed on the back, to the right: F. Léger.

Paris, Musée national d'Art moderne

136 MARCOUSSIS, LOUIS (pseudonym for LOUIS MARKOUS) - Warsaw 1878 - Cusset (Allier) 1941 - From 1903 on Markous worked in Paris.   For four years his art was greatly influenced by Impressionism, but then he adopted Cubism.   He took part in Villon's *Section d'or*.   An excellent engraver, he illustrated the works of his favorites poets, Apollinaire and Nerval.   He established his place amongst the Cubists by his poetic temperament.
STILL-LIFE WITH A CHEQUER-BOARD (1912) - Canvas 139×93 cm.   Signed and dated bottom right: Marcoussis 12.

Paris, Musée National d'Art Moderne

137 LA FRESNAYE, ROGER DE - Le Mans 1885 - Grasse 1925 - After studying at the Académie Julian, at the École des Beaux-Arts and at the Académie Ranson, where he came under the influence of Maurice Denis and Sérusier, he turned to Cubism around the year 1912 and carried out great compositions, which were interrupted by the First World War.   As a result of the war he contracted consumption, whereupon he went to live in Grasse where he eked out the last years of his life in constant ill-health.   He was no longer physically able to execute anything but works of rather small dimensions in which persist nevertheless all the grandeur, noble inspiration and classical concern with perfection that pervade his earlier compositions.
SEATED MAN (1914) - Canvas 131×162 cm.

Paris, Musée National d'Art moderne

138 MORANDI, GIORGIO - Bologna 1890 - Lives in Bologna - Studied at the Bologna Academy, and came into touch with modern art through the work of Renoir at the Venice Biennale in 1910, and the work of Cézanne at Rome in 1914.   After a short futurist and metaphysical interlude he turned in particular to the *Valori plastici* Group.   However, he remained isolated, and his art restored a pure poetic essence to everyday reality.
STILL-LIFE (1914) - Canvas 102×40 cm.   Signed and dated bottom left: Morandi, 1914.

Bologna, Giorgio Morandi

139 GRIS, JUAN (pseudonym for JOSÉ VICTORIANO GONZALÈS) - Madrid 1887 - Boulogne-sur-Seine 1927 - Gris made the acquaintance of Picasso in Paris in 1906, and from 1911 on he devoted himself to painting.   He came to analytical Cubism and produced some remarkable *collages*.

STILL-LIFE WITH FRUIT DISH (1914) - Oil and *papier collé* on canvas 95×65 cm.

Paris, Galerie Louise Leris

XXII LARIONOV, MICHEL - Tiraspol (near Odessa) 1881 - Lives in Paris - From childhood on he was attracted by painting and entered the Moscow Beaux-Arts in 1898.   In 1909 he exhibited a picture influenced by the first utterings of Cubism. In 1910 he inaugurated Rayonism, one of the first manifestations of truly abstract art.   In 1914 he settled in Paris with his wife Nathalie Gontcharova and did work for the *Ballets Russes*.
RAYONISM (1911) - Canvas 54×70 cm.   Signed in the bottom right-hand corner: M. Larionov. Signed and dated on the back: Larionov, Moscow, 1911.

Paris, Michel Larionov

140 GESTEL, LEO - Woerden 1881 - Blaricum 1941 - Studied under his father at the Amsterdam Academy of Art.   Left for Paris in 1904 with Jan Sluyters, where he came under the influence of Impressionism.   In 1908 he came under the influence of Divisionism, and in 1911 under that of Cubism.   After a long stay in Majorca he returned to Holland, where in his art he returned to Realism after the fashion of Bergen, where he settled down.
WOMAN STANDING (Cubist figure) (1913) - Canvas 182×95 cm.   Signed and dated bottom right: Leo Gestel 1913.

*Private collection
(on loan to the Stedelijk Museum, Amsterdam)*

141 SLUYTERS, JAN - Bois-le-Duc 1881 - Amsterdam 1957 - Studied art in Amsterdam.   He was awarded the *Prix de Rome*, after which he travelled for two years in Italy and Spain.   Then he settled down for a long time in Paris.   After having experimented in various current styles, he became the chief figure of avant-garde painting in the Netherlands.
CUBIST PORTRAIT OF A WOMAN (1914) - ' The movement, the dynamism are no longer translated by violent brushwork, but by the rhythm of flat planes into which the subject is broken down ' (H. Jaffé).   Canvas 202×176 cm.   Signed and dated bottom left: Jan Sluyters 1914.

Amsterdam, Jan Sluyters Jnr.

142 DUCHAMP-VILLON (pseudonym for RAYMOND DUCHAMP) - Damville (Eure) 1876 - Cannes 1918 - Brother of Jacques Villon and Marcel Duchamps. As a sculptor, at first he came under the influence of Rodin.   But around the year 1910, under the influence of Cubism, he began to produce extremely original work by means of interlocking planes and volumes.   In 1912 he worked with André Marc at the *Maison Cubiste*.   His ' Horse ' shows him to be one of the initiators of Cubist sculpture and one could even go as far as to say of modern sculpture in general.   He died as a result of the war.
THE HORSE (1914) - Bronze 44×36×44 cm.   Signed and dated bottom left: Duchamp-Villon, 1914.

Paris, Galerie Louis Carré

143 LIPCHITZ, JACQUES - Druskieniki (Lithuania) 1891 - Studied sculpture in Paris in 1909 at the École des Beaux-Arts and the Académie Julian. In 1913 he joined forces with Picasso and Gris. Through Cubism he developed a personal style, which tended increasingly towards the Baroque.

Lipchitz is really first and foremost a lyrical sculptor with a never failing source of invention.
SAILOR WITH A GUITAR (1914) - Bronze, height 80 cm.

Buffalo, Albright Art Gallery

144 BOCCIONI, UMBERTO - Reggio di Calabria 1882 - Sorte (Verona) 1916 - In 1898 Boccioni went up to Rome where he joined with Severini and Balla, then he went to France to study Impressionism.   On returning to Italy he met Marinetti in Milan in 1908.   In 1910 he signed the Futurist Manifesto and plunged with ardour into the fight for Futurism and very soon became one of its leading exponents.   A vigorous polemicist he defended his theories in numerous writings. — See 145, XXIII.
UNIQUE FORMS OF CONTINUITY IN SPACE (1913) - ' To give a body in movement, I am careful not to give its trajectory... but to fix the unique form that expresses its *continuity in space* ' (Boccioni, 1913).   Bronze, height 112 cm.

Milan, Galleria d'Arte Moderna

145 BOCCIONI, UMBERTO (biography see 144).
UNFLATTERING PORTRAIT (1913) - Bronze 60×47×40 cm.

*Birmingham (Michigan),
Mr. and Mrs. Harry Lewis Winston*

146 BALLA, GIACOMO - Turin 1871 - Rome 1958 - At the turn of the century he was closely associated with Boccioni and Severini, both of whom he encouraged to new experiments.   He devoted himself completely to Futurism, and he was one of the signatories of the Futurist Manifesto.   The importance of his work persisted beyond the end of the movement he represented and he influenced the following generation.
YOUNG GIRL RUNNING ON A BALCONY (1912) - Canvas 130×130 cm.   Signed and dated bottom left: Balla 1912.

Milan, Galleria d'Arte Moderna

XXIII BOCCIONI, UMBERTO (biography see 144).
DYNAMISM OF A CYCLIST (1913) - Canvas 100×30 cm.

Basle, Private collection

147 METZINGER, JEAN - Nantes 1883 - Very precocious, he was revolted by traditional teaching. He was first drawn to Neo-Impressionism and then to Fauvism.   Around the year 1908 he adopted Cubism of which he became one of the theoreticians.   Took part in Villon's *Section d'Or*, and in 1912 he published *Du Cubisme* in collaboration with Gleizes.
STUDY FOR THE PORTRAIT OF APOLLINAIRE (1910) - Exhibited by the artist at the Salon des Indépendants of 1910 (No. 52).   Pencil drawing on pink paper, 42×30 cm.   Signed and dated, bottom centre: J. Metzinger.

Paris, Musée national d'Art moderne

148 SIRONI, MARIO - Tempio Pausania (Sardinia) 1885 - Milan 1961 - After studying mathematics at Rome he was attracted to painting, but he did not join the Futurist movement until 1915. He displayed an individual personality and style which marked all his later work.   He was one of the founders of *Novocento* in 1920.
PORTRAIT OF THE ARTIST (1913) - Although Sironi did not join the Futurist movement until 1915, its influence is apparent in some of his earlier works.

Canvas 51,5×49 cm. Signed and dated, bottom left: Sironi, 1913.

Milan, Civica Galleria d'Arte Moderna

149 FEININGER, LYONEL - New York 1871-1956 - In 1887 he settled in Germany where he studied both in Hamburg and Berlin. He stayed on several occasions in Paris where he studied at the Académie Colarossi and frequented the circle of Matisse. He drew for a number of American weeklies, and from 1909 to 1913 his art developed in close touch with Cubism, and also with the *Brücke* and *Sturm* Groups. After the First World War he taught at the Bauhaus, and was one of the founders of the *Quatre Bleus*. In 1937 he left Germany for the U.S.A.
THE BRIDGE (1913) - Canvas 80×100 cm. Signed and dated top left: Feininger 13.

St. Louis, Missouri, Washington University

150 VILLON, JACQUES (pseudonym for GASTON DUCHAMP) - Damville (Eure) 1875 - Brother of Marcel Duchamp and Duchamp-Villon he settled in Paris in 1894 and did cartoon work. From 1906 onward he began to paint and came under the influence of Degas and Lautrec. In 1911 he adopted analytical Cubism and associated with the *Section d'Or* Group. His art developed systematically in the spirit of Cubism, or more precisely closely following a system of geometrical construction all his own and which he enlivens with a palette of ever increasing delicacy and richness. Villon is also a master of the art of engraving. He at present lives in the retiring peace of his atelier at Puteaux, which he has never left.
MARCHING SOLDIERS (1913) - Villon was triyng to convey the jerky movement of the soldiers by means of a play of coloured planes. Canvas 65×92 cm. Signed and dated bottom right: Jacques Villon 13.

Paris, Galerie Louis Carré

151 MACKE, AUGUST - Meschede (Germany) 1887 - Champagne Front 1914 - After studying at the Dresden Academy and the Beaux-Arts in Düsseldorf, Macke made numerous trips to Italy, Paris and London. He was friendly with Franz Marc, and joined the *Blaue Reiter* group. He also got to know Delaunay. In 1914 he went to Tunisia with Klee and Louis Molliet and did a large number of water colours whilst he was there. Unlike the other members of the *Blaue Reiter* group, Macke remained attached to visual experiences, though he interpreted them according to the principles of Fauvism and Cubism.
BRIGHTLY-LIT SHOP WINDOWS (1912) - Like the theme of ' people strolling ', that of the ' woman in front of a window ' was one that Macke went back to again and again. The big mirror allows him to catch the animated life of the street as it unrolls outside the frame of the composition. Canvas 105×85 cm. Signed and dated bottom right: Aug. Macke 1912.

Hanover, Städtische Galerie

152 MALEVITCH, CASIMIR (biography see 80). SUPREME (before 1915) - The artist gave the name of Suprematism to his abstract art and explained the principles in a manifesto published in 1915. Canvas 66×97 cm.

Amsterdam, Stedelijk Museum

153 KUPKA, FRANÇOIS (biography see 81). NOCTURNE (1910) - Probably the earliest, or one of the earliest, of Kupka's works that is really abstract. Canvas 66×66 cm. Signed bottom right: Kupka.

Paris, Galerie Louis Carré

XXIV MONDRIAN, PIET - Amersfoort (Amsterdam) 1872 - New York 1944 - Studied at the Amsterdam Academy. Between 1907 and 1910 he came under the influence of Fauvism. In 1911 he settled in Paris and this was the beginning of his Cubist period, which lasted until 1917. He was one of the founders of *De Stijl*, and he crossed the threshold of total abstraction. Subsequently he developed his ' neo-plastic ' style to greater and greater purity, and his work must be regarded as one of the corner-stones of modern art. — See 154.
COMPOSITION (1914) - Work from the Cubist period of the artist. Canvas 140×101 cm. Signed and dated in the bottom right-hand corner: P.M. 14.

Amsterdam, Stedelijk Museum

154 MONDRIAN, PIET (biography see XXIV). APPLE TREE IN BLOSSOM (about 1912) - Canvas 78×107 cm.

La Haye, Gemeentemuseum

155 KLEE, PAUL (biography see VII). ABSTRACTION: COLOURED CIRCLES JOINED BY BANDS OF COLOUR (1914) - Watercolour on paper 11,5×17 cm. Signed bottom left: Klee, and dated right: 1914, 218.

Berne, Paul Klee Stiftung

156 DELAUNAY, ROBERT (biography see I). CIRCULAR FORMS, SUN, TOWER (1913) - Canvas 130×130 cm. Signed and dated.

Paris, Private collection

157 LEWIS, PERCY WYNDHAM - Canada 1882 - London 1957 - After studying in London, Munich and Paris, Wyndham Lewis acquired a profound knowledge of avant-garde art of the continent. In 1913 he welcomed Marinetti to the post-impressionist and futurist exhibition in London, but his personal style tended to greater abstractionism and he was one of the founders of *Vorticism*, whose manifesto *Blast* he published in 1914.
COMPOSITION (1913) - Related to the series of designs for *Timon of Athens* exhibited at the second Post-Impressionist exhibition in London in 1912. Pencil, pen and watercolour, with pasted paper, 34×26,5 cm. Signed and dated bottom right: Wyndham Lewis 1913.

London, The Tate Gallery

158 ENSOR, JAMES (biography see 73). SKELETONS WARMING THEMSELVES (1889) - Canvas 75×60 cm. Signed and dated bottom left: Ensor 89.

Fort Worth, Texas, Robert F. Windfohr Collection

XXV ENSOR, JAMES (biography see 73). FALL OF THE REBEL ANGELS (1889) - Canvas 180×132 cm. Signed and dated in the bottom left-hand corner: Ensor 89.

Antwerp, Koninklijk Museum voor Schone Kunsten

159 MUNCH, EDVARD (biography see 72). SPRING EVENING IN KARL-JOHAN STREET IN OSLO (1892) - The artist has already acquired his definitive style: he wishes to paint the life of man and to express drama by accentuating colour and simplifying form. Canvas 84,5×121 cm. Signed bottom right: E. Munch.

Bergen, Rasmus Meyer Samlinger

160 VAN GOGH, VINCENT (biography see 69). PORTRAIT OF DR. GACHET (1890) - Painted at Auvers in June 1890, a few weeks before the artist's death. The first version of this work is in the Museum at Frankfurt. Canvas 68×57 cm. Not signed or dated.

Paris, Musée du Louvre

XXVI VAN GOGH, VINCENT (biography see 69). STARRY NIGHT (1889) - The starry night of Saint Remy is overflowing with richness. ' Van Gogh guides his life, his dramatic life, between heaven and earth, between the pitiful light of men and the incomparable light of heaven. ' Canvas

New York, Museum of Modern Art

161 REDON, ODILON - Bordeaux 1840 - Paris 1916 - After having studied in the atelier of Gérôme, he was taken up by the Symbolists in 1881 who regarded his art as related to their own. In his engravings he presented equivocal states of consciousness purely by means of chiaroscuro, whilst always remaining one of the most striking colorists of the French school. He went farthest in the exploration of what at that time was not yet called the subconscious.
THE CYCLOPS (1895-1900) - Signed bottom right: Odilon Redon.

Otterlo, Rijksmuseum Kröller-Müller

162 WILLUMSEN, JENS FERDINAND - Copenhagen 1863 - France 1958 - During his stay in Paris, Willumsen was connected with the Pont-Aven group and he exhibited with the Independents. In 1890 he met Redon, and under his influence Willumsen's art developed profoundly and rejoined the stream which flows from Gustave Moreau and ends in Surrealism. — See 237.
AFTER THE STORM (1905) - This artist reached his mature style in an expressionism comparable to that of Munch. His forceful colour is able to express the events of human life. Canvas 155,5 ×150 cm. Signed and dated bottom right: F.J.W. 1905.

Oslo, Nasjonalgalleriet

163 JOSEPHSON, ERNST - Stockholm 1851-1906 - In Paris from 1873 onwards, Josephson was attracted by Impressionism. In Sweden he headed the modernist movement against academism. In 1886 he founded the *Konstnärsförbundet*, an association of modernist artists, but after a while he fell out with his colleagues and retired to Brittany, where, in the following year, he had an attack of insanity. Returning to Sweden he continued his artistic career and the works he produced in this period have greatly influenced modern painting in his country.
AT THE SEA-SHORE (1894) - The exact subject of this picture remains a mystery. Wood 32×49 cm. Signed and dated bottom right: Ernst 18 27.10 94 Josephson.

Stockholm, National Museum

XXVII MUNCH, EDVARD (biography see 72). GIRLS ON THE BRIDGE (1901) - Canvas 136×125,5 cm. Signed in the bottom left-hand corner: E.M.

Oslo, Nasjonalgalleriet

164 DENIS, MAURICE (biography see 66). SOIR TRINITAIRE (1891) - This picture illustrates a theme from a poem by Adolphe Retté and is

characteristic of Denis' symbolist inspiration. Canvas 102×72 cm.

Louveciennes, Mme Dejan

165 NONNELL Y MONTURIOL, ISIDRO - Barcelona 1873-1911 - A pupil of Martinez Alter and of L. Graner, he lived in Paris. His paintings of bohemians and beggars seem to have influenced the young Picasso. At any rate, he represents a figure characteristic of *fin de siècle* Barcelona where Picasso passed his youth.
TWO GYPSIES (1903) - Canvas 136×136 cm. Signed and dated bottom right: Nonnell 1903.

Barcelona, Museum of Modern Art

166 PICASSO, PABLO RUIZ (biography see 122).
THE EMBRACE (1903) - A work of the 'Blue Period', in which the theme of the man and woman often recurs. Pastel 98×59 cm. Signed top right: Picasso.

Paris, Mme Jean Walter

167 SÉRUSIER, PAUL - Paris 1863 - Morlaix 1927 - After working at the Académie Julian he exhibited for the first time in Paris in 1887. The following year he met Gauguin at Pont-Aven, and it was decisive for his future. They worked together until Gauguin left for Tahiti. After that Sérusier's art adopted stricter formulas inspired by a symbolist spirit and based on the golden number.
THE TALISMAN (1888) - The first of the artist's works to show the influence of Gauguin; it was to have considerable importance for a whole younger generation of the Nabis. Wood 22×27 cm. Description on the back: 'Fait sous la direction de P. Gauguin' P. Sérusier 1888.

Formerly in the collection of Maurice Denis (Mme Boulet Denis)

XXVIII DERAIN, ANDRÉ - Chatou 1880 - Chambourcy 1954 - After studying at the Carrière Academy he formed a close friendship with Vlaminck, with whom he shared a studio at Chatou, hence the name 'Chatou school' given to the rather violent appearance which the two men gave to Fauvism. He later went through various other phases — Gothic, Byzantine, and Negro — ending in a hieratic and sobre stylization. Derain's personality was sophisticated and inclined to eclecticism, but he never lost the hope of returning to the great disciplines of Classicism. — See 177.
WESTMINSTER BRIDGE (1906) - Derain made a second journey to London in the spring of 1906. Whilst there he painted a number of his finest Fauvist compositions. Canvas 81×100 cm. Signed in the bottom right-hand corner: A. Derain.

Paris, Private collection

168 SICKERT, WALTER RICHARD - Munich 1860 - Bath 1942 - Born of an English mother and a Danish father, Sickert lived in England until 1900 when he went to Paris, where he became a friend of Degas. Son and grandson of painters, Sickert studied at the Slade and became a pupil of Whistler. He became one of the most influential Impressionist painters in England and always retained his contact with French painting.
THE DUTCHWOMAN (1905) - Canvas 51×40 cm. Signed bottom right: Sickert.

London, Peter Shand-Kydd Collection

169 SPILLIAERT, LÉON - Ostend 1881-1946 - A self-taught artist, Spilliaert generally preferred working in gouache, pastels and crayon to oils. His work inspired by his native town has a very personal style which touches on Symbolism. Sometimes recalls the Nabis and foreshadows certain Surrealist fantasies.
THE PINK HAT (1904) - Watercolour 58×49 cm. Signed and dated at the bottom near the middle: Léon Spilliaert 1904.

Ostend, Musée des Beaux-Arts

170 MARQUET, ALBERT - Bordeaux 1875 - Paris 1947 - Marquet went to Paris in 1890 where he studied at the École des Arts Décoratifs and then at the atelier of G. Moreau, where he met Matisse, whose friend he became. He adopted Fauvism from the beginning, but he always retained a certain moderation and a taste for more balanced harmonies and a simplification of form. His visual integrity makes him one of the great masters of French landscape.
PORTRAIT OF ANDRÉ ROUVEYRE (1904) - This boldly presented portrait dates from a period when Marquet was given to infusing into his fauvism a kind of lively, yet somewhat bitter Naturalism. It also serves to show off the artist's talents as a draughtsman. Rouveyre, cartoonist and writer, one of the best friends of Apollinaire, cuts a strange figure: he was one of those solitaries who possess only a few friends, but who are the cream of an epoch. Canvas 93×61 cm. Signed and dated bottom left: Marquet 1904.

Paris, Musée National d'Art Moderne

XXIX DUFY, RAOUL - Le Havre 1877 - Forcalquier 1953. In 1890 Dufy received a bursary which enabled him to study in Paris under Bonnat. Influenced by Pissarro, Boudin and Lautrec he came to Fauvism in 1905, and in this style showed all his usual vivacity. Then came a Cézanne period. It was only after the 1914-18 war that his art developed a personal style in its striking colours and independent line.
LA RUE PAVOISÉE (1906) - Flags waving from the windows of a street often inspired Manet and Monet, but the theme was a favourite one for the Fauves, who often treated it; and Dufy in particular seems to have loved it, since he painted it on a number of occasions. Canvas 81×65 cm. Signed and dated in the bottom right-hand corner: Raoul Dufy 1906.

Paris, Private collection

XXX MATISSE, HENRI - Le Cateau (near Cambrai) 1869 - Nice 1954 - After studying law Matisse went to the Académie Julian, and then, in 1895, to the atelier of G. Moreau. Attracted first by Impressionism and then by Neo-Impressionism the influence of Van Gogh led him to an exaltation of colour. From 1905 onwards his Fauvism was accentuated, and his development towards a stylisation of form and to coloured planes continued. Matisse may be regarded as the creator of 'pure' colour. His pictorial genius, his refined taste and his powerful sense of logic show up this daring revolutionary as one of the most perfect representatives of the long French tradition. — See 174, 175, 178.
LUXE, CALME ET VOLUPTÉ (1904-1905) - A work carried out in the technique of Neo-Impressionism, yet at the same time indicating the detachment of Matisse from something which was nothing more than an exercise for him. The title of this picture was inspired by Baudelaire's *Invitation au Voyage*, but in replacing the 'canals', the 'fields' and the 'rain-drenched sun' of Baudelaire by a strand, the blazing sun of the Midi, and free, naked bodies was Matisse perhaps, in opposition to the poet, proclaiming a new aesthetic and even perhaps a new ethic? Canvas 86×116 cm. Signed in the bottom right-hand corner: Henri Matisse.

Copenhagen, Statens Museum for Kunst

171 BRAQUE, GEORGES (biography see 130).
THE PORT OF ANTWERP (1906) - Canvas 50×61 cm.

Ottawa, National Gallery of Canada

172 VLAMINCK, MAURICE DE - Paris 1876 - Rueilla-Gadelière 1958 - At the age of twenty Vlaminck was a painter, a writer, a violinist and a racing cyclist. His art was spontaneous and popular and already possessed an extraordinary vigour. After coming into contact with Van Gogh and Matisse his painting became more vehement and vibrant composed of pure tones. His place is amongst the best of the Fauves. The influence of Cézanne caused his work to take on a more sober tone and to develop a more constructive character.
THE OUTING IN THE COUNTRY (1905) - The astonishing rhythm of the brushwork combines the artist's early Expressionist technique with Fauve colouring. Canvas 89×116 cm. Signed bottom left: Vlaminck.

Paris, Mme Marcelle Bourdon

173 DONGEN, KEES VAN - Delfshaven (Holland) 1877 - After beginning as a self-taught painter he established himself in Paris in 1897. In 1904 an exhibition of his work at Vollard's made him famous. His emphatic, rich and contrasted colours served him in particular for painting women and circus scenes. Up to 1913 he was one of the most famous of the Fauvist painters. After the war he became a society painter, often betraying a cruel streak.
ANITA (1905) - The model was a gipsy whom the artist had to follow from fair to fair so that he could finish his painting. Canvas 81×130 cm. Signed bottom middle: Van Dongen.

Monaco, Mme van Dongen

174 MATISSE, HENRI (biography see XXX).
THE GIPSY (1906) - This painting must date from the first months of 1906, and must have been done shortly after the *Woman in a Hat* shown at the notorious Salon d'Automne in 1905 which it resembles in Fauvist treatment. Canvas 55×46 cm. Signed bottom left: Henri Matisse.

Saint-Tropez, Musée de l'Annonciade

XXXI WOUTERS, RIK - Malines 1882 - Amsterdam 1916 - Son of a woodcarver, Wouters was initiated into the technique at an early age. He studied at the Malines and Brussels Academies. Later he took part in what was called the *Fauvisme brabançon* movement. In 1912 he went to Paris where he was seized with enthusiasm for the Impressionists. His most remarkable sculptures and paintings date from this period; by their colour and their movement they express an irresistible *joie de vivre*. Towards the end of his life, and under the influence of sickness, his art took on a tragic character. — See 184.
RED CURTAINS (1913) - Canvas 100×81 cm.

Brussels, P. Vermeylen Collection

175 MATISSE, HENRI (biography see XXX).
LA SERPENTINE (1909) - Bronze 56×25×18 cm.
Signed on the base: Henri Matisse 4/10.

Paris, Private collection

176 RODIN, AUGUSTE (biography see 56).
STUDY FROM NIJINSKI (c. 1911) - Rodin had often been inspired by dancing, and had made several statuettes and innumerable drawings on this subject. Bronze 18×6×9 cm. Signed.

Paris, Musée Rodin

177 DERAIN, ANDRÉ (biography see XXVIII).
THE BILLIARD PLAYERS (1913) - Canvas 140×88 cm.

Tokyo, Kabutoya Gallery

178 MATISSE, HENRI (biography see XXX).
LANE IN THE WOODS AT CLAMART (1912) - Barre dates this work by assuming that it is from the same time as the landscapes Matisse did during his stay in Morocco. Canvas 92×73 cm. Signed bottom middle: H. Matisse.

Paris, Private collection

179 ROUAULT, GEORGES (biography see 74).
MONSIEUR ET MADAME POULOT (1905) - This work was inspired by Léon Bloy's *Poor Woman*, and forms one wing of a triptych of which the others are entitled *Prostituée* and *Terpsichore*. It was exhibited at the Salon d'Automne of 1905. Léon Bloy completely misunderstood it. Watercolour on paper 70×52 cm. Signed and dated bottom left: G. Rouault, 1905.

Hem (Nord), M. Philippe Leclercq

180 CHAGALL, MARC - Vitebsk 1887 - Lives at Vence (Alpes Maritimes) - All his life Chagall has been profoundly affected by the traditions and customs of Jewish life, into which he was born. After studying at Vitebsk and Petersburg, where Bakst introduced him to the work of the Impressionists, he went to Paris in 1910, where at last he found personal style. He painted the Russia of his childhood, introducing symbols born of his own imagination. He returned to Russia in 1914, married and, like all the avant-garde Russian artists of the day, took an active part in the cultural movement encouraged by the revolution, which was eventually succeeded by the Stalinist reaction. Stayed in Berlin in 1922, after which he returned to France to remain there permanently with the exception of a period during the German occupation. — See XXXII.
HOMAGE TO APOLLINAIRE, WALDEN, CENDRARS AND CANUDO (1911-12) - Canvas 209×198 cm. Signed top middle: Chagall.

Eindhoven, Stedelijk van Abbe Museum

XXXII CHAGALL, MARC (biography see 180).
TO RUSSIA, ASSES AND OTHERS (1911) - Canvas 156×122 cm. Signed in the centre below: Chagall 1911 Paris.

Paris, Musée National d'Art Moderne

181 MINNE, GEORGES - Ghent 1866 - Laethem-Saint-Martin 1941 - Sculptor, sketcher and engraver, Minne studied at the academies in Ghent and in Brussels. His meeting with Maeterlinck was decisive for his art. In 1899 he became a member of the first group of artists to settle in Laethem. At first he was influenced by Rodin, and then he was more and more attracted by mediaeval art. His emaciated and mystical ado-

lescents and his motherhoods are contemplative and melancholic works which have had a profound influence on sculpture north of the Rhine.
THE RELICS-BEARER (1897) - Original plaster. Height 67 cm.

Ghent, Baron Georges Minne

182 LEHMBRUCK, WILHELM - Duisburg 1881 - Berlin 1919 - Son of a miner, Lehmbruck studied at the school of decorative arts in Düsseldorf. In 1905 he won a prize which allowed him to go to Italy, a country he subsequently visited on a number of occasions. From 1910 to 1914 he lived in Paris. At first the inspiration of his art was traditional, but he also came under the influence of Constantin Meunier and social naturalism. By 1911 he had developed a personal style which showed a certain affinity with the Symbolism of Minne. His elongated figures mirror an intense interior life and opened the way to a ' Gothicised ' expressionist style.
ADOLESCENT STANDING (1913) - Work conceived in Paris. There is also an engraving of the same subject. Bronze, height 241 cm.

Stuttgart, Mrs. Anita Lehmbruck

183 BOURDELLE, ANTOINE (biography see 121).
PENELOPE (1903-1915) - Bronze 120×45×35 cm. Not signed or dated. Third casting, made in 1915. The first version dates from 1903.

Paris, Mme A. Bourdelle

184 WOUTERS, RIK (biography see XXXI).
DOMESTIC CARES (1913) - One of the last works of the artist, who went blind shortly afterwards. Bronze, height 228 cm. Signed on the base, left: Rik Wouters.

Commune of Watermael-Boitsfort

XXXIII NOLDE, EMIL (pseudonym for EMIL HANSEN) - Nolde (Schleswig) 1897 - Seebüll 1956 - Originally a woodcarver, it was not until 1899 that he began to attend Hoeltzel's school of painting in Dachau. After that he worked at the Académie Julian in Paris. For two years he was a member of *Die Brücke* group, and in 1912 he settled in Berlin where he was associated with the *Blaue Reiter* group. He met Munch and Ensor. In 1913-14 he took part in an expedition to the Far East, travelling through Russia and Japan as far as New Guinea. Nolde's art is based on a profound appreciation of nature. A visionary and a mystic he gave a significance and a force of expression to colour which is unique in German Expressionism. — See 190, 191.
SLOVENES (1911) - The artist often shows an inclination towards grotesque stylisation, and it has been said of the faces in this picture that they are crepuscular and that the wearing of a mask deprives them of all relationship with a literary illustration. Canvas 79×69 cm. Signed in the top left-hand corner: Nolde.

Seebüll, Ada and Emil Nolde Collection

185 KOLLWITZ, KÄTHE - Königsberg 1867 - Moritzburg (Dresden) 1945 - After studying at Berlin, Berne and Munich she settled in Berlin with her husband in 1891. In 1904 she studied in Paris at the Académie Julian, and in 1907 in Florence where she was awarded the Villa Romana Prize. After that she went to Rome and Moscow. From 1928 to 1933 she taught engraving at the Berlin Academy. She is still regarded as one of

the most outstanding representatives of German graphic art during this particularly fertile period.
UNEMPLOYED (1909) - Etching.

Geneva, Private collection

186 MODERSOHN-BECKER, PAULA (biography see 75).
PORTRAIT OF THE ARTIST IN AN AMBER NECKLACE - Canvas.

Bâle, Kunstmuseum

187 BARLACH, ERNST - Wedel (Holstein) 1870 - Rostock 1938 - After studying at the School of Arts and Crafts and then at the Hamburg and Dresden Academies, Barlach left for Paris in 1895, where he took a course at the Académie Julian. Lived in Berlin, travelled to Russia and Italy. From 1910 he lived in Güstrow. Sculptor, engraver and poet, Barlach expressed his human and religious conceptions by means of a strict and archaic art form in a style both monumental and intense. See 188.
THE VANDAL (1910) - ' The figures of the Vandal and the Avenger become incarnations of gesture. The physiognomy fades away, movement becomes set in an expressive arabesque translating the sense of the theme '. Bronze, height 54,7 cm.

Hamburg, Hermann F. Reemtsma

188 BARLACH, ERNEST (biography see 187).
RUSSIAN BEGGAR-WOMAN WITH A CUP (1906) - The theme of ' the beggar ' inspired many of the artist's works after his visit to Russia in 1906. This belongs to his first deeply felt dramatic period, which is marked above all by a dense and expressive composition. Ceramic, height 29 cm. Inscribed: Cast from the studio of R. Mutz, Berlin.

Hamburg, Hermann F. Reemtsma

XXXIV SCHMIDT-ROTTLUFF, KARL - Rottluff 1884 - Lives in Berlin - Schmidt-Rottluff studied architecture in Dresden in 1905, where he met Heckel, Bleyl and Kirchner. With them he founded *Die Brücke* group, of which he was the youngest member. His work reflects the influence of Negro art and of Cubism, and is marked by monumental and constructive qualities. Its massive and stressed forms and its pure colours create a rhythm which is full of life.
NORWEGIAN LANDSCAPE (SKRYGEDAL) (1911) - The artist went to Norway in 1911 for an extended stay. The grandeur of nature there made a deep impression on him. With simplified landscapes he created striking works, stressing the barbaric side of nature, as for example in the twilight. Signed and dated in the bottom right-hand corner: Rottluff 1911.

Feldafing, Buchheim Collection

189 KIRCHNER, ERNST LUDWIG - Aschaffenburg 1880 - Frauenkirch 1938 - After studying architecture Kirchner went to Munich in 1903, where he turned to painting. In 1905 he was one of the founders of *Die Brücke*. By 1911 he was in Berlin, where he was a member of the *Sturm* group. It was in Berlin, inspired by the life of a great city, that he painted his most famous works. He committed suicide in 1938. His violent and uncompromising colouring is reminiscent of Fauvism, but instead of working for visual effects he placed the accent on emotivity and an aggressive character, which linked him to German Expressionism, to which he always remained faithful.

BERLIN STREET SCENE (1913) - The artist was at once fascinated and tormented by man as part of the anonymous rhythm of the street. A series of pictures on this subject expresses his passionate reaction to the world of the great city. Canvas 125 × 90 cm. Signed bottom left: E. L. Kirchner.

Stuttgart, Staatsgalerie

190 NOLDE, EMIL (pseudonym for EMIL HANSEN) (biography see XXXIII).
THE LEGEND OF MARIA AEGYPTIACA : AT THE PORT OF ALEXANDRIA (1912) - This picture forms the left wing of a triptych, of which the central panel shows *The Conversion* and the right *The death of St. Mary in the desert.* Canvas 86 × 100 cm. Signed bottom left: Emil Nolde.

Hamburg, Hamburger Kunsthalle

191 NOLDE, EMIL (pseudonym for EMIL HANSEN) (biography see XXXIII).
THE LAST SUPPER (1909) - This canvas begins the series of Nolde's paintings inspired by religion, of which the *Great Cycle of Life* of 1911 is the culmination. Canvas 88 × 108 cm. Signed and dated bottom right: Emil Nolde 1909.

Seebüll, Stiftung Ada und Emil Nolde

192 HECKEL, ERICH - Döbeln 1883 - Lives on Lake Constance - After first studying architecture, Heckel turned to painting. He was self-taught, and one of the founders of *Die Brücke* group. His paintings, engravings and drawings have a dreamlike and troubled character reflecting a high degree of deliberate spiritual tension.
TWO MEN AT TABLE (The Brothers Karamazov) (1912).

Hamburg, Hamburger Kunsthalle

193 MÜLLER, OTTO - Liebau 1874 - Breslau 1930 - Müller studied lithography first in Breslau and then at the Dresden Academy. In 1908 he went to Berlin, and in 1911 he joined *Die Brücke* group. His art is less aggressive than that of his colleagues. His favourite subject is the nude in paradisal surroundings, and the influence of Gauguin is clearly visible.
THREE GIRLS IN FRONT OF A MIRROR (about 1912) - Tempera on canvas 120 × 90 cm. Signed bottom right: O.M.

Feldafing, Buchheim Collection

XXXV MACKE, AUGUST (biography see 151).
KAIRUAN I (1914) - A few months before he was killed at the front Macke paid a visit to Tunisia with Klee and Molliet, where he painted only in water colours. The transparency of water-colours seemed to him to offer the best means of representing the brilliance of the light and air, ' as colourful and at the same time as clear as a stained-glass window. ' This ' degenerate ' picture, as he called it in a letter to his wife, was seized by the Nazi authorities in 1938. Water-colour on paper 20,5 × 24,5 cm.

Bolzano, E.S.F. Fohn Collection

194 KANDINSKY, WASSILY (biography see VI).
STUDY FOR IMPROVISATION NO. 8 (1910) - Painted in Moscow. The great archangel on the left with his sword and the fantastic vision of the Russian city above, evoke the image of the Last Judgement. Cardboard transferred to canvas 96 × 69,5 cm.

Wintherthur, Volkart-Stiftung

195 KANDINSKY, WASSILY (biography see VI).
LYRISM (HORSEMAN) (1911). This composition is closely comparable to the catalogue cover of the first *Blaue Reiter* exhibition in 1911, and constitutes the definitive expression of the horseman theme developed in a great number of variants. Canvas 96 × 100 cm. Signed and dated bottom right: Kandinsky 1911.

Rotterdam, Museum Boymans-van Beuningen

XXXVI MARC, FRANZ - Munich 1880 - Verdun 1916 - After studying at the Munich Academy Marc travelled in France, Italy and Greece. In 1909 he met Macke and, a year later, Klee and Kandinsky. In 1911 he discovered his particular line and produced a series of animal pictures. He was one of the founders of the *Neue Künstlervereinigung*, and of the *Blaue Reiter* group in 1912. He came under the influence of Kandinsky and then of Cubism and of Delaunay. His iridescent colouring, his symbolic values and his free style combined to form a cosmic harmony whose subjects played only a subordinate role.
TYROL (1913-1914) - Canvas 135,7 × 144,5 cm. Signed on the back: Tirol, fr. Marc.

Munich, Staatsgemäldesammlung

196 ROHLFS, CHRISTIAN - Niendorf (Holstein) 1849 - Hagen 1938 - After studying at the Weimar Academy of Arts, Rohlfs went to Berlin in 1890, where he came into contact with impressionist art, and subsequently met Munch. In 1900 H. Van de Velde introduced him to the problems of modern art, and the art collector Osthaus caused him to be appointed professor at the Volkswang Kunstschule in Hagen. In 1904 he joined with Nolde. His lyric art with its delicate nuances mirror the diverse influences he came under during the course of a long life. His interest and experiments extended to abstract art.
RED ROOFS (1913) - The originally clearly distinct forms of this artist have by 1912-13, become more stylized. The colour is simplified into a red-blue-yellow harmony. The subjects are dematerialized and grouped in a purely ornamental rhythm. Tempera on canvas 80 × 100,5 cm. Signed and dated bottom right: C.R. 13.

Karlsruhe, Staatliche Kunsthalle

197 GERSTL, RICHARD - Vienna 1883-1908 - After studying at the Vienna Academy of Arts and under the Secessionist H. Lefler, Gerstl became greatly attracted to music, and became a close friend of the composer Schönberg. Gerstl subsequently destroyed a great deal of his work, the most important of which was done from 1904 on to his death.
TWO SISTERS (about 1906) - This work is dated by the evidence of the models. It was offered by the artist as a ' test-piece ' in the entry competition to the special painting class at the Vienna Academy of Fine Arts. Canvas 175 × 150 cm.

Vienna, Österreichische Galerie

XXXVII KOKOSCHKA, OSKAR (biography see VIII).
PORTRAIT OF HERWARTH WALDEN (1910) - Herwarth Walden had invited Kokoschka to join the *Sturm* group in Berlin in 1910. They probably first met in 1900. This portrait is one of the best psychological interpretations carried out by the artist. Canvas 100 × 68 cm. Signed in the bottom right-hand corner: O.K.

Minneapolis, Mr. and Mrs. Samuel H. Maslon

198 SERVAES, ALBERT - Ghent 1883 - Lives in Switzerland - Servaes took evening courses at the Ghent Academy of Art. Settling down at Laethem he at first came under the influence of Minne, but from 1910 on he became an expressionist painter and his work foreshadowed that of Permeke, whose art owed a great deal to him in the beginning. Servaes took his subjects from peasant life and from the New Testament. A Golgotha of great dramatic ascerbity got him into difficulties with the Church.
THE RAISING OF LAZARUS (1911) - Canvas 96 × 99 cm. Signed and dated bottom right: Alb. Servaes 911.

Ghent, M. G. Crombé

199 PERMEKE, CONSTANT - Antwerp 1886 - Ostende 1952 - Son of a painter, Permeke took lessons as a free-lance at the Ghent Academy of Art and afterwards at the Bruges Academy. In 1906 he settled in Laethem-Saint-Martin, where he became the leader of the second group of artists there. Wounded in 1914 and transferred to England, where he was demobilised, he painted his first expressionist works, which were inspired by rural life. In 1918 he returned to Belgium and settled down permanently at Jabbeke in the country near Bruges. Permeke is the most outstanding figure of Flemish Expressionism. His monumental and spontaneous art, which harks back to man's most primitive feelings, places him amongst the great expressionist artists of the world.
MOONLIGHT (1913) - Canvas 138 × 92 cm. Signed bottom left: C. Permeke.

Brussels, Mme André Pisart

200 KOKOSCHKA, OSKAR (biography see VIII).
THE BRIDE OF THE WIND (1914) - Canvas

Bâle, Kunstmuseum

201 MODIGLIANI, AMEDEO - Livorno 1884 - Paris 1920 - Born in a Jewish middle-class family, Modigliani suffered a good deal of sickness as a child. He learnt the rudiments of painting from a landscape painter in his native town of Livorno. He went to Paris in 1906 and found himself amidst the full blossoming of Fauvism and the beginnings of Cubism. His first works reveal the influence of Lautrec, and later of Cézanne. Soon afterwards he went in for sculpture, and turned to the elements of Etruscan and Negro art and to the work of Brancusi. From 1913 he returned to painting and drawing, and it was then that he met Zborovsky who became his dealer and his friend. A straggling career of disorder, bohemian living, alcohol and genius makes Modigliani one of the legendary figures of the great saga of Montparnasse. He died in a charity hospital, and on the day of his burial his wife Jeanne Hébuterne committed suicide by throwing herself out of the window.
HEAD (1913) - At the Salon d'Automne of 1912 Modigliani exhibited seven pieces with the title ' Head ', and included in the classification of ' decorative ensemble '. Euville stone, height 62 cm.

London, The Tate Gallery

202 GAUDIER-BREZSKA, HENRI - Saint-Jean-de-Braye 1891 - Neuville Saint-Vaast 1915 - Settled in London in 1911 where he started to sculpt. He contributed to *Blast*, writing on the principles of Vorticism in sculpture. Killed at the front in 1915.
THE IMP (1914) - Veined alabaster 40,5 × 8 × 8,5 cm.

London, The Tate Gallery

203 BRANCUSI, CONSTANTIN - Pestisani Gorj (Rumania) 1876 - Paris 1957 - After studying at the Bucharest and Cracow Academies of Art, Brancusi reached Paris in 1902, stopping on the way in Zurich, Munich and Bâle. In 1906 he worked for a while with Rodin and exhibited his work for the first time. Two years later he created *Le Baiser*. From then on his art turned towards a stylisation of form in a pure and finished volume which has since exercised a great influence on contemporary sculpture. In 1937 he returned to his country of birth in order to execute some pieces of sculpture for the public gardens of Tugurju and an *Endless Column* 30 metres long of steel. He also visited India where he designed a temple of meditation for the Maharajah. He died a naturalised Frenchman in his atelier in the Impasse Ronsin.

THE SLEEPING MUSE (1909) - In his search for purity, Brancusi's art was sustained by a profound serenity which enabled him to affirm: ' It is pure joy that I am giving you '. Patinated bronze 27×30×17 cm., on a base of wood and wrought iron 31×50 ×43 cm. Signed and dated on the neck: C. Brancusi 1910.

Paris, Musée National d'Art Moderne

204 CHIRICO, GIORGIO DE - Volo (Greece) 1888 - Lives in Rome - Chirico studied first in Athens and then in Munich, where he came under the influence of Böcklin and Nietzsche, an influence which remained marked in the spirit of his art. In 1911 he went to Paris where he met Apollinaire, Picasso and Max Jacob. It was here that he began to create extraordinary works on unusual subjects which outstripped even Surrealism. On returning to Italy he founded the *Pittura metafisica*, which, together with Futurism, renewed the plastic arts in the country.

THE ENIGMA OF THE HOUR (1911) - Canvas 55×71 cm. Signed and dated bottom right: Giorgio de Chirico 1911.

Milan, Gianni Mattioli

XXXVIII SCHIELE, EGON - Tulln (Austria) 1890 - Vienna 1918 - After studying at the Vienna Academy of Art, Schiele came under the influence first of Klimt and then of Hodler, and later of Far-Eastern art. His work was related to the *Jugendstil* and he adopted an ornamental and graphic style whose inspiration was both mystical and erotic.

PORTRAIT OF THE ARTIST (1911).

205 PICASSO, PABLO RUIZ (biography see 122). THE STUDENT WITH THE PIPE (1913) - Oil, sand and paper 74×59,5 cm.

Paris, Private collection

206 PRAMPOLINI, ENRICO - Modena 1894 - Rome 1956 - After studying at the Rome Academy of Art he joined the Futurist group, and took part in the discussion which flared up in 1914 around the effort to substitute painted reality by the reality of the material object. His *collage d'objets* aroused the interest of Picasso and of Cocteau during their stay in Rome in 1917. He was a member of the *Dada* movement, Not for a moment, during the whole course of his career, did he lose his interest in avant-garde movements, or tire of aiding them with his inexhaustible inventiveness.

BÉGUINAGE (1914) - Collage on wood 18×22 cm.

Signed bottom right: E. Prampolini, and on the left ' Béguinage ' 1914.

Rome, Dr. Alessandro Prampolini

207 PICABIA, FRANCIS DE MARTINEZ - Paris 1879-1953 - Born of a Cuban father and a French mother, Picabia began to paint at the age of sixteen. After having come first under the influence of Impressionism and then of Cubism, his art turned towards abstraction. He created his most important works in the years 1912 and 1913. He exhibited at the Armory Show in New York, where he made the acquaintance of Stieglitz. Both painter and poet, Picabia took an original part in the experiments of the avant-garde of his time. — See XXXIX.

RUBBER (1909) - One can see in this watercolour the first signs of abstract art. Watercolour on paper 45,5×61,5 cm. Signed bottom left: Picabia.

Paris, Musée National d'Art Moderne

208 DUCHAMP, MARCEL (biography see XIII). COCOA-GRINDER NO. 2 (1914) - Canvas 64,5×54 cm. Title and date bottom left. A first version of this picture dates from 1913.

Philadelphia, Philadelphia Museum of Art (Louise and Walter Arendsberg Collection)

XXXIX PICABIA, FRANCIS (biography see 207). UDNIE (AMERICAN GIRL, OR THE DANCE) (1913) - According to Mme Gabrielle Buffet, this picture was inspired by the dancer Napierkovska whom the artist had seen dance on the liner bringing him back to Europe from New York. However, his recollection has parted company with any realistic image and has become only ' form and colour emancipated from their sensory qualities '. Canvas 300×300 cm. Signed and dated in the bottom left-hand corner: Picabia 1913. Title above in the middle: Udnie.

Paris, Musée National d'Art Moderne

XL WIENER, RENÉ - Nancy 1856-1939 - A member of a family of bookbinders, Wiener abandoned ancient styles and applied the process of pyrogravure of the working of leather, collaborating for instance with Toulouse-Lautrec and Victor Prouvé. — See XLVI.

PORTFOLIO FOR ENGRAVINGS (1894) - Camille Martin was responsible for the execution. The design includes references to the tools used in making engravings. Inlaid leather and pyrogravure. Signed C.M.

Nancy, Musée de l'École de Nancy

209 PAXTON, SIR JOSEPH - Milton Bryant (Bedfordshire) 1801 - Sydenham (London) 1865 - Horticulturalist. In 1826 he became superintendant of the Duke of Devonshire's gardens at Chatsworth. In 1836 he began to erect a great conservatory 300 feet in length, which was completed in 1840, and influenced Paxton's design for the Great Exhibition building, known as the Crystal Palace. Two engineers, Sir Charles Fox and Henderson were responsible for in its construction.

CRYSTAL PALACE, London (1851).

210 DARBY, ABRAHAM - 1750-1791 - English iron-master, appointed head of the Coalbrookdale factory at the age of 18. The Coalbrookdale bridge, built in 1777-81, was designed by the architect T.F. Pritchard.

BRIDGE AT COALBROOKDALE (1769) - With a span

of nearly a hundred feet it was the first iron bridge to be constructed.

211 TELFORD, THOMAS - Westerkirk (Dumfries-shire) 1757 - London 1834 - Civil engineer; he was first apprenticed to a stonemason. Became famous as the builder of numerous canals, aqueducts, roads and bridges both in England and Scotland.

MENAI SUSPENSION BRIDGE (1815) - Erected as part of the Hollyhead to Chester road.

212 LABROUSTE, HENRI - Paris 1801-1875 - One of the foremost graduates of the École des Beaux-Arts. Awarded the Prix de Rome at the age of twenty-three. Spent five years in Rome, a stay which introduced him to all the artistic problems of his day. He became the leader of the Rationalist school as opposed to the Academy. He was among the first to use iron and steel openly in public buildings. His ideas and his methods made him a pioneer for his generation.

BIBLIOTHÈQUE SAINTE-GENEVIÈVE, Paris (1843-1850).

213 BUNNING, JAMES B. - 1802-1863 - Son of a London Surveyor, he entered his father's office at the age of thirteen. He later held posts as surveyor to various public bodies and institutions. Designed Bethnal Green Union Workhouse in 1840. In 1843 he was appointed ' Clerk of the City's work's '. He built apart from the Coal Exchange, Holloway Prison 1852 and the Metropolitan Cattle Market 1855.

COAL EXCHANGE, London (1846-1849).

214 DUTERT, FERDINAND (Douai 1854-1906) and CONTAMIN, V. (1840-1893) - A pupil of Lebas and Ginain, Dutert worked in architectural ironwork and studied the rational use of ironwork in building. Contamin collaborated with Dutert in the building of the famous *Halle des Machines* at the Exhibition of 1889, which set the stamp on the triumph of iron and steel in modern construction and spread the knowledge of its multifarious possibilities.

HALL DES MACHINES, Paris International Exhibition (1889). - As one of the first examples of collaboration between architect and engineer it was a remarkable technical achievement.

215 WEBB, PHILIP - Oxford 1831 - Worth (Sussex) 1915 - Architect. Close friend of William Morris, for whose firm he produced many designs after having built for him Red House, Bexley Heath in 1859, which greatly influenced domestic architecture. — See 217, 220.

FIREPLACE, RED HOUSE, Bexley Heath, Kent (1860) - The interior details of the Red House are often deliberately rough and rustic. This fireplace is completely bare of ornament.

216 BROWN, FORD MADOX - Calais 1821 - London 1893 - Historical painter, Ford Madox Brown was one of the most curious and interesting figures of the English school of painting. He was pupil of Wappers at Antwerp. Later he was close to the Pre-Raphaelite group and influenced it considerably.

CHAIR (about 1860) - Ford Madox Brown also worked with Morris.

217 WEBB, PHILIP (biography see 215). FAIENCE TILE (1862).

218 MORRIS, WILLIAM - Walthamstow 1834 - London 1896 - Designer, craftsman, poet and

social reformer. Ruskin's lectures first turned him towards craft and social conditions. He was a friend of the Preraphaelites, and he founded his firm for craft-work and interior decoration in 1861. Towards the end of his life he occupied himself with typography, (Kelmscott Press). — See 219.
LILY CARPETING (1877).

219 MORRIS, WILLIAM (biography see 218).
TULIP CHINTZ (1875).

220 WEBB, PHILIP (biography see 215).
STANDEN, East Grinstead, Sussex (1892).

221 SHAW, RICHARD NORMAN - Edinburgh 1831 - Hampstead 1912 - Architect. Side by side with Webb the chief reformer of domestic architecture in England. His style was inspired by seventeenth century Dutch architecture, and the William and Mary and Queen Anne styles in England. His influence was wide and wholesome. — See 222, 223, 224.
BANSTEAD, Surrey (1884).

222 SHAW, RICHARD NORMAN (biography see 221).
NEW ZEALAND CHAMBERS, London (1872) - Destroyed during second World War.

223 SHAW, RICHARD NORMAN (biography see 221).
OLD SWAN HOUSE, Chelsea, London (1876).

224 SHAW, RICHARD NORMAN (biography see 221).
BEDFORD PARK, near London (1876) - The first garden suburb ever designed.

225 WHITE, STANFORD - New York City 1853-1906 - Architect. Collaborated with Henry H. Richardson in the designing of Trinity Church in Boston. Joined McKim, Mead and White and was the most brilliant designer in that firm.
W.G. LOW HOUSE, Bristol, Rhode Island (1887).

226 ARCHITECT UNKNOWN
5-9 ALDERMANBURY, London (about 1840).

227 SULLIVAN, LOUIS - 1856-1924 - After two years of study at the Massachusetts Institute of Technology in Boston, Sullivan went to the École des Beaux-Arts in Paris, where he studied under Vaudremer. He was the true precursor of modern architecture, though his stature was recognized only after his death. Frank Lloyd Wright was trained under him from 1887 to 1893.
GUARANTY BUILDING, Buffalo, New York (1894-1895).

228 MACKMURDO, ARTHUR H. (biography see 33).
TEXTILE DESIGN printed by Simpson and Godlec of Manchester for the Century Guild. Block-printed cotton (about 1884).
Walthamstow, London, William Morris Gallery

229 SUMNER, G. HEYWOOD - London 1853-1940 - Craftsman and illustrator.
BOOK COVER OF THE TRANSLATION OF ' UNDINE ' (1888).

230 ROUSSEAU, EUGÈNE - Paris 1827-1891 - Ceramist and worker in glass, Rousseau's works are preserved in the Musée des Arts Décoratifs in Paris and at the Musée des Céramiques at Limoges.
VASE of cased glass, height 20 cm. Signed: E. Rousseau (1884-1885). Bought from the artist in 1885 by the
Paris, Musée des Arts décoratifs

231 ROUSSEAU, EUGÈNE (biography see 230).
IMITATION JADE JARDINIÈRE (1884-1885) - Brought from the artist in 1885 by the
Paris, Musée des Arts décoratifs

232 GAUGUIN, PAUL (biography see 27).
PANEL FOR A CUPBOARD carved and painted in wood by the artist for his dining-room (1881).

233 GAUGUIN, PAUL (biography see 27).
CERAMIC CENTRE-PIECE for a table (1888).

234 GAUGUIN, PAUL (biography see 27).
CERAMIC PITCHER: earthenware modelled by Gauguin, baked and enamelled by Chaplet (1886-1887).
Paris, Musée des Arts décoratifs

XLI HOENTSCHEL, GEORG - 1855-1915 - Decorator and designer, Hoentschel was given the job of designing the pavilion of the Union Centrale des Arts décoratifs at the Exhibition of 1900.
VASE (1902) - Cylindrical in form, enamelled in deep brown with a large whitish couloure at the shoulder. Glazed earthenware. Height 28,5 cm. Diameter 5 cm. Signed G.H.
Paris, Musée des Arts décoratifs

XLII GALLÉ, ÉMILE (biography see 34).
VASE (1887) - Decorated with butterflies and dragonflies. Uncoloured crystal and translucent enamel en relief. Height 22 cm. Signature cut into the base: Émile Gallé, and monogram: E.G.
Paris, Musée des Arts décoratifs

XLIII LEVEILLÉ, ERNEST BAPTISTE
Ceramist and glass-worker, Leveillé was a pupil of Rousseau. In 1889 he won the Gold Medal of the *Exposition Universelle*.
GOBLET (ca. 1889) - Cylindrical shape with spiral sides. Plain glass, crackleware, marbled with green and red. Height 15 cm. Signed on the base: E. Leveillé, Paris.
Paris, Musée des Arts décoratifs

235 GAUGUIN, PAUL (biography see 27).
MAN WITH AN AXE.
New York, Lewyt Collection

236 BERNARD, ÉMILE - Lille 1868 - Paris 1941 - In 1888 during a stay at Pont-Aven with Gauguin he abandoned academic art and Impressionism to turn to Synthetism or Cloisonnism. From 1905 to 1910 he defended his theories in *La Rénovation esthétique*. Later his art became more conventional.
WALL-HANGING, Woman picking pears (1888).

237 WILLUMSEN, FERDINAND JENS (biography see 162).
VASE (1890) - Father, mother and child.
Copenhagen, Kunstindustrimuseet

XLIV BINDESBØLL, THORVALD - Copenhagen 1846-1908 - An architect by training, Bindesbøll designed furniture, silver, leatherwork, etc. However, he is best known as a ceramic artist. Under the influence of Far-Eastern art he developed a very individual style which was both abstract and independent and of a timeless spontaneity. — See 238.
DISH (1889) - Enamelled pottery - Sgraffito decoration. Diameter: 46 cm. Signed and dated: T.B. 99.
Copenhagen, Kunstindustrimuseet

238 BINDESBØLL, THORVALD (biography see XLIV)
PLATE with a floral design still in the naturalist tradition (1891) - Enamelled pottery with the decoration executed in sgraffito. Diameter 42 cm. Monogrammed and dated: T.B. okt 1891.
Copenhagen, Kunstindustrimuseet

239 GILBERT, ALFRED - London 1854-1934 - Sculptor. Studied in London, Paris and Rome. Amongst his best-known works are the Clarence Memorial at Windsor (1892) and the Shaftesbury Memorial Fountain (Eros) in Picadilly. — See 240.
TABLE CENTRE-PIECE made for the Golden Jubilee of Queen Victoria (1887) - Silver with inlays of mother of pearl and stones, 87×65×95 cm. (1887). Presented to the Queen by her officers.
In the collection of H.M. Queen Elizabeth II

240 GILBERT, ALFRED (biography see 239).
EROS: detail of base (1892).

241 VAN DE VELDE, HENRI - Antwerp 1863 - Zurich 1957 - Van de Velde began as a painter, but around the year 1893 he turned to architecture and craftsmanship. From 1899 to 1917 he worked in Germany and taught at Weimar. After a stay in Switzerland he was appointed a Professor at the University of Ghent. His principal works are the *Werkbund* Theatre in Cologne, the Kröller-Müller Museum at Otterlo, and the Library of Ghent University. He is equally important as a theoretical writer. — See 257.
' ENGELSWACHE ' TAPESTRY The lay-out of the forms give it an Art Nouveau character (1891).

242 OBRIST, HERMANN - Kilchberg (Zurich) 1863 - Munich 1927 - From 1888 he studied at the School for Decorative Arts in Karlsruhe, and subsequently studied sculpture in Paris. He was one of the founders of the *Vereinigten Werkstätten für Kunst und Handwerk* whose director he became.
' PEITSCHENSCHLAG ' EMBROIDERY (1892).

XLV VOYSEY, CHARLES F. ANNESLEY - 1857-1941 - Architect and designer of considerable international influence. In 1940 he was presented with the Gold Medal of the Royal Institute of British Architects. — See 243, 244, 279, 280, 281, 285, 286.
NYMPHEAS (1888) - Design for printed material. Paper 79×56 cm.
London, Royal Institute of British Architects

243 VOYSEY, CHARLES F. ANNESLEY (biography see XLV).
' WATER-SNAKE '. Wall-paper design (about 1890). Paper 44,5×42 cm.
London, Royal Institute of British Architects

244 VOYSEY, CHARLES F. ANNESLEY (biography see XLV).
FLOWERS AND LEAVES (about 1890) - Machine-printed cotton; printed for Newman, Smith and Newman. 56×81 cm.
London, Victoria and Albert Museum

245 LALIQUE, RENÉ - 1860-1945 - Jeweller and glass worker, Lalique studied at the Beaux-Arts in Paris, where he founded a glass works in 1885. His forms and designs were based on floral motifs. He also collaborated with Bing. — See 246, 247.
PENDANT, pearl and enamel (1900) - Exhibited a the Paris Exhibition in 1900. Length 10 cm. Signed: Lalique.
Paris, Musée des Arts décoratifs

246 LALIQUE, RENÉ (biography see 245).
BROOCH representing a peacock spreading its tail (1899) - Enamel on gold with precious stones.
Paris, Musée des Arts décoratifs

247 LALIQUE, RENÉ (biography see 245).
NECKLACE composed of a single semi-circular plaque with a filigree design of hazel-nuts and foliage in bas-relief: gold, translucent enamels and diamonds (1900). Height of the plaque; 5 cm; diameter 12 cm.
Paris, Musée des Arts décoratifs

248 CRANACH, WILHELM LUCAS VON - Stargard (Pomerania) Born in 1861 - A painter of portraits and landscapes, Cranach did maquettes for country houses in Silesia and his native Pomerania. Under the influence of the Russian Julovsky he also created objects d'art in precious metals.
BROOCH representing a jelly-fish smothering a butterfly: pure gold on multi-colour enamel enhanced with precious stones. Marked with an intertwined monogram of the letters W.C.L. (1900).
Berlin, Louis Werner

249 DAUM, the brothers AUGUSTE (1853-1909) and ANTONIN (1864-1930) - Stimulated by the success of Gallé at the Exhibition of 1889, the brothers Daum began to produce glassware in their works in Nancy, and after the Chicago Exhibition in 1893 their work achieved an international reputation.
' SORROWING AUTUMN CROCUSES ' (title borrowed from G. Deschamps) (1893) - Bottle-shaped purple glass; height 47 cm.
Paris, Musée National d'Art Moderne

XLVI WIENER, RENÉ (biography see XL).
BOOKBINDING (1893) - Binding for Flaubert's *Salammbô*. Design by Wiener. Leather work by Victor Prouvé, the bronze by Camille Martin. Inlaid leather and pyrogravure. Enamelled bronze corners. 42×45 cm. Signed on the back cover: Victor Prouvé 1913; above to the left the monogram: CM and VP. On the front cover the monogram: R.W.
Nancy, Musée de l'École de Nancy

250 KOEPPING, KARL - Dresden 1848 - Berlin 1914 - After studying chemistry he turned to painting in 1869. Also studied engraving at the Munich Academy. In 1878 he engraved for *Art*, and from 1896 on he contributed to *Pan*. He made a collection of Japanese objects d'art and took inspiration from his collection for his stained-glass designs.
DECORATIVE GLASS VASE-Height 31,3 cm. Diameter 8,5 cm.
Copenhagen, Kunstindustrimuseet

251 TIFFANY, LOUIS COMFORT - New York 1848-1933 - A painter and a worker in glass and jewellery, Tiffany studied under Innes, and then at Paris until 1878. Towards 1880 he took out patents for his oxidised iridescent glasswork, and founded a company which decorated numerous public and private interiors. His work won the Grand Prix at Turin in 1902. After the death of his father he devoted himself to jewellery. From 1918 onwards his house at Oyster Bay (Long Island) was the centre of a group of artists whose work he executed and whom he assisted financially when necessary.

GLASS VASE (1900) - Tiffany, who specialised in blown glass, was later to be imitated by the glass-makers of Bohemia.
Paris, Musée des Arts décoratifs

252 GALLÉ, ÉMILE (biography see 34).
BUTTERFLY BED (1904) - One of the last works of Gallé who watched its completion from an invalid chair. It is made of various precious woods and is incrusted with mother of pearl. The design is based on that of a giant moth.
Nancy, Musée de l'École de Nancy

253 PROUVÉ, VICTOR - Nancy 1858 - Sétif (Algeria) 1943 - Painter, engraver, sculptor and decorator, Prouvé studied in Nancy and Paris and subsequently worked for Gallé. After Gallé's death he was appointed President of the Nancy School, where he continued his work until after the 1914-18 war.
BOWL: ' Night ' - Bronze 45,5×79×48 cm. Signed and dated: V. Prouvé (1894).
Paris, M. Léon Meyer

254 MAJORELLE, LOUIS - Toul 1859 - Nancy 1929 - After studying in Paris, Majorelle took over the ceramics workshop of his father. The success of Gallé led him to carry out original research, and after the Exhibition of Paris in 1900 his intensely personal style received wider and wider recognition.
TABLE (1902) - A three-leaf clover design supported on three console legs decorated with water-lily stems, mahogany, varnished tamarind and gilded bronze; height 85 cm.
Paris, Musée des Arts décoratifs

255 CHARPENTIER, ALEXANDRE - Paris 1856 - Neuilly 1909 - Ornamental sculptor. Charpentier was a member of the *Cinq*, and then of the *Six* group. He was famous for his bronze plaques, which he often used for furniture and bindings.
MUSIC-STAND (1901) - Element of an ensemble made up of a quartet piece and two stands: waxed hornbeam; 122×144 cm.
Paris, Musée des Arts décoratifs

256 GAILLARD, EUGÈNE - 1862-1933 - Decorative furnisher, collaborator of Bing. Author of *A propos de mobilier*.
DOUBLE-SEAT (canapé) (1911) - Decorative motifs based on the water-lily stem and leaf: polished Brazilian rosewood, silk decorated with stylised blue and yellow chrysanthemum flowers, woven by the firm of Cornille frères; 99×138 cm.
Paris, Musée des Arts décoratifs

257 VAN DE VELDE, HENRI (biography see 241).
DESK AND CHAIR (1896) - Only four were produced. The long curvilinear design of two opposing arcs is characteristic of van de Velde's furniture. Natural oak. Desk: 76×261×100 cm. Chair: height, 73,5 cm; height of seat,44 cm; area 61,5×48,5 cm.
Nuremberg, Germanisches National museum

XLVII VALLIN, EUGÈNE - Herbevilliers (Vosges) 1856 - Nancy 1922 - Vallin served his apprenticeship with his uncle in Nancy. His uncle was a manufacturer of religious furnishings, and in his atelier Vallin came across Viollet-le-Duc's ' Dictionnaire d'Architecture '. Vallin produced a good deal for Gothic and Neo-Gothic churches. In 1895 he freed himself from pastiche, and there-

after in his furniture he sought to create a harmony between nature and constructive logic.
DINING ROOM (1903-1906) - The ensemble designed for M. Masson in Nancy was transferred to Paris in 1917, and its installation in a Paris apartment necessitated reductions. Leather panels, ceiling and sideboard carvings by Victor Prouvé. The wood is cedar. Copper lampstand designed by Vallin. Glass by Daum. Ceiling signed and dated: V. Prouvé 1906.
Nancy, Musée de l'École de Nancy

258 ECKMANN, OTTO - Hamburg 1865 - Badenweiler 1902 - Eckmann studied at Hamburg, Munich and Nuremberg, and in 1894 he adopted the *Jugendstil* in his typographical creations, in which the stylisation of form always harked back to the natural model. His furniture designs were accurate and structural.
ARMCHAIR made for the new palace at Darmstadt. Two curved wooden struts decorated with brass plaques act as intermediary supports between the back of the chair and the back legs. The surface of the seat area itself slopes backwards: beech, brass and upholstered leather (about 1900). Total height 102 cm.; seat area 60×63 cm.; height in front 45 cm.; behind 36 cm.
Wolfsgarten, Prince Ludwig von Hesse

259 RIEMERSCHMID, RICHARD - Munich 1868-1957 - Architect, decorator and painter, Riemerschmid studied at the Munich Academy from 1888 to 1890. In 1897 he was one of the founders of the *Vereinigten Werkstätten für Kunst und Handwerk* and he took part in the Paris Exhibition of 1900 He was Director of the School for Decorative Arts in Munich from 1912 to 1924, and in 1926 he became Director of the Cologne Polytechnic. — See 302, 303, 317, 318, 332.
ARMCHAIR for a dining-room (1903) - The design is simple and restrained; the back is moulded to the shape of the human body: mahogany; height 99,5 cm.; seat 54×47 cm.
Munich, Stadtmuseum

260-261 GAUDÍ, ANTONIO (biography see 44).
ARMCHAIR FROM THE CASA CALVET (1898-1904) - The design avoids all rectilinear and traditiona forms.

262 GAUDÍ, ANTONIO (biography see 44).
BENCH FROM SANTA COLOMA DE CERVELLÓ (Colonia Güell) (1898-1914) - Wood 117×65 cm.

XLVIII GAUDÍ, ANTONIO (biography see 44).
CRYPT OF SANTA COLOMA DE CERVELLÓ (1898-1914).

263 GAUDÍ, ANTONIO (biography see 44).
CRYPT OF SANTA COLOMA DE CERVELLÓ (Colonia Güell) (1898-1914).

264 GAUDÍ, ANTONIO (biography see 44).
CASA MILÁ AT BARCELONA (1905-1910) - This building is known as ' la Pedrera ' (the Quarry).

265 GAUDÍ, ANTONIO (biography see 44).
CASA BATLLÓ: façade (1905-1907).

266 GAUDÍ, ANTONIO (biography see 44).
CHURCH OF THE SAGRADA FAMILIA, pinnacle (detail) (about 1924).

XLIX-L Gaudí, Antonio (biography see 44).
DETAILS FROM GÜELL PARK (1900-1914).

267 ENDELL, AUGUST (biography see 35).
FACADE OF THE ATELIER ELVIRA IN MUNICH (1896) - The really revolutionary element in this façade was the fantastic abstraction of the decorative motif in red and turquoise stucco. The decoration was removed in 1933 and the house was completely destroyed in 1944.

268 ENDELL, AUGUST (biography see 35).
ATELIER ELVIRA, Munich: staircase (1896) - The light-fitting shoots upwards like a rocket from the undulating bannister rail.

269 HORTA, VICTOR (biography see 47).
HOUSE, formerly the Hôtel A. Solvay, Brussels (1895-1900).

270 HORTA, VICTOR (biography see 47).
STAIRCASE FROM A HOUSE, formerly the Hôtel A. Solvay, Brussels (1895-1900).

271 HORTA, VICTOR (biography see 47).
STAINED GLASS WINDOW FROM A HOUSE, formerly the Hôtel A. Solvay, Brussels (1895-1900) - The glass is set in a metal framework.

272 HORTA, VICTOR (biography see 47).
HOUSE, formerly Hôtel Horta (1898-1899).

273 SEHRING, BERNHARD - Edderitz 1855 - Berlin 1932 - Sehring is primarily known in the architectural field for the theatres he built, for instance those of Düsseldorf, Bielefeld and Berlin.
TIETZ DEPARTMENT STORE (1900) - The glazing is more extensive than in almost any other façade of the period.

274 GUIMARD, HECTOR (biography see 45).
ENTRANCE TO A PARIS MÉTRO STATION (PORTE DAUPHINE) (1899-1904) - Components of cast iron attached to a metal framework.

275 GUIMARD, HECTOR (biography see 45).
ENTRANCE TO CASTEL BÉRANGER, a block of flats, 14, rue Lafontaine, Paris (1897-1898).

276 GUIMARD, HECTOR (biography see 45).
IRONWORK (on the upper part of the building), Castel Béranger, Paris (1897-1898).

277 GUIMARD, HECTOR (biography see 45).
TRANSLUCENT STAIRCASE WALL, Castel Béranger, Paris (1897-1898).

278 MACKMURDO, ARTHUR H. (biography see 33).
DESK (1886) - Oak 99 × 68,5 × 56 cm.

279 VOYSEY, CHARLES F. ANNESLEY (biography see XLV).
GILL HEAD, Lake Windermere (1898).

280 VOYSEY, CHARLES F. ANNESLEY (biography see XLV).
STUDIO HOUSE, West Kensington, London (1891).

281 VOYSEY, CHARLES F. ANNESLEY (biography see XLV).
ENTRANCE TO VODIN HOUSE, Pyrford Common, Surrey (1902).

282 PRIOR, EDWARD SCHRÖDER - Greenwich 1852-1932 - The most original architect in the Arts and Crafts group. Professor at Cambridge from 1912 to 1932. Produced some outstanding books on English mediaeval architecture.
HOME PLACE, Kelling (1904-1906).

283 LUTYENS, SIR EDWIN LANDSEER - London 1869-1944 - His early architecture was influenced by Shaw, Voysey and the Arts and Crafts. From 1906 on he turned to Palladianism and an eighteenth century style, introducing Neo-Georgianism. Architect of the New Delhi, also designed the British Embassy building in Washington and the Cenotaph in Whitehall.
TIGBOURNE COURT, Surrey (1897).

284 LETHABY, WILLIAM RICHARD - Barnstaple (Devonshire) 1857 - 1931 - Architect. Wrote a great deal on the theory and history of architecture. He was responsible with Sir G. Frampton for the establishment of the Central School of Arts and Crafts, whose principal he was from 1893 to 1911. Designed the Eagle Insurance Building in Birmingham in 1900.
BROCKHAMPTON CHURCH, interior (1900-1902).

285 VOYSEY, CHARLES F. ANNESLEY (biography see XLV).
CLOCK (about 1906) - Built by C.F. Nielsen: ebony with ivory inlays, decorated with yellow silk and topped by a brass ball; 40,5 × 19,5 cm.
London, Geffrye Museum

286 VOYSEY, CHARLES F. ANNESLEY (biography see XLV).
TEAPOT: brass (about 1896) - 14 × 18 cm.
London, Victoria and Albert Museum

LI MACKINTOSH, CHARLES RENNIE - Glasgow 1868 - London 1928 - Studied at the Glasgow School of Arts. Assistant and later partner in the firm of Honeyman and Keypie. He designed, furnished and decorated various mostly private buildings, and also the Scottish pavilion at the Turin Exhibition. He settled in London in 1913 and finally abandoned architecture in 1920. He retired to Port-Vendres. — See 289, 290, 293, 294, 295, 296, 297, 298, 299, 300.
PAIR OF DOORS (1904) - Designed for one of the rooms at the 'Willow Tea-Rooms' in Glasgow. Painted wood, beaten metal, leaded and mirrored glass. Each wing: 195,5 × 68,5 cm.
Glasgow, The House of Frazer

287 ASHBEE, CHARLES ROBERT - 1863-1942 - Architect, designer and author, Ashbee founded the Guild and School of Handicraft in 1888, and subsequently moved into the country to Chipping Campden. He exhibited regularly at the Arts and Crafts Exhibition and also at the Vienna Secession. The Guild was discontinued owing to the First World War. — See 291.
BOWL WITH LID (1899-1900) - Made by the Guild of Handicraft: silver. The lid is enamelled and decorated with a precious stone; marked with Ashbee's personal stamp: C.R.A.
London, Victoria and Albert Museum

288 GIMSON, ERNEST - 1864-1920 - Studied architecture from 1881 to 1884. At the advice of William Morris he joined J.D. Sedding, remaining with him from 1886 to 1888. From 1901 on he designed furniture and other work in metal. His designs were executed by a group of craftsmen at Cirencester, and subsequently in his own workshops — the Daneway House Workshops.
CABINET WITH SEPARATE BASE (1908): ebony with mother of pearl inlays and metal handles; 118 × 73 × 39,5 cm.
Leicester, Museum and Art Gallery

289 MACKINTOSH, CHARLES RENNIE (biography see LI).
GLASGOW SCHOOL OF ART (1897-1909).

290 MACKINTOSH, CHARLES RENNIE (biography see LI).
PENDANT WITH CHAIN (1902) - Made by Margaret Macdonald, Mackintosh's wife: silver and pearls; pendant 5 × 11,5 cm; chain 59 cm.
Edinburgh, Mrs M. N. Sturrock

291 ASHBEE, CHARLES ROBERT (biography see 287).
PENDANT (about 1900) - Made by the Guild of Handicraft - Gold and silver with decorations in enamel and pearls.
Cheltenham, E. Scott Cooper

292 MACDONALD, the sisters MARGARET (1865-1933) and FRANCES (1874-1921) - Margaret Macdonald was a designer and worker in metals, stained glass and embroidery. In 1900 she married Charles Rennie Mackintosh and collaborated with him in much of his work. Trained like her sister at the Glasgow School of Arts, Frances was a teacher there from 1907 onwards. She worked sometimes alone and sometimes in collaboration with her sister. In 1899 she married J.H. McNair and collaborated with him in the designing of furniture and stained glass.
MIRROR FRAME 'HONESTY' (about 1896) - Embossed pewter: 71 × 74 cm.

293 MACKINTOSH, CHARLES RENNIE (biography see LI).
GLASGOW SCHOOL OF ART, pilaster in the committee room (1906-1909).

294 MACKINTOSH, CHARLES RENNIE (biography see LI).
GLASGOW SCHOOL OF ART, wrought-iron emblem on the main staircase (1906-1909).

295 MACKINTOSH, CHARLES RENNIE (biography see LI).
GLASGOW SCHOOL OF ART, arch on the roof (1906-1909).

296 MACKINTOSH, CHARLES RENNIE (biography see LI).
PROJECT FOR A CONCERT HALL (1898) - It was exhibited at the Glasgow Exhibition in 1901 but was not awarded a prize.

297 MACKINTOSH, CHARLES RENNIE (biography see LI).
CHAIR, designed for the principal bedroom of Hill House (Helensburgh) (1902) - Ebonised wood; 140,5 × 40,5 × 33,5 cm.
Helensburgh, M. T. C. Lawson

298 MACKINTOSH, CHARLES RENNIE (biography see LI).
TABLE, designed for the hall of Hill House (Helensburgh) and similar to those designed by Voysey

(1902) - Ebonised wood with mother of pearl inlays 63,5×68,5×68 cm.

Helensburgh, W. G. Blackie

299 MACKINTOSH, CHARLES RENNIE (biography see LI).
TABLE (about 1900) - Enamelled white wood and inlayed with ivory roses 61×61,5×49,5 cm.

Glasgow, University

300 MACKINTOSH, CHARLES RENNIE (biography see LI).
ARMCHAIR (about 1902) - Enamelled white wood. The back is of cloth with a stencilled design; 114×70×53 cm.

Glasgow, University

301 RIEMERSCHMID, RICHARD (biography see 259).
GLASS (1912).

302 RIEMERSCHMID, RICHARD (biography see 259).
CHAIR FOR A MUSIC-ROOM (1899) - Well adapted for this purpose in that it has a low back giving full support to the back but also freedom of movement to the arms.

Frankfurt, Museum für Kunsthandwerk

303 BEHRENS, PETER - Hamburg 1868 - Berlin 1940 - Architect, decorator, painter, modeller, engraver and designer of type, he studied fitrs at Karlsruhe and then at Düsseldorf. He was a founder member of the *Vereinigte Werkstätten*. From 1905 on he abandoned the embellishments of the *Jugendstil* for a resolute constructivism. He exercised a profound influence on the technique and taste of Germany. — See 319, 320, 321.
BOTTLES (1898).

Munich, Stadtmuseum

304 EIFFEL, GUSTAVE (biography see 42).
THE EIFFEL TOWER, Paris - 984 feet high. It was begun on 26th January 1887 in spite of considerable opposition and was finished on 15th April 1889.

305 DE BAUDOT, ANATOLE - Sarrebourg 1834 - Paris 1915 - Architect and theoretician. De Baudot was a pupil of Labrouste and Viollet-le-Duc. As an Inspector of Historic Monuments he carried out the restoration of numerous ancient buildings, and as a government architect he was responsible for a great deal of varied building. As a teacher he defined the use of reinforced materials along the lines he had himself employed at Saint-Jean de Montmartre.
SAINT-JEAN DE MONTMARTRE, Paris (1894-1902) - The main door incorporated in the belltower. The architect made use of prefabricated components and had the supporting towers built in brick.

306 HENNEBIQUE, FRANÇOIS - Neuville-Saint-Vaast (Pas-de-Calais) 1842 - Bourg-la-Reine 1921 - Was contractor at Courtrai and Brussels before going to Paris. From 1879 to 1888 he studied the combination of iron and concrete, and in 1892 he took out patents and introduced the plate girder, an innovation adopted since all over the world.
FACTORY (SPINNING-MILL), Tourcoing, France (1895). Hennebique was one of the first architects to study the possibilities of the structural combination of steel and concrete.

307 PERRET, the brothers AUGUSTE (Brussels 1874 - Paris 1954) and GUSTAVE (Brussels 1875 - Paris 1952) - Auguste and Gustave Perret were the sons of the man who was responsible for the stone-work of the royal conservatory at Laeken. On the death of their father the two brothers collaborated closely and signed their plans A.G. Perret. The fruitful collaboration of the two brothers contributed to the originality of more than one architectural solution. They were the first to use reinforced concrete in the architecture of private buildings, and they developed its use both structurally and aesthetically. — See 308.
BLOCK OF FLATS, 25 *bis* rue Franklin, Paris (detail) (1902) - Infil panels of faïence tiles with a typically Art Nouveau leaf-design.

308 PERRET, AUGUSTE (biography see 307).
BLOCK OF FLATS, 25 *bis* rue Franklin, Paris (1902) - The concrete skeleton constitutes the essential architectural form of the building.

309 GARNIER, TONY (biography see IV).
SLAUGHTERHOUSE AT LA MOUCHE, LYONS (1909-1913) - Garnier was one of the first architects to give importance to the outward appearance of factories and other buildings of a similar nature.

310 MAILLART, ROBERT - 1872-1940 - Swiss engineer, inventor of the 'mushroom ceiling' technique in which he applied the principles of organic continuity and structural integrity. In 1901 he began to apply these principles to the bridges that made his name famous.
TAVANASA BRIDGE (1905) - The supporting span and the road surface constitute a single structural unity.

311 BERG, MAX - Berlin 1870-1947 - After studying at the College of Technology in Berlin, Berg became architect to the town of Breslau, where he designed the Centenary Hall of the 1913 exhibition. Later he withdrew from architecture.
CENTENARY HALL, Breslau (1910-1912).

312 HOFFMANN, JOSEF - Pirnitz (Moravia) 1870 - Vienna 1956 - A pupil of Otto Wagner, Hoffmann was one of the founders of the Vienna Secession. In 1903 he founded the *Wiener Werkstätte*, and for the next thirty years it was inspired by him. The Palais Stoclet in Brussels (1905-1911) represents a synthesis of the fundamental principles of Otto Wagner and the theories of Art Nouveau in a harmonious combination of architecture, decoration and furnishings. — See 313, 314.
PALAIS STOCLET, Brussels (1905-1911) - Exterior seen from the entrance gate. This building is a true synthesis of architecture with interior decoration and furniture.

313 HOFFMANN, JOSEF (biography see 312).
PALAIS STOCLET, Brussels, hall (1905-1911).

314 HOFFMANN, JOSEF (biography see 312).
PALAIS STOCLET, Brussels, dining room (1905-1911) - Marble veneer and mosaics by Klimt.

315 LOOS, ADOLF - Brno 1870 - Vienna 1933 - Loos was one of the pioneers of modern architecture in Austria. Son of a sculptor he studied in Dresden and in the United States. From 1897 onwards he adopted a style which eschewed all ornament and sought to obtain its artistic effect by the articulation of planes and the utilisation of beautiful materials.
STEINER HOUSE, Vienna (1910) - Uncompromisingly austere, it looks forward to the 1930's.

LII KLIMT, GUSTAV (biography see 112).
THE KISS (1909) - Design for the mosaic of the dining-room of the Palais Stoclet in Brussels. Water-colour and gouache, paper on wood 192 ×118 cm.

Strasbourg, Musée des Beaux-Arts

316 TAUT, BRUNO - Königsberg 1880 - Ankara 1938 - A pupil of Fischer in Munich, Bruno Taut collaborated in Berlin with his brother and with F. Hoffmann. In 1931 he was a teacher of the College of Technology in Berlin. In 1932 he was invited to Moscow, and from there he went to Japan, and finally he became a professor at Istanbul.
GLASS HOUSE, at the exhibition of the *Werkbund*, Cologne (1914) - This circular building with its impressive dome was designed merely to symbolise the use of glass in new architecture.

317 RIEMERSCHMID, RICHARD (biography see 259).
LINOLEUM designed for the Delmenhorst factory (1912).

318 RIEMERSCHMID, RICHARD (biography see 259).
TEA-SET (1914).

319 BEHRENS, PETER (biography see 303).
A.E.G. ASSEMBLY SHOPS, Berlin (1909) - Behrens, who became architect to the company, not only saw to the construction of new buildings but also designed appliances and even letter-headings.

320 BEHRENS, PETER (biography see 303).
TWO ELECTRIC KETTLES made by A.E.G. (1912).

321 BEHRENS, PETER (biography see 303).
TWO VENTILATORS made by A.E.G. (1912).

322 RIETVELD, GERRIT THOMAS - Utrecht 1888 - Lives in Utrecht - Dutch architect and decorator — See 323.
ARMCHAIR (1908) - Pine; 85,5×55×40 cm.

Utrecht, Centraal Museum der Gemeente

323 RIETVELD, GERRIT THOMAS (biography see 322).
ARMCHAIR (1917).

324 ROHDE, JOHAN - Randers (Jutland) 1856 - Copenhagen 1935 - At first a painter, and considerably influenced by Maurice Denis, he turned to designing furniture and silverware. Collaborated with Jensen. He had a decisive influence on production and was responsible for introducing European trends into his own country. — See 326.
TEAPOT (about 1906) - Silver, made by Georg Jensen; 7×12,5 cm. with the monogram G. J. and dated: 1906.

Copenhagen, H.P. Rohde

325 JENSEN, GEORG - Copenhagen 1866-1935 - A goldsmith, Jensen was also a sculptor and a ceramic artist. After a stay in Paris he began to make jewellery in inlaid silver, and worked generally in silver, creating his own individual style. His work became known more widely at the exhibitions in Essen and Cologne, and by 1910 he had won an international reputation.
CUTLERY (about 1908) - Silver.

Copenhagen, Georg Jensen

326 RODHE, JOHAN (biography see 324).
CUPBOARD designed by Johan Rohde and made for

the personal use of the artist by the brothers H.P. and L. Larsen (1897) - Mahogony 148 × 133,3 × 36 cm.

Copenhagen, H.P. Rohde

327 GROPIUS, WALTER - Berlin 1883 - Lives at Lincoln (U.S.A.) - Gropius studied architecture in Munich and Berlin from 1903 to 1907. In 1919 he succeeded van de Velde in Weimar at the art school, which he converted into the famous *Bauhaus*. The *Bauhaus* with a teaching staff composed of men like Klee, Kandinsky, Feininger, Schlemmer and Moholy-Nagy rapidly became one of the great centres of the international modern movement. It removed to Dessau in 1925. Gropius left it in 1928 and was replaced by Mies van der Rohe. In 1932 it again moved, this time to Berlin. A year later the school was disbanded. Its members dispersed in the face of the Nazi storm. Gropius went as a refugee to the U.S.A., taught at Harvard and still exercices a potent influence on American architecture.
FAGUS FACTORY at Alfeld on the Leine (1911-1914) - A synthesis of modern industrial architecture; the supporting elements are retracted, which makes the walls look like a mere curtain of transparent glass.

328 WRIGHT, FRANK LLOYD - 1869-1959 - Wright collaborated with Louis Sullivan from 1887 to 1893, and a publication of his work in Berlin in 1910 inaugurated the growing influence of America on Europe. All his activity was imbued with a passion for experiment, a love of nature and great faith in liberty and organic unity.
MARTIN HOUSE, Oak Park, Buffalo (1906).

329 SAUVAGE, HENRI - Rouen 1873-1932 - A pupil of Duray and Pascal, Sauvage collaborated with Frantz Jourdain on the Samaritaine building. He was responsible for numerous modern buildings in Paris, including the he house at No. 26 rue Vavin.
BLOCK OF FLATS at 26 rue Vavin, Paris (1913) - Here can be seen the newly evolved principle of ' terraced ' floors. The revetment of ceramic tiles is designed to keep the façade of the building light.

330 PARKER, BARRY (1867-1947) and UNWIN, SIR RAYMOND (1863-1940) - Architects and town-planners. They were commissioned to design Letchworth, the first of all garden-cities. In 1907 Sir Raymond Unwin went to live in Hampstead in connexion with the design of the Hampstead Garden suburb. His book *Town Planning in Practice*,

published in 1909, greatly influenced his generation.
— See 330, 331, 333.

330 PARKER, BARRY and UNWIN, SIR RAYMOND (biography see 330).
HOUSE AT LETCHWORTH GARDEN CITY (begun 1904).

331 PARKER, BARRY and UNWIN, SIR RAYMOND (biography see 330).
HOUSE AT LETCHWORTH GARDEN CITY (begun 1904).

332 RIEMERSCHMID, RICHARD (biography see 259).
INDUSTRIAL GARTEN CITY for the textile factories at Hagen, Westphalia (1907) - Drawing from an aerial view. The garden city movement that originated in England soon stimulated a keen interest in Germany. Some important projects were carried out on these lines by big industrialists like Krupp. Riemerschmid was one of the first to adhere to this movement and to treat with some regard to aesthetic considerations plans which were originally of a purely social nature.

333 PARKER, BARRY and UNWIN, SIR RAYMOND (biography see 330).
HOUSE, HAMPSTEAD GARDEN SUBURB (begun 1907).

NOTES ON THE IN-TEXT ILLUSTRATIONS

BERGSON, HENRI-LOUIS - Paris 1859-1941 - Bergson began his teaching career in 1881 equipped with a diploma in philosophy. His *Essai sur les données immédiates de la conscience* was published in 1889, and his *Matière et Mémoire* in 1897. The two essays contain the essentials of his thought, which is based on intuition of duration. From 1900 omwards his lectures at the Collège de France made him famous. His philosophy has exercised a decisive influence on his time.
p. 8 ' ESSAI SUR LES DONNÉES IMMÉDIATES DE LA CONSCIENCE '. Title-page (1889) - Thesis submitted to the University of Paris for the *doctorat ès lettres*. In this work, which is of capital importance, Bergson — without touching again on the problem of metaphysics — introduces a new method of envisaging the problems of knowledge, and he ' sets out to show how a wrong evaluation of psychological states leads to an indissoluble contradiction between the doctrines which affirm and those which deny free will '.

Paris, Bibliothèque Nationale

EINSTEIN, ALBERT - Ulm 1879 - Princeton (New Jersey) 1955 - After studying in Munich, and then in Milan and Zurich, Einstein published his first work in 1905 on the quantum theory and on relativity. His famous work on the general theory of relativity was published in 1913. One of the greatest physicists in the history of science, Einstein not only gave the world a new form of physics but also certain new ways of thought.
p. 8 ' EINE NEUE BESTIMMUNG DER MOLEKÜL-DIMENSIONEN ' (A new Determination of Molecular Dimensions) Title-page (1905) - In his doctoral thesis Einstein developed his first theory of relativity by dwelling on the fact that a result can appear different to different observers. Gra-

dually however relativity overcomes apparent paradoxes, and from ' special relativity ' Einstein arrived from 1915 on at a ' generalised theory of relativity ' and although its form has not yet been definitively laid down it already dominates all physics, and even geometry.

Paris, Bibliothèque Nationale

FREUD, SIGMUND - Freiberg (Moravia) 1856 - London 1939 - As a neurologist and psychiatrist, Freud revolutionised clinical psychology by his technique of exploring the unconscious. In 1910 he founded the International Psycho-analytical Society, and his fame became world wide. His lectures at the University of Vienna in 1914 were of tremendous influence. A veritable intellectual phenomenon, Freud was amongst those who have deeply influenced human culture and changed the history of human thought.
p. 8 ' THE INTERPRETATION OF DREAMS ' (1900) Title-page - One of the earliest of Freud's works to make an impression on the learned world.

Paris, Bibliothèque Nationale

p. 12 THE JUDGE'S PANEL FOR THE PARIS SALON (1885).

Paris, Union centrale des Arts décoratifs, ' Maciet ' collection

p. 15 DESIGN FOR THE PALACE OF ELECTRICITY at the Paris Universal Exhibition (1900) taken from *L'Encyclopédie du Siècle*.

Paris, Bibliothèque Nationale

NIETZSCHE, FRIEDRICH - Röcken 1844 - Weimar 1900 - Nietzsche began as an admirer of Greek culture, and in his *Birth of Tragedy* (1871) he made his famous distinction between the ' Apollonian '

and ' Dionysiac ' spirits. His health was precariou and this, together with a natural preference for solitude, made his life a very solitary one. He had few friends — one of them was Richard Wagner, but the relationship ended in a violent break and the most terrible satirical denunciations from Nietzsche. He wrote his famous *Also Sprach Zarathustra* (1883-85) in the solitude of Sils-Maria. His later life was passed under the shadow of insanity, but his influence after his death has been profound.
p. 18 ' ECCE HOMO ' (1908) - End-papers. Autobiography written by Nietzsche in 1888 and published in 1908 after his death by the Insel Verlag in Munich with ornaments by Van de Velde: *Ecce Homo*, or how one becomes what one is. The work is in four parts: 1. Why I am so wise; 2. Why I have known it long; 3. Why I write such good books; and 4. Why I am such a fatality. In this last testament Nietzsche has painted his own spiritual portrait and expressed most clearly the uncompromising violence of his philosophy.

Starnberg, Dr Friedrich Wichmann

MALLARMÉ, STÉPHANE - Paris 1842 - Vulaines (Seine-et-Marne) 1898 - Teacher of English, first in the provinces and then in Paris, Mallarmé led a very quiet and uneventful existence. His whole attention was devoted to a wonderfully rich spiritual life, of which his published works represent only a small fragment. But they are among the rarest and greatest poems in the world's literature. All the young poets of the Symbolists professed themselves his disciples. They formed a fervent cult and on his ' Tuesdays ' crowded into his rooms in the rue de Rome.
p. 20 ' UN COUP DE DÉS JAMAIS N'ABOLIRA LE HASARD ' (1897) - This poem, which was printed

with a very unusual typographical lay-out, is one of the last and most difficult of Mallarmé's works, and consequently one that sums up most completely his metaphysical and poetic ideas. It was first published in the review *Cosmopolis*, May, 1897.

Paris, Bibliothèque Sainte-Geneviève

MALLARMÉ, STÉPHANE
p. 20 MANUSCRIPT PAGE FROM ' L'APRÈS-MIDI D'UN FAUNE ' (1876). *L'Après-midi d'un Faune* was begun in 1865 during Mallarmé's Tournon years. Later he took it up again and brought it to the state that we now known. It was not published until 1876. Claude Debussy's symphonic poem *Prélude à l'Après-midi d'un Faune* was first performed in 1894 at the Société Nationale.

Paris, Bibliothèque Nationale

IBSEN, HENRIK - Skien 1828 - Christiana (Oslo) 1906 - The most famous Norwegian play-wright, his work extended over half a century until 1890 when, with Maeterlinck and Strindberg, he turned to what one can call the ' theatre of the soul '. On the verge of Symbolism and Pre-Expressionism, his dramas of ideas owe their power of evocation to strongly marked characters which have given the greatest actors an opportunity to enhance their fame.
p. 22 POSTER FOR ' AN ENEMY OF THE PEOPLE ' by Henrik Ibsen (1893) - Poster by Vuillard for the first French performance — announced as a single performance — of Henrik Ibsen's play *An Enemy of the People* translated from the Norwegian by Chennevière. The main character Stockmann, who has revealed the fact that the water which serves the thermal spa of which he is the doctor is polluted, finds himself condemned and execrated by his fellow citizens, and he is driven out and has to begin his career afresh; nevertheless he is happy because he is at peace with his conscience, and reckons himself ' amongst the most powerful men in the world because he is the most alone '. In France the leading role was created by Lugné-Poë in 1893, and played again by Georges Pitoeff in 1939. Ibsen wrote the play in Italy in 1882, and it aroused a great deal of discussion.

Paris, Musée national d'Art moderne

HUYSMANS, JORIS KARL - Paris 1848-1907 - Began as one of the Médan group, but he broke with Naturalism by the publication of *A Rebours* (1884), which marks a deep distate for reality, and a passionate curiosity for symbolist and decadent novelties, occult knowledge, and the *mystique* of Catholic ritual. Huysman's conversion is represented, among other works, by *En Route* and *La Cathédrale*.
p. 54 ' A REBOURS ' (1884). Title-page. - Writing of this work of Huysmans, Barbey d'Aurevilly declared: ' After such a book all that is left for the author is to blow his brains out or throw himself at the foot of the Cross '. In fact, Huysmans was converted to devout Catholicism soon afterwards. It has often been said that as his hero Des Esseintes, Huysmans took Robert de Montesquiou, out of whom Proust was later to make M. de Charlus. Whatever the truth of the matter this character, at once both mystical and libertine, both drawn and attracted by the Faith, repelled by nature and everything natural, is extremely characteristic of the anxiety of the age.

Paris, Bibliothèque Nationale

MAETERLINCK, MAURICE - Ghent 1862 - Orlamande 1949 - Took part in the Belgian symbolist movement with *Serres Chaudes*, followed by *Quinze Chansons* and the curious plays beginning with *La Princesse Maleine* which aroused the enthusiasm of Mirbeau. One of them, *Pelléas et Mélisande*, set to music by Debussy, is an immortal masterpiece of both poetry and music. His nature books, above all *The Life of the Bee* (1901) had a resouding success. During the last war Maeterlinck lived in the U.S.A.
p. 54 ' SERRES CHAUDES ' (1889). Title-page.

Paris, Bibliothèque Sainte-Geneviève

VALÉRY, PAUL - Sète 1871 - Paris 1945 - Starting writing in 1890, in ten years he produced only two slim volumes and a few poems. Then for fifteen years he wrote nothing. In 1917 the *Jeune Parque* appeared, which immediately marked him out as one of the leading poets of the time, and drew attention to his earlier works. Many of his poems arise out of particular occasions, but all have a common unity of thought, stemming clearly from Mallarmé but having a specially personal significance.
p. 54 ' LA SOIRÉE AVEC MONSIEUR TESTE ' (1906). Title-page of the original edition published by the ' Éditions Bonvalet-Jouve '. It had already appeared in the review *Le Centaure*.

*Paris, Bibliothèque Sainte-Geneviève,
Collection ' Doucet '*

COCTEAU, JEAN - Maison-Laffite 1889 - French poet, Cocteau was elected a member of the Académie Française in 1955 after having been among the leaders of the avant-garde. He touches on the dramatic in all his poems, but enlivens them with continual ingenious devices. He has also written ballets: *Les Mariés de la Tour Eiffel;* and novels, *Les Enfants terribles;* plays, *La Voix humaine, L'Aigle à deux têtes;* and films, art criticism, and so on. He has also lavished his inexhaustible vitality an painting and drawing.
p. 58 STRAVINSKY COMPOSING ' LE SACRE DU PRINTEMPS ' (1913) - Drawing for the *Revue musicale* May-June 1939.

DUFY, RAOUL (biography see XXIX)
p. 61 ILLUSTRATION FOR ' LE BESTIAIRE ' BY GUILLAUME APOLLINAIRE - *Le Bestiaire* or *Le Cortège d'Orphée* appeared in 1911 with illustrations by Raoul Dufy. In very short poems, perfect in their form and extremely expressive, Apollinaire represents the characteristics trait of a particular animal, indicating at the same time the symbolism with which it is charged for him. The verses reproduced here refer to Pegasus the horse. The poems were set to music by Poulenc.

Paris, Bibliothèque Sainte-Geneviève

KIRCHNER, ERNST LUDWIG (biograhy see 189).
p. 62 MANIFESTO OF ' DIE BRÜCKE ' (1906) - This association of artists was born in 1903 with the meeting of Kirchner, Bleyl, Heckel and Schmidt-Rottluff. Their first exhibition was in the Seifert lamp-factory at Dresden in 1905.

Cologne, Dumont-Schauberg Bildarchiv

MUNCH, EDVARD (biography see 72).
p. 62 ' PORTRAIT OF MALLARMÉ ' (1896) - Lithography (40,1×28,9 cm.), produced by Munch during his stay in Paris. Munch also did another portrait of Mallarmé as an etching.

Oslo, Municipal Collection

p. 63 COVER OF THE GERMAN SATIRICAL WEEKLY ' SIMPLICISSIMUS ' (No. 38. 4th Year) - This illustrated satirical weekly was founded in 1896 by Albert Langen. Thomas Theodor Heine, a famous caricaturist, was an established contributor. It was one of the most virulent expressions of the German revolutionary spirit. *Simplicissimus* ceased publication in 1942, and was started again in 1954 by Olaf Iversen.

Marbach, The Schiller Museum

p. 63 COVER OF NO. 14 OF THE REVIEW ' DER STURM ' - Cultural and artistic weekly, founded in Berlin in 1910 by Herwarth Walden. In 1912 Walden also opened an art gallery under the same name: *Der Sturm*. *Der Sturm* (The Storm) was responsible for a big movement in the artistic world which a great influence, and the gallery successfully introduced all the avant-garde painters.

KIPLING, RUDYARD - Bombay 1875 - London 1936 - Born of a family long established in India, Rudyard Kipling was brought up in England but returned to India when he was 17 and took up journalism. He was living there when *Plain Tales from the Hills* was published in 1887. Later came his best known works: *The Jungle Book* (1894), *Kim* (1901), etc. He was a prodigious story-teller and at the same time a considerable poet. One can see in him one of his own typical ' Englishman '. He gives a fascinating portrait of imperialist England, conscious of its vitality but at the same time animated by extraordinary poetry and fantasy.
p. 105 TITLE-PAGE OF THE 1907 EDITION OF ' THE JUNGLE BOOK ' - *The Jungle Book*, which recounts the adventures of Mowgli, first appeared in 1894. Mowgli was the boy lost in the forest who was adopted by the animals and brought up by a wolf to obey the laws of the jungle whereby he became a sort of king of the animals. This was followed by the *Second Jungle Book* (1895). The edition from which the illustration is taken was designed by the author himself.

London, Macmillan and Co.

p. 106 COVER OF THE FIRST ISSUE OF ' LA NOUVELLE REVUE FRANÇAISE ' (1909) - This critical and literary monthly appeared for the first time in February 1909 under the editorship of Jacques Riviere, Jacques Copeau, Jean Schlumberger and André Gide. A preliminary number was published in 1908. The N.R.F. has counted, and still counts, amongst its contributors almost every well-known figure amongst writers, painters, philosophers and so on. Since its foundation it has fought against the frivolous debasement of literature, and it has played an important role in French letters. Its publication was interrupted during the Second World War, but it re-appeared in 1953 under the editorship of J. Paulhan and Marcel Arland.

Paris, Bibliothèque Sainte-Geneviève

PÉGUY, CHARLES - Orléans 1873 - Marne 1914 - Modestly provincial in origin, Péguy had a normal schooling, dividing his admiration between Bergson and Jaurès, preaching Socialism and throwing himself into the Dreyfus affair with the republicans. In his famous little bookshop in the rue de la Sorbonne, he published his *Cahiers de la Quinzaine*, where many of the most promising younger writers made their first appeerence. All the political and moral questions of the time

were discussed in the *Cahiers*, Péguy's own contributions being marked by feeling and a very personal style. The poet in him was not less remarkable than the prose writer. He eventually broke with his left-wing friends and became a Catholic, but a very individual Catholic: his *Jeanne d'Arc* is his greatest religious work. He was killed at the battle of the Marne by a bullet in the head.
p. 106 A COVER OF THE 'CAHIERS DE LA QUINZAINE' - This issue called *Notre Jeunesse* is one of the most brilliant and profound works to spring from the Dreyfus affair.

Paris, Bibliothèque Sainte-Geneviève

APOLLINAIRE, GUILLAUME (pseudonym of APOLLINARIS DE KOSTROWITZKY) - Rome 1880 - Paris 1918 - French poet, author of *Alcools* (1913), *Calligrammes* (1918), *Les mamelles de Tirésias* (1918), a heroic comedy, a sort of manifesto, in which, incidentally, the word 'surrealist' was coined for the first time. For the author the word defined a tendency in art which had 'never served to affirm any creed, or any artistic or literary affirmation'. As an art-critic, Apollinaire was one or the first defenders of modern painting; he was the friend of many great artists, in particular the Cubists. During the 1914-18 war he was wounded, stayed in hospital in Paris and resumed his literary work, but fell ill again and was buried on the very day of the armistice.
p. 108 'LE POÈTE ASSASSINÉ' (1916). Cover - This long fantasy is particularly valuable because it is full of autobiographical details. In the love-affair between the poet Croniamantal and Tristouse Ballerina one can recognise the stormy liaison between Apollinaire and Marie Laurencin. Cappiello's design on the cover looks like a prophecy.

BARRÈS, MAURICE - Charmes (Vosges) 1862 - Neuilly-sur-Seine 1923 - As a young writer Barrès made himself known by his curious trilogy *Culte du Moi* and *Ennemi des Lois*, works whose aesthetic is essentially anarchist. With *Du sang, de la volupté et de la mort*, the aestheticism turns to romanticism, and the style becomes one of the most melodious and captivating since Chateaubriand. But politics came to attract him, he forgot his poetic myths and became a *député*, created 'nationalism', and with the outbreak of war put his talents at the service of his country with a most ardent patriotism — or in his own words 'jusquauboutisme'.
p. 108 'DU SANG, DE LA VOLUPTÉ ET DE LA MORT' - Title-page (1894). Published in 1893; complete edition in 1894; definitive edition in 1909.

Paris, Bibliothèque Sainte-Geneviève

GAUGUIN, PAUL (biography see 27).
p. 109 ILLUSTRATION FOR 'NOA NOA' (1895-1899). (in Maori: adoring). During the winter of 1893-94 Gauguin collaborated with Charles Morice in setting down the memories of his first visit to Tahiti. Part of this first version was published in the *Revue Blanche* (1897). During his second stay in Tahiti, Gauguin revised the text, and the revised version was published in Paris in 1900. He illustrated the book with drawings and water-colour paintings, some of which were compositions he had already done in oils. The folio volume of 182 pages is illustrated with 59 water-colour drawings and coloured woodcuts, 18 black and white woodcuts, and various photos and engravings. The book describes the customs of the Tahitians and the life the author led amongst them.

Paris, Musée du Louvre, Cabinet des Dessins

WORRINGER, WILHELM - Aix-la-Chapelle (Aachen) 1881 - Worringer studied in Germany and Switzerland. He lectured in Berne and afterwards became a professor of art at Bonn, Königsberg and Halle. He came under the influence of Nietzsche and campaigned against the 'intellectual sterility' of the day. 'The true Expressionism of the age', he insisted, 'lies in the new way our mind sees things and not in the way our eyes see things'.
p. 110 COVER OF THE THIRD EDITION OF 'ABSTRAKTION UND EINFÜHLUNG' (1911).

MÉLIÈS, GEORGES (biography see 94).
p. 112 'THE CONQUEST OF THE POLE' (1912) - Drawing in pen and wash on paper 35×28 cm. 'If this film is still triumphant in retrospect today' writes G. Sadoul, 'it is because it preserves intact the primitive qualities of an art in its infancy'. This film was one of the last ones made by Méliès before he was ruined.

Paris, Cinémathèque française

VERNE, JULES - Nantes 1828 - Amiens 1905 - Passionately interested in the scientific discoveries of his day, Jules Verne set out to write 'scientific novels'. His ingenious works displayed an extraordinary ability to previsage scientific discoveries. His first work of this kind, *Five Weeks in a Balloon*, was immediately successful, and the general public is interested in his work down to the present day.
p. 113 'TRIP TO THE MOON', illustrated by Émile Bayard (1901) - In 1865 Jules Verne published an adventure novel *De la terre à la lune*, which he subsequently incorporated in its entirety in the longer book of the same title published in 1870. An enormous projectile equipped with scientific instruments is shot out of a cannon. However, an unexpected encounter with a meteor throws it out of its trajectory so that it skims the moon without landing on it. On rocky mountains friends of the lunar travellers follow their interplanetary course through a giant telescope. Finally the projectile returns to earth and falls into the Pacific, and the lunar travellers are rescued by a corvette. Éditions Hetzel 1902.

Paris, Bibliothèque Nationale

LARIONOV, MICHEL (biography see XXII)
p. 114 'SERGE DE DIAGHILEV', drawing taken from the book *Les Ballets russes* by Pierre Vorms.

Éditions P. Vorms

BEARDSLEY, AUBREY VINCENT - Brighton 1872 - Menton 1898. English artist and engraver. Self-taught, infant-prodigy, he achieved fame early by the brilliance of his technique. An admirer of Morris and Burne-Jones, he joined the Pre-Raphaelite Brotherhood. His drawings, engravings and posters — the style refined, elegant and decorative, the spirit fantastic and sensual — had an effect on the growth of the *Jugendstil* in Germany. Paul Klee was certainly influenced by Beardsley in 1904-1905.
p. 127 TITLE-PAGE OF OSCAR WILDE'S 'SALOMÉ' by Beardsley (1907). This play was written by Wilde in French, at the request of Sarah Bernhardt, and was put on at the Théâtre de l'Œuvre on February 12 th, 1896. It had a triumphant success, but was banned in London for religious reasons. Richard Strauss's opera, with libretto by Hedwig Lochmann, was likewise refused a licence by the Austrian censor and was first performed in Paris at the Théâtre du Châtelet (1907).

REDON, ODILON (biography see 161).
p. 127 THE EYE, LIKE A STRANGE BALLOON, AIMS AT THE INFINITE (1882) - One of six lithographs from the series *A Edgar Poe*, published in Paris in 1882. Signed in the top right-hand corner: Odilon Redon.

New York, Philip Hofer Collection

VALLOTTON, FÉLIX (biography see 114).
p. 131 THE EXECUTION - Woodcut (1894) 14,9×9 cm., japan-paper. Signed in the bottom right-hand corner: F.V.

Paris, M. Vallotton Collection

p. 135 THE FUTURIST MANIFESTO (1910) - In February 1909 the poet Filippo Tommaso Marinetti published his *Manifeste de la poésie futuriste*. At the beginning of 1910 Boccioni and a few others met Marinetti at Milan and decided to address a manifesto to the young artists. A second manifesto was launched the same year. One of the signatories, Carlo Carrà, relates in his *Mémoires* that 'this bold and open appeal to rebellion... had an effect like an electric shock'. Many Frenchmen, including Apollinaire, ranged themselves with Italian Futurism.

NOLDE, EMIL (biography see XXXIII).
p. 149 PROPHET (1912) - Woodcut.

KANDINSKY, WASSILY (biography see VI).
p. 151 DER BLAUE REITER. ALMANACH. Title-page (1912) - Kandinsky had painted a canvas called *The Blue Knight*, and an important artistic movement formed under this title. Kandinsky opened his own art-school in Munich, where he had lived since 1896. The sole object of the group was to gather together young artists and to organise exhibitions of their paintings so as to make known avant-garde painters to the whole world. The *livre almanach* of *Blaue Reiter* expresses the theories of its supporters, who if they admit to all these artistic principles, affirm their hatred of academism and of *la nature extérieure*.

KLEE, PAUL (biography see VII).
p. 152 VIRGIN IN A TREE - Etching (1903) - One of the artist's earliest works. Monogram and date in the centre at the bottom: P.K. 03.

KUBIN, ALFRED - Leitmeritz (Bohemie) 1877 - Zwickledt (Upper Austria) 1958 - In 1898 began to study in Munich with Schmid-Reutte and Gysis. Travelled to Paris and Italy in 1905. In 1906 he settled in Zwickledt. He illustrated with lithographs many of the world's literary masterpieces.
p. 152 DIE ANDERE SEITE - Illustration by the author.

p. 233 SIGNET OF THE WILLIAM MORRIS FIRM (c. 1861) - In 1861 Morris and several of his architect and painter friends opened a shop which was intended to put within the reach of the general public everyday objects, furniture, wall-paper, materials, tiles, stained glass, etc., to be both well designed and well made.

MACKMURDO, ARTHUR H. (biography see 33). p. 237 WREN CITY CHURCHES - Frontispiece (1883) - Designed by the author for his book in which he defends Wren's churches in London which were being threatened with demolition.

MACKMURDO, ARTHUR H. (biography see 33). p. 237 SIGNET OF THE CENTURY GUILD (1884) - Mackmurdo under the influence of Morris's teachings in 1882 founded the Century Guild ' so

that all branches of art might be in the hands of the artist rather than the tradesman '.

WHISTLER, JAMES MCNEIL - Lowell (Massachusetts) 1834 - Paris 1903 - American painter. Came to Paris at the age of twenty and later lived in London. He started as an Impressionist but soon turned to more decorative values. p. 237 BUTTERFLY SIGNATURE.

GAUGUIN, PAUL (biography see 27). p. 238 AUX ROCHES NOIRES - Poster for the Café Volpini exhibition (1889) - In 1889 an ' Exhibition of Impressionist and Synthetist painting ' took place at Volpini's in the Champ de Mars. The catalogue states: ' Available on request — album of lithographs by Paul Gauguin and Émile Bernard ', (the latter had added a few pages to Gauguin's collection).

LEMMEN, GEORGES - Brussels 1865 - 1916 - Son of an architect, he studied drawing and in 1899 joined *Les Vingt*. Painter and engraver, Lemmen collaborated with van de Velde and van Rijsselberghe in the renewal of the decorative arts. He also joined the group of the *Libre Esthétique*. p. 239 CATALOGUE FOR ' LES VINGT ' (1891) - Frontispiece of the catalogue for the exhibition organised by *Les Vingt*, in 1901.

VAN DE VELDE, HENRI (biography see 241). p. 239 DOMINICAL - Frontispiece (1892) - *Dominical*

is the first collection of verse by the symbolist poet Max Elskamp of Antwerp.

VAN DE VELDE, HENRI (biography see 241). p. 241 INITIAL LETTERS FOR THE REVIEW ' VAN NU EN STRAKS ' (1896) - Flemish avant-garde review founded by van de Velde in 1890. He collaborated in the editing of the first numbers and it is thanks to him that their typography is so remarkably successful.

ECKMANN, OTTO (biography see 258). p. 241 COVER FOR RUSKIN'S ' SEVEN LAMPS OF ARCHITECTURE ' (c. 1908).

ECKMANN, OTTO (biography see 258). p. 241 DESIGN FOR A TYPE-FACE - The design and decorative aspects of typography intrigued Eckmann. He gave renewed energy to the art of typographical forms in Germany.

GAUDÍ, ANTONIO (biography see 44). p. 245 PLAN OF THE CASA MILÁ (begun in 1905).

MACKMURDO, ARTHUR H. (biography see 33). p. 247 EXHIBITION STAND, LIVERPOOL (1886) - From a drawing of the time. Objects belonging to the *Century Guild* were exhibited on this architecturally remarkably independant and progressive stand.

MACKINTOSH, CHARLES RENNIE (biography see LI). p. 248 HOUSE OF AN ART-LOVER (1902) - In 1901 Alexander Koch, a publisher from Darmstadt, instigated a competition on the theme *Haus eines Kunstfreundes*, in which Mackintosh came second. This reproduction (55,5×39 cm.) is included in the *Meister der Innenkunst* (Ed. A. Koch, Darmstadt).

HOFFMANN, JOSEF (biography see 312). p. 249 DESIGN FOR AN INTERIOR (1900) - Hoffmann shared the views of his master Otto Wagner, believing that the unity of architecture, décor and furnishing was indispensable.

BEHRENS, PETER (biography see 303). p. 250 A.E.G. CATALOGUE (1908) - Since 1907 Behrens had been the artistic adviser of the A.E.G. (Allgemeine Elektrizitäts Gesellschaft) in Berlin. He showed himself to be an industrial designer of the first order.

EIFFEL, GUSTAVE (biography see 42). p. 251 SECTION THROUGH THE STATUE OF LIBERTY, NEW YORK (1886) - A statue 46 metres high by the sculptor Bartholdi, which France presented to the U.S.A. in 1886.

PERRET, AUGUSTE and GUSTAVE (biography see 307). p. 252 SKELETON OF THE THÉÂTRE DES CHAMPS-ÉLYSÉES (1911-1914) - The framework is of concrete.

GARNIER, TONY (biography see IV). p. 253 INDUSTRIAL CITY - Plan (1901-1904) - One of the views of the Industrial City as designed by Garnier while he was on a scholarship of the Academy in Rome.

WRIGHT, FRANK LLOYD (biography see 328). p. 257 PLAN OF THE MARTIN HOUSE, BUFFALO, U.S.A.(1903) - An early example of Wrights freedom in making interior spaces interpenetrate.

SANT'ELIA, ANTONIO - Como 1888 - Killed on the Carso Front 1916 - Sant'Elia studied architecture in Como, Bologna and Milan. His work, confined to the years 1913-1915, is known to us from numerous drawings and projects which are fertile in inventiveness and gave promise of a great future. In 1914 he signed the *Manifesto of Futurist Architecture*. His ' ideal town ' was destined to remain in the experimental stage, but thanks to his intense preoccupation with the relationship between man and his surroundings it had a great influence. p. 259 SKYSCRAPER - Design (1913).

358

INDEX

Ordinary numerals refer to pages.
Numerals in bold type refer to black and white plates.
Roman numerals refer to colour plates.